History of Universities

VOLUME XI

1992

History of Universities

VOLUME XI

1992

Oxford University Press

1992

History of Universities is published annually as a single volume.

Editor:
Laurence Brockliss *(Magdalen College, Oxford)*

Assistant Editor:
Mark Curthoys *(Christ Church, Oxford)*

Bibliography Editor:
John Fletcher *(University of Aston in Birmingham)*

Editorial Board:
R. D. Anderson *(University of Edinburgh)*
P. Denley *(Westfield College, London)*
C. Fascione *(Rome)*
W. Frijhoff *(Erasmus Universiteit, Rotterdam)*
N. Hammerstein *(University of Frankfurt)*
D. Julia *(Institut Universitaire Européen, Florence)*
N. G. Siraisi *(Hunter College, New York)*

*Papers for publication in History of Universities as well as
books for review should be sent to the editor, Dr. L. W. B. Brockliss,
Magdalen College, Oxford, OX1 4AU, United Kingdom.*

A leaflet 'Notes to OUP Authors' is available on request from the editor.

*Details of subscription rates and terms are available from
Oxford Journals Subscription Department, Walton Street,
Oxford OX2 6DP, United Kingdom.*

*British Library Cataloguing in Publication Data
(data available)
ISBN 0 19 822001 4*

*Library of Congress Cataloguing Publication Data
(data available)*

*Typeset by Latimer Trend & Company Ltd, Plymouth
Printed in Great Britain by
Biddles Ltd, Guildford and King's Lynn*

Contents

Articles

Research in Progress

Conference Reports

Essay Review

Book Reviews

viii   *Contents*

Bibliography

The Visitation of the Collège de Cluny, Paris, 1386

Thomas Sullivan, OSB

On April 30 and May 1, 1386, the prior of La Voûte-Chilhac, Maurinus de Monteclaio, concluded his visitation tour of the Cluniac province of France with an inquiry *super statu et gubernatione* of that Order's house of studies in Paris, the Collège de Cluny.* Normal procedure in the Cluniac visitation system provided a battery of questions concerning the house to be visited, some of which could be answered by personal observation and some of which demanded interviews of those living in the house or near by.[1] Armed with such a questionnaire, Maurinus de Monteclaio heard testimony from five witnesses—two members of the college itself and three priors of the Order of Cluny; his nine questions focused on the student personnel of the college and their sponsoring monasteries, the college's reputation, and steps to be taken for the reformation of the college. A notary was present to record in third-person form the responses of the first four witnesses; he received the deposition of the fifth witness and copied it word for word, joining it to the evidence of the first group of witnesses.

The fortunate survival of this testimony—edited and presented by Dom Gaston Charvin, O.S.B, in his *Statuts, chapitres généraux, et visites de l'Ordre de Cluny*[2]—affords historians of the Cluniac Order and of the medieval university a unique window through which to view the world of the university-monk. The historian is further blessed by the survival of not only the minutes of the general chapter of the Order held in 1385 during which Maurinus de Monteclaio's visitation tour was commissioned[3] but also the minutes of the general chapter meeting at Cluny only thirteen days after the visitation of the Collège de Cluny in 1386.[4] These latter minutes report the actions taken by de Monteclaio during his visitation of the college and, combined with the responses to the prior's questions, not only further our knowledge of the Cluniac visitation system but more importantly give us an immediate experience of the problems that arise when the demands of monastic and university life overlap. These texts—the notarial report of the prior's interviews and the chapter minutes—are the only firsthand records we have of a visitation of the Collège de Cluny during the Middle Ages and indeed appear to be the only extant visitation records of any of the Parisian monastic colleges in the Middle Ages.

This is not to say that the Order of Cluny was uninterested in its foundation at Paris; the affairs of the college were of major concern to general chapters from its establishment in 1260 until its suppression at the Revolution. A house of studies was a major undertaking for any religious community, involving great expense in both money and personnel, and demanded constant vigilance from superiors and administrators. But a house of studies at the university afforded an opportunity not to be missed, that of combining the stability and routine of the cloistered life with the most advanced and sophisticated theological training of the schools.[5] Of the seventeen or so colleges successfully founded at the University of Paris in the thirteenth century, eight were intended for regular clergy: canons, mendicants and monks.[6] Of these eight, three were monastic and included the Benedictine Collège de Saint-Denis (founded as early as 1229; refounded around 1263),[7] the Cistercian Collège Saint-Bernard, founded in 1246,[8] and the Cluniac Collège de Cluny, founded in 1260.[9] The fourteenth century would see the foundation of only one monastic college at Paris, that of the Collège de Marmoutier in 1328.[10]

The founder of the Collège de Cluny, Abbot Yves de Vergy (*rexit* 1257–1275), hoped a house of studies in Paris would serve as a remedy for abuses in the Order. Of the opinion that his monks gave themselves over to irregularities because they did not know what to do with themselves, he thought to substitute a taste for learning, especially in the theological sciences, for a penchant for that which would be harmful to the monastic life.[11] During the one hundred twenty-five years between the college's foundation by Abbot Yves and the visitation of 1386, the college's affairs, disciplinary as well as financial, had frequently been on the agenda of the general chapters. The fourteenth century, for instance, saw five sets of statutes published, either on the abbot's authority or by the general chapter's, meeting annually at Cluny, four prior to the 1386 visitation.[12] In addition, the records of the general chapters are sprinkled with complaints—from the monk-scholars, the *prior scolarium*, or the superiors of the Order—about the payment of the pensions or their inadequacy. In 1352, the abbot of Cluny was urged to visit the Collège de Cluny personally, to see if he could restore order to the house since there were only a few benefiting from the educational opportunities offered and more not only wasting the pensions paid but above all bringing shame on the whole Order.[13]

1. The general chapter of 1385

When, however, the 'definitors' of the general chapter of the Order of Cluny met at Cluny in the spring of 1385, their concerns were not focused on the Collège de Cluny but on the spiritual and temporal disintegration which, in their view, characterized the Order and which, if not quickly checked, would lead to ruin and destruction.[14] Alleging that the divine office was not celebrated as it should be, that monks were accused of various crimes, and that some were not wearing the habit appropriately, the chapter fathers stated that neither the monastic rule nor religious life was observed—monks lived as seculars, rebellious and disobedient. This regrettable situation they attributed to the poor administration of some of the Order's superiors. There were many other problems, they said, which for the sake of brevity they would not mention but which would lead to the dishonour of the Order, the loss of souls, and the scandal of many if not addressed.

To remedy this lamentable situation, the 'definitors' first directed Abbot Jean de Damas-Cozan (*rexit* 1383–1400)[15] and the community of the monastery of Cluny to write to the pope, the king and other princes in the name of the general chapter. At the same time, they commanded that two priors be sent to the papal court at Avignon[16] and to the French royal court to seek help in restoring the monastic observance of the Order of Cluny. These same two priors were appointed extraordinary visitors of the Cluniac provinces of France, Auvergne, and Provence; one of the two was to visit each province entirely and both could delegate their considerable powers of visitation to others for those places not easily accessible. Invested with full authority for correction, punishment, and subpoena, the visitors could deprive monks of their livings, could assign them to other priories or imprison them; they could place benefices in the hands of the abbot of Cluny, suspend monks from administrative posts, make them return to their cloisters, and even appeal to the secular arm for help, should the situation so warrant. In short, the visitors had the powers of the abbot of Cluny, were he present.

The 'definitors' also ordered that the two priors have letters from the abbot of Cluny granting these powers of visitation and that the visitors' authority should extend until the next general chapter (i.e., May 13, 1386). The approaching feast of Pentecost was designated as the best time to begin the tour.

Chosen for this important task were the prior of La Voûte-Chilhac, Maurinus de Monteclaio, mentioned above, and the prior of Trouhaut. Why the assignment fell to them in particular is unclear. The priory of Trouhaut, in the diocese of Langres, was small—two monks and their superior—and apparently unimportant.[17] The name of the prior of Trouhaut in 1385 is unknown, as are his dates of appointment and demission (though by 1390 the priory was held *in commendam* by the Cardinal de Neufchâtel[18]). Happily more information concerning Maurinus de Monteclaio is available, allowing us to suggest that he began ruling as prior of La Voûte-Chilhac in about 1385 and ended his governance there around 1403.[19] If these dates are reliable, we learn that de Monteclaio was a doctor of canon law and that as prior of La Voûte-Chilhac, his first important administrative assignment for the Order was this extraordinary visitation of 1385–1386. The authorities appear satisfied with his work, for he was chosen in subsequent chapters as 'definitor', visitor and emissary of the general chapters.[20]

Considerations raised at the chapter of 1385 about the Order's tepid observance and its spiritual and temporal collapse—concerns which brought about the call for the visitation and the appointment of the two visitors—reflect the condition of the Order of Cluny beginning in the first decades of the fourteenth century and lasting until the reforms initiated by Abbot Jean de Bourbon in the mid-fifteenth. This period of Cluniac history saw in France not only the epidemic of 1348–1349, the Hundred Years' War (*c.* 1337–1453) and wars between the Armagnac and Burgundian factions (1410–1435), but also an economic recession with its resulting crises in the distribution of commodities and in the fluctuation of prices, salaries, and revenues. The distress felt by the fathers of the general chapter was the result not only of these external forces, complicated in turn

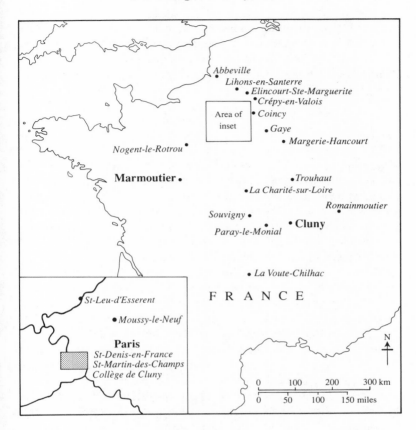

Abbeville
Lihons-en-Santerre
Elincourt-Ste-Marguerite
Crépy-en-Valois

Area of inset

Coincy

Gaye

Margerie-Hancourt

Nogent-le-Rotrou

Marmoutier

Trouhaut
La Charité-sur-Loire

Souvigny

Romainmoutier

Cluny

Paray-le-Monial

La Voute-Chilhac

St-Leu-d'Esserent

F R A N C E

Moussy-le-Neuf

Paris
St-Denis-en-France
St-Martin-des-Champs
Collège de Cluny

N

0   100   200   300 km
0   50   100   150 miles

by the Avignon papacy (1309–1376) and the Great Schism (1378–1417), but also the absence of successful reforming initiatives from among those most responsible for the direction of the Order, men appointed by means of the pontifical reserve and *commendam* systems.[21]

2. The Visitation of the Parisian College

The minutes of the general chapter of 1386 reveal that the two priors carried out their assignment with admirable zeal, visiting approximately seventy-seven houses in the three provinces and correcting

abuses in place or citing numerous monks—priors, scholars, obe-
dientiaries, and other malefactors—to appear before the court of the
abbot of Cluny.[22] As mentioned above, the last house visited by
Maurinus de Monteclaio, on April 30 and May 1, 1386, was the
Collège de Cluny.

2.1. *Witnesses*

Visitations presumed the sworn oath and testimony of everyone
assigned to a particular house. In his visitation of the Collège de
Cluny, Maurinus de Monteclaio personally heard the testimony of
only two members of the college itself and that of the prior of
Moussy-le-Neuf. The members of the college interviewed were the
prior scolarium, Jacobus Heraudi, a monk of the Cluniac priory of
Gaye, a member of the college for fifteen years and a bachelor of
theology, and Baudetus de Cise, a monk of La Voûte-Chilhac who
had come to the college within the year. The value of the testimony
of the college's prior is obvious; that of its newest member is less
evident. As prior of La Voûte-Chilhac, de Monteclaio may have felt
that the testimony of a monk of his own monastery might be more
forthright; perhaps, too, he valued the insights of someone fresh to
the scene. Three additional witnesses called were Cluniac dignitaries
– the first, an unnamed prior of Moussy-le-Neuf, the second two,
Jocerandus de Canobio, prior of Crépy-en-Valois, and Henricus de
Iserpanno, prior of Souvigny. The value of the testimony of both
Jocerandus de Canobio and Henricus de Iserpanno is readily
apparent: both priors had long experience in administration, each
one of his own house and both more widely in the Order; both
priories were responsible for *bourses* demanded by the Order of
Cluny for support of students at the college; and each prior had a
student in the college, both of whom had been resident for fourteen
years and were bachelors in theology. In addition, de Iserpanno is
noted in 1389 as having been promoted to the doctorate in canon
law and would be expected to be familiar with the demands
university life placed on a monastic setting.[23] The testimony of the
prior of Moussy-le-Neuf, and the probable reason for his inclusion
as a witness, states that he resided in Paris and was aware of the
scholars' reputation in the city since '. . . *quasi omni die talia videt vel
audit*'.[24]

2.2. *Student personnel*

As *prior scolarium* of the Collège de Cluny, Jacobus Heraudi was best prepared to answer any questions concerning the scholars living in the college: their names, their sponsoring monasteries, and the nature and length of their studies.[25] In his testimony, he listed twenty-three monasteries of the Cluniac Order that were held to the annual payment of *bourses* for the maintenance of students at the Collège. Since the important priories of La Charité-sur-Loire and St-Martin-des-Champs were required to support two students each, the total number of students supported by these obligatory *bourses* and therefore the minimum number of students expected to be working in the college was twenty-five. Heraudi's statement indicates, however, that at the time of the visitation there were resident only fifteen scholars plus himself as their prior—i.e., sixteen students rather than the required minimum of twenty-five. An additional student from the priory of Coincy was expected but had not arrived by the time of the visitation. Thus a total of sixteen students from fifteen monasteries (La Charité-sur-Loire had sent its required two) were resident in the spring of 1386. Earlier figures indicate a fluctuation in the number of residents that concerned the superiors of the Order: a letter of Pope Honorius IV in 1286 speaks of forty students dwelling at the college;[26] a university census report, dated between 1329 and 1336, indicates a total of only thirteen monks living there, including the prior;[27] and a petition to Clement VI in 1344, requesting permission for a cemetery, mentions that there were and had been in the past at least twenty-five scholars at the college.[28]

The other Parisian Benedictine colleges seem to have had an academic population much smaller than that of the Collège de Cluny, though it is frequently difficult to establish with certainty the exact number of students living in the colleges at any one specific time. The accounts for the abbey of Saint-Denis-en-France indicate that in the year 1336–1337, six new students were admitted to the Collège de Saint-Denis. Abbot Gui des Castres established in 1339 that the membership of the college should include ten monks and a master. In 1411, ten students resided in the college. In 1474, there were six students, a master or instructor, a prior general, and a prior '*ordinatus ad solicitatem causarum*', as well as two servants. Fourteen years later, documents inform us that the monks of the Collège de Saint-Denis in 1488 numbered five students and their master.[29]

Statutes issued for the Collège de Marmoutier in 1390 established that there should be only six scholars, one of whom was to be the master.[30]

Fifteen of the sixteen students resident at the Collège de Cluny in 1386 are noted by their prior as engaged in a particular discipline: seven studied grammar, one logic, and seven were bachelors in theology. Placed in the context of fourteenth-century legislation prescribing both a course of studies for students of the Collège de Cluny and a guaranteed length of stay, the condition of the college in 1386 can be evaluated and the concerns expressed by the superiors understood. There are three fourteenth-century *cursus*; the first is dated to 1314 and is found in the statutes of Abbot Henri de Fautrières. While mentioning no specific number of years for theology, it allows two years for the study of logic (the *summulae*, old logic and new logic), three years for the study of philosophy (the *libri naturales et philosophiae*), and then the study of theology (Sacred Scripture and the *Sentences*).[31] In 1344 the 'definitors' of the general chapter lamented that the college was not producing doctors and bachelors in theology according to its stated purpose. The chapter therefore legislated that after seven years of study in logic or philosophy, a student must be prepared to lecture in these disciplines or lose his *bourse*. If, after studying a further seven years in theology, a monk-scholar is not prepared to lecture in theology, he too would be deprived of his *bourse*. The fathers decreed finally that any scholar holding a *bourse* for twelve years who had not yet begun lecturing in the discipline for which he had received the pension would be deprived of his pension and be returned to his monastery.[32] In 1383, only three years before the visitation under discussion here, the grand prior of Cluny, Raymond de Cadoèn, acting in the place of the ailing abbot, Jacques de Cozan, had promulgated the following for the Collège de Cluny: students were to be allowed four years for the study of logic and philosophy and nine years for the study of theology (i.e., the baccalaureate after five years and the doctorate after four additional years).[33]

The Order's legislation had also determined how long a period of study a student would be guaranteed at the college, granting each student a *quinquennium* once the student had been officially received and presented proofs of competence. It was decreed in 1301 that no-one (priors and deans included) had authority to dismiss a student from the college, even after the *quinquennium* was completed, without the express permission of the abbot of Cluny. This regulation had been introduced because good and capable students were removed from the college and replaced by relatives, friends, and even countrymen of those who had the right to place students in the college.[34] The statutes of 1314 allowed priors and deans the right to recall students of theology hearing lectures on the Bible to preach and give good example in their home monasteries. This 'right of recall' was permitted only if the students were not *'dispositos ad perfectionem in facultate theologica consequendum'* and only if they had already finished their allotted five-years' study.[35] By the end of the fourteenth century, however, the situation was apparently reversed from that of 1301. Scholars were still guaranteed the *quinquennium* but could not stay even a month longer without the abbot of Cluny's explicit permission, under pain of excommunication.[36]

As noted above, seven of the fifteen students were grammarians. One monk, resident only a half-year, was working on the *Disticha Catonis*, a favourite beginner's manual in grammar. Two more were reading the *Doctrinale* of Alexander of Villedieu, intended for use by young scholars already somewhat proficient in grammar. The other four monks were Summulists, that is, students at an advanced level of grammar, attending lectures on the *Summulae*. The Summulists, in their study of speculative grammar, had entered the most advanced level of preparatory learning, a stage completed usually by the age of twelve or thirteen years.[37] The length of time the grammarians at the Collège de Cluny spent in residence, judged in the light of the progress made and expected, lends weight to the witnesses' complaints about the scholars' inadequate preparation for university studies. The college was founded primarily for studies in philosophy and theology, yet half its members in 1386 were still engaged in preparatory training—and some were spending inordinate amounts of time at this introductory level. Johannes de Murato of St-Leu-d'Esserent, resident in the college for eight years, was still a Summulist. Ludovicus Episcopi, a monk of St-Martin-des-Champs, had been a member of the college for twelve years and was still studying the *Doctrinale*.

Of the remaining eight monks, Petrus de Morcourt of Lihons-en-Santerre studied logic and had been a student for twelve years. His seven colleagues were all bachelors of theology: one, Bartholomeus de Matiscone had begun lecturing on the *Sentences*, and the other,

Guillelmus de Costa, was listed as the next to be promoted to the doctorate in theology. All of the bachelors had been resident in the college between thirteen and twenty years, averaging a little over fifteen years each. The complaint of 1344 that the college was producing no graduates for the Order seems to have been heard, for the college's production of graduates was reaching a respectable level by 1386. Of all the monks resident in 1386, only one is known to have proceeded to the doctorate in theology, Bartholomeus de Matiscone, who appears in 1409 at the Council of Pisa as abbot of Molesme and a master in theology.[38] Others in residence appear to have advanced to the licentiate: Guillelmus de Costa in theology and Johannes de Murato in canon law.

2.3. *The college's reputation*

When responding to the visitor's questions concerning the reputation of the college, each of the witnesses painted a dismal picture of the college community. Henricus de Iserpanno, the prior of Souvigny, gave the most negative response, almost bitter in tone, though he insisted that he spoke with a good conscience rather than out of bad zeal.[39] He claimed that the college was almost destroyed, as were the other colleges of the Order,[40] primarily because the common life was neglected, because there was no one to demand that the laws and statutes of the college be kept, and because evildoers were defended and the good left unsupported.

The prior of Souvigny also claimed that the provincial vicars harmed the college, as did the prayers and requests of the laity. Though what he intended by this statement is not immediately clear, it is likely that the entrance requirements of the college were undermined because the powerful—both within the Order and outside—brought pressure on the administrators of the college to admit either unprepared or unworthy students. The vicars referred to were officials appointed by the abbot of Cluny as his personal representative in each of the ten Cluniac provinces, competent to intervene in the temporal and disciplinary affairs of the province committed to them.[41]

An additional problem contributing to the disorder of the house, according to de Iserpanno, was the division of the college along linguistic lines. The prior of Souvigny was referring to the linguistic duality of France, divided as it was into the *langue d'oc* and the *langue d'oil*. Monasteries from both regions were represented at the Collège de Cluny in 1386, although those from the *langue d'oil* predominated.[42] These difficulties could have been avoided if the monk-students had obeyed college statutes demanding that Latin be spoken at all times within the college, except with the laity.[43] De Iserpanno's final complaint was that the endowment of the college was not well managed.

Jacobus Heraudi alleged in his testimony that the scholars had not followed the statutes of the Order for over thirty years and that they had a bad reputation, an opinion reiterated by the prior of Moussy-le-Neuf who, as stated above, claimed he saw and heard on a daily basis what the scholars did. All the witnesses testified that the scholars were quarrelsome, disobedient, fought with one another, ran about Paris without a *socius*, refused to attend the university sermons, and would not take meals together. They would not wear their habits, bore arms within the cloister (and were therefore by definition excommunicate and irregular), and played at dice and other forbidden games. Beyond this catalogue of crimes, the prior of Souvigny stated, a diligent investigator could find even more should he try.[44]

3. Recommendations

All of the witnesses, with the exception of Baudetus de Cise, who only that year had begun his studies at Paris, were willing to give counsel concerning its regeneration. Their recommendations fall into three categories: the first dealing with the students themselves, the second with the pensions involved in their upkeep, and the third with the exercise of authority within the house vis-à-vis the statutes and the prior.

3.1. *Improve the qualifications of the students*

The first piece of advice given recommended that superiors should send to the Collège de Cluny only those who were properly trained in the *scientia primitiva*—preparatory studies in grammar. This was a point well made, given the level of study current at the college in 1386. The expense of maintaining a student was very high, and funds were expended needlessly on students ill-prepared for study. Jacobus Heraudi proclaimed that the students were hardly ready for philosophy, much less the study of theology, and the prior of Crépy-en-Valois, Jocerandus de Canobio, urged that the college statutes regarding admission of students should be followed, mentioning too that unprepared students were being admitted by dispensation of the abbot of Cluny.[45]

According to the statutes, any student wishing to pursue studies at the Collège de Cluny was instructed to present himself to the abbot of Cluny or to the *prior scolarium* of the college for a preliminary examination that would assure the officials of the Order that the candidate had the requisite credentials to profit from a stay at the college.[46] The ability to learn was considered adequate preparation if the applicant could not show sufficient acquired learning.[47] The statutes preferred that the prospective student be well-versed in the *scientia primitiva*, that is, that he have at least enough grammar to study dialectic; better though that he be prepared by the study of logic for that of philosophy.[48] In 1336, Benedict XII's *Summi magistri* had likewise required the candidate to be instructed in the *scientia primitiva*, as well as regular in observance, docile and honest, pure in faith, and endowed with an aptitude for learning.[49] Cluniac statutes warned examiners not to show favoritism but encouraged them to admit only the good and the docile.[50]

If the Cluniac Order had established an educational system comparable to that of the mendicant orders, one that promoted the study of the *scientia primitiva* within the important monasteries of the Order, perhaps theology rather than grammar would have dominated the studies of the scholars of the Collège de Cluny in 1386. An attempt made earlier in the century seems to have come to nothing. At the general chapter of 1314, the 'definitors' ordered that at Cluny and other important monasteries, *studia* be organized for the study of theology, law, philosophy, and grammar. A commission was established, composed of the abbot of Cluny and four prominent men of the Order, to act as a steering committee for this project. Their instructions were to determine how many *studia* to organize, which monasteries should house them, how many students were to train at each *studium*, and how these students were to live and study. Once the *studia* were established, the rectors of each location would choose and examine prospective students.[51] Unfortunately, there is no further trace of this committee in the records of the Order, nor does it seem to have had, if indeed it ever functioned, any effect on the educational level of the houses of the Order.

The priors of Moussy-le-Neuf and Souvigny also proposed that troublemakers be expelled from the college—not only those who were unworthy of the opportunity of studying at the university or were morally unfit, but also those who were academically unsuited. If five or six of the current scholars were removed, things would soon be peaceful enough and the scholars would manage themselves well. Letters had already been sent to the abbot of Cluny about them, Henricus de Iserpanno stated, asking him and the general chapter to expel them.[52]

3.2. *Improve the financial situation*

Unlike some of the other monastic colleges, the Collège de Cluny at its foundation was given neither a large endowment nor rents that would assure it a necessary and steady income in a time of prolonged political and economic crisis, such as the fourteenth century. The college's income depended primarily on a fixed number of pensions or *bourses* owed annually by designated priories and deaneries of the Order of Cluny, as mentioned above, supplemented by taxes, aids, and subsidies. Attendance at the Collège de Cluny was not restricted to monks from houses paying *bourses*, nor was the obligation remitted if the house had no student to send. Unfortunately, payment of *bourses* or pensions was not always made—to bad effect. Two witnesses at the inquest of 1386 urged that the abbot of Cluny see to the collection of the *bourses*, since students were obliged by statute to leave the college if payments were not made; often they returned to the college only after two or three years, by this time corrupt and morally reprehensive, perhaps having run about the countryside seeking to have their pensions paid. Jacobus Heraudi suggested that if the scholars had enough to live on, they would make more progress in five years than they presently did in twenty and that the Order of Cluny would have a hundred good clerics— which it did not now have![53]

Collection of the *bourses* was, and always remained, a frustrating endeavour for the administrators of the Order and the college;

recourse was had to financial penalties and even to excommunication. In 1260, those delinquent in payment were held to double payment of the *bourse*;[54] in 1294, a penalty of three *sous* per day was assessed for tardy remittance.[55] Other chapters demanded that those priors who had not made full payment remain at Cluny after the general chapter until the debt was paid in full, until all arrears were taken care of, or at least until suitable arrangements had been made promising full compensation.[56] In 1365, the general chapter decided to visit the sins of the fathers on the heads of the children: a scholar whose prior had not fully paid what was due could receive nothing from the college beginning two months after the date the payment was due.[57] The ultimate penalty was excommunication, and the priors of 1395 were warned that if full payment were not made they would be excommunicated *ipso facto* and could be absolved only by the abbot of Cluny or his grand- or claustral-prior.[58] But, the witnesses in 1386 claimed, even if the pensions were paid in full, they were not adequate to maintain a scholar for the whole year but only a half-year and, when wine and wheat were expensive, only a quarter-year. The frequently changing value of the *bourse*, due most likely to the prolonged inflationary trend of the late thirteenth and fourteenth centuries attests to the difficulties the college had in meeting expenses.

The original value of the *bourse* was established at fifteen *livres parisis*.[59] Originally judged sufficient *pro victu et vestitu* over the period of one year, this amount soon proved inadequate and in 1314 circumstances threatened a mid-year closing of the school since the pensions were not adequate, owing to the '*caristiam rerum monetariumque mutationes*'. This early closing was forestalled when the general chapter of 1314 voted a supplement of sixty *sous* for each student's pension.[60] In 1319, Pope John XXII intervened with the general chapter on the students' behalf, stating that the present pension was not sufficient for a year's board, however moderate.[61] In line with the papal suggestion, the general chapter of 1320 voted to increase the pension according to an academic scale: twenty *livres parisis* for scholars, thirty for bachelors in theology, and forty for theology masters.[62] Only sixteen years later Benedict XII's *Summi magistri* increased the pensions paid for scholars in Paris to forty *livres tournois* (thirty-two *livres parisis*); masters in theology were to receive sixty *livres tournois* (forty-eight *livres parisis*), and the *prior scolarium* was to receive twenty *livres tournois* (sixteen *livres parisis*) in addition to his regular *bourse* as a scholar or master.[63] The priors of the Order seemed to ignore this legislation and were still paying only twenty *livres parisis* as the basic pension in 1392.[64]

One remedy for the financial difficulties offered by two of the witnesses, the priors of Moussy-le-Neuf and Crépy-en-Valois, was the reduction of the number of scholars either by one-third or one-half. Jocerandus de Canobio further suggested that this reduction be extended to all the colleges of the Order.[65] In the past this solution had been attractive in many ways, both to the superiors of the Order and to the students themselves. The latter saw that if there were fewer students in the college, there would be more *per capita* income for those already in residence. Resident students had periodically refused to receive newcomers into the college and rejected replacements for those of their number deprived of their pensions.[66] The Order's administrators in 1295 saw reduction as a means of satisfying debts and decided that scholars from four houses would be sent home for a year's time.[67] A reduction of the number of students by half was ordered in 1306, '*propter deteriorationem monete*', although the priors were expected to continue full payment of the *bourse*. The general chapter, aware of the hardship this radical stratagem would cause the sponsoring monasteries of those dismissed, made provision to reduce by one the number of monks those monasteries were expected to maintain at home.[68]

Jocerandus de Canobio offered another possible and partial solution to the college's financial difficulties. Priors owing pensions whose monasteries were in the vicinity of the Collège de Cluny and who had students there should pay the pension in kind—wheat and wine—rather than in cash. The college would then be supplied with wheat and wine at a good price and could use the money saved to purchase other necessities.[69] There are two points to consider in relation to de Canobio's suggestion: what priories did he envision taking part in this programme and how would his suggestion prove advantageous? He does not mention his own monastery of Crépy-en-Valois, about thirty-six miles from Paris, as an example of a monastery in the vicinity of Paris but does speak of St-Leu-d'Esserent, approximately twenty-six miles from the city and St-Martin-des-Champs, in the capital, as possibilities. The only other *bourse*-paying monastery close to the city was Longpont, fourteen miles south of Paris. These three houses then—St-Leu-d'Esserent,

St-Martin-des-Champs, and Longpont—appear to be those de Canobio had in mind as nearby and likely participants in his scheme. Though the prior of Crépy-en-Valois does not make clear how money would be saved, he likely presumed that these local priories would not charge the current rates for wheat and wine, or that payment in kind would eliminate payments to middlemen whose need for profit would necessarily raise the price to the college. Wheat prices were high in the late fourteenth century: Miskimin has plotted the price of wheat in France for the period 1365 to 1395, showing a famine price for wheat in 1369. In 1384, wheat prices had reached their fourth highest level since 1365, a level unsurpassed until famine prices were again reached in 1392. Perhaps it was this 1384 price level that provoked de Canobio's suggestion in the spring of 1386.[70]

The difficulties priors had in paying the pensions are understandable, given the economic and political conditions of the period, and should have met with sympathy by at least two of the witnesses. Ruined by the ravages of the Hundred Years' War and having lost more than half his revenues, Henricus de Iserpanno, prior of Souvigny, would be forgiven part of his debt to the apostolic *camera* by command of the pontifical commissary on May 31, 1386, about four weeks after he testified concerning the Collège de Cluny. In return for this significant favour, he was obliged to offer three masses for the intention of the pope.[71] In 1374, Jocerandus de Canobio, as prior of Crépy-en-Valois, found himself unable to pay an annual pension of two hundred *livres* owed the abbot of Cluny; his revenues, he said, had been reduced by two-thirds, '*propter guerras, mortalitates et alias pestes sive sterilitates, que in regno Francie (proh dolor) diutius viguerunt et vigent de presenti.*'[72]

3.3. *Restore discipline in the college*

The last of the witnesses, Henricus de Iserpanno, stated very clearly that restoration of order in the college depended on the appointment of a new *prior scolarium*—someone worthy, non-beneficed, and not a member of the college. If the new prior were to collapse under the pressure of laymen or other monks of the Order (presumably allowing unprepared students into the college), de Iserpanno wanted him excommunicated or deprived of his living in the college. In addition to this new *prior scolarium*, the 'definitors' and general chapter should appoint someone to oversee the reformation of the college, someone who could also act as the prior's protector. This new official should be someone who lived in Paris, should be from among the advisors of the abbot of Cluny, should be capable in word and deed, and should be holy.[73]

De Iserpanno's suggestions concerning the restoration of authority within the college are practical and intelligent, considering that the *prior scolarium* was chosen annually from among the students by the abbot of Cluny to rule over them and considering that he was probably close in age and academic achievement to those over whom he had been given authority. Expected to be both scholar and administrator, the *prior scolarium* had to govern with the insufficient funds provided by the Order and the insufficient obedience preferred by the monk-scholars.[74] De Iserpanno, when suggesting that someone not a member of the college be appointed *prior scolarium*, apparently wished to establish an authority within the college functioning on the same footing as the other priors and deans within the Cluniac Order. Cluniac priors were chosen by the abbot of Cluny from among the whole monastic population of the Order; his choice was not limited to the members of the house needing the new prior. Priors within the Cluniac Order served at the pleasure of the abbot of Cluny; they were not appointed as prior on an annual basis as at the Collège de Cluny.[75]

The appointment of an official delegated to oversee the reformation of the college and to fortify the position of the *prior scolarium*, though perhaps only a temporary position, would strengthen the *prior scolarium* vis-à-vis both the students and the other authorities, such as the provincial vicars and important members of the laity seeking inappropriate favors. The combination too of a local protector and a strong *prior scolarium* could have fostered sufficient local autonomy, similar to other priories of the Order, allowing the community of the college to develop, take pride in, and maintain an appropriate monastic discipline.

The statutes of the Collège de Marmoutier, published in 1390, established for the *magister* of the Collège de Marmoutier the type of protector demanded by de Iserpanno for the *prior scolarium* of the Collège de Cluny in the person of the prior of Notre-Dame-des-Champs, a dependency of Marmoutier in the city of Paris less than a half-mile from the Collège de Marmoutier. If the *magister* of the Collège de Marmoutier found himself unable to solve quarrels arising among the members of the college or found the scholars rebellious or disobedient, he was authorized to call the trouble-makers before the prior of Notre-Dame-des-Champs and, in the presence of the chapter of Notre-Dame-des-Champs and the schol-ars of the college, the two officials were to decide on punishments appropriate to the offence.[76] A comparable solution for the Collège de Cluny would have established perhaps the prior of St-Martin-des-Champs as the protector of the *prior scolarium* of the Collège de Cluny. There is no indication that such a solution to the problems of the college was ever attempted.

The prior of Souvigny also wanted the scholars to observe the statutes of Abbots Simon de la Brosse and Jacques de Cozan regulating life at the Collège de Cluny and issued respectively in 1365 and in 1383.[77] A glance at both sets of statutes indicates that matters deserving primary attention were residence, financial payments, academic exercises, and monastic discipline—all issues addressed again in the visitation of 1386. Perhaps the prior felt that regulations for the good order of the house were already in place; all that was needed was to enforce those statutes and strengthen the position of the *prior*. If his suggestions concerning the restoration of authority were to be implemented, de Iserpanno had no doubt that the college would prosper.[78]

3.4. *Restore common life in the college*

Before concluding his recommendations, de Iserpanno strongly advised that members of the college, with the exception of the *bacallarii formati*[79] (and presumably those of higher rank), no longer be allowed the use of *camerae*, that is, private rooms '*quia ex hoc pendet omne malum et dissolutiones.*'[80] At the heart of this suggestion was a concern for two elements central to cenobitic monastic life throughout the middle ages—the integrity of the cloister and the obligation to live in community, which entailed a common table and a common dormitory.

The principle of the common dormitory had begun to weaken already in the thirteenth century, when the division of the dormitory into quasi-private rooms by erecting dividers, low or high, or even constructing rooms within the dormitory became acceptable.[81] In his legislation of the mid-1330s for monks and canons, Pope Benedict

XII forbade cells or private rooms for religious, except in the infirmary, authorizing only room dividers of some sort; he did permit, however, the use of private rooms for study during the day.[82] The first alarm concerning private chambers at the Collège de Cluny was sounded in 1342 when superiors reported that they had heard that the scholars of the college did not sleep in the dormitory nor did they eat together in the refectory but dined in chambers. The chapter forbade the students to eat or sleep in the chambers except in case of necessity, and then only with the permission of the prior or subprior.[83] Abbot Simon de la Brosse's statutes in 1365, however, allowed masters, priors, *bacallarii formati*, and the sick the privilege of their own private rooms.[84]

The offence to common life represented by the private chambers was perhaps seen as less serious than the possible violation of the integrity of the cloister. In general, the statutes of both the Collège de Cluny and the Order of Cluny held that it was best that women be restricted from entering the precincts of the monasteries and the college, particularly women of suspect virtue (and these especially after Compline). Though female guests of noble status could be received on special occasions into the Collège, never were they to be allowed into the monks' private rooms, whether they be the scholars' studies or an individual's living quarters.[85]

4. The *procès verbal*

It was customary in the Order of Cluny to prepare a *procès verbal* or minutes of the proceedings of the visitation of each house for the use of the members of the general chapters. From this detailed report the visitors prepared a résumé enabling the chapter to acquaint itself at a glance not only with the condition of the house in question but with the events of the visitation as well. After the general chapter, the visitors then made a summary of the résumé, including the decisions of the general chapter, to serve as the basis for the following year's visitation of that monastery. This last form, which we will label as the précis, was the one usually included in the minutes of the general chapter.[86] Fortunately, the minutes of the chapter of 1386 include this third form of the *procès verbal*, drawn up by Maurinus de Monteclaio during or after his visitation of the Collège de Cluny in 1386.[87] His précis has three brief sections: the

first assesses the general condition of the college, the second delin-
eates the visitor's decisions, and the third reports the 'definitors''
instructions to the abbot of Cluny concerning the college.

The first section notes—as one would expect from the testimony
given at the inquest—that there was great dissension among the
scholars of the college, to such a degree that they were unwilling to
obey their prior. The précis relates then the decisions which the
Maurinus de Monteclaio made during the visitation: namely that
two scholars, Petrus de Merduno and Robbertus Parisiensis, were
deprived of their pensions—the latter for having been present in the
college ten years (note that Jacobus Heraudi claimed thirteen) and
having done and learned nothing. This accusation is difficult to
credit since Robbertus Parisiensis was a bachelor in theology and
had accomplished this level within the fourteen years deemed
appropriate by the general chapter of 1344. Parisiensis immediately
appealed against the visitor's decision, sought his *apostolos*, and was
instructed to attend the upcoming general chapter to receive them.[88]

The prior then cited two of the monks, Bartholomeus de Matiscone and the *domnus de Bris* (perhaps a scribal error for Bardo
Debas or de Bas), before the court of the abbot of Cluny to answer
various charges contained in the citation but not mentioned in the
précis (except for the accusation that de Matiscone was *bricosus* or
quarrelsome). The précis then notes that the 'definitors' of the
chapter instructed the abbot of Cluny to do whatever he felt was best
concerning the deprivations and citations. The 'definitors' themselves, however, approved what the visitors had ordered, ratified it,
and gave thanks for the work done.

The conditions revealed by the extraordinary visitation of the
Collège de Cluny in 1386—a state of general disorder—mirror the
dislocation which monastic life in particular and the church in
general suffered in the fourteenth and fifteenth centuries. Marcel
Pacaut attributes the decline of the Cluniac Order in the late Middle
Ages both to the external forces it endured and to its inability to
reform itself.[89] These factors are operative too in the malaise of the
Collège de Cluny in 1386. The effects of such external forces as
economic turmoil are apparent in the recurring financial difficulties
already described and in the constant concern which the material
status of the college caused the general chapters of the Order of

Cluny, especially during the fifteen years following the visitation of 1386.[90] The superiors of the Order, however, cannot be faulted for neglecting reform in the college—they hoped for a house where the *disciplina* of the cloister and the *doctrina* of the university[91] could be so combined as to produce holy and learned monks for the good of the church and the renown of the Cluniac Order. The difficulty lay rather in accomplishing such a reform—and for that the scholars in the college needed the 'good zeal' called for in c.72 of Benedict's *Regula* rather than the 'bad zeal' they frequently exhibited throughout the whole of the late Middle Ages.[92]

Conception Abbey
Conception
Missouri 64433
USA

Appendix

Cluniac personnel involved in the visitation of 1386

1. **BUETI**, Johannes, scholar of the Collège de Cluny since 1366, maintained by the prior of Margerie–Hancourt, a bachelor of theology by 1386 (*SCGV*, iv. 185 [see note 2 below]).
2. **CAN**, Johannes, scholar of the Collège de Cluny since 1384, maintained by the dean of Paray-le-Monial, noted as beginning studies in logic (*SCGV*, iv. 185).
3. **CANOBIO** (Chameneux), Jocerandus de, witness at inquiry concerning the Collège de Cluny in 1386 (*SCGV*, iv. 187–8); prior of Crépy-en-Valois 1365–1388 (*Gallia Christiania...* (16 vols.; Paris, 1715–1865), x. 1489–90); twice 'definitor' of the general chapter of the Order of Cluny (1374, 1377) (*SCGV*, iv. 89, 119); four times visitor of the Cluniac province of France (1366, 1378, 1382, 1386) (*SCGV*, iv. 30, 130, 162, 185); mentioned as *subcamerarius* of Cluny in 1370 (*SCGV*, iv. 71); appealed for help from Gregory XI in managing a debt owed to the abbot of Cluny (1374);[93] died March 27, 1388 (*GC*, x. 1490).
4. **CISE**, Baudon (Baudetus) de, scholar of the Collège de Cluny, received in 1386, maintained by the prior of La Voûte-Chilhac,

Maurinus de Monteclaio (*SCGV*, iv. 185); witness at inquest held that year (*SCGV*, iv. 186–7).

5. **COINCY**, scholar of, appears to have been appointed as a scholar but had not yet arrived at the college by April 30, 1386 (*SCGV*, iv. 185).

6. **COSTA**, Guillelmus de, scholar of the Collège de Cluny since 1368, maintained by the prior of Longpont; by 1386 a bachelor of theology (*SCGV*, iv. 185); appointed by Abbot Jacques de Cozan *prior scolarium* in 1383 (*CUP*, iii. 662 [see note 26 below]); mentioned in 1385 in the Johannes Blanchart case as one licensed in theology with no deposition from or deliberation by the Faculty of Theology (*CUP*, iii. 359, 365 [#1511]); licensed again in theology in 1387, presenting himself perhaps for a second time in order that normal procedures of the Faculty of Theology could be followed (BN MS Latin 5657a: fol. 10r).

7. **DEBAS** (de Bas, de Bris?), Bardo, scholar of the Collège de Cluny since 1372, maintained by the prior of Souvigny, Henricus de Iserpanno, a bachelor of theology of 1386 (*SCGV*, iv. 185); likely the *domnus de Bris* cited by Maurinus de Monteclaio at the general chapter to appear in the presence of the abbot of Cluny concerning the accusations made against Bartholomeus de Matiscone (*SCGV*, iv. 237); appears in 1394 on a *rotulus* of the University of Avignon seeking benefices of Pope Benedict XIII as a formed bachelor in theology and a student in canon law in his third year and as prior of the Cluniac house of Autheuil-en-Valois, a dependency of Nanteuil-le-Haudouin.[94]

8. **ELINCOURT**, scholar of, newly received into the Collège de Cluny, maintained by the prior of Elincourt-Ste-Marguerite, studying grammar (*SCGV*, iv. 185).

9. **EPISCOPI**, Ludovicus, scholar of the Collège de Cluny for twelve years (since 1374), maintained by the prior of St-Martin-des-Champs, studying grammar (*SCGV*, iv. 185).

10. **GONTIER**, Michael, scholar of the Collège de Cluny, maintained by the prior of La Charité-sur-Loire, resident for two-and-a-half years, finishing preparatory studies for logic (*SCGV*, iv. 184).

11. **HERAUDI**, Jacobus, *prior scolarium* of the Collège de Cluny and a bachelor of theology in 1386, maintained by the dean of Gaye, resident at the college fifteen years (*SCGV*, iv. 185); a witness at inquiry (*SCGV*, iv. 184–5). The necrology for St-Martin-des-Champs presents, under the date of October 24 (no year is given), a

Jacobus Gueraldi (Giraudi), prior of Moussy-le-Neuf, who left substantial bequests to both St-Martin-des-Champs and Moussy-le-Neuf in return for anniversary remembrances in prayer.[95] It is possible that Jacobus Heraudi and Jacobus Gueraldi are one and the same person, though Jacobus Gueraldi's obituary notice does not mention a degree in theology, as would be customary.

12. **ISERPANNO** (Isserpan, Isserpent), Henricus de, witness at inquiry concerning Collège de Cluny in 1386 (*SCGV*, iv. 188); prior of Souvigny 1370–1412;[96] 'definitor' of general chapter seven times (1373, 1383, 1390, 1394, 1400, 1402, 1404) (*SCGV*, iv. 83, 173, 277, 347, 413, 458, 496); appointed five times visitor of the abbey of Cluny (1373, 1392, 1395, 1399, 1404) *SCGV*, iv. 88, 301, 363, 401, 496); once appointed visitor for the Cluniac province of France (1389) (*SCGV*, iv. 276); noted as *decretorum doctor* in 1389 (*SCGV*, iv. 276); complaints about his administration of Souvigny were made at general chapters in 1406 and 1408 (*SCGV*, iv. 529, 554); he died in 1412.[97]

13. **MATISCONE**, Bartholomeus de, scholar of the Collège de Cluny for fourteen years (since 1374), in 1386 a bachelor of theology lecturing on the *Sentences*, maintained by the prior of Crépy-en-Valois, Jocerandus de Canobio, who gave testimony at the inquiry of 1386 (*SCGV*, iv. 185); cited by Maurinus de Monteclaio at the general chapter of 1386 to appear in the court of the abbot of Cluny to defend himself against the charge of being quarrelsome (*SCGV*, iv. 237); in 1391, licensed in theology at the University of Paris, ranking tenth in ten (BN MS Latin 5657a: fol. 10v); probably the Bartholomeus de Matiscone present at the Council of Pisa in 1409 and described as regent-master in theology at the University of Paris, abbot of the Benedictine house of Molesme,[98] ruling there *c.* 1395–1427 (*Gallia Christiana*, iv. 739).

14. **MERDUNO** (Morduno), Petrus de, scholar of the Collège de Cluny for thirteen years and a bachelor of theology in 1386, maintained by the prior of Romainmoutier (*SCGV*, iv. 185); deprived of his scholastic pension at the Collège de Cluny by Maurinus de Monteclaio, visitor of the college in 1386 (*SCGV*, iv. 237).

15. **MONTECLAIO**, Maurinus de, visitor of the Collège de Cluny in 1386 (*SCGV*, iv. 184); prior of La Voûte-Chilhac, ruled between 1385 and sometime before 1406 (noted as *prior modernus* in 1385 [*SCGV*, iv. 183]); in 1385, appointed representative of the Order of

Cluny, along with the prior of Trouhaut, to the papal court and the royal court (*SCGV*, iv. 183); at the same time appointed visitor, with the prior of Trouhaut, to the Cluniac provinces of France, Auvergne, and Provence (*SCGV*, iv. 183); reported on inquiry concerning the Collège de Cluny to general chapter in 1386 (*SCGV*, iv. 237); five times appointed 'definitor' of the general chapter (1390, 1392, 1396, 1399, 1401) (*SCGV*, iv. 277, 301, 372, 401, 432); three times appointed visitor of the abbey of Cluny (1386, 1397, 1402) (*SCGV*, iv. 317, 347, 484); once again visitor of the Cluniac province of Auvergne (1394) (*SCGV*, iv. 370); sent to the papal court to plead for Cluniac priories held *in commendam* (1396) (*SCGV*, iv. 372); listed as a *decretorum doctor* when chosen to inform the king's council on the state of the Order of Cluny (1399) (*SCGV*, iv. 404).

16. **MORCORT**, Petrus de, scholar of the Collège de Cluny for twelve years, studying logic, maintained by the dean of Lihons-en-Santerre (*SCGV*, iv. 185).

17. **MOUSSY-LE-NEUF**, prior of, witness at inquiry concerning the Collège de Cluny in 1386 (*SCGV*, iv. 186). Moussy-le-Neuf was a dependent priory of St-Martin-des-Champs in the diocese of Paris; during his testimony, the prior stated he had lived in Paris and claimed to be familiar with the situation and reputation of the scholars of the college (*SCGV*, iv. 186).

18. **MURATO**, Johannes de, scholar of the Collège de Cluny for eight years, was finishing grammar studies in 1386 and was maintained by the prior of St-Leu-d'Esserent (*SCGV*, iv. 185). When Bego de Murato, a licentiate in theology and possible former *prior scolarium* of the Collège de Cluny, was named abbot of Fleury in 1404, a Johannes de Murato was among those taking possession of Fleury in Bego de Murato's name. The text notes this Johannes de Murato as a bachelor in canon law and prior of Bolbec, a dependency of the abbey of Bernay, formerly held by Bego de Murato, who would later serve as Bego de Murato's procurator.[99]

19. **PARISIENSIS**, Robbertus, bachelor in theology, resident of the Collège de Cluny for thirteen years by 1386, maintained by the dean of Nogent-le-Rotrou (*SCGV*, iv. 185); Maurinus de Monteclaio deprived him of his *bourse* at the college '. . . *quia fuit scholaris per decem annos et nihil fecit, neque profuit in scientia* . . .'; Parisiensis appealed against the decision and was given a date to appear before the court of the abbot of Cluny (*SCGV*, iv. 237).

20. **RAMBAUT**, Petrus, scholar at the Collège de Cluny for three years, maintained by the prior of Abbeville; he was completing his grammar studies (*SCGV*, iv. 185).

21. **TROUHAUT**, prior of, appointed extraordinary visitor of the Cluniac provinces of France, Auvergne, and Provence by the general chapter in 1385 (*SCGV*, iv. 183); priors of Trouhaut appear each year in the records of the Order of Cluny from 1378 through 1386, but it is not clear that all these are one and the same person; in 1378, the prior of Trouhaut appears as a 'definitor' of the general chapter, listed fourteenth out of fifteen in seniority (*SCGV*, iv. 121); in 1383, he is a 'definitor' listed seventh in seniority (*SCGV*, iv. 163); in 1386, the prior of Trouhaut is again a 'definitor', this time holding the twelfth place (*SCGV*, iv. 189); at the same chapter he is named visitor of the church of Cluny (*SCGV*, iv. 250). Based on his loss of position in seniority between 1383 and 1386, one could suggest that the prior of Trouhaut, appointed extraordinary visitor in 1385, had been appointed prior sometime between 1383 and 1385. Such a suggestion is very tentative—one's position in the seniority listing of the 'definitors' could change from year to year, depending on who was elected 'definitor'. More senior priors of the Order could serve one year, and the prior of Trouhaut's position could be lower; priors junior in service could be elected the next year and the prior of Trouhaut's position could be elevated. It should be noted that the priory of Trouhaut was held *in commendam* by 1390 (*SCGV*, iv. 278).

22. **VOMITIS**, Stephanus, scholar of the Collège de Cluny for only a half-year by 1386, began his grammar studies that year, maintained by the prior of La Charité-sur-Loire (*SCGV*, iv. 184).

REFERENCES

* The author is grateful to the National Endowment for the Humanities for a grant which enabled him to finish work on this article and to Canon Astrik Gabriel, O. Praem. and Professor John Van Engen of The Medieval Institute of the University of Notre Dame for their hospitality during his time spent there. Thanks are owed also to Professors Theodore Goudge and Stephen E. Fox, of the Geo-Technical Services division of Northwest Missouri State University in Maryville, Missouri, for their kindness and skill in producing the map accompanying the text.

1. The Cluniac visitation system is discussed in some detail in Guy de Valous, *Le Monachisme clunisien des origines au XVᵉ siècle* Archives de la France monastique, nos. 39–40 (2 vols.; Ligugé, 1935; 2nd ed. rev., Paris, 1970), ii 95–114.
2. *Statuts, chapitres généraux et visites de l'Ordre de Cluny*, ed. Gaston Charvin (9 vols. and supplement; Paris, 1965–82), iv. 186–8. Hereinafter abbreviated as *SCGV*.
3. *SCGV*, iv. 183.
4. *SCGV*, iv. 237.
5. See Stephen Ferruolo, *The Origins of the University: The Schools of Paris and their Critics, 1100–1215* (Stanford, Ca. 1985), p. 313, for a discussion of the origins of the houses of study for the religious orders at the University of Paris.
6. The presence of the *monachi nigri* at the medieval university is surveyed by Ursmer Berlière, 'Les Collèges bénédictins aux universités du Moyen-Age', *Revue Bénédictine*, 10 (1893), 145–58, and by Jean Leclercq, 'Les Études universitaires dans l'ordre de Cluny', *Mélanges bénédictines publiées à l'occasion du XIVᵉ centénaire de la mort de Saint-Benoît par les moines de l'abbaye de Saint-Jerôme de Rome* (Abbaye de Saint-Wandrille, 1947), pp. 351–71. See also James E. Sullivan, 'Studia monastica: Benedictine and Cluniac Monks at the University of Paris, 1229–1500', Ph.D. dissertation Univ. of Wisconsin–Madison (1982).
7. Donatella Nebbiai dalla Guarda, 'Le Collège de Paris de l'abbaye de Saint-Denis-en-France (XIIIᵉ-XVIIᵉ siècle),' in *Sous la Règle de Saint-Benoît: Structures monastiques et sociétés en France du moyen-age à l'époque moderne* (Geneva, 1982), pp. 461–88.
8. Edmond Kwanten, 'Le Collège Saint-Bernard à Paris, sa fondation et ses débuts', *Revue d'histoire ecclésiastique*, 43 (1948), 443–72; Louis J. Lekai, 'The Cistercian College of Saint Bernard in Paris in the Fifteenth Century', *Cistercian Studies*, 6 (1971), 172–9; Pierre Dautrey, 'Croissance et adaptation chez les cisterciens au treizième siècle. Les débuts au collège des Bernardins de Paris', *Analecta cisterciensia*, 32 (1976), 122–215.
9. Pierre Anger, *Le Collège de Cluny* (Paris, 1916).
10. The Collège de Marmoutier has received little attention from historians both of the medieval university and of medieval monasticism. Treatment of the college's history has been relegated to histories of the city of Paris: see Adolphe Berty and L. M. Tissersand, *Topographie historique de vieux Paris: Région centrale de l'université* (Paris, 1897), pp. 269–71, 489–92, and Michel Félibien, *Histoire de la ville de Paris* (5 vols.; Paris, 1725) i. 570–2 and iii. 395–8.
11. Anger, *Le Collège de Cluny*, p. 14.
12. These statutes, with the exception of those promulgated in 1365, are published in *SCGV*. The statutes for 1301 are found in *SCGV*, i. 83; for 1314, in *SCGV*, i. 130–7; for 1383, *SCGV*, iv. 167–9; for 1399, *SCGV*, iv.

406–8. The statutes published in 1365 can be found in Th.J. Sullivan, 'The Collège de Cluny: Statutes of Abbot Simon de la Brosse (1365),' *Revue Bénédictine*, 98 (1988), 169–77.

13. *SCGV*, iii. 460–1.

14. The text describing the sad state of the Cluniac Order and the commissioning of the visitation of the Cluniac provinces of France, Auvergne and Provence can be found in *SCGV*, iv. 183–4. The definitors of the Cluniac general chapters numbered fifteen in the fourteenth century. Elected by the members of the chapter, their task was to act as the chapter's executive committee while the chapter was in session; the definitors were delegated the legislative, administrative, and judicative powers of the chapter. Their duties included naming provincial visitors for the coming year, receiving the reports of the previous year's visitations, and ordering corrective measures which such reports might necessitate. They also arbitrated disputes and, at the end of each general chapter, confided to a few of their number the care of urgent affairs until the next general chapter. For general information concerning definitors and their role at general chapters of the religious orders, see Jacques Hourlier, *L'Âge classique (1140–1378)*. *Les Religieux* (Paris, 1974), pp. 383–5. The 'definitors' and their role in the Cluniac general chapters are discussed in Valous, *Le Monachisme clunisien*, ii. 86–90.

15. When Abbot Jacques de Cozan died on his way to Avignon at Lyon on July 16, 1383, Pope Clement VII appointed the deceased abbot's grandnephew, Jean de Damas-Cozan, as abbot of Cluny, who would rule until 1400. His abbacy is described briefly in: *Dictionnaire d'histoire et de géographie ecclésiastique* (Paris, 1913-), xiii. 103.

16. At the death of Pope Gregory IX at Rome in March, 1378, Cluny declared her allegiance to Clement VII, who took up residence at Avignon. See Jean Leclercq, 'Cluny pendant le Grand Schisme d'Occident', *Revue Mabillon*, 32 (1942), 119–32.

17. *Bibliotheca cluniacensis*, ed. Martin Marrier and André Duschesne, (Paris, 1614; repr. Macon, 1915), col. 1708.

18. *SCGV*, iv. 278.

19. This tentative dating is suggested by the distinct cluster of references in the administrative records of the Order of Cluny to a prior of La Voûte-Chilhac between 1385 and 1403, named in *SCGV*, iv. 186, as visitor to the Collège de Cluny in 1386.

20. See Appendix, #15.

21. Marcel Pacaut, *L'Ordre de Cluny* (Paris, 1986), pp. 232–4, 254–65.

22. *SCGV*, iv. 189–95 (Auvergne), 209–34 (Provence), 234–37 (France).

23. *SCGV*, iv. 276.

24. *SCGV*, iv. 186.

25. *SCGV*, iv. 184–6, presents the text of Jacobus Heraudi's testimony.

26. *Chartularium universitatis parisiensis*, eds. H. Denifle and E. Chatelain (4 vols; Paris, 1889–97), i. 571. Hereinafter abbreviated as *CUP*.
27. *CUP*, ii. 661–2.
28. *CUP*, ii. 548.
29. Nebbiai dalla Guarda, 'Le Collège de Paris de l'abbaye de St-Denis-en-France', pp. 464–5.
30. Félibien, *Histoire de la ville de Paris*, iii. 396; *CUP*, iii. 538 (#1588).
31. *SCGV*, i. 131, #95.
32. *SCGV*, iii. 392–3.
33. *SCGV*, iv. 167.
34. *SCGV*, i. 83, 95.
35. *SCGV*, i. 134, #104.
36. *SCGV*, i. 159–60, #105.
37. Astrik Gabriel treats of the *scientia primitiva* in 'Preparatory Teaching in Parisian Colleges in the Fourteenth Century', in *Garlandia: Studies in the History of the Medieval University* (Frankfurt-am-Main, 1969), pp. 97–124.
38. Hélène Millet, 'Les Pères du Concile de Pise (1409): edition d'une nouvelle liste', *Mélanges de l'Ecole Française de Rome: Moyen Age–Temps Modernes* 93 (1981), 744 (#263).
39. For the text of Henricus de Iserpanno's testimony, see *SCGV*, iv. 188.
40. By 1386, the Order of Cluny supported for the education of its monk at universities, in addition to the Collège de Cluny in Paris, the monastery of St-Pierre-des-Cuisines in Toulouse, founded in 1067 and established as a college by the abbot of Moissac, Bernard de Montaigu (1286–90) [cf. C. E. Smith, *The University of Toulouse in the Middle Ages* (Milwaukee, 1958), pp. 87, 117, 118, and 120] and the Collège de St-Martial in Avignon, established in 1379 by the abbot of Cluny, Jacques de Cadols (1374–83) [cf. Guy de Valous, 'Un collège clunisien: le prieuré collège de Saint-Martial à Avignon', *Revue Mabillon*, 18 (1928), 284–301].
41. For further information about the vicars and their duties, see Valous, *Monachisme clunisien*, ii 45–54.
42. See Philippe Wolff, *Western Languages*: AD 100–1500 (New York and Toronto, 1971), pp. 146–57.
43. See Sullivan, 'Collège de Cluny', 176, #22.
44. *SCGV*, iv. 184–88.
45. *SCGV*, iv. 186, 187.
46. *SCGV*, i. 83, #95; 131, #94; iv. 167.
47. *SCGV*, i. 131, #94; iii. 392; iv. 167.
48. *SCGV*, iii. 392.
49. *Concilia Magnae Britanniae et Hiberniae*, ed. D. Wilkins (4 vols.; London, 1737), ii. 595.
50. *SCGV*, i. 83, #95; 131, #94.
51. *SCGV*, ii. 373–4.

52. *SCGV*, iv. 186, 188.
53. *SCGV*, iv. 186, 187.
54. *SCGV*, i. 253.
55. *SCGV*, ii. 75.
56. *SCGV*, i. 145; i. 160, #106; ii. 273; iv. 120.
57. Sullivan, 'Collège du Cluny', 175, #16.
58. *SCGV*, iv. 368.
59. *Bullarium sacri ordinis Cluniacensis*, ed. P. Symon (Lyon, 1680), p. 171.
60. *SCGV*, ii. 373.
61. Symon, *Bullarium*, p. 171.
62. Anger, *Collège de Cluny*, p. 19.
63. Wilkins, *Concilia*, ii. 596.
64. *SCGV*, iv. 314.
65. *SCGV*, iv. 186, 187–88.
66. *SCGV*, iii. 335 (1342), 414–5 (1345); iv. 131 (1378).
67. *SCGV*, ii. 90.
68. *SCGV*, ii. 255. Sometime in the fourteenth century, a register of monasteries and their dependencies, as well as the statutory number of monks assigned to each house, was published; it is presented in the *Bibliotheca cluniacensis*, cols. 1705–56.
69. *SCGV*, iv. 187.
70. Harry A. Miskimin, *Money, Prices, and Foreign Exchange in Fourteenth Century France* (New Haven and London, 1963), p. 68, fig. 9.
71. Léon Côte, *Contributions à l'histoire du prieuré de Souvigny* (Moulins, 1942), p. 168.
72. Heinrich Denifle, *La Désolation des églises, monastères et hôpitaux en France pendant la guerre de cent ans* (2 vols.; Macon, 1897; repr. Brussels, 1965), i. 709–10.
73. *SCGV*, iv. 188.
74. A discussion of the responsibilities of the *prior scolarium* of the Collège de Cluny may be found in Sullivan, 'Studia monastica', pp. 40–7.
75. Valous, *Monachisme clunisien*, i. 191.
76. Félibien, *Histoire de la ville de Paris*, iii. 397(#25). The statutes also presume that the *procurator* of the college will normally be the prior of Notre-Dame-des-Champs, giving the *magister* of the college additional support in the day-to-day affairs of the college. See Félibien, *Histoire de la ville de Paris*, iii. 396(#1).
77. The statutes published in 1365 can be found in Sullivan, 'Collège de Cluny', 160–77; those published in 1383 have been presented in *SCGV*, iv. 167–9.
78. *SCGV*, iv. 188: '... [E]t si isto isto modo fiat, non dubito quin prosperetur.'
79. The *baccalarius formatus* was a student in theology in the third and final phase of his bachelorship, lasting, according to university regulations in 1335, for four years. The duties of a 'formed bachelor' are discussed in

Gordon Leff, *Paris and Oxford Universities in the Thirteenth and Fourteenth Centuries: An Institutional and Intellectual History* (New York, 1968; repr. Huntingdon, New York, 1975), p. 167.
80. *SCGV*, iv. 188.
81. See Pierre Minard, 'Du dortoir à la cellule', *La Vie bénédictine*, 46 (1938), 17–25.
82. Hourlier, *L'Âge classique*, p. 292.
83. *SCGV*, iii. 336.
84. Sullivan, 'Collège de Cluny', 176, #19.
85. *SCGV*, i. 63, 107, 157; Sullivan, 'Collège de Cluny', 174, #10. The Cluniac texts do not make a distinction between private chambers as studies and private chambers as living quarters and probably the scholars did not either.
86. Valous, *Le Monachisme clunisien*, ii. 105.
87. The text relating to the Collège de Cluny is presented both in *SCGV*, iv. 237 and *CUP*, iv. 15(#1730), with a significant difference between the two concerning the dating of the text, perhaps a result of the use of different manuscripts as the basis of the editions. The editors of the *CUP* date the text to April 23, 1396; Charvin dates the text to May 13, 1386, which is obviously correct, given the sequence of events and the correspondence of names between the original testimony and the summary of the résumé.
88. *Dictionnaire de Droit Canonique* (Paris, 1935–65), i. 690–8, *s.v.* '*Apostoli*'. *Apostoli* were letters addressed by an inferior judge (in this case, Maurinus de Monteclaio) to a superior judge (in this case the abbot of Cluny) testifying that a decision had been the subject of an appeal. Without *apostoli*, the appeal could not proceed to a superior court.
89. Pacaut, *L'Ordre de Cluny*, p. 233.
90. *SCGV*, iv. 249, 313, 368, 394, 406, 409, 412, 430, 446–7.
91. Ferruolo, *The Origins of the Medieval University*, p. 313.
92. *Règle de saint Benoît*, ed. and comment. Adalbert de Vogüé and Jean Neufville (Sources Chrétiennes 181–186; Paris, 1971–2), clxxxii. 670–1.
93. See above, note 57.
94. *Les Statuts et privilèges des universités françaises depuis leur fondation jusqu'en 1789*, ed. Marcel Fournier (3 vols.; Paris, 1890–1892; repr. Aalen, 1970), ii. 35(#1270).
95. Wolf-Dieter Heim, Joachim Mehne, Franz Neiske, Dietrich Poeck, *Synopse der cluniacensischen Necrologien*, published under the direction of Joachim Wollasch (2 vols.; Munich, 1982), p. 525. This information was kindly brought to my attention by Dr. Franz Neiske of the Institut für Frühmittelalterforschung, Westfälische Wilhelms-Universität in Münster.
96. Léon Côte, *Moines, sires et ducs à Souvigny. Le Saint-Denis Bourbonnais* (Paris, 1966), pp. 177–84.

97. Côte, *Moines, sires et ducs à Souvigny*, p. 177.
98. Millet, 'Pise', p. 744(#263).
99. Johannes Berland, 'Deux abbés auvergnats de Saint-Benoît-sur-Loire: Jean de la Tour (1358–1371) et Begon de Murat (1404–1414)', *Revue Mabillon*, 60 (1982), 103–15.

Law and Gospel: The Importance of Philosophy at Reformation Wittenberg

Sachiko Kusukawa

Everything the papacy has instituted and ordered serves only to increase sin and error. What else are the universities, unless they are utterly changed from what they have been hitherto, than what the book of Maccabees calls *gymnasia epheborum et graecae gloriae*? What are they but places where loose living is practised, where little is taught of the Holy Scriptures and Christian faith, and where only the blind, heathen teacher Aristotle rules far more than Christ? In this regard my advice would be that Aristotle's *Physics, Metaphysics, Concerning the Soul,* and *Ethics,* which hitherto have been thought to be his best books, should be completely discarded along with all the rest of his books that boast about nature, although nothing can be learned from them either about nature or the Spirit.... I dare say that any potter has more knowledge of nature than is written in these books. It grieves me to the quick that this damned, conceited, rascally heathen has deluded and made fools of so many of the best Christians with his misleading writings. God has sent him as a plague upon us on account of our sins.[1]

Such criticism of Aristotelian philosophy by Martin Luther is all too famous, and, compared to his other remarks, even mild.[2] As if in stark contrast, however, twenty-five years after Luther had written these words, Philip Melanchthon, Luther's friend and ally, wrote the following regulations for the Wittenberg arts faculty:

... there shall be ten lecturers of languages and of philosophy: two inspectors of the college ... of whom one shall teach natural philosophy (*physicen*) and the second book of Pliny's [*Historia naturalis*].... The eighth shall be a natural philosophy lecturer who shall teach Aristotle's *Physica* and Dioscorides and shall be a pointer-out (*monstrator*) of herbs.... The tenth shall be a lecturer of the Greek language.... He shall also incorporate some epistle of Paul. . . . The same lecturer shall be the moral philosophy lecturer. . . . whoever the moral philosophy lecturer shall be, he shall teach Aristotle's Greek *Ethica* verbatim. But he should diligently discriminate between the different kinds of teachings: the Law of God, the Gospel, philosophical precepts and civil matters on behaviour, and shall distinguish between the sects of philosophers and shall illustrate these precepts with examples.[3]

It seems as if Melanchthon was prescribing the very Aristotelian philosophy which Luther had rejected. The views of Luther and Melanchthon, who taught side by side at the University of Wittenberg and who were engaged in the Reform of the Church, thus seem strangely incompatible. However, the seeming contradiction between these two passages should in fact be understood as highlighting the significant transformation that philosophy as a university discipline underwent (as I shall be arguing) at the hands of Melanchthon: Melanchthon had created a new kind of philosophy which was at once compatible with and useful for Lutheran theology.[4] The kind of philosophy developed by Melanchthon was substantially different from the one that Luther had been objecting to, and we need to look into the historical context in order to understand why they wrote about philosophy in the way that they did. When we recognize Melanchthon's reasons for needing a philosophy with a new and positive meaning, we shall also be able to appreciate the unity of what on first inspection looks like a piecemeal collection of philosophical studies in the 1545 statutes and to understand what place philosophy occupied at Wittenberg.

By 1517 Luther had reached a new understanding of justification and accordingly he proceeded to re-interpret the whole Bible. Luther's message of the Word of God was twofold:

The Law is the Word in which God teaches and tells us what we are to do and not to do, as in the Ten Commandments. Now wherever human nature is alone, without the grace of God, the Law cannot be kept, because since Adam's fall in Paradise man is corrupt and has nothing but a wicked desire to sin. . . . The other Word of God is not Law or commandment, nor does it require anything of us; but after the first Word, that of the Law, has done this work and distressful misery and poverty have been produced in the heart, God comes and offers His lovely, living Word, and promises, pledges, and obligates Himself to give grace and help, that we may get out of this misery and that all sins not only be forgiven but also blotted out. . . . See, this divine promise of His grace and of the forgiveness of sin is properly called Gospel.[5]

As often depicted by Lucas Cranach, both Law and Gospel constituted the core of Luther's understanding of justification by faith alone.[6] The knowledge that however hard one tried to follow the Law, i.e. what one should do or not do, human beings cannot merit salvation on their own, denied the validity of works righteousness promoted by the Papacy. Instead Luther claimed that people are justified by faith in the crucified Christ alone. Luther passionately preached and wrote about what he believed to be the true message of the Gospel, justification by faith alone. At the same time he vigorously attacked whatever stood in the way of establishing the Gospel.

It was as part of his call for Reform of the Church that Luther attacked Aristotle. For, his home university, Wittenberg, since its foundation in 1502, had been teaching an arts curriculum that was dominated by Aristotle and essentially orientated towards the kind of theology that Luther opposed. By 1508 students wishing to take the BA degree at Wittenberg had to hear the lectures on Petrus Hispanus' *Summulae Logicales*, on Aristotle's *Analytica Priora*, *Analytica Posteriora*, *Topica*, and *Sophistici Elenchi*, and on grammar, while those wishing to take the MA degree were required to hear the lectures on the new and old logic as well as on Aristotle's *Physica*, *De anima*, *De caelo et mundo*, *De generatione et corruptione*, *Meteorologica*, *Parva naturalia*, *Ethica* and *Metaphysica*, and mathematics. These lectures were offered in three different ways (*viae*): the ways of Thomas Aquinas, of Duns Scotus, and of Gregory of Rimini.[7] Although it is now customary for Reformation historians to note the statutory prescription of the way of Gregory of Rimini in the light of Luther's debt to medieval nominalism,[8] here by contrast I wish to stress the predominance of Aristotelian philosophy in this arts curriculum as well as the Scholastic nature of the philosophy which was being practised at Wittenberg.[9]

The commentaries of Petrus Tartaretus and of Martin Polich von Mellerstadt which we know were used at Wittenberg,[10] were typically 'Scholastic' in that they followed the method and authority of the Schoolmen, using the *quaestio* method whereby statements of Aristotle which seem to contradict himself, the Schoolmen or the Church, are resolved by logical reasoning and distinctions often drawn from other Scholastic authorities.[11] Thus the best human rational knowledge was attained on the basis of logic, Aristotle, Scholastic authorities, and the teaching of the Church.[12] All of Aristotle's nature books, the *Metaphysica* and the *Ethica*, one after another, were commented upon in this way. The study of the *Metaphysica* in particular lent powerful support to theology as a rational examination of the various modes of the being of God,[13] while Scholastic natural philosophy provided theology with the grounds for elucidating certain doctrines such as that of the Eucharist, and theology in turn guided for instance the way the universe as God's creation should be understood.[14]

Though the extent of humanist scholarship at Wittenberg, even before the foundation of the University, has been carefully documented by historians interested in tracing the background of (Luther's) 'Biblical humanism',[15] it has to be stressed that insofar as philosophy teaching was concerned, humanism had minimal influence at Wittenberg.[16]

Although it may be an exaggeration to claim that Luther denied the validity of any form of philosophy,[17] it is nevertheless noteworthy that whenever he spoke of Aristotelian philosophy he usually meant philosophy as taught in the universities and he did not speak of that philosophy in kindly terms. During the early years of the Reformation, it was primarily by pointing out his differences with and the shortcomings of the Papacy, that Luther fought to establish his message of the Gospel. He vigorously attacked the teachings and institutions of the Papacy. As Luther saw universities as one of the institutions maintaining and perpetuating the errors of the Papacy, and indeed saw the Scholastic kind of philosophy (as taught at Wittenberg) as an important part of an intellectual system for Roman Catholic theology, his attack on Aristotelian philosophy was also harsh and often vitriolic.

At Wittenberg, Luther actively campaigned to remove Scholastic philosophy from the curriculum: he petitioned that Aristotle's *Ethica* which he regarded as 'the worst enemy of grace' should be dropped from degree requirements[18] and that the Thomist way of teaching logic and philosophy be abolished altogether.[19] In his writings such as the *Disputation Against Scholastic Theology* and *An Address to the Christian Nobility of Germany*, he strongly called for the comprehensive abolition of Aristotelian philosophy from the universities. As people started to embrace the new Lutheran faith at

Wittenberg, they began to refuse to teach Scholastic philosophy too. For instance, Melanchthon's disaffection with Aristotle and philosophy became such that he flatly refused to teach Aristotle's *Physica*[20] and announced his total distrust of human reason:

... what else do the philosophers teach but external works? When they discuss the virtues, do they not relate all things to external works and those fictitious, elicited acts? But they are blind leaders of the blind. Therefore, it is hoped that God will change our minds from the judgement of human reason and from philosophy to spiritual discernment. For the blindness of human reason is such that we cannot recognize the full nature of sin or righteousness without the light of the Spirit. All the capacities of human reason are mere shadows.[21]

Furthermore, Johann Dölsch, hitherto lecturer on Aristotle's *De anima*, begged to be discharged from his teaching on the ground of 'his new faith'.[22] It is impossible to tell whether or when Scholastic philosophy was abandoned altogether at Wittenberg because the official records of the University are patchy with respect to philosophy teaching from 1521 onwards. Yet, we may reasonably assume from the above instances that when most of the members of the University became adherents of the Lutheran faith, the teaching of Scholastic philosophy could hardly have been tolerated.[23]

It is not until 1545 that we read a full official endorsement of the teaching of philosophy, in the form of statutes of the arts faculty, as quoted at the beginning. As a comparison with the 1536 (re-) foundation document indicates, however, the 1545 statutes were not so much stipulating a new set of texts or lectures as confirming a pre-existing structure of teaching: natural philosophy and moral philosophy lectures had been prescribed in the arts faculty from 1536.[24] We know that in practice the teaching of Aristotelian philosophy had been restarted much earlier than 1545. For instance, when Melanchthon's commentary on Aristotle's *De anima*, the *Commentarius de anima*, was published in 1540, it was immediately put to use in the lectures.[25] Vitus Amerbach also taught the *De anima*, but apparently in deliberate opposition to Melanchthon's interpretation.[26] It seems that Aristotle's *De anima* and other of his nature books were taught at an even earlier date, during the early 1530s, by Johann Feltkirch (Velcurio).[27] The earliest example we have, in fact, of Aristotelian philosophy being positively taught at Reformation

Wittenberg is Melanchthon's lectures on Aristotle's *Ethica (Nico-machea)*. Melanchthon made his intentions known in 1527 that he wished to teach Aristotle's *Ethica* and taught it frequently from 1532 until the year of his death.[28]

It is through this *Ethica* that Aristotelian philosophy was re-introduced positively into the arts curriculum at Wittenberg. This marked a striking reversal of attitude on Melanchthon's part towards philosophy. As I have argued elsewhere, Melanchthon's re-evaluation of philosophy should be understood as his response to the disturbances caused by the Anabaptists.[29] His experience during a visitation to Thuringia in 1527 convinced Melanchthon of the utmost need to argue against civil obedience if Luther's cause was to survive in dissociation from the evangelical radicals.[30] Moral philo-sophy thus became for Melanchthon a legitimate study sanctioned by Christ:

> Jesus Christ does not take away civil manners (*civiles mores*) from Christian teaching, but rather, requires them. He also approves philosophy or reasoning (*rationem*) teaching about civil manners, just as He also approves of civil magistracy and bears witness that He is the author of civil government, in Romans 13 [.1] 'the powers that be are ordained by God'. He nevertheless demands even of those who do not have the Holy Spirit that they be checked by civil justice.[31]

Moral philosophy was thus to furnish Melanchthon with a strong basis for the claim that even those without faith (such as the Anabaptists) should comply with civil law. Melanchthon is, how-ever, careful to draw a clear distinction between this and the message of the Gospel, a distinction which previous kinds of philosophy did not keep:

> ... it is not philosophy but inane dreams, when we judge about the divine Will from reason.... those who taught that we are justified by our own merits were confusing philosophy with Christian teaching.... Thus to affirm as certain what reason or philosophy cannot affirm, or rather what are placed beyond the judgement of reason and of philosophy, this indeed is empty deceit ... The Gospel is the teaching of spiritual life and of justification in the eyes of God; but philosophy is the doctrine of the corporeal life (*doctrina vitae corporalis*); just as you see that medicine serves health, the turning points of storms serve navigators, so civil behaviour

serves the common peace of all men. The use of philosophy in this way is very necessary and approved of by God ...[32]

By confining philosophy to deal with the external welfare of man, as opposed to his spiritual welfare, the realm of Gospel, Melanchthon now claims for philosophy a positive and necessary role. Indeed, as the teaching about how to regulate external actions—what to do and not do in civil life – Melanchthon gives philosophy a status of (Lutheran) Law:

Philosophy is neither gospel nor any part of it, but it is a part of divine law. For it is the law of nature itself divinely written in men's minds, which is truly the law of God concerning those virtues which reason understands and which are necessary for civil life. For philosophy, properly speaking, is nothing other than the explanation of the law of nature. . . . To oversimplify, philosophy is the law of God as far as reason understands law ...[33]

This re-evaluation and re-definition of philosophy meant that a completely new set of textbooks became necessary. Melanchthon wrote a set of philosophical textbooks, writings whose content and format are largely dictated by their didactic use, which were published and used frequently in the latter half of the sixteenth century.[34] Instead of proceeding meticulously along the text of Aristotle with expanded commentaries in the form of *quaestiones*, Melanchthon proceeded by summarizing Aristotle's arguments (often rearranging them), sometimes omitting topics and at other times adding material from other ancient or contemporary authors. Each section was headed by questions such as 'what is moral philosophy?', 'what is the soul?', 'what is the world?' etc., followed straightaway by brief and succinct answers, often reinforced with testimonies from other classical and contemporary authors. Although 'catechetical'[35] in nature and seemingly eclectic, it is precisely because they are 'textbooks' that we may all the more appreciate from them the clear goal Melanchthon set for philosophy in the universities.

In the *Philosophia moralis epitome* (1538),[36] Melanchthon firmly sets out the importance of moral philosophy: although it cannot teach salvation as the Gospel does, it is nevertheless praiseworthy as a part of divine Law.[37] As a creature of God made in His image, the Christian man's goal is 'to follow divine Law and true philosophy, i.e. to acknowledge God, obey Him, reveal and illustrate His Glory and maintain human society according to God.'[38] In moral philosophy, which deals with external actions in civil life, man's goal is to pursue virtue which is defined, according to Aristotle, as 'a habit, which inclines the will to obey right reason.'[39] Not all philosophical opinions are true, and philosophy is true only when it contains demonstration.[40] On the basis of Romans (1.19, 20), Melanchthon claims that there exists in man 'natural law', or innate knowledge. 'Honour your parents', 'Obey the laws of magistrates' are just such precepts of natural law for Melanchthon.[41] This is the basis from which moral philosophy can demonstrate, following his criteria of demonstration ('principles' [innate knowledge], universal experience, and syllogistic reasoning),[42] the truth of certain laws, such as the following:

> Actions which disturb the society of mankind are to be prohibited.
> Thefts, freebooting and the like disturb the society of mankind.
> Therefore thefts, freebooting and the like should be prohibited.
> The major premise is a principle. The minor premise has the evidence of experience and both are therefore most certain. What the lawyers call the law of nature, or strictly speaking law of the peoples is nothing unless it is knowledge of certain principles of behaviour and civil life.[43]

By positing knowledge of (civil) good and bad, and the desirability of civil obedience as part of the knowledge innate in man, Melanchthon's moral philosophy lends support to various laws and regulations pertaining to social order. The duty of magistrates to punish the impious and support the faithful is discussed in particular detail. In terms of proper conduct in civil life, Melanchthon further draws on Aristotle's *Ethica* when explaining the ideas of moderation, temperance, and the various types of civil justice. It is impossible to miss the lesson: the necessity of obeying God's will on the one hand and of obeying civil law of magistrates on the other.

The *Commentarius de anima* (1540)[44] on which Melanchthon had been working for seven years, was unusual for a commentary of its time in that it contained in its first part an extensive discussion on Galenic anatomy.[45] Melanchthon drew extensively on Galen's teleological explanation of the human body in order to point out that every single part of the human body was created by God according to Providential design. For instance, Melanchthon was prepared to doubt the existence of a 'natural spirit' since its use seemed to be superfluous.[46] Furthermore, his discussion of the traditional topics of the *De anima*, such as his account of the rational soul, followed the basic tenets of Lutheran theology. Melanchthon was adamant that the human will had no spiritual freedom to attain salvation, and he redefined 'synteresis', which used to denote man's power to avoid sin and aspire for eternal life, to mean only knowledge of civil good and bad.[47] Melanchthon's *Commentarius de anima*, guided by Lutheran principles, was written in order to demonstrate that God had created every part of the human body and soul, namely the whole man, for a certain purpose. This provided the starting point of moral philosophy for Melanchthon:

Moral philosophy takes from natural philosophy this proposition: the nature of man was created for a certain purpose. This is demonstrated in natural philosophy, but not confirmed in moral philosophy. But it is accepted in moral philosophy as a hypothesis, namely a firm proposition, which is taken from elsewhere so that it may be the starting point of moral philosophy.[48]

As we can readily see from the list of *loci*, principal topics to be learned, in Melanchthon's *Initia doctrinae physicae* (1549),[49] the whole of his natural philosophy was designed to demonstrate the starting point for moral philosophy. The list starts with God, Providence, the world, the heavens, followed by the powers and movements of planets, the elements, matter, form, privation, causes, etc., fate, comets, metals, ending with the parts of man, the vegetative, sensitive, appetitive, locomotive, and intellective soul, the intellect, the will, freedom of the human will, causes of vice and virtue, and the end of man.[50] As is obvious, the *Commentarius de anima* covered the gamut of topics on man. The *Initia doctrinae physicae*, which incorporated discussions of Aristotle's *Physica, De generatione et corruptione, Meteorologica* and *De caelo*, was to cover the rest of the topics. However, there were topics which Aristotle did not deal with comprehensively or sufficiently and hence Melanchthon used, for instance, for the astrological part of the *Initia*, Ptolemy's *Tetrabiblos*.[51] For knowledge of plants and herbs, Dioscorides or Nicander was used;[52] Ptolemy's *Geographia* was also read in order to teach how God had purposefully designed the earth,[53] and the second book of Pliny's *Historia naturalis* was regarded as a useful text which demonstrated God's Providential plan in the

physical universe.[54] Melanchthon's natural philosophy thus set out
to prove the existence of God's Providence in the physical universe
which, as I argue elsewhere, was a specifically Lutheran view of
God's governance over creation.[55]

Melanchthon re-evaluated philosophy when he saw that civil
disturbances caused by the radical evangelicals were jeopardizing
Luther's cause. He thus wrote a new textbook on moral philosophy
which set forth the idea that the civil virtue of man lay in abiding by
civil law and magistrates. Melanchthon reinforced his point about
moral philosophy by demonstrating its starting point in a natural
philosophy about the human soul. He then even went further to
prove that absolutely everything in this world was created for a sure
purpose, thus leaving no room of doubt as to God's Providential
design in creation, including man and political orders.

This is therefore the unity of philosophy teaching which lay
behind the statutes of 1545: the second book of the *Historia naturalis*
introduced beginners to the idea of a physical universe which was
governed by a Providential God; a natural philosophy lecturer
taught, using Aristotelian teleology and commentaries by Melanchthon, that absolutely everything including humans were created by
God for a specific purpose, and moral philosophy taught that this
purpose of human beings was the pursuit of civil virtue. This whole
system of philosophy was developed by Melanchthon when he saw
that the radical wing of the evangelical movement was seriously
jeopardizing Luther's cause. And we may also detect Melanchthon's
concern personally to see to the establishment of a new kind of
moral philosophy, as the 1545 statutes stipulate it is to be read by the
Greek teacher, a post that Melanchthon occupied most of the time.[56]
The notable absence of the teaching of the *Metaphysica* is also
consistent with Melanchthon's view that philosophy does not prove
theological truths.[57]

As Melanchthon himself painstakingly pointed out, philosophy
was a knowledge of Law, not of the Gospel, in that it did not teach
about salvation. That this new philosophy was no longer part of a
logically rigorous system of thought crowned by theology did not
mean, however, that it became independent of theology either. In
fact it was developed in conformity with the tenets of Lutheran
theology in order to counter a civic problem that Melanchthon's as
well as Luther's cause was facing at the time. The status of 'Law'

accorded to philosophy indicates precisely the Lutheran reformulation of the value of philosophy.

Both Law and Gospel were necessary and were taught alongside one another at Wittenberg. As the 1545 statutes stipulate, every morning after rising, philosophy students were to read a chapter of the Old Testament and when they came back to their chamber in the evening, they were to read a chapter of the New Testament. Such readings were to be accompanied by prayers based on the reading. On feast days they were required to go to chapel and learn where to join in the prayers. After these public assemblies, they were to recite the catechism of Christian teaching and respond to questions concerning articles of faith and important topics such as the difference between law and gospel, what sin is, what faith is, and what the correct use of the sacrament should be.[58] Thus the study of philosophy and the Gospel, however different, were not to be separated.

The importance of philosophy was clearly understood in practice also at Wittenberg. Lecturers stated in their lecture advertisements the goal of their subject unequivocally: the second book of Pliny's *Historia naturalis* was an excellent introduction to natural philosophy;[59] the *De anima* taught the basis of moral philosophy;[60] Dioscorides demonstrated the Providence of God in nature[61] and moral philosophy taught various forms of (civil) virtue.[62] As for the way these lectures were in fact taught, we have only limited information. For instance, it is fairly obvious that students were expected to buy a copy of the text, notwithstanding the fact that the University Library was one of the few libraries at the time which lent out books to students and lecturers.[63] Printed texts were welcome by lecturers while manuscripts seem to have circulated frequently among students.[64] A major shortage of supply of texts sometimes obliged the lecturers to lecture on another text on the related topic.[65] Greek or Greek and Latin texts of Aristotle seem to have been often used in lectures[66] while Melanchthon's commentaries were also used.[67] It is unclear how the Greek/Latin text stood in relation to Melanchthon's commentaries in the lectures. We also know that the same lecturer sometimes gave lectures from different texts in the same week.[68] While we can discern no fixed *order* in which various texts were read in the lectures, the *De anima*, the *Physica*, the *Meteorologica* and Dioscorides were frequently taught, with all lecturers acknowledging the goal of philosophy set by Melanchthon.

Further, from disputation records we know that philosophical topics were frequently debated. Subjects included 'temperaments', 'the office of magistrates', 'the formation of the foetus', 'philosophy', 'comets', 'powers of the soul', 'ethical and physical causes of human action', 'different powers in man', 'parts of the human body', and 'physical principles of things.'[69] In one instance, we have a fairly detailed list of disputation topics, printed at the end of the 1548 edition of the *Commentarius de anima*: God gave man innate knowledge; this innate knowledge is very useful for man; true philosophy is built on demonstrations; moral philosophy is part of divine law and the difference between Law and Gospel should be retained.[70] Virtually all the crucial points in Melanchthon's philosophy are covered.

It is striking how most students and lecturers disputed and wrote about philosophy in virtually the same way as Melanchthon did.[71] The 'catechetical' textbooks and disputations seem to have ensured a uniform understanding of philosophy at Wittenberg to the extent that, even forty years after his death, it could be observed that 'all who were true disciples of Melanchthon employed a very similar style and form of oration in speaking and writing, moulded and turned out in imitation of their most erudite preceptor'.[72]

In a divisive world which saw the rise of the radical evangelicals, the Roman Catholics' attempt to label all evangelicals as disruptive,[73] and the deepening of rifts amongst the evangelicals on the interpretation of the Lord's Supper, there was an increasing necessity to maintain correct teaching of faith. Melanchthon regarded education as essential for theologians in order to maintain the purity of doctrine.[74] After having re-evaluated philosophy as 'Law', Melanchthon thus devoted himself to establishing it through writing textbooks and teaching it. A uniform understanding of philosophy was effectively achieved at Wittenberg under Melanchthon.

To conclude, the difference in the attitudes of Luther and of Melanchthon towards philosophy may be explained thus: Luther tried to remove the Scholastic kind of Aristotelian philosophy which was incompatible with his theology; Melanchthon developed a new philosophy which was based on Lutheran principles and was, from Melanchthon's point of view, crucial to ensuring the survival of

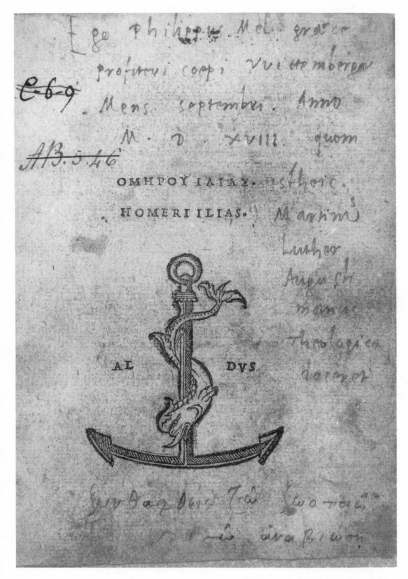

Fig. 1.   Title page of Melanchthon's copy of Homer's *Iliad* (Venice, Aldus Manutius, 1504). Ultra-violet photography. Reproduced by permission of the Syndics of Cambridge University Library.

Luther's cause. In other words, Luther vigorously attacked Scholastic Aristotelian philosophy in his campaign to establish the message of the Gospel; while Melanchthon devoted himself to developing and establishing a knowledge of Law by utilizing Aristotelian philosophy. And this difference may in fact be due to the different vocations they respectively pursued. Melanchthon's inscription on his copy of Homer's *Iliad* is quite symbolic in this regard (fig. 1). It reads:

I, Philip Melanchthon, began teaching the Greek language at Wittenberg in September 1518 when at this very place Martin Luther, the Augustinian monk, was teaching theology.[75]

Luther the theologian attacked Scholastic philosophy which was a hindrance to his theology; Melanchthon the Greek teacher, teaching in the arts faculty, found a new meaning for philosophy in support of Luther's cause.

So long as we do not assume a singular and static identity for Aristotelian philosophy in the universities we may thus appreciate that the attitudes of Luther and Melanchthon towards philosophy as quoted at the beginning of this paper are not contradicting each other. After all, we must remember how varied and dynamic Aristotelian philosophy in the universities could be in this period.[76] As for *why* certain people chose to write a particular kind of Aristotelian philosophy in the way that they did, the historical context in which those words were written may provide an answer.

Christ's College
Cambridge
CB2 3BU

REFERENCES

1. Martin Luther, 'To the Christian Nobility of the German Nation concerning the Reform of the Christian Estate' (1520), *Luther's Works*, ed. J. Pelikan and H. T. Lehmann (55 vols.; St. Louis, 1955–76), xliv. 200f., trans. C. M. Jacobs, revised J. Atkinson. The Latin reference is to 'a school for youths and for Greek glory', namely pagan religion perpetuated by the wrong kind of education, in II Macc. 4.9.

2. For lists of Luther's invectives against Aristotle, see G. Rokita, 'Aristoteles, Aristotelicus, Aristotelicotatos, Aristotelskunst', *Archiv für
   Begriffsgeschichte*, 15 (1970), 51–93, and F. Nitzsch, *Luther und Aristoteles, Festschrift zum vierhundertjährigen Geburtstage Luther's* (Kiel,
   1883), 35–51.

3. 'In hac Witebergensi academia constitutum est ab illustrissimo principe
   et domino Johanne Friderico duce Saxoniae electore . . ., ut lectores
   linguarum et philosophiae sint decem: Duo inspectores collegii, . . .,
   quorum . . ., alter physicen et secundum Plinii. . . . Octavus physicus, qui
   Aristotelis physica enarret et Dioscoriden ac monstrator sit herbarum. . . . Decimus lector graecae linguae, qui subinde repetat gram-
   maticen graecam et hos scriptores: Homerum, Hesiodum, Euripidem,
   Sophoclem, Theocritum. . . . interdum vero misceat aliquam Pauli epis-
   tolam, ... idem lector sit ethicus, ... enarrabit autem ethicus, quisquis
   erit, graeca Aristotelis ethica ad verbum. sed diligenter discernet genera
   doctrinarum, legem dei, evangelium, praecepta philosophica et civilia
   de moribus, dijudicabit sectas philosophorum et illustrabit praecepta
   exemplis.' 'Leges collegii facultatis liberalium artium, quas philosophia
   continet' (1545), *Urkundenbuch der Universität Wittenberg. Vol. I.
   1502–1611*, ed. W. Friedensburg (Magdeburg, 1926), 267f.

4. For a study focusing on natural philosophy made 'Lutheran' by
   Melanchthon, see S. Kusukawa, 'Providence Made Visible: The Crea-
   tion and Establishment of Lutheran Natural Philosophy', Ph.D. thesis
   (Cambridge, 1991).

5. As quoted in C. C. Christensen, *Art and the Reformation in Germany*
   (Athens, Ohio, 1979), 126.

6. P. Althaus, *The Theology of Martin Luther*, trans. R. C. Schultz
   (Philadelphia, Pa., 1970), 251–73, and T. M. McDonough, *The Law and
   the Gospel in Luther* (Oxford, 1963).

7. '[P]reterea suorum preceptorum litteris fidem faciant baccalaureandi, se
   audivisse Petrum Hispanum, novam et veterem logicam Aristotelis,
   priorum, posteriorum analyticorum, topicorum quatuor, elencorum,
   necnon grammaticam; magistrandi vero novam et veterem logicam,
   libros phisicorum, de anima, de celo et mundo, de generacione et
   corrupcione, metheororum, parva naturalia, ethicorum, methaphisi-
   cam, necnon mathematicam. . . . indifferentur profiteatur via Thome,
   Scoti, Gregorii. estate quinta, hieme sexta legatur major logica per illas
   tres vias; estate septima, hieme octava libri phisicorum et de anima,
   quibus finitis parva naturalia, similiter per tres vias. hora duodecima
   minor logica, id est Petrus Hispanus, similiter per tres vias, secunda libri
   ethicorum et post illos methaphisica, item in mathematica, tercia
   grammatica;' 'Statuta collegii artistarum' (1508), *Urkundenbuch*, 54, 56.

8. See H. A. Oberman, '*Via antiqua* and *via moderna*: Late Medieval
   Prolegomena to Early Reformation Thought', *From Ockam to Wyclif*,
   ed. A. Hudson and M. Wilks (Oxford, 1987), 445–63, and the collection

of essays in *Gregor von Rimini: Werk und Wirkung bis zur Reformation*,
ed. H. A. Oberman (Spätmittelalter und Reformation, 20; Berlin, 1981).
For a summary discussion of the 'German phenomenon' of the *viae*, see
A. L. Gabriel, '"Via antiqua" and "via moderna" and the Migration of
Paris Students and Masters to the German Universities in the Fifteenth
Century', *Antiqui und Moderni: Traditionsbewusstsein und Fortschritts-
bewusstsein im späten Mittelalter*, ed. A. Zimmermann (Miscellanea
mediaevalia, 10; Berlin, 1974), 439–83, and J. H. Overfield, *Humanism
and Scholasticism in Late Medieval Germany* (Princeton, N. J., 1984),
49–60.

9. The best treatment of the arts curriculum at pre-Reformation Wittenberg is still G. Bauch, 'Wittenberg und die Scholastik', *Neues Archiv für
Sächsische Geschichte und Altertumskunde* 18 (1897), 285–339.

10. The *Clarissima singularisque totius philosophie nec non metaphysice
Aristotelis magistri Petri Tatareti [sic] exposicio ac passuum Scoti
allegatio* was printed at Wittenberg (in 1504) at the request of Sigis-
mund Epp, an Augustinian and the first dean of the arts faculty at
Wittenberg: *Urkundenbuch*, 6; *Martini Polichij Mellerstadij exquisita
cursus Physici collectanea* (Leipzig, 1514); Bauch, 'Wittenberg', 326f.
We have little direct evidence of how, if at all, Aristotelian philosophy
was taught in the way of Gregory of Rimini.

11. For a concise introduction to the *quaestio* technique, see J. Marenbon,
Later Medieval Philosophy (1150–1350): An Introduction, (London,
1987), 25–34.

12. The 'scholastic method' has been defined by J. A. Weisheipl as
'essentially a rational investigation of every relevant problem in liberal
arts, philosophy, theology, medicine and law, examined from opposing
points of view, in order to reach an intelligent, scientific solution that
would be consistent with accepted authorities, known facts, human
reason, and Christian faith', in *New Catholic Encyclopedia*, ed. The
Catholic University of America (17 vols.; Washington, 1967, 74, 79), xii.
1145.

13. C. H. Lohr, 'Metaphysics', in *Cambridge History of Renaissance
Philosophy*, ed. C. B. Schmitt and Q. Skinner (Cambridge, 1988),
538–84.

14. For the use of natural philosophy for the doctrine of transubstantiation,
see E. D. Sylla, 'Autonomous and Handmaiden Science: St Thomas
Aquinas and William of Ockham on the Physics of the Eucharist', in
The Cultural Context of Medieval Learning, ed. J. E. Murdoch and
E. D. Sylla (Boston Studies in the Philosophy of Science, 26; Dortrecht,
1975), 349–96; for theological issues reflected in natural philosophy, see
J. E. Murdoch, 'The Analytic Character of Late Medieval Learning;
Natural Philosophy Without Nature', in *Approaches to Nature in the
Middle Ages: Papers of the Tenth Annual Conference of the Center for
Medieval and Early Renaissance Studies*, ed. L. D. Roberts, (New York,

1982), 171–213. For the theological orientation of the arts curriculum in general, see also R. McInery, 'Beyond the Liberal Arts', in *The Seven Liberal Arts in the Middle Ages*, ed. D. L. Wagner (Bloomington, Ill. 1983), 248–72.

15. For a study of humanism at pre-Reformation Wittenberg, see M. Grossmann, *Humanism in Wittenberg 1485–1517*, (Bibliotheca Humanistica et Reformatorica, 11; Nieuwkoop, 1975).

16. I take 'humanism' to mean 'the general tendency of the age to attach the greatest importance to classical studies, and to consider classical antiquity as the common standard and model by which to guide all cultural activities', following P. O. Kristeller, *Renaissance Thought: The Classic, Scholastic and Humanist Strains* (New York, 1961), 95. Although Chilian Reuther at Wittenberg adopted a textbook containing a new translation of the *De anima* by Johannes Argyropulos, it was attached to a commentary on the *De anima* by Thomas Aquinas, whom Reuther followed, Grossmann, *Humanism* 65, 73f. It should be noted, moreover, that humanist scholarship and Scholastic philosophy are not necessarily mutually exclusive categories, see Overfield, *Humanism*.

17. For a study of the place of reason and philosophy for Luther, see B. A. Gerrish, *Grace and Reason: A Study in the Theology of Luther* (Oxford, 1962).

18. 'Disputation Against Scholastic Theology', thesis 41, *Luther's Works*, xxxi. 12; Luther to Spalatin, 2 September 1518, E. G. Schwiebert, *Luther and His Times: The Reformation From a New Perspective* (St Louis, Missouri, 1950), 299.

19. Luther to Spalatin, 9 December 1518, *Luther's Works*, xlviii. 95f.

20. 'De physicis quod scribis, mihi videtur, si sit legendus Aristoteles plus frugis fecero in dialecticis, quae instaurare queam, et omnino nova isti universo orbi artium dare coniuncta cum rhetoricis, ut debent, id quod opinor non est in proclivi cuivis facere. Sed Physicorum Aristotelicorum adeo frigida sunt ὑπομνήματα ut nihil possit incommodius legi.' Letter to Spalatin, 13 March 1519, *Corpus Reformatorum Philippi Melanthonis Opera quae supersunt omnia*, ed. C. B. Bretschneider and H. E. Bindseil (28 vols; Halle and Brunswick, 1834–60) [*CR* hereafter], i. 75. Cf. Luther's letter to Spalatin of the same date, *Luther's Works*, xlviii. 111–15, and note 23 below.

21. 'Loci Communes Theologici' (1520) trans. L. J. Satre and revised W. Pauck, in *Melanchthon and Bucer*, ed. W. Pauck (The Library of Christian Classics, 19; London, 1969), 47. For a more comprehensive onslaught on Aristotelian philosophy by Melanchthon, see 'Didymi Faventini i.e. Philippi Melanthonis adversus Rhadinum pro Luthero Oratio' (1521), *CR*, i. 286–358.

22. See Letter of Friederich the Wise to Spalatin, 29 September 1519, *Urkundenbuch*, 90f. Dölsch, according to the report of the 1516 visitation, was teaching natural philosophy in the *via Scoti*. At the time of his

plea to the Elector, Dölsch was probably teaching the *De anima*. Ibid., 77, 100. For Dölsch, see F. Kropatscheck, 'Zur Biographie des Joh. Dölsch aus Feldkirch (gest. 1523)', *Zeitschrift für Kirchengeschichte*, 21 (1901), 454–7.

23. Spalatin seems to have wanted the lecture on Aristotle's *Physica* to continue, see *Urkundenbuch*, 117.
24. '[D]ie neunde lection soll teglich sein in phisica, die zehende in morali philosophia.' *Urkundenbuch*, 177.
25. 'Decrevi igitur enarrare librum de anima hic editum, ac polliceor auditoribus diligentiam et fidem.' Erasmus Flock's lecture advertisement (1540), in *Scriptorum publice propositorum a professoribus in Academia Witebergensi, Ab anno 1540, usque ad annum 1553*, Tomus Primus (Wittenberg, 1560), B8ʳ; 'Et quia libellus de anima clarissimi praeceptoris nostri D. Philippi Melancthonis, videtur conducere scholasticorum studijs, decrevi eum enarrare . . .' Jacob Milich (1540), ibid., B8ᵛ.
26. Amerbach's commentary, *Quatuor libri de anima* (Strassburg, 1542), differs substantially from Melanchthon's in the interpretation of 'entelechy' and of the importance of anatomy. For Amerbach's disaffection from Wittenberg, see W. Friedensburg, *Geschichte der Universität Wittenberg* (Göttingen, 1926), 226.
27. For Velcurio's editions, see C. H. Lohr, *Latin Aristotle Commentaries*. Vol. II. *Renaissance Authors* (Florence, 1988), 474; for the difference between the Velcurio editions, see Kusukawa, 'Providence Made Visible', ch. 3.
28. Melanchthon taught the *Ethica* in the years 1532, 1533, 1543, 1544, 1545, 1546 and 1560. Mostly he concentrated on the fifth book which deals with the ideal of (civil) justice as the abiding by civil law. For Melanchthon's lecture list, see K. Hartfelder, *Philipp Melanchthon als Praeceptor Germaniae* (Berlin, 1889), 555–65.
29. Kusukawa, 'Providence Made Visible', ch. 2. Standard biographies of Melanchthon such as C. L. Manschreck, *Melanchthon: The Quiet Reformer* (New York, 1958), R. Stupperich, *Melanchthon*, trans. R. H. Fischer (London, 1966), and P. Petersen, *Geschichte der Aristotelischen Philosophie im Protestantischen Deutschland* (Leipzig, 1921), 38–48, do not relate Melanchthon's 'Aristotelianism' to the impending threat of Anabaptism. Although it should be noted that modern studies, such as G. H. Williams, *The Radical Reformation* (London, 1962), indicate that Anabaptism did not necessary imply civil disobedience, see J. S. Oyer, *Lutheran Reformers Against Anabaptists; Luther, Melanchthon and Menius and the Anabaptists of Central Germany* (the Hague, 1964), 239–42, and especially Melanchthon's letter to the Elector, 27 December 1521, in *CR*, i. 513f. Cf. H. Engelland, 'Introduction', in *Melanchthon on Christian Doctrine: Loci Communes 1555*, trans. C. L. Manschreck (New York, 1965), xxvif.

30. For Melanchthon's experience in the Thuringian visitation of 1527, see Oyer, *Lutheran Reformers*, 140–78.
31. 'Neque vero tollit [Christus] christiana doctrina civiles mores, sed eos exigit, et philosophiam seu rationem praecipientem de civilibus moribus approbat, sicut et civiles magistratus approbat, et testatur, se authorem esse civilium ordinationum, Roman. decimo tertio: omnia, quae ordinata sunt, a Deo ordinata sunt. Et ab his qui non habent spiritum sanctum, tamen exigit, ut frenentur civili iusticia.' 'Disputatio' (1527), *CR*, xii. 694.
32. 'Non est enim philosophia, cum de divina voluntate ex ratione iudicamus, sed sunt inania somnia,. . . . Et admiscuerunt doctrinae christianae philosophiam, qui docuerent, quod nostris meritis iustificemur. . . . Sic pro certis adfirmare, quae ratio aut philosophia non potest adfirmare, imo quae prorsus sunt extra iudicium rationis aut philosophiae posita, ea est inanis deceptio. . . . Sed Evangelium est doctrina vitae spiritualis et iustificationis coram Deo, Philosophia vero est doctrina vitae corporalis, sicut vides medicinam valetudini servire, navigantibus discrimina tempestatum, mores civiles communi hominum tranquillitati. Est autem huiusmodi usus necessarius et a Deo probatus, . . .' Ibid., 695.
33. 'Epitome Ethices' (1532), translated by R. A. Keen, *A Melanchthon Reader* (New York, 1988), 204.
34. For editions of Melanchthon's textbooks on Aristotle, see Lohr, *Latin Aristotle Commentaries*, 254–8. For a survey of trends in philosophical textbooks, see C. B. Schmitt, 'The Rise of the Philosophical Textbook', in *The Cambridge History of Renaissance Philosophy*, 792–804.
35. Schmitt, 'The Rise of the Philosophical Textbook', 798.
36. For editions of Melanchthon's ethical writings, see Lohr, *Latin Aristotle Commentaries*, 257f. For the *Philosophiae moralis epitome* (which is based on an earlier, [unpublished] 'Epitome Ethices' of 1532 and now translated by Keen in *A Melanchthon Reader*, 203–38), I have used the edition in *Melanchthons Werke im Auswahl*, ed. R. Stupperich (6 vols.; Gutersloher, 1951–55), iii. 152–301.
37. 'Magna igitur laus est philosophiae moralis, quod est pars legis divinae e sapientia Dei, etiamsi non est Evangelium.' *Melanchthons Werke im Auswahl*, iii. 158.
38. 'Cum philosophia moralis sit pars legis Dei, ut supra dictum est, prorsus idem finis est hominis secundum legem divinam, et secundum veram philosophiam, videlicet agnoscere Deum, eique oboedire, et eius gloriam patefacere et illustrare, et tueri societatem humanam propter Deum.' Ibid., 163f.
39. 'Virtus est habitus, qui inclinat voluntatem ad oboediendum rectae rationi.' Ibid., 174.
40. Melanchthon's re-evaluation of philosophy is paralleled in his concern in his dialectic textbooks to establish methods of drawing *certain* conclusions (i.e. demonstration). For a summary of the various changes

in Melanchthon's dialectic textbooks, see W. Risse, *Die Logik der Neuzeit. Vol. I. 1500–1640* (Stuttgart, 1964), 79–109.

41. Cf. Melanchthon's earlier pronouncement on 'natural law': 'The law of nature, therefore, is a common judgement to which all men give consent. . . . This knowledge is not the product of our mental powers, but it has been implanted in us by God. I am not concerned to make this agree with the philosophy of Aristotle. For what do I care what that wrangler thought?' 'Loci communes Theologici' (1520), in Pauck, *Melanchthon and Bucer*, 50.

42. Melanchthon gave three criteria of demonstration by which certain knowledge can be attained: principles or 'common axioms' innate in man; universal experience, such as fire is hot; and syllogistic reasoning. *De dialectica libri quatuor* (Wittenberg, 1531), L5^{r-v}.

43. 'Facinora quae perturbant societatem generis humani, sunt prohibenda
    Furta, Latrocinia, et simila perturbant societatem generis humani.
    Ergo furta, Latrocinia, et similia sunt prohibenda.
    Major est principium. Minor testem habet experientiam, utraque igitur certissima est, Et quod Iurisconsulti vocant Ius naturae aut gentium proprie nihil est, nisi principiorum quorundam de moribus de civili vita, noticia.' Melanchthon, *De dialectica libri quatuor* (Wittenberg, 1531), L6^{r-v}.

44. It should be noted that the *Liber de anima*, first printed in 1552, which is reproduced in all modern editions (e.g. *A Melanchthon Reader*, 239–89; *Melanchthons Werke im Auswahl*, iii. 305–72; *CR*, xiii. 1–178) is considerably different from the *Commentarius de anima* in that the *Liber* adopts much material from Andreas Vesalius' *De fabrica corporis humani libri Septem* (Basel, 1543). For a brief summary of the difference between the two editions, see V. Nutton, 'Anatomy of the Soul in Early Renaissance Medicine', *The Human Embryo: Aristotle and the Arabic and European Traditions*, ed. G. R. Dunstan, (Exeter, 1990), 136–57.

45. Melanchthon first mentions working on the *De anima* on 8 November 1533, see his letter to Johannes Naevius, *CR*, iv. 1021. For a survey of works on and editions of the *De anima* in this period, see H. Schüling, *Bibliographie der psychologischen Literatur des 16. Jahrhunderts* (Hildesheim, 1967). For an earlier juxtaposition of anatomical knowledge (following Mundinus) and Aristotle's *de anima*, see Magnus Hundt, *Antropolgium de hominis dignitate, naturae et proprietatibus . . . de mentis partibus et membris humani corporis etc* (Leipzig, 1501).

46. *Commentarius de anima*, 135^v. For Melanchthon's theory of spirits, see D. P. Walker, 'Medical Spirits and God and the Soul', in *Spiritus, IV Colloquio Internazionale Roma, 7–9 gennaio 1983* ed. M. Fattori and M. Bianchi (Lessico Intellettuale Europeo, 32; Rome, 1984), 223–29.

47. *Commentarius de anima*, 216ᵛ–217ʳ. See also C. Bauer, 'Melanchthons Naturrechtslehr', *Archiv für Reformationsgeschichte*, 42 (1951), 64–100, and J. T. McNeil, 'Natural Law in the Thought of Luther', *Church History*, 10 (1941), 211–27. For medieval interpretations of 'synteresis', see O. Lottin, *Psychologie et morale aux XIIᵉ et XIIIᵉ siècles* (5 vols.; Louvain, 1948), i. 104–349, and the literature cited in note 1 of R. A. Greene, 'Synderesis, the Spark of Conscience, in the English Renaissance', *Journal of the History of Ideas*, 52 (1991), 195.

48. 'Philosophia moralis ex Physica assumit hanc propositionem: Natura hominis condita est ad certum finem. Id in physicis demonstratur, non confirmatur in Philosophia morali. Sed recipitur, tanquam hypothesis, id est, firma propositio, aliunde assumta, ut sit inchoatio doctrinae moralis.' *Erotemata dialectices* (1547), in *CR*, xiii. 650.

49. For editions of the *Initia doctrinae physicae*, see Lohr, *Latin Aristotle Commentaries*, 256. For an analysis of the interest shown by historians of science in Melanchthon's different treatment of Copernicus in the two editions of the *Initia doctrinae physicae*, see B. Wrightsman, 'Andreas Osiander and Lutheran Contributions to the Copernican Revolution', Ph.D. thesis (Wisconsin, 1970). The basic format and content of the *Initia* . . . took shape by 1543, as is clear from a manuscript now in the Vatican Library (Manuscriptorum Latinorum Bibliothecae Palatinae 1038) 'Physicae seu naturalis philosophiae compendium', which I believe grew out of Melanchthon's lectures on Ptolemy's *Tetrabiblos*, see Kusukawa, 'Providence Made Visible', ch. 4.

50. *Initia doctrinae physicae* (Wittenberg, 1549), 26ʳ–27ᵛ.

51. Melanchthon himself taught the *Tetrabiblos* in 1535, 1536, 1537, 1543, 1544, and finally in 1545, Hartfelder, *Philipp Melanchthon*, 555–66.

52. See Melanchthon's lecture advertisement on Nicander in *CR*, x. 82. Valerius Cordus heard one of Melanchthon's lectures on Nicander in the 1530s [Valerius Cordus, *Annotationes in P. Dioscoridis De medica materia libros V* (Strassburg, 1561), biiʳ]. Dioscorides was taught by Cordus (1540), Caspar Cruciger, and Sebastian Theodoricus (1546). For a further list of names, see K. H. Dannenfeldt, 'Wittenberg Botanists During the Sixteenth Century', in *The Social History of the Reformation*, ed. L. P. Buck and J. W. Zophy, (Columbus, Ohio, 1972), 223–48. For Theodoricus' lectures, see *Scriptorum publice propositorum . . . Ab anno 1540 usque ad annum 1553*, 211ʳ⁻ᵛ.

53. See Melanchthon, 'De astronomia et geographia', *CR*, xi. 292–8. It should be noted that geography was not regarded as an independent discipline at the time, see D. N. Livingstone, 'Science, Magic and Religion: A Contextual Reassessment of Geography in the Sixteenth and Seventeenth Centuries', *History of Science*, 26 (1988), 269–94. For the importance of God's Providence in Lutheran geography, see M. Büttner, *Regiert Gott die Welt?* (Stuttgart, 1975).

54. The earliest we have of the teaching of the second book of Pliny's *Historia naturalis* specifically is 1531, see Melanchthon, 'De ordine discendi', *CR* xi, 210. A series of commentaries on the second book of the *Historia naturalis* specifically came from the hands of Wittenberg scholars such as Jacob Milich and Bartholomaeus Schonborn. For a study on the astronomy read in the second book of the *Historia naturalis*, see B. S. Eastwood, 'Plinian Astronomy in the Middle Ages and Renaissance', in *Science in the Early Roman Empire: Pliny the Elder, his Sources and Influence*, ed. R. French and F. Greenaway (London, 1986), 197–251. For a full survey of commentators of Pliny, including these men, see C. G. Nauert, Jr., 'Caius Plinius Secundus', *Catalogus Translationum et Commentariorum: Mediaeval and Renaissance Latin Translations and Commentaries*, 4 (1980), 297–422.

55. Kusukawa, 'Providence Made Visible', chs. 3–4.

56. The reading of the *Ethica* as the Greek teacher's responsibility was copied in the statutes at Leipzig (1580), see J. S. Freedman, *Deutsche Schulphilosophie im Reformationszeitalter (1500–1600): Ein Handbuch für den Hochschulunterricht* (Münster, 1984), 35.

57. The subsequent return of the *Metaphysica* into Reformed universities during the late sixteenth century probably reflects the nature of theological dispute amongst the evangelicals, which required precise definitions of terms pertaining to the nature of Christ. See Lohr, 'Metaphysics', 620–30.

58. *Urkundenbuch*, 272f.

59. 'Hunc ordinem, et consensum corporum coelestium, qui certe admonent nos de opifice Deo, considerare et utile et iucundum est. Ac mihi curae erit, hunc consensum mutationum aeris cum coelo in his Plinij Meteoris magna ex parte ostendere. Illustrat autem ea Plinius multis historijs et ego plures addam. Quare magnopere adhortor scholasticos, ut hanc partem studiose audiant, quae quidem etiam praeparabit rudiores, ut postea Physicen avidius audituri, et facilius percepturi sint. Incipiam autem tractatum Plinij de Meteoris . . .' Paulus Eberus (1544?), *Scripta quaedam in Academia Witenbergensi a Rectoribus, Decanis et aliis eruditis quibusdam viris publice proposita ab anno MDXLIIII usque ad finem anni quadragesimi quinti* (Wittenberg, 1545), Cii^v-Ciii^r.

60. 'Et quia libellus de anima clarissimi praeceptoris nostri D. Philippi Melanthonis, videtur conducere scholasticorum studijs, decrevi eum enarrare. Ac hortor scholasticos, ut hanc partem Philosophiae inprimis et ament et colant. . . . Fateri omnes necesse est, Ethicam doctrinam utilem esse vitae, ac moribus. At fontes sunt in doctrina de Anima. . . . Non enim frustra Deus has noticias nobis indidit, vult esse vitae regulas, vult esse vincula societatis humanae . . .' Andreas Aurifaber (1540), in *Scriptorum publice propositorum . . . Ab anno 1540 usque ad annum 1553*, 8^v, 9^v, 10^r; 'Nunc inchoabo librum de Anima, in quo non solum usitatas

descriptione potentiarum organa et totius humani corporis ἀνατομὴν, humorum species et alia multa complectemur. Nec ulla pars Physices utilior est, aut ingenijs liberalibus iucundior. Nam ad tuendam valetudinem, et ad mores regendos, membrorum atque organorum cognitione opus est.' Jacob Milich, in *Scriptorum publice propositorum . . . Ab anno 1540 usque ad annum 1553*, 24ʳ.

61. 'Hactenus enarravi doctrinam de Anima dulcem et necessariam ordine discentibus. Nunc adiungam alias duas Philosophicas materias . . . Die Lunae et die Martis singulis septimanis, enarrabo Pontani μετέωρα. . . . Die vero Iovis et Veneris enarrabo Dioscoridem, ut Herbarum, et fruticum appellationes et naturas aliquo modo discant Iuniores. Nam et herbas ipsas, quas gignit haec regio, monstrabo, et nomina usitata in lingua vernacula addam. Et quidem inchoabo enarrationem a frumentorum appellationibus. Est enim turpis negligentia, horum ipsorum frumentorum et olerum, quibus vescimur, naturas et nomina ignorare. Est autem tota doctrina de stirpibus cum ob alias causas iucunda et utilis, tum vero ideo etiam digna consideratione, quia manifestum testimonium est providentiae divinae'. . . . (1548), in *Scriptorum publice propositorum . . . Ab anno 1540 usque ad annum 1553*, 211ʳ⁻ᵛ.

62. 'Arbitror omnibus sanis persuasum esse, utilem esse lectionem Ethicorum Aristotelis Nam et in vita communi opus est nosse virtutum descriptiones . . .' *Scripta quaedam . . . proposita ab anno MDXLIIII usque ad finem anni quadragesimi quinti*, Aiiijᵛ.

63. '. . . ut adolescentes invitentur ad Physicen, et alias Philosophiae partes, rursus incipiam enarrationem Quadripartiti [Ptolemy's *Tetrabiblos*], ac proximo die veneri inchoabo praefationem primi libri, Interim scholastici, qui codices non habent, et haec studia amant, libros emant.' Melanchthon (*c*. 1544), *Scripta quaedam . . . proposita ab anno MDXLIIII usque ad finem anni quadragesimi quinti*, D8ʳ. Although the University Library was accessible to (poor) students and lecturers alike, it is not clear at present what role books in the Library had for students' instruction. For the formation and purpose of the library, see E. G. Schwiebert, 'Remnants of a Reformation Library', *The Library Quarterly*, 10 (1940), 494–531.

64. '. . . ut his proximis mensibus physica hic excudiantur, eam editionem expectandam esse censui. Erit enim emendatior, et locupletior ijs libellis, qui nunc manu scripti circumferuntur.' Paulus Eberus, *Tertius liber scriptorum quae in Academia Vitembergensi publice proposita sunt* (Wittenberg, 1549), A7ᵛ.

65. 'Physicos libros Aristotelis praelegam, iam enarraturus eram μετέωρα Sed scio exempla deesse, Ideo nunc dulcissimum carmen Pontani, quod inscripsit μετέωρα, enarrabo, quod profecto dignum est cognitione. . . . Spero autem aliquanto post Graeca et latina exempla aliquot librorum Aristotelis, qui sunt utiliores, editurus esse Typographos, quae cum

haberi poterunt, ipsum textum interpretabimur' Sebastianus Theodoricus, 10 May 1546, *Scriptorum publice propositorum* ... *Ab anno 1540 usque ad annum 1553*, 161ᵛ–162ʳ.

66. 'Cum autem et Ecclesiae Dei, vitae communi, doctrina de anima utilissima sit, Aristotelis textum Graecum hora 3. quae mihi attributa est, enarrabo.' Sebastianus Theodoricus, 5 Sept. 1546, *Scriptorum publice propositorum* ... *Ab anno 1540 usque ad annum 1553*, 177ᵛ.

67. 'Ego quoque ex sententia Praeceptorum libellum physicae, Vvitebergae editum, praelegam.' Sebastianus Theodoricus (1552), *Scriptorum publice propositorum* ... *Ab anno 1540 usque ad annum 1553*, 421ʳ.

68. '... Deo iuvante, inchoaturum esse Physicen quam dictabo, atque ita deinceps singulis septimanis, biduum libro de Anima, et deinde biduum Physicis tribuemus et operam dabimus, ut res vitae et moribus utiles, et cognitione dignas proponamus ...' Paulus Eber (1545), *Scripta quaedam* ... *proposita ab anno MDXLIIII usque ad finem anni quadragesimi quinti*, F7ᵛ.

69. 'Melchior Fendius de Temperamentis' (1536), *Die Baccalaurei und Magistri der Wittenberger philosophischen Facultät 1518–1537 und die ordentlichen Disputationen 1536–1537 aus der Facultätsmatrikel*, ed. J. Köstlin (Halle 1888), 26. 'Philippus de officio Magistratus ...'; 'Melchior de formatione foetus' (1538); 'Vitus Winshemius de Philosophia'; 'Ambrosius de Philosophia et sectis'; 'Christannus de Cometis'; 'Paulus Eberus de Potentiis animae' (1539); 'Ioannes Aurifaber Vratislaviensis de Philosophia' (1540), *Die Baccalaurei und Magistri der Wittenberger philosophischen Facultät 1538–1546 und die öffentlichen disputationen derselben Jahre aus der Facultätsmatrikel*, ed. J. Köstlin (Halle, 1890), 22f. 'Caspar Peucerus de causis liberarum actionum hominis ethicis et physicis, et differentibus in homine potentiis' (1554); 'Decanus ipse de partibus humani corporis' (1556); 'Caspar Peucerus de principiis rerum physicis' (1557). *Die Baccalaurei und Magistri der Wittenberger philosophischer Fakultät 1548–1560 und die öffentlichen disputationen derselben Jahre aus der Fakultätsmatrikel*, ed. J. Köstlin (Halle, 1891), 30.

70. 'Die 7 Junii. 1. Deus indidit mentibus hominum lucem quandam, e qua excusitata sunt extructrae artes vitae utiles, quas Deus vult extare. Vult annorum spacia esse definita, vult cognosci remedia et usum, ad quem opus est aliqua Physices cognitione, vult vitam hominum certis legibus regi, quae congruant ad discrimen honestorum et turpium, inditum mentibus humanis, vult et sermonem constare certis legibus, ut doceri homines possint etc.... 6. Una est igitur Philosophia, scilicet vera doctrina quae demonstrationibus constat.... 24. Philosophia moralis quae demonstrationes habet, pars est legis divinae, Sed promissio Evangelij propria de reconciliatione propter filium Dei, prorsus aliud genus est doctrinae, ignotum rationi et Philosophiae. Disputatio.' *Commentarius de anima* (Wittenberg, 1548), X4ʳ, X4ᵛ, X6ʳ.

71. Students of Melanchthon often recommended similar plans of study. See for instance, Paul Eber, 'Ratio studendi generalis scholasticis olim praescripta, per Dominum Doctorem Paulum Eberum', in *Institutiones literatae, sive de discendi atque docendi ratione Tomus tertius* (Torun, 1588), 203–14.

72. As trans. in L. Thorndike, *A History of Magic and Experimental Science* (8 vols.; London, 1923–58), v 378, from Joannes Ferinarius, *Narratio historica de vita et morte . . . J. Curei . . . philos, et medici etc.* (Liegnitz, 1601). For the 'School of Melanchthon', see further Petersen, *Geschichte der Aristotelischen Philosophie*, 109–27.

73. E.g., '303. [= 403] Proprium et genuinum est verbo dei, seditiones et tumultus excitare: hinc non habeo fortiorem probationem, doctrinam meam esse a deo, nisi quia suscitat discordas dissensiones et tumultus. Lutther. Vnde multi eorum saepe publice testati sunt ad plebem. Evangelium velit habere sanguinem. Zuinglius et alii.' [Johannes Eck], *Articulos 404 partim ad disputationes. . . . partim vero ex scriptis pacem ecclesiae perturbantium extractos, Coram divo Caesare Carolo V . . ., Ioan. Eckius minimus ecclesiae minister, offert se disputaturum . . .* (Ingolstadt, 1530), Diii^v.

74. See 'De puritate doctrinae in Ecclesia conservanda' (1536), *CR*, xi. 272–8, and 'De coniunctione scholarum cum ministerio Evangelii' (1543), *CR*, xi. 606–18.

75. 'Ego Philippus Mel. graece / profiteri coepi Wittembergae / Mens. Septembri. Anno / M. D. XVIII. quom / istheic / Martinu^s / Luther / Augusti / moncus / Theologica / doceret.' Inscribed on the title-page of the Greek text of Homer's *Iliad* (Venice, 1504), now in Cambridge University Library (classmark Adv. d. 13. 4), my transcription.

76. See C. B. Schmitt, *Aristotle and the Renaissance* (London, 1983), and id., *The Aristotelian Tradition and Renaissance Universities* (London, 1984).

The Teaching of Philosophy at Seventeenth-Century Zurich[1]

Wolfgang Rother

By a decree of 29 September 1523 the Zurich City Council consented to the establishment of a school of theology according to the plans drawn up by the reformer Ulrich Zwingli.[2] On 19 June 1525 the *Prophezei*—as Zwingli called the new school, though the name *lectorium* (or *lectiones publicae*) and later *Carolinum* became common—was inaugurated. The main purpose of Zwingli's school was the instruction of reformed ministers. The teaching of the early professors was limited to a critical exegesis of the Bible, which mainly consisted in the comparison of the original text and the Latin translation. After Zwingli's death (1531) the lessons ceased to be exclusively Biblical. The students were systematically taught Latin, Greek, and Hebrew. The Latin lessons were combined with an introduction to rhetoric and dialectic. The professor of Greek was not only entrusted with the explanation of the philological, but also the philosophical aspects of the texts he read with his students. In 1541 Konrad Gesner (1516–1564) was asked to give lessons on physics; in 1558 his lectureship was transformed into an ordinary professorship. From then on, there were five chairs in the Zurich *lectorium*: two for theology, one for Greek, one for Latin, rhetoric and dialectic, and one for physics; the professor of physics was also responsible for the teaching of ethics.

The curricular discussions of the late sixteenth century culminated in the school reform of 1601, which followed the Strasbourg model of Johannes Sturm.[3] This reform, framing a tripartite system of academic instruction, resulted in the foundation of the *Collegium Humanitatis*, which was interpolated between the Latin school and the *Carolinum*. The courses at the *Collegium Humanitatis* were given by four professors, the first teaching Latin and Greek, the second logic and rhetoric, the third Hebrew, and the fourth the New

Testament. At the *Carolinum* there were two ordinary chairs for theology, one for Greek, one for logic, and one for physics. Moreover, there were lectureships for Hebrew, history, rhetoric, and ethics. The students were about twelve or thirteen years old when they entered the Latin school, which they left about five years later. So they began their higher education at the age of seventeen or eighteen, though some were only sixteen or seventeen, while others were already twenty or twenty-one years old. The studies at the *Collegium Humanitatis* (henceforth: Hum.) and the *Carolinum* (henceforth: Carol.) normally lasted another four or five years.[4] Twice a year, in spring and in autumn, the students had to pass oral and written exams. The final exams were the *philosophicum* and the *theologicum*, after which the candidates had to preach their trial sermons prior to ordination.[5]

The sources for the doctrinal aspects of the teaching of philosophy are the printed disputations composed by the professors and their handbooks written for educational use.[6] As the philosophical chairs were only those for logic and physics,[7] the following presentation will focus on their respective professors.[8] It should be noted, however, that the writings of these professors very often dealt with ethical and metaphysical topics.

The early seventeenth-century Zurich professors of logic seem to have been more or less strict Aristotelians. The physician Johannes Rudolf Simler (1568?–1611, prof. log. Hum. 1602–1605, Carol. 1605–1611) published several Aristotelian theses.[9] Nothing is known about his predecessor at the *Carolinum*, Jakob Ulrich (prof. 1576–1605). Simler's successor Heinrich Erni (1565–1639, prof. graec. Hum. 1602–1611, log. Carol. 1611–1612, theol. 1611–1639) held about two dozen disputations on theology, but none while professor of logic. Johannes Jakob Breitinger (1575–1645, prof. log. Hum. 1605–1611), the later *antistes* and delegate at the Synod of Dord, was the author of some disputations[10] on Aristotelian logic, in which he referred to Rudolf Goclenius and Clemens Timpler. Johannes Rudolf Lavater (1575?–1625, prof. log. Hum. 1611–1612, Carol. 1612–1625) quoted in his logical and metaphysical theses[11] not only Aristotle, but also Clemens Timpler and Bartholomäus Kecker-mann. Lavater's successors Jost von Kusen († 1630, prof. log. Hum. 1612–1625, Carol. 1625–1630), Johannes Waser (1595–1629, prof. log. Hum. 1625–1629), Johannes Rudolf Brunner (1582–1639, prof.

log. Hum. 1629–1639), and Johannes Jakob Thomann (prof. log. Hum. 1635–1649) seem to have published no disputations; Brunner was the author of a logic handbook.[12] The theologian Johannes Rudolf Stucki († 1660, prof. log. Carol. 1630–1639, theol. 1639–1660) published a lot of theological, but also some philosophical disputations.[13] His successor, also a theologian, Johannes Wirtz (1591–1658, prof. log. Carol. 1639–1651, theol. 1651–1658), mainly wrote logical disputations,[14] in which he quoted, besides Aristotle of course, Rudolf Goclenius, Bartholomäus Keckermann, Clemens Timpler, and Franco Burgersdijk. The philosophical disputations of Johannes Heinrich Hottinger (1620–1667, prof. log. Carol. 1651–1655, theol. Heidelberg 1655–1661, Zurich 1661–1667) mostly dealt with theological topics.[15] And another theologian, Johannes Heinrich Heidegger (1633–1698, prof. theol. Steinfurt 1659–1666, eth. Zurich 1666–1668, theol. 1668–1698) held, while teaching ethics at Zurich, a series of disputations on Christian morals.[16]

Heinrich Lavater (1560–1623), who after his study of philosophy and medicine at Lausanne, Geneva, Marburg, Heidelberg, Basle, Padua, Bologna, and Pisa became professor of physics at Zurich, a post which he held for thirty-five years (1588–1623), published — besides a lot of theses mainly on physics[17] — a handbook, in which he 'corrected' the Aristotelian philosophy of nature by the doctrines of the Holy Scripture.[18] His successors, Johannes Caspar Lavater († 1637, prof. phys. 1623–1637)[19] and Johannes Rudolf Giger († 1662, prof. phys. 1637–1662)[20], both of them physicians as well, have only left a few disputations. Giger's authorities are — besides German Protestant school philosophers and Iberian scholastics — mainly David Derodon, Franco Burgersdijk and his Leyden successor Adriaan Heereboord. But, according to Giger, the true philosopher is not the man who only repeats the doctrines of Aristotle and others, but the man who is able 'to perceive and penetrate nature itself and the essence of things'.[21] Giger was the first Zurich professor to refer to Descartes: 'videatur cumprimis accuratum de fulminis generatione judicium Ren. Des Cartes, Nob. Galli, qui novum veluti & lucidissimum sydus philosophiae illuxit'.[22] Giger's successor, Johannes Heinrich Lavater (1611–1691), who combined the offices of the professor of physics and the municipal physician of Zurich for nearly thirty years (1662–1691), did not leave any writings.

Caspar Waser (prof. log. Hum. 1649–1658, Carol. 1658–1667)[23] accepted the Cartesian definition of philosophy as *habitus evidenter discurrendi de rebus*,[24] and defended the Cartesian distinction between material or extended and immaterial or thinking substance.[25] The *ens perfectissimum* exists necessarily.[26] The natural perception of God is, he conceded, true, but it is not perfect and sufficient for salvation.[27] In his many disputations, which mainly dealt with logical topics, Waser not only quoted Aristotle, but also the Cartesian Johannes Clauberg and the Leyden professors Franco Burgersdijk and Adriaan Heereboord.

Johannes Lavater (1624–1695),[28] who taught for forty years at Zurich (vicarius prof. log. Hum. 1655–1657, prof. log. Hum. 1658–1667, Carol. 1667–1695), was also on the whole quite benevolent towards Cartesian philosophy. For his students, he wrote an *Ontosophia*,[29] in which he defined philosophy as a *habitus*, which leads the human mind by the light of nature and by divine grace to truth, and which leads the human will to the love of God and to man's beatitude (p. 1). The objects of ontosophy are: substance, mode, and accident; the principles and attributes of substance; essence; existence; subsistence; unity; truth; goodness; perfection; place, time, and duration. In his theses Lavater taught that logic provides the remedies for the maladies of the mind, which are divided into the maladies of notions (obscurity, confusion, ignorance), maladies of judgement (precipitation, doubt, error), and the malady of memory (forgetfulness).[30] Whereas in this Cartesian-inspired presentation doubt is supposed to be a malady, Lavater acknowledged in a later disputation[31] that doubt leads to certainty, not referring to Descartes, but to Augustine's *De trinitate* (Book 10, Chapter 10). Lavater argued against both *superstitiosa antiquitas* and *ambitiosa novitas*, and invited his audience to discard all prejudices and to search for the simple truth.[32] Lavater's writings are full of Cartesian doctrines, such as the belief that the principle of evidence (i.e. clear and distinct perception[33]) is the only and the most certain way for the search after truth in philosophy.[34] He defended the Cartesian rules of method.[35] He followed Descartes' distinction between extended and thinking substance,[36] of which man consists.[37] Further Cartesian positions included: animals do not have souls;[38] there are innate principles;[39] the image of God is innate to the human mind;[40] the existence of God can be demonstrated from the idea of the most perfect being;[41] the demonstration of God from the Bible is the strongest proof, the demonstration from nature the most evident.[42] Lavater maintained that the object of physics is the extended natural body: it is divisible, but not *in infinitum*; the smallest particles being the atoms, which are solid and impenetrable.[43] In this understanding of matter, Lavater (although quoting Descartes' *Principles of Philosophy*) seemed to be more Gassendist than Cartesian. In his theses on fountains and rivers (1664) Lavater referred mainly to Descartes' *Principles* (Part 4, §§ 64 and 66), and to Henricus Regius' *Philosophia naturalis* (Amsterdam, 1654, Book 3, Chapter 2), but also to Daniel Sennert, Sébastien Basson, and Pierre Gassendi. Lavater wrote in addition three remarkable disputations on deaf-mutes, their cognition, and their instruction (1664–1665). As a whole, his mechanism turns out to be rather eclectic.

Johannes Lavater's successors, Johannes Rudolf Hofmeister (prof. log. Hum. 1668–1697) and Johannes Jakob Lavater (†1725, prof. theol. Hum. 1684–1695, eth. Carol. 1695–1697, log. Hum. 1697–1710, theol. Carol. 1711–1725), did not leave any philosophical writings. Johannes Rudolf Ott (1642?–1716, prof. eth. 1681–1695, log. Carol. 1695–1716) was the author of a voluminous *Ethica christiana*,[44] and of three small handbooks[45] on logic and metaphysics. Logic is divided into a noetic and a critical part, i.e. the doctrines of syllogism and of method. The handbook on metaphysics follows, as the author already indicates in the title, the handbook of Johannes Lavater. Ott's conclusion announces 'the general division of being' into God and his creation, divided in turn (as Descartes teaches) into immaterial substance or mind and material substance or body.[46] In his ethical theses[47] Ott argues theologically, referring to the precepts of the Decalogue. But in the other disputations,[48] there are a lot of Cartesian arguments: a discussion of the *cogito* as the first principle of philosophy;[49] an analysis of error as the result not of doubt, but of precipitation;[50] a critique of prejudice[51] as the source of error;[52] an account of the *substantia cogitans* and *extensa*,[53] and their union.[54] The two writings on the errors of disputants (1703, 1705) can be compared with Samuel Werenfels' famous critique of logomachy.[55]

Johannes Heinrich Schweizer (1646–1705) studied in Zurich, Geneva, Basle, Strasbourg, and Heidelberg, became a professor of philosophy and Greek in Hanau (1665–1666), then a minister in Birmensdorf near Zurich (1667–1684), and at last professor of Greek and Hebrew in Zurich (1684–1704). He published an 'Aristotelian-Cartesian' handbook of physics,[56] in which he discusses 454 questions, beginning with: 'Quid est philosophia?' Answer: a *habitus*, which leads reason from innate ideas, which are known *per se*, to the perception of things, and which guides the will to acting according to virtue.[57] Schweizer also adapted Hugo Grotius' *De iure belli et pacis* as a handbook,[58] and provided an edition of Johannes Clauberg's *Ontosophia* for scholastic use.[59] A summary of this work is to be found as an appendix to the *Compendium physicae*. In addition under the pseudonym *Benignus Ericus Arborator* he defended the argument for the existence of God,[60] which Descartes developed in his fifth *Meditation*, in response to its rejection by Samuel Werenfels as a sophism.[61] In his disputations[62] Schweizer defended mainly Cartesian theses, but nonetheless he was not afraid to confess sympathy with Aristotle, too. Among positions sustained we find: the *cogito*;[63] the Cartesian belief that the way to real knowledge is to begin by doubting everything;[64] the doctrine that the mind is better known than the body;[65] the demonstration of God from his idea;[66] the existence of innate principles;[67] the union of mind and body;[68] the definition of movement according to Aristotle's *Physics* (III, 3);[69] and of repose according to Jacques Rohault's *Traité de physique* (Paris, 1671, I, 10);[70] the definition of the world according to Aristotle's *De mundo*;[71] and a reference to the experiment with the aeolipile (a wind instrument) and to Descartes' *Météores* (IV, 3) for the explanation of the wind.[72]

After Johannes Heinrich Lavater's death in 1691, two successors were elected. The first of them, Salomon Hottinger (1649–1713, prof. phys. 1691–1713), a physician, who had graduated at Basle University in 1672, wrote an *Idea physicae nov-antiquae* for his students.[73] In the first part, *physica generalis* (pp. 1–28), he treats of the principles and causes of natural bodies and their affections. The second part, *physica specialis* (pp. 29–200) is much more comprehensive, dealing with the world, the elements, the imperfectly and perfectly mixed bodies, plants, animals, and man (defined as *substantia constans ex corpore organico et mente finita*, p. 187). For the most part Hottinger's disputations[74] were scientific. Subjects discussed included: bread (1696–1697), milk (1704), wine (1707–1712), crystals (1698), lightning and thunder (1698–1700), life (1706–1707). Hottinger claimed allegiance to the eclectical school of philosophy and stressed that the eclectic philosopher is free of every prejudice.[75] However, he owed much to the Cartesians, believing that method is the core of logic (with reference to Descartes'

Discours de la méthode and to Clauberg).[76] He also defended innate principles,[77] the 'Copernican-Cartesian' system[78] and the Cartesian beast-machines.[79] On the other hand, he emphasized that Holy Scripture is the guide of the book of nature, too.[80] The other successor was Johannes von Muralt (1645?–1733, prof. phys. 1691–1733), who—like his colleague—had taken his MD at Basle in 1672. Since 1688 he served as the municipal physician of Zurich. In his disputations[81] he discussed questions, which were rather medical than strictly physical. Noteworthy are his two works on anatomy,[82] and his two physical handbooks,[83] both of which follow more or less the same order, the *Systema physicae experimentalis* being the more comprehensive. The *Physica generalis* (pp. 3–104) deals with the principles of physics, nature and monsters, quantity and figure, movement, repose, place, and time. The *Physica specialis* is divided into two parts, the first of which (pp. 105–230) describes the heavens and the stars, and contains a discussion of the world systems of Ptolemy, Copernicus and Tycho. Von Muralt himself favours the semi-Copernican hypothesis as taught by the seventeenth-century Danish astronomer Christian Longomontanus (pp. 128–132). Next von Muralt presents the four elements: in his discussion of the air he refers to the pneumatical experiments of Robert Boyle (pp. 188f.) and to barometric experiments (p. 192). Finally the meteors are treated. The second part (pp. 233–323) is on man, i.e. the principles of the human body; chyle and milk; water and saliva; bile; blood; bones, cartilage, ligaments, tendons; skin; fat and muscles; intestines; stomach; ending with the rational soul (pp. 320–323).

Conclusion.—As to the doctrinal aspects, the teaching of philosophy at seventeenth-century Zurich can be divided into three different periods, which correspond to the general evolution of European academic philosophy at that time.[84] The first period is that of Aristotelianism (sometimes corrected by Christian doctrines), which seems to last until the 1650s. The authorities most frequently mentioned in the disputations are—besides Aristotle himself—contemporary German Protestant scholastic philosophers, such as Rudolf Goclenius, Clemens Timpler, and Bartholomäus Keckermann, or the Leyden professor Franco Burgersdijk, whose handbooks were used all over Europe. During that period philosophy was still propaedeutic with respect to theological instruction. The second period is that of the penetration of Cartesian philosophy, though at first this was not a pure Cartesianism, but an Aristotelo-Cartesian eclecticism. The first Zurich reference to Descartes to have been traced is in a thesis of 1654 by Johannes Rudolf Giger, but it is possible that Cartesian philosophy entered much earlier into the courses, because Giger had taught physics since 1637. A representative of the eclectic *philosophia novantiqua* was the mid-century professor Caspar Waser. Johannes Lavater, who published an *Ontosophia* (Zurich, 1679), and his later successor Johannes Rudolf Ott seem both to have been real Cartesians, whereas Johannes Heinrich Schweizer with his *Compendium physicae aristotelico-cartesianae* (Basle, 1685) and much later Salomon Hottinger with his *Idea physicae nov-antiquae* (Zurich, 1708) continued the tradition of eclecticism. On the other hand, there can be found no trace of Aristotelianism in Hottinger: he was a more or less strict Cartesian with strong scientific interests, thus preparing the way for the third period, which is characterized by an enthusiasm for experimental philosophy. The first Zurich representative of this new current was Johannes von Muralt, who became professor in 1691 and who published a *Systema physicae experimentalis* (Zurich, 1705–1708). As a result, it can be concluded that in the course of the seventeenth century the teaching of philosophy at Zurich departed totally from Zwingli's original educational purpose. With the introduction of Cartesianism[85] and later of experimentalism,[86] philosophy ceased to be a merely propaedeutic discipline, a preparation for the study of theology, and received a certain autonomy.

Brühlstrasse 43
CH-5412 Gebenstorf
Switzerland

REFERENCES

1. This article is a revised and annotated version of a paper read at the British Society for the History of Philosophy Conference on *The History of Philosophy in Universities*, Magdalen College, Oxford, 9–11 April 1991. My study of the sources available on Zurich were undertaken with regard to a comprehensive survey of seventeenth-century Swiss philosophy to appear in Ueberweg's *Grundriss der Geschichte der Philosophie*, Basle, Schwabe (cf. note 84 below). This survey will also include sections on Basle, Berne, Lausanne, and Geneva.

2. For the early history of Zwingli's school of theology, see Hans Nabholz, 'Zürichs Höhere Schulen von der Reformation bis zur Gründung der Universität 1525–1933', in Ernst Gagliardi, Hans Nabholz and Jean Strohl, *Die Universität Zürich 1833–1933 und ihre Vorläufer* (Zürich, 1938), pp. 3–29.

3. For the curriculum after the school reform cf. Nabholz, 'Zürichs Höhere Schulen', pp. 30–39.

4. Ibid., pp. 11, 14, 33f.

5. Ibid., pp. 14, 32.

6. Those sources are kept in the *Zentralbibliothek* of Zurich.

7. In this respect the teaching of philosophy at Zurich follows the pattern of other Protestant academies, at least in Switzerland. There were no chairs of metaphysics at Basle, Berne, Lausanne or Geneva. Only Basle University had an ordinary professorship for ethics; at Geneva, the professor of Greek was entrusted with the ethical instruction of the students. At the *Carolinum* there were, as mentioned above, lectures on ethics. It may be remembered in this context, that also in the French Protestant academies initially only chairs of logic and physics were set up: cf. Laurence W. B. Brockliss, *French Higher Education in the Seventeenth and Eighteenth Centuries. A Cultural History* (Oxford, 1987), p. 186.

8. In the course of the seventeenth century, there were 24 professors, who taught logic and physics at Zurich. It is a rather striking fact that a quarter of them (i.e. six professors) belonged to the Lavater family. Since the Reformation, the Lavaters, who received their citizenship in the fifteenth century, were one of the leading Zurich families and very influential in the city, the church, and higher education. A famous descendant of this family was the physiognomist Johann Kaspar Lavater (1741–1801). There was a similar phenomenon at Basle University, where many professors of philosophy were recruited from the Burckhardts, but also the Zwingers and later the Bernoullis.

9. 'De philosophia & disciplinarum liberalium, quae sub ea continentur, distributione' (1602); 'De logica, eius origine, natura, partibus cum annexa physiologica de vitae humanae beatitate' (1603); 'De praedicamentorum gradibus, cum annexa dyodecade ethica de temperantia' (1603); 'De termine vocis simplicis' (1605); 'Theses miscellae' (1609); 'De natura et definitione logicae' (1610); 'De forma' (1610).

10. 'Disputatio I. de artis logicae definitione e genere, subiecto, et fine constitutiva' (1606); 'II. de artis logicae distributione, e generalissimis cogitandi, seu cogitationes dirigendi medijs constituta' (1607); 'III. de praedicamentorum toto homogeneo, et praecipuo hujusque doctrinae usu, quem quidem logicus spectare solet' (1608).

11. 'Decas problematum philosophicorum προθεωρίας ἕνεκα logicis disputationibus praemissa' (1604); 'Disputatio I. metaphysica, continens προθεωρίαν de natura habitus metaphysici' (Hanau, 1605:

Lavater was *rector* at Hanau before his professorship at Zurich); 'II.
. . . de natura systematis metaphysici' (1605); 'De tribus necessitatis affir-
mativae legibus de omni; per se; et universim' (1614); 'Disputationum
logicarum I. . . . de natura logicae in genere' (1614); 'II. . . . de termino
vocis' (1619); 'These miscellae' (1619); 'De nihilo' (n.d.).

12. *Compendiolum Logicum* (Zurich, 1635) in 8°. Mentioned by Hans Jakob
Leu, *Allgemeines Helvetisches, Eydgenössisches, Oder Schweitzerisches
Lexicon* . . . (Zürich, 1747–1765), iv. 373; no copy found.

13. 'Theses logicae quaestionibus controversis illustratae' (1633); 'De syllogismo' (1635); 'Currus moralis rotae quaternae, seu methodus quatuor
virtutum cardinalium' (1635); Theses logicae, physicae, ethicae, metaphysicae (Saumur, 1652).

14. 'De syllogismi definitione' (1643); 'De artis logicae definitione e genere,
objecto, & fine' (1644); 'Analecta positionum de circulo logico; ubi
simul sophisticum circulum in fidei dogmatis asserendis a pontificiis,
non item ab orthodoxis committi demonstratur, lucique editur' (1644);
'De philosophiae natura' (1644); 'De logica ex theologiae regno non
proscribenda' (1645); 'Theses philosophico-theosophicae' (1645);
''Αγγελογραφία stylo thetico conscripta' (1645); 'De praedicamentis'
(1646); 'De abstractione, abstracto, & concreto' (1646); 'De proposi-
tione propria et impropria' (1647); 'De toto et parte' (1648); 'De causis'
(1649); 'De definitione' (1649); 'De coelo' (n.d. [1649/50]); 'De sensuum
testimonio' (1650); 'Theses logicae' (1650).

15. 'Examen philosophiae historicae, ex primo, post Christum natum,
seculo institutum' (1652); 'De philosophia exulante, et superbiente'
(1652); 'De philosophia ancillante' (1652); 'De usu praedicamentorum
in theologia' (1652); 'De substantia et accidente, et vario utriusque in
theologia usu' (1653); 'De subsidiis ἀναλύσεως logicae materialis sacrae' (1654); 'De syllogismo sophistico, ejusque solutione' (1654).

16. 'Ethicae christianae disputatio I., de summo bono fine ultimo actionum
humanarum' (1666); 'II., de affectibus, eorumque ἡγεμονίᾳ seu recto
regimine' (1666); 'III., de virtute morali' (1667); 'IV., de honestate et
bonitate morali' (1667); 'V., de opere legali et evangelico, nec non de
virtutibus gentilium' (1667); 'VI., de lege, norma virtutum et actionum
moralium, prior' (1667); 'VII., de lege, posterior, in specie de lege morali
decalogo comprehensa' (1668); 'De imperio et subiectione' (1667).

17. 'De coelo tam astrifero quam ultramundano' (1612); 'De terraemotu'
(1613); 'De elementis' (1614); 'De metallis' (1616); 'De veritate sive vero
et falsitate sive falso' (1616); 'Theses meteorologicae' (1618); 'De
cometis' (1619); 'De animae rationalis essentia' (1621).

18. *Epitome Philosophiae Naturalis, Ex Aristotelis summi Philosophi libris
praecipue concinnata, & passim ex sacris correcta, Pro Schola Tigurina*
(Zurich, 1621).

19. 'Theses physicae ex parte eiusdem generali depromptae' (1634); 'De
terrae motu' (1635).

20. 'Theses miscellae, physico-metaphysicae' (1654); 'Theses ex jucundissimis physicorum viretis delibatae' (1654).
21. 'Thes. misc.' (1654), annexum 9.
22. 'Thes. phys.' (1654), thes. 7.
23. 'Disputationum logicarum I. . . . de natura logicae in genere' (1659); 'II. de artis logicae divisione' (1661); 'III. de termino vocis' (1662); 'IV. de termino rei in genere, et de categoriis, seu praedicamentis in specie' (1663); 'V. de categoria substantiae prima' (1663); 'VI. . . . secunda' (1664); 'VII. de accidente prima' (1664); 'VIII. . . . secunda' (1665); 'IX. de quantitate prima' (1666); 'X. . . . secunda' (1666); 'XI. . . . tertia, continens quaedam problemata doctrinam ejus, & varias affectiones, tum illustrantia, tum vero probantia' (1667); 'De metaphysicae existentia, et ab aliis disciplinis differentia' (1661); 'Isagoge in coelestis sapientiae sacrarium, hoc est, disputatio praeliminaris de recto rationis humanae in rebus theologicis & fidei usu' (1661); 'De affectionibus entis in genere, & de unitate in specie' (1662); 'De methodo' (1662); 'Theses ex universa philosophia' (1663); 'Isagoge in philosophiae sacrarium, seu disputatio prooemialis I., de philosophiae ortu, ejusque acquirendae modo' (1665); '. . . II., de philosophiae fine et usu' (1667); '. . . III., naturam philosophiae ex causis suis internis, objecto item, subjecto, definitione et divisione explicans' (1668).
24. 'Ex univ. philos.' (1663), thes. I, 2.
25. 'De cat. subst.' (1663), pneumatica, no. 3; 'Ex univ. philos.' (1663), thes. II, 2.
26. 'De affect. ent.' (1662), thes. 68.
27. 'De cat. subst.' (1663), pneumatica, no. 6.
28. 'De fontium ac fluminum origine' (1664); 'De mutorum ac surdorum ab ortu sermone, auditu, cognitione atque institutione, I.' (1664); 'Schola mutorum ac surdorum . . . II. . . . de eorundem cognitione, ac institutione' (1665); '. . . III. . . . de eorundem institutione' (1665); 'De amicitia' (1666); 'De atomis I.' (1666); '. . . II., in qua, quae corporis essentia sit, indagatur' (1667); 'Theses philosophicae' (1667); 'Theses philosophicae' (1668, 7 pp.); 'Theses philosophicae' (1668, 1 p.); 'De anima separata' (1669); '. . . demonstratur, omnipraesentiam corporis Christi esse figmentum' (1671); '. . . demonstratur, existentiam atque veracitatem Dei opt. max. fundamentum esse omnis certitudinis, quae in cognitione humana datur' (1671); '. . . demonstratur, unum corpus non posse esse in pluribus locis' (1672); 'Theses philosophicae' (1672); 'Theses miscellaneae' (1673); 'De origine mundi' (1673); 'De mundi interitu' (1674); 'Theses miscellaneae' (1675); 'De duratione mundi' (1676); 'De animae immortalitate, ex nature & sanae rationis lumine demonstrata' (1676); 'De cognitione Dei naturali' (1676); 'De errorum humanae mentis origine, causis, mediisque illos evitandi' (1676); 'Theses philosophicae' (1677); 'Theses miscellaneae' (1679); 'De substantia' (1681); 'Theses philosophicae' (1682); 'Theses philosophicae' (1683).

29. Ontosophiae, Seu Scientiae Catholicae, Rudimenta, Per Disputationes illustrata (Zurich, 1679).
30. 'Thes. philos.' (1668, 7 pp.), cap. 5.
31. 'Thes. philos.' (1683), thes. 6.
32. 'Thes. philos.' (1668, 1 p.), thes. 1.
33. 'De error.' (1676), thes. 25–31; 'Thes. philos.' (1677), thes. log. 4.
34. 'Thes. misc.' (1679), thes. log. 3.
35. 'De error.' (1676), thes. 40–41.
36. 'Exist. Dei' (1671), thes. 10; 'Thes. misc.' (1673), thes. 13; 'Thes. philos.' (1677), thes. met. 6; 'De subst.' (1681), thes. 25.
37. 'Thes. philos.' (1668, 1 p.), thes. 8–9; 'Thes. misc.' (1675), thes. 4; 'Thes. philos.' (1677), thes. met. 7; 'Thes. misc.' (1679), thes. phys. 5.
38. 'Exist. Dei' (1671), coroll. phys. 2.
39. 'Unum corpus' (1672), epimetra, no. 1.
40. 'De cogn. Dei' (1676), thes. 8.
41. 'Exist. Dei' (1671), thes. 25; 'De cogn. Dei' (1676), thes. 5; 'Thes. philos.' (1683), thes. 8.
42. 'De mut. I.' (1664), epimetra pneum. 2.
43. 'De atom. I.' (1666); 'De atom. II.' (1667); 'Thes. misc.' (1675), thes. 5; 'Thes. philos.' (1677), thes. phys. 1.
44. Ethica Christiana Juxta Decalogi Praecepta Ex Disputationibus publicis enata & in Compendium contracta (Zurich, 1692). – . . . Editio Secunda (Zurich, 1700).
45. Logicae Doctrinae Compendium una cum Brevi Epitome Praeceptorum Nobilissimae Scientiae Metaphysicae in Publicum usum Scholae Tigurinae Conscriptum (Zurich, 1708); Compendium Logici Compendiolum Brevius In pleniores Institutiones Isagogicum Majori Praemittendum (Zurich, 1708); Brevis Epitome Praeceptorum Nobilissimae Scientiae Metaphysicae Ex accuratissimo antecessoris nostri Clarissimi Lavateri Systemate conscriptum (Zurich, 1708).
46. Epit. met., Cap. 27.
47. 'De votis' (1681); 'Theses ethico-politicae' (1681); 'De virtutibus specialibus V. & VI. praecepti in decalogo' (1691); 'De virtutibus VII. VIII. IX. & X. praecepti in decalogo' (1691); 'De dependentia creaturae a Deo in esse, fieri et operari' (1695).
48. 'Theses philosophicae' (1682); 'Theses philosophicae' (1688); 'Theses philosophicae' (1692); 'Theses logicae' (1696); 'De origine ac progressu philosophiae, et pacifico illius studio' (1697); 'Theses philosophicae' (1697); 'De argumento testimonii' (1699); 'De causa in genere, et necessario illam inter et effectum illius nexu in specie' (1701); 'De communioribus disputantium erroribus I.' (1703); 'II. de . . . erroribus, eorumque causis aliquot et remediis' (1705); 'De substantia' (1707).
49. 'De virtut. V. & VI. praec.' (1691), appendix 3.
50. 'De arg. test.' (1699), coroll. 1.
51. 'Thes. philos.' (1697), thes. 1.

52. 'De caus.' (1701), p. 10.
53. 'Thes. philos.' (1688), thes. 8; 'De arg. test.' (1699), coroll. 6.
54. 'De subst.' (1707), p. 16.
55. Samuel Werenfels, *Dissertatio de logomachiis eruditorum I–VII* (Basle, 1688–1692; Amsterdam, 1702).
56. *Compendium Physicae Aristotelico-Cartesianae Methodo Erotematica in usum Tyronum adornatum. Adjecta est ad calcem Ontosophia Claubergiana in Theoremata & Axiomata succincte digesta* (Basle, 1685).
57. *Comp. phys.*, p. 1; cf. also 'Thes. philos.' (1665), p. 4.
58. *Hugonis Grotii Jus Belli Et Pacis In Compendio Institutioni Scholasticae aptatum, & subinde castigatum, Opera Joh. Henrici Sviceri* (Zurich, 1689).
59. *Johannis Claubergii Ontosophia, quae vulgo Metaphysica vocatur, Notis perpetuis In Philosophiae & Theologiae Studiosorum usum illustrata, a Joh. Henrico Suicero. In calce annexa est Claubergii Logica Contracta* (Zurich, 1694).
60. *Epistola Apologetica ad Deoduraeum Gentangulum, in qua Argumentatio Cartesii pro Existentia Dei contra Judicium Reginense asseritur & vindicatur* (Ulm, 1700).
61. *Judicium de Argumento Cartesii Pro Existentia Dei Petito Ab Ejus Idea* (Basle, 1699).
62. 'Theses exhibentes breve & succinctum theoreticae philosophiae theatrum' (Hanau, 1665); 'Exercitationum logicarum III. ... de recte formanda apprehensione simplici, agens de idearum origine in genere, & de ideis innatis in specie' (Hanau, 1666); 'De cognitionis humanae elementis' (1691); 'De existentia Dei' (1691); 'De corporum naturalium motu' (1691); 'Specimen philologiae S. Novi Testamenti in explicatione principii Epistolae ad Ephesios ostensum' (1691); 'Dissertatio philologica II., qua doctrina de electione in cap. I. ad Ephesios vers. 4. contenta explicatur, & a variis παρερμηνείαις, Grotianis praecipue, vindicatur' (1692); 'De mundo universe spectato' (1692); 'De Deo, mente & corpore, nec non de mentis cum corpore unione' (1692); 'De angelis malis' (1694); 'De corporum naturalium quiete' (1694); 'De ventis' (1694); 'De corporis et animi conjunctione' (1694); 'De magistratus iure circa sacra' (1695); 'Dissertationum philologicarum, in Epistola S. Pauli ad Colossenses I.' (1697); 'II.' (1697); 'III.' (1697); 'IV.' (1697).
63. 'De cogn.' (1691), § 26.
64. Ibid., § 27.
65. Ibid., § 32.
66. Ibid., §§ 60–66; cf. also 'De exist. Dei' (1691).
67. 'Diss. philolog. IV' (1697), coroll. 2.
68. 'De Deo' (1692); 'De conjunct.' (1694).
69. 'De corp. nat. mot.' (1691), thes. 7.
70. 'De corp. nat. quiet.' (1694), thes. 6.
71. 'De mundo' (1692), p. 5.

72. 'De ventis' (1694), thes. 12.

73. *Idea Physicae Nov-Antiquae, Seu Eclectico-Reconciliatricis (una cum Compendiolo ex hac Idea extracto,) in usum Scholae Tigurinae Jussu Superiorum conscripta* (Zurich, 1708).

74. 'Ἀρτολογία, seu disputationum de pane, hujus natura, usu legitimo, et noxio abusu, I.' (1696); 'II.' (1696); 'III.' (1697); 'Κρυσταλλολογία, seu dissertatio de crystallis, harum naturam, ad mentem veterum & recentiorum per sua phenomena explicatius tradens' (1698); 'Βροντολογία physico-sacra, seu dissertatio de fulmine, hujus naturam, in genere, secundum suas causas, & affectiones proponens' (1698); 'Βροντολογία specialis, potiora fulminis adjuncta, fulgur, tonitrum, & ictum fulmineum εἰδικῶς sistens' (1700); 'Theses philosophicae' (1699); 'Theses philosophicae miscellaneae' (1699); 'Theses philosophicae miscellaneae καταλλακτικαί' (1703); 'Specimen physiologiae sacrae' (1704); 'Γαλακτολογία generalis & specialis, seu dissertatio de lacte, variis hujus speciebus & partibus: butyro, sero & caseo' (1704); 'Βιο-γραφία physico-sacra, seu dissertatio de vita, hujus natura, essentia, intervallis, seu aetatibus, cumprimis etiam de incommodis senii, juxta illustrem locum, Eccles. XII. 3–8, tandem de opposita vitae morte' (1706); '. . . pars altera' (1707); 'Physica generalis et specialis juxta historiam creationis ex Genes. cap. I. κατ᾽ ἐπιτομὴν proposita' (1706); 'Οἰνολογία seu dissertationum de vino I., sistens hujus causam efficientem; primam, secundam, instrumentalem; item materiam & sic naturam vitium, uvarum atque musti' (1707); 'II., sistens vini causam formalem, id est naturam & essentiam' (1710); 'III., continens hujus causam formalem; per se et per accidens; seu varium, legitimum vini usum, cum opposito & noxio ejusdem abusu' (1712); 'Theses physico-philosophicae' (1709); 'Schediasma ontologico-onomatologicum, sistens entis nomen & divisionem nominalem' (1709); 'Liber naturae ex Psalmo XIX, v. 1–7, propositus' (1711); 'Theses philosophicae' (1713); 'De necessitate & utilitate logicae' (1713).

75. 'Thes. philos. misc.' (1699), thes. 1.

76. 'De necess. log.' (1713), p. 10.

77. 'Thes. philos.' (1699), thes. 1.

78. 'Thes. philos. misc.' (1703), thes. 28; 'Lib. nat.' (1711) pp. 16f.

79. 'Thes. philos. misc.' (1703), thes. 9.

80. 'Spec. phys. sacr.' (1704), thes. 23; cf. also 'Phys. ex Genes.' (1706).

81. 'Disputationum physicarum de humoribus microcosmum irrigantibus I., chyli et lactis naturam per theses explicans' (1695); 'II., sanguinis et lymphae naturam . . . explicans' (1697); 'III., bilis naturam . . . explicans' (1698); '. . . de oeconomia corporis animati, seu microcosmi IV.' (1700); '. . . de sanitate, seu microcosmi V.' (1702); 'Dissertatio physica integram naturam per compendium traditam experimentis variis illustrans' (1703); 'De lapidibus' (1711).

82. *Exercitationes Medicae, seu Experimenta Anatomica De Humoribus In Corpore nostro circumfluentibus. Videlicet: Chylo, Lympha, Bile, Et Sanguine* (Zurich, 1675); *Vade Mecum Anatomicum, Sive Clavis Medicinae, Pandens Experimenta De Humoribus, Partibus, Et Spiritibus Adornata* (Zurich, 1727).

83. *Scientiae Naturalis Seu Physicae Compendium Pro Scholae Carolinae Auditoribus adornatum* (Zurich, 1694); *Systema Physicae Experimentalis Integram Naturam illustrans* (Zurich, 1705–1708): in three parts with separate title-pages. Part 1: *Physica Generalis* (1705) pp. 3–104; Part 2: *Physicae Specialis Pars Prima. Uranologia, Stoicheiologia & Meteorologia; De Coelo, Elementis, & Suspensis* (1707) pp. 105–230; Part 3: *Physicae Specialis Pars Secunda. Anthropologia, seu Microcosmus* (1708) pp. 233–323.

84. To avoid giving a long list of recent studies on philosophy teaching in the seventeenth century, I refer to the respective contributions in *Grundriss der Geschichte der Philosophie. Begründet von Friedrich Ueberweg. Völlig neubearbeitete Ausgabe. Die Philosophie des 17. Jahrhunderts*, ed. Jean–Pierre Schobinger [vols. 1–3], Helmut Holzhey and Wilhelm Schmidt-Biggemann [vol. 4] (Basle, Schwabe). – Vol. 1: Iberian Peninsula and Italy. Vol. 2: France and The Netherlands. Vol. 3: England. Vol. 4: Germany, Scandinavia, Eastern Europe. Vol. 3 has already appeared; the other vols. are at present prepared for the press. The contributions to Ueberweg's *Grundriss* are quite representative of the actual state of historical research on philosophy teaching.

85. The Zurich professors took up Descartes more or less about the same time as other Protestant professors (cf. the respective articles in Ueberweg's *Grundriss*, note 84: e.g. for the Netherlands by Paul Dibon, for Germany by Wilhelm Schmidt-Biggemann and Walter Sparn, for Switzerland by Wolfgang Rother), although his promotion was sometimes very controversial, for instance at Berne, where the City Council issued a prohibition of the teaching of Cartesian philosophy in April 1669, which was renewed in 1671 and 1680.

86. In Zurich the development of an interest in experimental philosophy was relatively late, compared e.g. with Basle or Geneva. The Basle professor of mathematics Samuel Eglinger, who possessed a collection of scientific instruments and a *laboratorium chymicum*, seems to have performed experiments as early as the 1670s. In 1676 Jakob Staehelin and Jakob Roth gave private courses, where they showed chemical experiments to their students. The most important Basle experimental philosopher of that time was the famous Jakob Bernoulli [cf. Wolfgang Rother, 'Die Philosophie an der Universität Basel im 17. Jahrhundert. Quellen und Analyse', Ph.D. thesis (Zurich, 1980), pp. 139–147, and *idem*, 'Zur Geschichte der Basler Universitätsphilosophie im 17. Jahrhundert', *History of Universities*, II (1982) 170–171]. At Geneva Jean–Robert Chouet seems to have performed experiments from 1670 [cf.

Michael Heyd, *Between Orthodoxy and the Enlightenment. Jean–Robert Chouet and the Introduction of the Cartesian Science in the Academy of Geneva* (London, 1982), pp. 88–102]. It must be emphasized, moreover, that at Basle and Geneva the experiments were really carried out, whereas there is no evidence that the Zurich professors of the period did so. They seem to have only *discussed* the experiments and results of others in their lessons and disputations. The developments at Zurich were in a certain sense anticipated by the developments at Basle, where in fact a number of Zurich professors (among them Johannes von Muralt) had studied and taken their medical degrees.

Philosophy in the Eighteenth-Century Dissenting Academies of England and Wales[1]

Alan P. F. Sell

Those who were nurtured philosophically at a time when that ancient discipline was straitjacketed by the conviction not only that philosophy was simply 'talk about talk', but that the most interesting kinds of talk should be proscribed; when the writings of all (especially the idealists) who had preceded Moore, Russell, and Wittgenstein were viewed by some with patronizing disbelief—people thus scarred in their youth whose wounds have yet to heal, will simply have to swallow hard when turning to eighteenth-century philosophy. For here almost anything goes; philosophers will turn their minds to all manner of questions—sometimes out of interest, frequently because they are spurred on by controversy and—not least in the Dissenting academies—because of a shortage of teachers. The more philosophically talented tutors would glide elegantly from logic to metaphysics to ethics to theology and back again, and even the less gifted were expected to familiarize students with all of these fields. Their efforts were generally worthy, their results sometimes unfortunate. Nor was the need of polymaths soon over. When at the end of our period—in 1804—John Pye Smith delivered his inaugural address at Homerton Academy (1730–1820), he listed the subjects he intended to cover: natural philosophy, astronomy, chemistry, natural history, logic, ontology, philosophy of the human mind, composition and rhetoric, history, mathematics, Hebrew, Greek, Latin, and English.[2] Two years later Pye Smith assumed the theological chair. All of which seems awesome, especially when one recalls reports (no doubt malicious and ill-founded) of some in our own time who experience difficulty in keeping one chapter between themselves and their students in one discipline. Our awe must be tempered, however, by the realization that the post-Renaissance

explosion of knowledge was in its adolescence, our modern disciplines had yet to receive their now-familiar shapes,[3] and the progressive eighteenth-century person was expected to have a nodding
acquaintance with many things. But deeper than the matter of
personal interest, or the requirements of controversy, or the shortage of teachers, many Dissenters would have endorsed the words of
Thomas Barnes at the opening of Manchester Academy in 1786:

Of all subjects, DIVINITY seems most to demand the aid of kindred, and
even of apparently remoter sciences. Its objects are, GOD and MAN: and
nothing, which can either illustrate the perfections of the one, or the nature,
capacities, and history of the other, can be entirely unimportant. But how
extensive a field do these subjects open? Natural Philosophy, in its widest
sense, comprehending whatever relates to the history or properties of the
works of Nature, in the Earth, the Air, the Ocean, and including Natural
History, Chemistry, &c. has an immediate reference to the one—and to the
other belong, all that Anatomy and Physiology can discover relating to the
body, and all that Metaphysics, Moral Philosophy, History, or Revelation
declare concerning the mind. But here again the field still opens upon us.
For History, as well as Revelation, demands the knowledge of Languages;
and these again, of Customs and of Arts, of Chronology and Manners—the
stream of science still branching out into more and wider channels. And to
the highest finishing of the mind are necessary, those subjects which belong
to cultivated Taste, which regulate the Imagination and refine the Feelings,
and which give correctness to vigour, and elegance to strength.[4]

In a word, those who were seriously concerned with the ways and
works of God and humanity, and who wished to provide university-
level education to those otherwise excluded from it, could not
consistently balk at a curriculum which ran over the whole field of
available knowledge.

With the reference to exclusion from the universities of Oxford
and Cambridge we return to the beginning of our period. In bald
summary of a very complicated story we may say that the continuing
influence of the medieval idea of the unity of the realm was thrown
into relief by Henry VIII's disengagement of the English Church
from that of Rome. The conviction was fostered that an important
constituent of the cement of national unity was religious uniformity.
Hence the attempts to secure such uniformity by legislation, which
were so stoutly resisted by the Separatist harbingers of English
Dissent. In the wake of the Civil War and under Cromwellian rule,

the lot of Dissenters was easier. But reaction against them set in with the Restoration of the monarchy in 1660. The times were politically and religiously turbulent, and once again the authorities set themselves to secure religious uniformity as a mainstay of national unity. To this end a series of five measures (known to the Dissenters of the time as 'the five-thonged whip') found their way to the statute books. The Corporation Act of 1661 excluded Nonconformists (Roman and Dissenting) from holding civil office. Between 1660, when the Convention Parliament's Act restored sequestered clergy to their livings, and 1662, and speeded by the Act of Uniformity of the latter year, some two thousand clergymen were ejected from their livings because they could not in conscience give their 'unfeigned assent and consent' to the Book of Common Prayer of the Church of England. The Act applied also to schoolmasters and university teachers, and among the ejected in the latter category was John Owen, Dean of Christ Church and formerly Vice Chancellor of Oxford University. There followed the Conventicle Act (1664), which prohibited religious meetings of five or more persons over the age of sixteen (other than members of the same household); and the Five Mile Act (1665), which was designed to separate ejected ministers from their former pastorates by imposing penalties upon any of them who resided within five miles of any corporate town, or of the place in which they had formerly ministered. The provisions of the first Conventicle Act were reinforced by those of the Second, in 1670.[5]

If the Act of Uniformity excluded Dissenting teachers from the ancient universities, the university statutes effectively excluded Dissenting students; for at Oxford all entering students were required to subscribe to the doctrines of the Thirty-Nine Articles of the Church of England, and all members of that university were prohibited from having relations with any Dissenting societies. Some degrees at Cambridge were open only to those who were members of the Church of England, while other degrees were awarded only upon the candidate's subscription to the articles of the Thirty-sixth Canon of the Church of England.[6]

Under the circumstances described the earliest Dissenting academy tutors lived dangerously. For example, threatened by the penalties of the Five Mile Act, Richard Frankland migrated with his academy (1669–98) on no fewer than five occasions between 1683 and 1689.[7] The arrival of William of Orange in 1688 was, however,

soon followed by the enactment of what has come to be known as
the Toleration Act of 1689—despite the fact that the term 'toleration' appears neither in the title of the Act nor anywhere in the text.[8]
Without repealing earlier adverse legislation, the Act permitted
orthodox Protestant Dissenters (not Roman Catholics, Socinians or
Jews) to organize and to be protected under the law. Such Protestants, who assented to the doctrines of the Thirty-Nine Articles of
the Church of England (with a concession to Baptists on their
doctrinal *raison d'être*), were enabled to establish more permanent
academies.

The Toleration Act did not meet with universal approval. To
some it did not go far enough; but what disturbed the orthodox
Dissenters were the attempts to repeal it which flared up intermit-
tently until 1734, when George II ordered that charges against Philip
Doddridge be dropped. The narrowest squeak was in 1714. The
Schism Bill requiring the closure of Dissenting academies was passed
in June 1714, and was to have reached the Statute Book on 1
August. But on that very day Queen Anne died—unparalleled
evidence of a favourable Providence in the eyes of many Dissenters,
as witness the sermon said to have been preached in London by the
Congregationalist Thomas Bradbury (known to Queen Anne herself
as 'bold Bradbury') on II Kings ix: 34: 'Go, see now this cursed
woman, and bury her, for she is a king's daughter'. The textual
reference is, of course, to Jezebel.

As Dissenters were free to worship and to educate their young in
accordance with their consciences, so many felt increasingly free to
think for themselves. Thus, when the Presbyterian divine John
Taylor looked back on the Glorious Revolution of 1688 from his
vantage point in the 1740s he was moved to eulogize: 'LIBERTY at
the Revolution, O bright auspicious Day! reared up her heavenly
Form, and smiled upon our happy Land . . . Men began freely to use
their Understandings; the Scriptures were examined with more
Attention and Care, and their true sense, setting aside human
Comments, and especially the Jargon and Sophistry of School-
Divinity, was sought after.'[9] The widely-shared optimism could not
but influence the attitude of many a Dissenting tutor and student—
especially those in the more liberal academies. But the use of the
term 'liberal' prompts our final preliminary observation.

The labelling of academies and divines alike is a hazardous
undertaking. Some establishments and teachers were more open to

'advanced' thought with its accompanying doctrinal change than others; but matters were seldom tidy either ecclesiastically or theologically. Ecclesiastically, it by no means followed that a student entering a Presbyterian, Congregational or Baptist academy would remain within the fold. Thus, Timothy Goodwin, the future Archbishop of Cashel had studied at Samuel Cradock's academy at Wickambrook, Suffolk (1678?–1696), where he was a contemporary of Edmund Calamy. Josiah Hort, later Archbishop of Tuam, was at Thomas Rowe's notable academy (founded at Newington Green *circa* 1666, and continued by Rowe at Clapham and Little Britain until his death in 1705), whose alumni included Isaac Watts, Daniel Neal, John Evans, and Henry Grove, later of Taunton Academy (1670?–1759). Again, the lay Presbyterian tutor Samuel Jones of Tewkesbury Academy (1708?–1724) nurtured both the future Bishop Joseph Butler and Thomas Secker. The latter came to Tewkesbury following studies under the Independent Timothy Jollie at Attercliffe (1690–1720?). He 'preached as a Probationer at Bolsover, but failed to get an invitation to the pastorate.'[10] He did, however, subsequently manage to become Archbishop of Canterbury. From Ebenezer Latham's Presbyterian Academy at Findern (1710?–1754) emerged John Wiche the General Baptist, and Ferdinando Warner, who became an Anglican and published among other things *A full and plain Account of the Gout . . . with some new and important Intstructions for its Relief* in 1768, the year of his death—from gout. This unhappy coincidence, as his biographer drily remarks, 'destroyed the credit of his system'.[11] Joseph Priestley, the first student under the Congregationalist Caleb Ashworth at Daventry (1728–1789), became the leading Unitarian of the latter part of the eighteenth century, while from the moderately Calvinistic Bristol Baptist College (1679, continuing) there issued General Baptists, Unitarians and a Sandemanian.[12]

Theologically, the Congregational Fund Board's academy which, from 1752, was conducted successively at Ottery St. Mary (John Lavington), Bridport (James Rooker), Taunton (Thomas Reader) and Axminster (James Small) was decidedly evangelical, as was that at Mile End under John Conder's tutelage from 1755–1781. Indeed, with reference to the latter Priestley wrote, 'My Aunt, and all my relations, being strict Calvinists, it was their intention to send me to the academy at *Mile-end*, then under the care of Dr. Cander [*sic*]. But, being at that time an Arminian, I resolutely opposed it, especially upon finding that if I went thither, besides giving an *experience*, I must subscribe my assent to ten printed articles of the strictest calvinistic faith, and repeat it every six months.'[13]

Other academies were notably open and progressive—supremely the 'Athens of the North' established at Warrington in 1757. John Taylor, the first divinity tutor there exhorted his students thus:

I, I do solemnly charge you, in the Name of the God of Truth, and of our Lord Jesus Christ,... that in all your Studies and Inquiries of a religious Nature, present or future, you do constantly, carefully, impartially and conscientiously, attend to Evidence, as it lies in the holy Scriptures, or in the Nature of things, and the Dictates of Reason; cautiously guarding against the Sallies of Imagination, and the Fallacy of ill-grounded Conjecture. II, That you admit, embrace, or assent to, no Principle or Sentiment, by me taught or advanced, but so far as it shall appear to you to be supported and justified by proper Evidence from Revelation, or the Reason of things. III, That, if at any time hereafter, any Principle or Sentiment by me taught or advanced, or by you admitted and embraced, shall, upon impartial and faithful Examination, appear to you to be dubious or false, you either suspect or totally reject such Principle or Sentiment. IV, That you keep your Mind always open to Evidence. That you labour to banish from your Breast all Prejudice, Prepossession, and Party-zeal; ... and that you steddily assert for yourself, and freely allow to others, the unalienable Rights of Judgment and Conscience.[14]

Between the decidedly evangelical and the equally decidedly liberal academies were some which, according to one's viewpoint, provided a varied theological diet or emitted mixed theological signals. Thus at Daventry, according to Priestley, 'Our tutors ... were of different opinions, Dr. Ashworth taking the orthodox side of every question, and Mr. [Samuel] Clark, the sub-tutor, that of heresy, though always with the greatest modesty.'[15] When William Bull, later tutor at Newport Pagnell (1783–1820), entered Daventry Academy in 1759, four years after Priestley's departure, the staunch Calvinist found a number of Arians among his fellow students; and in 1762, when Samuel Morton Savage was appointed divinity tutor at Hoxton (1701–1785) his colleagues were the Arian Abraham Rees and the Socinian Andrew Kippis.[16]

Against the background thus sketched, and following some remarks upon the philosophical inheritance flowing down from the earliest academies,[17] we shall first investigate philosophy (including logic, metaphysics, natural theology, and ethics) as it appears in academy curricula, and then briefly review the philosophical contributions of Dissenting academy teachers and alumni. In each case we shall present our findings in relation to our rough categories of more liberal, more conservative, and more mixed (that is, more theologically diverse) academies.

I

In 1790 Gilbert Wakefield was appointed classical tutor at the liberal Hackney College (1786–1796), where he proved to be a 'troubler of Israel'. He published a tract in repudiation of public worship;[18] he taught Greek without accents—'against which he was as violent as he was against the Trinity';[19] he deemed systematic doctrinal teaching to produce 'a harvest of *theological coxcombs*',[20] and he lamented that 'in these institutions young men are dosed with such infusions [of metaphysics, morals, history, and politics] to a degree that makes even the strongest stomach regurgitate under the operation.'[21] Wakefield resigned before completing his first year in post and he was, to put it mildly, atypical. For the most part the place of philosophy in the Dissenting academies was unquestioned (though, as we shall see, the attention paid to it in some conservative academies was minimal).[22] Indeed, added zeal was provided by the realization that here as elsewhere there were new ideas to be propounded. If Aristotle's syllogistic stranglehold was upon Oxford, the Dissenting tutors made sure that Ramus and, later, Locke were heeded by their students. Ramus (1517–1572) had pioneered the application of reason well outside the confines of scholastic logic, and his ideas were transmitted through such Cambridge Puritans as William Perkins and William Ames,[23] Oxford scholars doing little to propagate his work, and for the most part noticing him only with a view to attacking his views. The observation of Irene Parker[24] that when Henry Fleming went up to Queen's College, Oxford, in 1678, he read the same logic texts as those prescribed at Sheriffhales (1663–1697) and Shrewsbury (1680?–1715?) Academies—except that the latter recommended Ramus, who was apparently unknown to Fleming— is suggestive; for John Woodhouse of Sheriffhales, Francis Tallents of Shrewsbury, and Richard Frankland of Rathmell, who also used Ramus, were all Cambridge men. Frankland's pupil, James Clegg, informs us that where logic was concerned, 'One Tutor was a Ramist but we read ye Logick both of Aristotle and of Ramus, and within the Compass of the first year I was thought an acute disputant in that way.'[25] Another Rathmell alumnus, Renald Tetlaw, left a list of authorities used in the academy. They include the Cartesian Heereboord on logic and ethics, and the same author's commentary on Burgersdyck's logic; Ramus's logic with Downame's commentary upon it; the logic of the Aristotelian Smiglecius, the *Ars Cogitanda* of Le Clerc, with Govean, Milton, and others for good measure. The metaphysicians Fromenius and Barlow, the philosophers Colbert, Eustache and Descartes, and the ethics of the Cambridge Platonist Henry More all came under review.[26] This broad approach, and the use of some of the authors already named, was adopted by John Woodhouse at Sheriffhales,[27] by James Owen at Shrewsbury,[28] and by John Ker at Bethnall Green (1680?–1708?).[29] It was continued at the Manchester Academy (1699–1713) under Frankland's pupil John Chorlton.

As for Locke, whose period of exile in Holland is by no means insignificant, his *Essay* was proscribed at Oxford in 1703[30] (though read by some under cover), but was the epistemological staple at a number of the Dissenting academies, as we shall see. Although the Cambridge intellectual impetus was of primary importance, we ought not to leave the impression that all Oxford alumni were intellectually hidebound. Matthew Warren, for example, who had been educated at St John's College, Oxford, became tutor at Taunton Academy (1670?–1759), to which town he had moved in 1687, and where he remained until his death in 1706. Of him it was written, 'Tho' bred himself in the Old Logic and Philosophy, and little acquainted with the improvements of the New, yet he encouraged his pupils in a freedom of enquiry, and in reading those books which would better gratify a love of truth and knowledge, even when they differed widely from those writers on which he had formed his own sentiments.'[31] Thus, while Franco Burgersdyck of Leiden's logic was studied in class, 'Locke [already], Le Clerc and Cumberland were guides to [the students'] just thinking, close reasoning and enlightened views in their closets.'[32] Neither should it be thought that all early academies were beacons of philosophic light. Though a pupil of Frankland, Timothy Jollie, estimable as he was in inculcating practical divinity, 'forbad the Mathematicks, as tending to scepticism & infidelity',[33] and gave no instruction in logic. Of his

Attercliffe Academy (c. 1690–1714) it was said that 'only the old philosophy of the schools was taught there, and that neither ably nor diligently'.[34]

After 1690 promising Dissenting students did not need to stay at home awaiting the influx of continental and Scottish ideas. Under the Common (that is Presbyterian and Congregational) Fund (1690) and, following the breakdown of the 'Happy Union' of Congregationalists and Presbyterians, the Presbyterian Fund (1693), to which resource was later added Dr. Williams's Trust (1706), scholars went to study in Scotland, Holland, and Halle. Of those who became philosophical tutors, Samuel Jones had been at Leiden, Samuel Benion at Glasgow, and John Aikin, Philip Doddridge's first student at Northampton (1729–1751),[35] at Aberdeen, where he moved in an Arian direction. In Scotland a prominent open-minded line flowed down from Francis Hutcheson, who had been educated at James M'Alpin's philosophical Dissenting academy at Killyleagh (1690s–1724), Co. Down,[36] and who, in 1710, proceeded thence to Glasgow, among whose influential professors were Gershom Carmichael and John Simson. The latter had studied under the orthodox Reformed theologian Marckius in Leiden, but was himself suspected of heresy though never deposed.[37] Carmichael, who became Glasgow's first professor of moral philosophy in 1727,[38] was poised between the older scholasticism and the new experimentalism, and it was the latter on which Hutcheson, influenced by Locke, was to fasten. Hutcheson succeeded Carmichael in 1730, and his supporter and theological colleague, William Leechman, who had been nurtured at Edinburgh in William Hamilton's nest of Moderates (and Hamilton was a friend of Simson), lectured to crowded classes in an undogmatic manner, and had himself attended Hutcheson's classes prior to his appointment.[39]

If it be true that 'By their honours ye shall know them', then of the fifteen out of some forty Dissenting philosophy tutors who received Scottish DDs during the eighteenth century, Aberdeen awarded eleven (including one from each of its colleges to Philip Doddridge), of which nine went to conservative or moderate thinkers, and two to theological liberals; Glasgow, at Leechman's suggestion honoured the liberal John Taylor in 1756 (though for his Hebrew scholarship, not for his as yet unpublished critique of Hutcheson's moral theory); and Edinburgh admitted three liberals only, of whom the first, in 1743, was Caleb Rotheram of Kendal Academy (1733–1753)—and this for a thesis in which 'he ably refutes the notion strongly insisted on by many sceptical writers, and somewhat incautiously admitted even by Mr. Locke, "that the probability of facts depending on human testimony must gradually lessen in proportion to the distance of time when they happened, and at last become entirely evanescent"'.[40]

On the foundation of the philosophical authors already mentioned, we may proceed to note the philosophical works prescribed at (to use very rough categories) more liberal, more conservative, and more mixed academies. It must be said that the evidence is incomplete, and this for two reasons. In the first place, until Philip Doddridge pioneered the provision of academy libraries distinct from the tutors' personal collections,[41] students were at the mercy of their tutors' own books. Early tutors were sometimes on the run; most tutors were impecunious; and some, like Ebenezer Latham professed a wide range of subjects, ministered to a local church, and served the district as physician. None of these circumstances was conducive to reading, let alone to maintaining comprehensive libraries. It is therefore all the more impressive a tribute to John Shuttlewood of Sulby Academy (1680–1688) that his student Thomas Emlyn, who resigned because Shuttlewood 'had very few books, and them chiefly of one sort', went to Oxford, and sated himself in the Bodleian, subsequently returned to Shuttlewood for teaching and example which were not to be found among the dreaming spires.[42] Secondly, there is the matter of teaching through the medium of English. Among the Dissenting pioneers of the use of English in preference to Latin was Charles Morton (1627–1698) of Newington Green Academy. In Scotland Hutcheson introduced the practice at Glasgow, and Leechman followed suit. When Doddridge adopted the practice his powerful example ensured that henceforth English was the normal medium of instruction in the Dissenting academies. But there resulted a serious time-lag in the provision of translated texts by continental authors. This threw the onus very much upon the tutors, who had to refer to foreign sources in their own lectures—and that they sometimes did so to the point of indigestion may be seen from surviving manuscripts.

As to the more liberal academies: at Whitehaven (1708–1729) Thomas Dixon,[43] according to the manuscript notes of Henry Winder at Manchester College, Oxford, made reference to Bacon,

Newton and Locke—and not least to the Locke-Limborch correspondence. Thomas Hill, who founded the academy at Findern in 1710, required his students to read Le Clerc for logic and Fromenius for metaphysics. His successor Ebenezer Latham,[44] however, prescribed Carmichael and Locke on logic, but nothing on metaphysics or ethics. At the age of 16, in 1704, Latham had left James Owen's Shrewsbury Academy for Glasgow University, whose professor of philosophy, as we saw, was Carmichael. At Warrington students had the first sight of what became John Taylor's *An Examination of Dr. Hutcheson's Scheme of Morality* and *A Sketch of Moral Philosophy*. These were published in 1760, the latter being designed to introduce students to Wollaston's *Religion of Nature Delineated*.

Isaac Watts's *Treatise on Logic* (1724) was used in such more conservative institutions as Bristol Baptist Academy and Newport Pagnell (Independent) Academy; and in the more liberal centres at Carmarthen and Warrington. Doddridge's *Lectures on Pneumatology, Ethics and Theology* were likewise widely used in academies of all hues. What seems to emerge from a study of the more conservative academies is that from about 1730 onwards philosophy— especially epistemology and metaphysics—begins to take a back seat in the curriculum—if, indeed, it is present at all. It is not difficult to divine the reasons for this. On the one hand there is the concern of the theologically orthodox to 'guard the Ark' against a rationalism which was turning many in an Arian, and even a Socinian direction. On the other hand there is the influence of the Evangelical Revival, which fostered the establishment of academies exclusively devoted to ministerial training rather than to the providing of a broad university-level education, with consequent pressure on the curriculum from the homiletic, practical, and professional directions.

The history of the Baptist Academy at Bristol reveals the subtle change. There Bernard Foskett lectured on a variety of subjects including logic, ontology, and ethics from 1720–1758. And there in 1744 student John Collett Ryland wrote a detailed description in his diary of his proposed academic work for the year. Of particular interest to us are the following remarks:

1. Go thro' Dr. Watts's Logick twice. 2. Then thro' his Scheme of Ontology twice ... N.B. Also read quite perfectly thro' Mr. Lock's Essay on Hum. Understanding, and sometimes when Mr. Fosket requires it give an account of it. ...

1. Make my Self (i.e. in God's Strength) a Perfect and Compleat Logician and Metaphysician—from Dr. Watts's 2 Treatises on those Subject—But if possible I'll excell the Dr. Watts in both those Sciences—and Correct and improve and inlarge where he's Defective. 2. Read Correct and Explain and make Remarks on Mr. Locks Treatise before Mentioned ... Get a Large Knowledge of Moral Philosophy as founded on Reason and Scripture [on which subject Foskett used Pufendorf].[45]

Foskett was succeeded by Hugh Evans, and during his term of office a student, Thomas Dunscombe, reported on the work he had done during the year 1770–1771. From this statement, and from a subsequent one written a year later, it would seem that whereas in both years Watts's *Logic* had been studied, that work was the sole representative of the philosophical disciplines. Alongside it went the Baptist John Gill's high Calvinistic theology, and a good deal of Hebrew and classics.[46] In 'A Catalogue of a Few Useful Books' presented to one of his leaving students in 1773, Dr Evans recommends the following of philosophical interest: Doddridge on the evidences—'a *very* valuable performance'; Boyle on natural and revealed religion; Jonathan Edwards, 'the most rational, Scriptural divine and the liveliest Christian the world was ever blessed with', on freewill and other topics; and, under 'Miscellaneous', Derham's *Astro* and *Physico-Theology*, Locke's *Essay*, and Watts's *Improvement of the Mind*.[47] These last are clearly 'runners up' to substantial lists of doctrinal, practical, and historical works. And this, to repeat, is the impression conveyed also by the newer conservative academies.

Thus Homerton Academy, for the training of ministers only, was established by the orthodox Calvinists of the King's Head Society shortly after that body's formation in 1730. On 22 May 1754 Thomas Gibbons recorded in his diary that he had informed the governing bodies of his intention to teach 'Logick, Metaphysics, Ethics, Rhetorick, Stile in gener:, Pulpit Stile', and that this was approved. On 26 May 1758 he writes: 'Lectured at Mile End. Poorly in the afternoon with the Head-Ach. Blessed be God that poorly as I was, I finished the last Lecture of the four years' course of Lectures at the Academy, & hereby have acquired a Sett of Lectures for my whole future life, or so long as I may continue in the Tutorship.' Before we deem this unforgiveable slackness, let us recall that Gibbons was pastor for forty years at Haberdashers' Hall, and that on 1 March 1755, at a time when he felt that his pastoral work was under threat from too much lecture preparation, he wrote, 'My business as a Pastor is first to be taken care of. My Business as a Tutor is only secondary.'[48] The fact remains that Gibbons's ability to keep abreast of newer philosophical developments must seriously have been curtailed.

The Abergavenny Academy (1757) was established by the Congregational Fund Board as a result of the Board's dissatisfaction with the liberalizing tendencies of Carmarthen Academy. Logic and ethics are specified in the course of instruction, but not metaphysics or epistemology.

At Trevecka, opened on the Countess of Huntingdon's birthday, 24 August 1768, the philosophical disciplines were, with the exception of logic, conspicuous by their absence from the list of subjects to be studied: 'Grammar, logic, rhetoric, ecclesiastical history, natural philosophy and geography, with a great deal of practical divinity and languages';[49] but Trevecka was a special place, where evangelical Calvinist preachers were to be trained, where tutors and students alike had to subscribe to fifteen Calvinistic articles, and where the entire syllabus could be set aside if Fletcher of Madeley, President of the College, was seized with a concern for the students' souls:

Languages, art, sciences, grammar, rhetoric, logic [a passing mention], even divinity itself . . . were all laid aside when he appeared in the school-room among the students. His full heart would not suffer him to be silent. He *must* speak, and they were readier to hearken to this servant and minister of Jesus Christ than to attend to Sallust, Virgil, Cicero, or any Latin or Greek historian, poet, or philosopher they had been engaged in reading. And they seldom hearkened long before they were all in tears, and every heart caught fire from the flame that burned in his soul.[50]

At the second Hoxton Academy—that is, the Independent one established in 1778, Robert Simpson, who had studied under James Scott at Heckmondwike, was at the helm. He was 'distinguished for his consistent and systematic theology which was in every particular Calvinistic.'[51] He taught the three 'R's': 'Ruin, Redemption, and Regeneration', and expected his students to preach with 'Animation, Affection and Application'—and, no doubt, with Alliteration. There is no evidence of philosophical studies in the Hoxton curriculum until 1803, when logic makes its appearance. Nonetheless, among Hoxton's alumni was George Payne (though he had also been a Dr Williams scholar at Glasgow University), who taught at Blackburn and Exeter Independent colleges, and was said to have 'a genuine gift for metaphysical speculation'.[52] Much the same is true of the missionary enthusiast David Bogue's Gosport Academy (1780?), where the Bible reigned supreme, where students were expected to have had a definite conversion experience, and in whose curriculum philosophy was conspicuous by its absence. Yet from here emerged the historian James Bennett, who became tutor at Rotherham Academy (1795–1820) in 1813, following the death of Edward Williams. There, among other things, he taught logic and the history of philosophy.

The origins of the Newport Pagnell Academy are unusual in that the moving force was the Anglican evangelical clergyman John Newton who, supported by likeminded colleges, persuaded William Bull the Independent to lead the new institution. Bull had been under Caleb Ashworth's open-minded tutelage at Daventry, but, staunch evangelical Calvinist that he was, he was more than happy with the prescriptions which Newton laid down in his *A Plan of Academical Preparation for the Ministry*.[53] A letter from Newton to Bull contains the intriguingly paradoxical assertion: 'Many persons are seriously thinking of a new academy, on *liberal* grounds, for preparing young men for the ministry, in which the greatest stress might be laid upon truth, life and spirituality, and the least upon modes, forms, and non-essentials.'[54] At once we see that this 'liberal' academy is for ordinands only, that piety is to be the main objective, and it takes little imagination to guess what the 'non-essentials' might be. If we are at a loss, Newton will illuminate us. In his *Plan* he declares that the Bible is his body of divinity, and that he prefers Paul's letters 'to any human systems I have seen'. He does not wish the tutor to be 'seduced by the specious sounds of candour and free enquiry'. Of the list of books recommended for study, Ashley Smith justly writes, 'The most striking characteristic ... is its out-of-dateness. These were the standard texts of fifty or more years before'.[55] Watts's *Logic and Improvement of the Mind* were approved for study, but of other branches of philosophy Newton writes, 'I have no great opinion of metaphysical studies. For pneumatology and ethics I would confine my pupils to the Bible.' Out, too, went the evidences, which had loomed so large at Doddridge's Northampton and Ashworth's Daventry: Newton had no patience for the probing of first principles. In a letter to Newton Bull contemplated the future with some alarm: 'I expect the time will come when [the friends of Jesus] will not dare to say anything but what may be proved by *"Cicero de Officiis"* or "Wollaston's Religion of Nature" '.[56] There is no suggestion, however, that future ministers needed to be equipped to address such a state of affairs should it come to pass.[57] Overall the more conservative academies were least hospitable to the philosophical disciplines: their supporters had seen the baneful influence of rationalism both upon more liberal academies and, thence, upon church life at large.[58]

We turn finally to those academies which were mixed in that while generally moderate and intellectually open and having a broad curriculum for lay and ministerial students alike, more liberal or more conservative tendencies were found among their staffs and students.

As we have seen, over a period of time the Carmarthen Academy became so generally Arminian and even Arian in complexion that the Congregational Fund Board withdrew its financial support. It must be emphasised, however, that the change occurred because of the spirit of open enquiry in which the academic work was done, and not because of the indoctrination of students by subversive tutors. As D. Elwyn Davies has rightly reminded us,

R.T. Jenkins has argued that to blame Perrot for producing Arminians like Jenkin Jones (1700–42), for some years the only public advocate of Arminianism in Wales, is an example of confusing *post* with *propter*. It would be just as ridiculous to hold Vavasour Griffiths (d. 1740), the successor of Perrot, (despite his unimpeachable orthodoxy) responsible for the Arians Richard Price and Jenkin Jenkins. It was not so much the theological teaching of the Tutor that produced the Arminians and Unitarians, as the liberal atmosphere and tolerant attitude prevailing within the College.[59]

Thus Samuel Thomas, who had himself studied under Perrot; who was 'certainly an Arminian and probably an Arian';[60] whose manner was frigid, and whose lectures were boring; and who was theologically the last straw as far as the Congregational Fund Board was concerned, nevertheless used Watts's *Logic*, Pufendorf on ethics, and Locke's *Essay*, just as many more conservative tutors did. To these, however, he added Hutcheson and the Anglican Arian Samuel Clarke. Thomas served from 1743 until his death in 1766, and his student, Noah Jones, writing in 1764, confirmed the texts as just given.[61]

At Hoxton Academy (1701–1785)[62] the manuscript *Institutiones Ethicae* of the learned John Eames (who himself published nothing) was used by his pupil and successor, Abraham Rees, its Latin notwithstanding. For information concerning Samuel Jones's course at Tewkesbury we are indebted to Thomas Secker's letter to Isaac Watts. According to Secker, Jones's students were allowed 'all imaginable liberty of making objections against his opinion, and prosecuting them as far as we can.'[63] More specifically:

Our *Logic*, which we have read once over, is so contrived as to comprehend all *Heereboord*, and the far greater part of *Mr. Locke's* Essay, and [Le. Clerc's] the *Art of Thinking*. What *Mr. Jones* dictated to us was but short, containing a clear and brief account of the matter, references to the places where it was more fully treated of, and remarks on, or explications of the authors cited, when need required. At our next lecture we gave an account both of what the author quoted and our tutor said, who commonly then gave us a larger explication of it, and so proceeded to the next thing in order. He took care, as far as possible, that we understood the sense as well as remembered the words of what we had read, and that we should not suffer ourselves to be cheated with obscure terms which had no meaning. Though he be no great admirer of the old *Logic*, yet he has taken a great deal of pains both in explaining and correcting *Heereboord*, and has for the most part made him intelligible, or shewn that he is not so.

Sadly, after a time, Jones began 'to drink too much ale and small beer and to lose his temper, and most of us fell off from our applications and regularity'.[64]

John Jennings, the Independent tutor at the Kibworth-Hinckley Academy from 1715–1723, who had been a student under Timothy Jollie, clearly favoured a more extensive curriculum than he. Jennings's most illustrious pupil, Philip Doddridge, declared that 'Mr. Jennings encourages the greatest freedom of enquiry, and always inculcates it as a law, that the scriptures are the only genuine standard of faith.' At the same time, 'Mr. Jennings does not follow the doctrines or phrases of any particular party; but is sometimes a Calvinist, sometimes an Arminian, and sometimes a Baxterian, as truth and evidence determine him.'[65] In his letter to Thomas

Saunders of 16 November 1725[66] Doddridge provided a full account of Jennings's course, from which we learn that Burgersdyck's *Logic* was dealt with in about six lectures, and supplemented by Jennings's own system, 'a great deal of which was taken from Mr. Locke'. Metaphysics appears in a list of 'Miscellanies' which included Fortification and Psalmody, while in ethics Grotius, Pufendorf and Wollaston were read. During the eighth half year a brief historical account of ancient philosophy was given.

Doddridge continued in the line of Jennings at his celebrated Northampton Academy (1729–1751).[67] According to his pupil Job Orton logic was studied,[68] while ethics and pneumatology were incorporated within the divinity course, as were studies of the nature and properties of the human mind, the theistic proofs, the nature of moral virtue, natural law, the immortality of the soul, and the necessity of revelation. Orton remarks that 'In his Lectures of *Philosophy, History, Anatomy*, &c [Doddridge] took Occasion to graft some *religious* Instructions on what he had been illustrating, that he might raise the minds of his Pupils to GOD and Heaven.'[69] Doddridge paid particular attention to the proofs of Christianity, a subject which he thought was 'more largely and accurately exhibited than in any other place of education I have ever heard of.'[70] As to teaching method, he 'referred [students] to Writers on both Sides, without hiding any from their Inspection.'[71]

Following Doddridge's early death in 1751, his Academy was continued at Daventry by his chosen successor, Caleb Ashworth. Ashworth's assistant from 1760 was Noah Hill, of whom Belsham said, 'of Logic and Mathematics he knew but little';[72] and of whom another says, 'He was particularly clear and excellent in his mathematical lectures'.[73] The latter writer notes that Hill lectured on logic, the philosophy of the human mind, the first principles of moral philosophy, and natural theology. Hill was succeeded by Thomas Belsham in 1771, and with reference to his logic course Timothy Kenrick wrote on 10 June 1775, 'We entered immediately after Xmas on Logic, and have now finished it; we always followed Dr. Watts' plan, except in a very few instances.'[74] When Belsham became divinity tutor in 1781 his course included logic, the doctrine of the human mind, the existence and attributes of God, the first principles of ethics, and the evidences of revealed religion.[75] Of particular importance is the fact that Belsham was the first Dissenting tutor to teach materialistic and neccessarian philosophy.[76]

When Belsham, by now a decided unitarian, honourably resigned from Daventry Academy in 1789, he was replaced by John Horsey. Horsey, trained at the more conservative Homerton Academy, reintroduced Doddridge's lectures. The clientele now comprised ordinands only, but the tradition of free intellectual enquiry was maintained. Though orthodox himself, Horsey, in his inaugural address, outlined his policy in terms which would have found the approval of more liberal tutors: 'It is not the design of this institution, and it is very far from my inclination, to usurp any authority over Conscience, or to cherish Bigotry or party zeal.' He continued, 'My object is not to stamp infallibility on any human system of Religion ... but ... to promote a Scriptural Christianity.'[77] Horsey's manuscript lectures on logic and ethics are extant. In the latter he compared various systems of logic, and then expounded Watts, suitably amended and enlarged by reference to other writers. Lant Carpenter, who entered the Academy in 1797, wrote to his mother, explaining that he was giving 'very close attention to the study of the doctrine of Necessity', and stating that the works of Locke and Hartley had been read 'with great care'.[78] All of which was too much for the recently appointed classical tutor, David Saville, a Scot and a Calvinist to boot. He anonymously advised the Coward Trustees that the Academy was 'tinctured not a little with Socinian principles', and Horsey was informed by a letter of 15 June 1798 that the Trustees had decided to close the Academy—and so it was.[79]

Thirty years later, Horsey's posthumous *Lectures to Young Persons on the Intellectual and Moral Powers of Man* were published in his memory. In the preface he writes,

The following Lectures took their rise from some peculiar circumstances attending my situation at the time when they were drawn up. Having had the honour and the felicity of presiding for the space of eight years over the Academical establishment supported by the Trustees of the late William Coward, Esq., without the slightest censure from them, collectively or individually, but receiving, on the contrary, in the most handsome terms, repeated testimonies of their approbation,—the ninth year became exceedingly uncomfortable, by the introduction of a very unsuitable classical tutor. The connexion was in consequence dissolved, and the Academy removed to Wymondley in Hertfordshire.

The passing events of the period led to the construction of the following Work, as an exercise pleasant in itself, and a seasonable relief to the mind, under no small share of misrepresentation, and consequent unmerited censure.[80]

We may conclude this section with some general observations on the teaching methods employed. The evidence suggests that in the earlier academies the tendency was to keep students' noses in the texts, so to speak. The emphasis was upon memorizing content and subsequently regurgitating it orally. Thus Toulmin's account of the procedure at Sheriffhales is not untypical: 'In all lectures, the authors were strictly explained and commonly committed to memory, at least as to the sense of them. On one day, an account of the lecture of the preceding day was required before a new lecture was read: and on Saturday a review of the lectures of the five days before was delivered. When an author had been about half gone through, they went that part over again; and so the second part passed under a second perusal; so that every one author was read three times.'[81] Henry Grove pursued an intermediate course, 'confining himself to no system in divinity, but the scriptures, directing his students to the best writers on the several subjects of enquiry',[82] while Doddridge and other later tutors devised their own systems, and worked through them systematically. To some students the systematic method had the disadvantage of either encouraging false discipleship by elevating extra-biblical authorities to undue prominence, or of inducing a scepticism on important questions prompted by the disagreement of acknowledged authorities upon them.[83] But if the newer method lacked appeal for some, Strickland Gough, in 1730, lamented the time 'usually wasted in old systems of logick and metaphysicks'.[84] Our investigation of the extant materials suggests that the backhanded compliment which John Rippon paid to Bernard Foskett of Bristol Baptist Academy has a wider application: 'If it be conceded that Foskett's method of education was limited rather than liberal, severe rather than enchanting, employing the memory more than the genius . . . in a word, if it be granted that Mr. Foskett is not the first of tutors . . . it is a debt of honour, to acknowledge that some good scholars and several of our greatest ministers were educated by him.'[85] At least Rippon stopped short of referring to a benign overruling Providence.

II

What contributions to philosophy were made by the tutors and alumni of the eighteenth-century Dissenting academies? We shall proceed chronologically through the tutors, placing them within the rough categories of more liberal, more conservative, and mixed academies. This will enable us to draw comparisons, though we shall, of course, be able only very sketchily to allude to the tutors' philosophical concerns.

Joshua Oldfield (1656–1729) taught at Coventry Academy from 1693, and at Southwark (later, Hoxton Square) from 1699. He had read philosophy at Christ's College, Cambridge, under Cudworth and More, and it is possible[86] that he also studied under John Shuttlewood at Sulby Academy. To these acquaintances he added that of Locke, whom he met at the time of the latter's work on his paraphrases of Paul's letters.[87] In 1707 Oldfield published, *An Essay towards the Improvement of Reason*, in which Cartesian, Platonist and Lockian emphases are discernible. Thus, he is with empiricists in his conviction that where things, words, and notions are concerned, 'Nature seems commonly to lead Men to begin with the first of these'; on the other hand his declaration that 'The first thing of which we are aware is our own awareness', would warm a Cartesian heart; while in ethics he follows the Cambridge Platonist Henry More in according conscience the role of judging the value of notions presented to the intellect.[88] Eclectic and ambivalent Oldfield may have been, but he does at least present some of the major philosophical options which lay before philosophers as the eighteenth century opened.

With Henry Grove (1684–1738), Warren's successor at Taunton, we come to a much more prolific author, and one who, though holding Locke in high esteem, was by no means intellectually subservient to him. This emerges, for example in his *An Essay towards the Demonstration of the Soul's Immateriality* (1718), on the cover of which Plotinus is quoted. The crux of his case is that '*Matter* cannot *think*; and if so, *unquestionably the soul is immaterial*'.[89] Accordingly, having stated Locke's view that 'If to the individuals of each species God had not superadded a power of propagation, the species had perished with those individuals', Grove expostulates:

Is this reasoning worthy of so great a Philosopher? Excepting the instances of sense and spontaneous motion in animals . . . in which Mr. *Locke* begs the question, all the other properties which Mr. *Locke* saith are superadded to *matter*, really conclude no more than that *matter* may be figured and moved by almighty power in ten thousand ways, than which nothing more true; and therefore because the qualities of *matter* may be acted upon and new modified, *matter* may receive a new quality of a kind perfectly differing from all the qualities it was possessed of before; than which, in my opinion, nothing can be more false.[90]

Grove moves towards his conclusion, concluding not with a QED, but with 'an act of devotion'.

Grove's special love was ethics, and here again, on the question of the freedom of the will, he found himself at odds with Locke. He agrees with Locke that 'Liberty is a power to act or not to act', but regrets that Locke added 'according to the preference of the mind' — which, he says more than once, '*is not free*'. Grove goes to some lengths to refute Locke, utilizing both logic and imagination thus:

Let us suppose a man locked into a room in company with a tempting Harlot, who imploys all her charms and cunning to draw him into sin; and that he *prefers* to stay there. I ask, whether he be free in this preference or not? If not, he is guilty of no fault therein, since no action can be culpable that is not free. If he be free, then it follows, that he has a *power to will* or *not to will* his stay; in other words, that he is free as willing.[91]

Grove's ethics were grounded in his conviction that we are obliged to love God and to show benevolence towards other intelligent beings. We are, moreover, under the commands of God; but these, though challenging, are not the sole ground of our obedience. Rather, we are to love God because 'he hath made us capable of loving him, and both by his perfections and benefits challenges our love . . . [I]f [these] are good reasons why we should love God, now that he commands it, they must be equally reasons for love antecedent to the consideration of any command whatsover.'[92] With this emphasis upon the primacy of the intellect over the will, Grove was revealing indebtedness to Cudworth, and laying a trail which both John Taylor and, more definitively, Richard Price were soon to follow.

It remains only to note that in his curriculum at Taunton Grove was among the first, if not the first, to separate ethics from theology.

Though he asserted the religious basis of ethics, and insisted, in
quasi–Newtonian fashion, upon God's orderly governance of a
morally ordered world, the time would come when others would feel
free to dispense with that foundation.[93] However, while Grove was
attacked by the high Calvinist John Ball of Honiton for his alleged
elevation of reason above Scripture,[94] he does not appear to have
been rebuked by any for his 'Pelagian' or 'Stoical' treatment of
ethics apart from theology—unlike his contemporaries at Yale, of
whom Cotton Mather wrote, 'There are some unwise things done
about which I must watch for opportunity to bear public testimony;
one is the employing so much time upon Ethik in College, a vile form
of paganism.'[95]

On the philosophical side John Taylor (1694–1761), trained at
Derby/Findern and Whitehaven, and tutor at Warrington, was
concerned, as we have seen, to refute Hutcheson's moral sense
theory by opposing to it a theory in the line of Cudworth, Clarke,
Grove, and Price. He also wished to introduce his students to
Wollaston's *The Religion of Nature Delineated*. Taylor objects to
what he understands as Hutcheson's reduction of all virtue and
religion to benevolence. He maintains that there are virtues to be
cultivated in addition to benevolence, among them proper self-love.
Whereas happiness is agreeable sensations, or feelings of the mind,
virtue is right action; and virtue cannot be commanded, it can be
exercised only in freedom. On conscience Taylor declares that it 'is
not a distinct Faculty in the human Soul; but the Judgment of our
Minds concerning our Actions; or it is our Apprehensions of Right
and Wrong, either directing, or reflecting upon, our own Conduct.'[96]
As to the moral sense, since reason shows us which actions are
virtuous and which are not—as it does—the moral sense is redun-
dant.[97] What Taylor overlooks is that Hutcheson regarded his moral
sense as a means of perception only, and in no way denied that
reason had plenty of work to do in its wake.[98]

Of Thomas Amory (1701–1774), Grove's pupil, biographer,
editor and successor at Taunton, Alexander Gordon wrote, 'In all
his literary work he was a dull, honest, serviceable man.'[99] No doubt
his was not an original mind, and he left no complete philosophical
works for our perusal, though he did contribute the concluding eight
chapters to Grove's *System of Moral Philosophy*. However, his
sermons and prefaces furnish evidence of the ideas typically received
and popularly communicated by the more liberal tutors, and are to

that extent interesting. Thus, in his sermon at the ordination of William Richards, we find Amory's apologetic *credo*:

> As to the great Doctrines therefore of *Natural Religion*, which the *Gospel* takes for granted, and which are the foundations of our Faith in any Divine Revelation, because these can only be proved by reasonings on the nature of things, the frame of the world, and the like; we must, by arguments of this sort, addressed to the Reason of Men, endeavour to establish in them the belief of the Being, Perfections, and moral Providence of God; of the moral and essential differences of characters and actions, and of a future state of recompences ... As all men therefore are obliged to receive these Truths, and are *capable* of discerning the evidences of them; all they, whom we would confirm in the faith of these, have a right to demand from us *rational grounds for their faith.* To require that they should believe, without good reasons, what we affirm on these heads, is to exalt ourselves into *Lords of Faith,* and degrade them to a level with *brutes.*[100]

In similar vein, Amory's preface to an address to young men begins thus: 'The main Doctrines and Duties of the Christian Religion are not only agreeable to Reason, but may be proved immediately by it: These, on Account of their internal Evidence and Excellency, claim our Belief and Regard, as well on Account of the Revelation which delivers and enjoins them.'[101]

Here we have characteristic emphases of the rational Dissenters: the Gospel is grounded in the doctrines of natural religion; these can be proved and commended to reasonable beings; such beings are required to, and are capable of, assent to the proofs (no noetic effects of sin here); and to refuse to offer rational grounds for faith is to tyrannize and dehumanize others. But however wide the consensus on such matters, liberal Dissenters could differ in emphasis on other points—not least on philosophical ones. Thus in a sermon on Psalm 145: 9 entitled, 'Goodness proved to be a Divine Perfection', Amory declares that God's goodness is demonstrated, *inter alia*, by the moral sense he has planted in us; and in a note he writes, 'In proof of this, see Hucheson's [sic] *Inquiry* concerning moral Good and Evil.'[102] Amory would thus appear to be more favourably disposed towards Hutcheson than Taylor, for example.

Like Amory, John Aikin (1713–1780) who, following training at Kibworth, began to lean towards Arianism whilst at Aberdeen University, left no philosophical works. That he was a most highly regarded tutor at Warrington is clear, however, from the remarks of

John Yates. Yates refers to Aikin 'Who, though little known to the world, because he was restrained by an aversion to public notice from ever being an author, possessed an union of genius, learning and eloquence, which eminently qualified him for preparing youth for the office of the sacred ministry.'[103] William Enfield was more specific concerning Aikin:

The first object of his researches was, to discover those truths which are the foundation of moral wisdom. Subjects merely speculative he occasionally examined, either in the way of amusement, or in the ordinary course of instruction. But those questions which are intimately connected with the conduct of life, and the happiness of rational beings, he studied with a degree of attention and solicitude, which discovered a deep sense of their importance.

Whilst he readily acknowledged the existence, and the powerful operation, of original principles in human nature, he was no advocate of that indolent philosophy (so well adapted to the spirit and manners of the present age) which has raised an unnatural contest between *Reason* and *Common Sense*, and instructed men to trust to their feelings rather than to their understandings. He thought it the duty of every rational being to employ his powers of reasoning and judging in the search of truth, and to endeavour to deduce the practical rules of life and manners from such theoretical propositions as have been established by conclusive argumentation ...

The same rational and Christian principles, which gave him such elevation and strength of mind, likewise taught him the lessons of humility and charity.[104]

The most eminent philosopher to be trained in a Dissenting academy, to remain a Dissenter, and to become a Dissenting tutor was undoubtedly Richard Price (1723–1791).[105] He was educated under Samuel Jones[106] at Pen-twyn, Vavasor Griffiths at Chancefield, and John Eames in London. Time would fail to tell of his polymathic activities, but we must refer to a puzzle surrounding his tutorial activities at Hackney College (1786–1796). How much teaching did he do? Herbert McLachlan cites Belsham as saying that Price gave no lectures at all at Hackney; his biographers as saying that Price's tutorial experience was brief; and sides with William Broadbent, a student who wrote to the *Christian Reformer* as follows: 'The good Doctor had only three pupils to attend upon him ... and gave but very few lectures at all ... both Tutor and Pupils being better pleased to fill up the lecture hours in agreeable conversation on philosophy or politics, rather than employ it in difficult and abstruse calculations.'[107] There is no good reason to doubt the accuracy of Broadbent's statement, and it is sad that Price did not meet with the same success in tutoring as had attended his efforts in other fields. From our point of view his lasting memorial is his work of 1758, *A Review of the Principal Questions and Difficulties in Morals*. He here set his face against the sensationalism of Hutcheson, the scepticism of Hume and the several varieties of teleological ethics which were then current and, in the wake of Cudworth and Clarke, defended the objectivity of morals along epistemological lines. We are aware of moral principles which are self-evident to our understanding, divine in origin, and which place us under obligation. We have the capacity freely to meet, or to deny our obligations, and virtue lies in the willing fulfilment of them. Although the principles of morality originate in God, they are not expressions of an arbitrary or capricious divine will. For Price, supremely in the case of God, the intellect has primacy over the will: God ordains what is good; things are not good because he ordains them.

However much or little of this Price managed to communicate to his students at Hackney, his point was not lost upon others. Thus Andrew Kippis at Price's interment in 1791:

By his moral writings he has laboured, with distinguished ability, to build the science of Ethics on an immutable basis: and what he has advanced on the subject will always stand high in estimation, as one of the strongest efforts of human reason in favour of the system he has adopted. For myself, I scruple not to say, that I regard the treatise referred to [i.e. the *Review*] as a rich treasure of valuable information, and as deserving to be ranked among the first productions of its kind. With respect to the other ethical writings of our friend, every one must admire the zeal, and earnestness, and strength with which he endeavours to lead men into pious views of God, of Providence and of Prayer, and to promote the exercise of devout and amiable dispositions.[108]

In endorsement of Kippis's last point here, Priestley, in the following month, declared in his memorial address for Price that 'No person well acquainted with Dr. Price could say, that rational sentiments of christianity are unfriendly to devotion.'[109]

But the reference to Priestley (1733–1804) brings us to that polymath, who taught at Warrington Academy and later, *gratis*, at Hackney during its declining days. We may stay only to note Priestley's critique of Scottish Common Sense Philosophy (1774);[110] his indebtedness to Hartley for his denial of spirit-matter dualism in his *Disquisitions relating to Matter and Spirit* (1777); and his work on philosophical necessity, which provoked the celebrated controversy with Bishop Samuel Horsley. Reactions to Priestley were varied, and some were hostile. Thus, in the *Life* of Bishop Horne the biographer, William Jones, remarks, 'I have often wondered secretly, why this good man [i.e. Horne] should have felt as if he was called upon to encounter a writer of Dr. Priestley's disposition ... That Dr. Priestley is a man of parts, a versatile genius, and of great sagacity in philosophical experiments, is well known and universally allowed: but let any person follow him closely, and he will see, that if ever there was a wise man, of whom it might be said, *that the more he learnt, the less he understood*, it will be found true of Dr. Priestley.' Indeed, as Horne said, Priestley was a man, '*who is defying all the world, and cannot construe a common piece of Greek or Latin.*'[111] But Horne and his biographer were evangelicals. On which note let us see what philosophy was produced by those who taught in the more conservative academies of the eighteenth century.

As far as published works are concerned the harvest is slight, even from the older more conservative academies, which offered university-style education without regard to students' career intentions; and as for the newer conservative academies, formed under the impetus of the Evangelical Revival with the objective of producing pastors and preachers only, and sometimes requiring students to supply evidence of conversion and to subscribe to Calvinistic articles, the philosophical products are more meagre still. Indeed, the only substantial published work of any philosophical interest by a philosophical tutor from this class of academies is Thomas Ridgley's *A Body of Divinity wherein the Doctrines of the Christian Religion are expounded and defended. Being the substance of several lectures on the Assembly's Larger Catechism* (1731).

Ridgley (1667?–1734) is thought to have been educated under the Particular Baptist John Davison of Trowbridge. In 1712 he succeeded Isaac Chauncy as divinity tutor at the Congregational Fund Board academy at Moorfields. In his *Body of Divinity* he is especially concerned to repudiate the charge that such doctrines as those of election, particular redemption and efficacious grace are inconsistent with 'the moral perfections of the divine nature'.[112] Against encroaching Arminianism and Arianism he intends to uphold the doctrine of the Trinity, and is concerned that some ways of explicating the eternal generation of the Son and the procession of the Spirit have given encouragement to Arians. Alexander Gordon declares that in seeking to avoid the latter pitfall, Ridgley 'denudes' his system of those doctrines, and 'is essentially Sabellian'.[113] In fact, he strove to maintain the independence of the divine persons in their personalities and their essence. How far he succeeded, we need not here enquire.

More to our purpose is the position Ridgley accords to reason. Reason is important, though subordinate to revelation. By revelation we become aware of such a doctrine as that of the Trinity, and reason's task is to prove both the truth of the doctrine, and the fact that we are under obligation to assent to revealed truth: 'what is false cannot be the object of faith in general.'[114] Reason, however, yields only relative security in matters of faith, and we can be saved from being 'tossed to and fro, and carried about with every wind of doctrine' only if our hearts are 'established with Grace'.[115]

Ridgley's system was in use at Bristol Baptist Academy under Bernard Foskett (1685–1758), whose manuscript lectures on *Pneumatology* are extant.[116] Foskett begins optimistically enough: 'Pneumatology by some stil'd the special part of Metaphysicks, by Mr. Lock a branch of Physics must be agreeable to every student's Mind because it is a Discourse of Spirits.' By the time he reaches the end of page three he has announced that thinking beings are immaterial; that the fact that we are 'Ridles to our Selves' shows only that 'the Soul is derived and dependent on some other Being who for wise Reasons has been pleased to limit its knowledge of itself', and that 'We have an original Freedom of Choice, and are not blindly, determined, by Fate and Necessity.' He next pronounces upon the relation of reason and revelation: reason, despite its best efforts, cannot produce full knowledge of God. Hence 'We should receive what Revelation discovers of the divine Being, the Trinity and hypostatic Union, and not with the Socinians and others object their Repugnancy to Natural Reason—for there are as great seeming absurdities in our Notions of God's Eternity, Immensity &c. which are universally own'd.'[117] He proceeds to discuss the essence and immateriality of the soul, siding on occasion with Locke, but more generally with the Cartesians, Cudworth and Grove; and then considers the nature and origin of ideas (with a reference to 'Mr. Leibniz'); he passes to the faculties of the soul and the will, to affections and passions; to the soul's ubiquity, its union with the body, and its immortality. In this last connection he again cites Grove with approval. In his second Book Foskett has essays 'Of angels' and 'Of God' separated by some blank pages. We do not need to designate Foskett an original philosopher, but at least we can say that he reflected upon the available theoretical options, presented both sides of the several arguments, and drew his own conclusions. In so doing he appears to have been the most thorough of all the more conservative academy tutors.

Abraham Taylor (fl. 1727–1740) was appointed to the Clerkenwell-Deptford Academy of the King's Head Society at its inception in 1730. He was noted for his staunch Calvinism (though this did not prevent a controversy with the equally staunch Calvinist John Gill) and his harsh temper. He has left us manuscript *Lectures on Natural and Revealed Theology* which appear to be largely a regurgitation of Marckius, and *An Introduction to Logick, with a few Lectures on Perception, the first part of that Science.* Never averse to *ad hominem* argument, Taylor asserts: 'If we consider matters justly and impartially, we must conclude, that Adam our common parent, impair'd his intellectuals greatly by his fall . . .'[118] Even so, the world owes a great debt to Aristotle in the matter of orderly reasoning.[119] Sufficient of Taylor's manner and attitudes will become plain from one further quotation:

The Popish writers have run into great confusion in endeavouring to make free thinking consistent with implicit faith in the dictates of their church; and Mr. Locke, who let his admirers say what they will of him, was no better than a Socinian in principle, and but a mean Divine for that sort, and no great friend of revelation, has interlarded his work with a great many subtleties, which tend to bring persons to have a mean and low view of what is properly mysterious. These men were certainly persons of deep thought, and penetrating genius, but their learning was very inconsiderable, and their reading was not large. This, in a particular manner, was true of Mr. Locke. Those that knew him personally were satisfied, that, as to ancient literature he was but very superficial.[120]

Thomas Gibbons (1720–1785) began his higher education under Abraham Taylor, but on 3 January 1737, he addressed a letter to the King's Head Society in which he expressed his wish to leave the Academy. His complaints were that Taylor taught no logic, that his lectures on the introduction to divinity took up too much time and were excessively concerned with classical learning, and that Gibbons was required to ask permission to leave the premises at other than stated times. The Society found in favour of Taylor, and discharged Gibbons from its care.[121] Gibbons completed his education under John Eames, and eventually, in 1754, became tutor in logic, metaphysics, ethics, rhetoric and belles lettres at his original *alma mater*, by this time located at Mile End. Gibbons wrote on a variety of subjects: numerous elegies and a two-volume work on *Female Worthies* are among his works; but on logic, metaphysics and ethics he did not commit himself in print. His personal confession of faith at his ordination does, however, mark him an an eighteenth-century man in his starting point, but as a traditional Calvinist in his conclusion. For he sets out from 'the Evidences derived from the Light of Nature', proceeds to the obligations of duty, but then affirms that over and above all of this, 'I believe we are indebted to the Light of a Verbal Revelation from God'—and so he proceeds to summarize his position on the cardinal doctrines of the Reformed faith.[122]

Among Gibbons's pupils was Caleb Evans (1737–1791), who became president of the Bristol Baptist Academy in succession to his father Hugh (who had himself succeeded Foskett, and whom Caleb had assisted since 1758), in 1781. Though always on the conservative side theologically, we gain the distinct impression that this institution is now being 'warmed up' by the Evangelical Revival. Thus, of Caleb Evans a student expostulates, 'Oh, how often has he in prayer, and in advice, melted over us.'[123] This puts us much more in mind of a Fletcher of Madeley than of an Abraham Taylor. There can be no question that Evans's supreme objective was the production of godly ministers of the Word. Like many of these, and according to the candid John Rippon, he seems to have been quite effective 'off the cuff': 'He never professed himself to be a *profound* metaphysician . . . yet his mind was enriched with numerous combinations of thought, with a taste cultivated and pure, and a memory eminently accurate.

Warm and occasionally rapid in his manner, he sometimes succeeded more through a kind of natural felicity than previous
study.'[124]

Given John Newton's aversion to the idea of students' being 'put
upon the needless and hurtful attempt of proving first principles',[125]
it is hardly surprising that William Bull (1738–1814) of Newport
Pagnell Academy left no philosophical remains—an achievement in
which he was emulated by tutors at the evangelical academies at
Gosport and elsewhere. We can understand the pressure upon
conservative academies to equip sound ministers; from the relative
silence in class and in authorship on philosophical questions we may
hazard the guess that philosophy is becoming more of an enemy
than once it was. But are ministers fully equipped unless they are
able to face the scepticism of a Hume or the materialism of a
Priestley? The philosophical record of the conservative Dissenting
tutors is not encouraging to those who would return a negative
answer to this question.

We now turn to the philosophical contribution of those who
taught in academies in which a broad spectrum of views was not
only tolerated, but welcomed. We may begin with John Jennings (d.
1723), trained at Attercliffe, Independent minister at Kibworth, who
opened his Academy there in 1715, and removed it with him to
Hinckley in 1722. His *Logica in usum Juventutis Academicae* (1721)
covers ninety-eight pages, and is replete with references to Locke,
whose *Essay, Conduct of the Understanding*, and *Method of Common
Places* appear in Jennings's 'Syllabus Librorum', together with
Descartes's *Meditations* and *Discourse on Method*, and seventeen
other works. Jennings, while introducing his students to a variety of
authors, was not reluctant to adjudicate between them. Thus, for
example, he refers to Malebranche's *Recherche de la Vérité* and sides
with Locke against the Frenchman's view that God communicates
ideas of phenomena to the human mind directly from his own mind.
Locke had argued that this would have made the creation of matter
unnecessary, and that it is as conceivable that God had ordained the
union of sensory perception with mind as that all ideas were in
Him.[126]

Jennings's outstanding pupil was Philip Doddridge (1702–
1751).[127] In his own tutorial work Doddridge was much indebted to
the breadth and style of Jennings's course, and from his friend

Samuel Clark of St Albans he received advice while a student which he never forgot:

I am sensible of the difficulties pneumatology has attending it. The only method of extricating oneself out of them is to see that we have clear ideas of all the terms we use, whether single, or connected with propositions, and that we take nothing for granted without sufficient evidence; and, which flows from the other two, that we do not pretend to reason upon things about which we have no ideas: that is, that we do not pretend to impossibilities. Mr. Locke's Essay is so useful to direct the mind in its researches, that methinks it should have been read before you entered upon pneumatics. . . . As to your contemplations upon the being and attributes of God, take heed of suffering your mind to rest in barren speculations. Whatever clear and enlarged ideas you attain to of the divine excellencies, see that they have proportionable effect upon the soul, in producing reverence, affection, and submission.[128]

We thus find that Doddridge, though he disagreed with Locke's interpretation of particular verses, was in general sympathy with Locke's approach to Paul's epistles,[129] though he felt that, like Pearce (*sic*) and Benson he erred 'in too great a fondness for new interpretations'.[130] Again, and given the ever-present scrutiny of eagle-eyed high Calvinists, he took the risk of enunciating a favourable interpretation of Locke's widely suspect view that the fundamental of Christianity is that Christ is the Messiah. He grants that 'a question arises concerning the extent of those words: perhaps it may be sufficient to answer it by saying, that wherever there appeared to be such a persuasion of the dignity of Christ's person and the extent of his power, as should encourage men to commit their souls to his care, and to subject them to his government, those who professed such a persuasion were admitted to baptism by the apostles, and ought to be owned as Christians.'[131] Further, Doddridge fully accepted the position of Baxter and Locke that the Christian religion has a rational basis, and that its truth can be argued for: hence, for example, his rebuttal of Henry Dodwell's *Christianity not founded on Argument* (1741). But that he was no slavish follower of Locke is seen from Doddridge's challenges to Locke on such matters as personal identity, the liberty of indifference, and miracles.[132] Doddridge is rightly remembered more for his hymns, his temperate theology and his personal marrying of head and heart, than for his philosophy. But there is always a place for the journeyman in philosophy, who will present and digest a variety of views in a balanced manner, so that they who run may read. That, following Doddridge's death in 1751, the more evangelical tutors ceased to attempt even this task is, as we have seen, disquieting.

Not the least of the tributes to Doddridge is that his *Lectures* were used by Samuel Morton Savage (1721–1791) at Hoxton Academy (1701–1785), and by his pupil and chosen successor, Caleb Ashworth (1722–1775). Neither of these left any philosophical writings, though the former presented his case for a broad curriculum in the ordination charge he delivered to Samuel Wilton on 18 June 1766, while the latter, on taking up his tutorial work, was cautioned by Job Orton thus: 'Especially warn the students against metaphysical and philosophical prayers, but *let not your animadversions be severe, as the good Doctor's often were, when he thought they were not evangelical, which intimidated and discouraged many of his pupils. Errors that will naturally mend by years* and *experience should be gently treated*.'[133] There spoke a wise pastor.

The last two notable philosophical tutors in the moderate and theologically mixed academies flourished during the second half of the eighteenth century. They are the contemporaries Thomas Belsham (1750–1829) who, as we saw, on adopting unitarian views left Daventry for Hackney; and John Horsey (1754–1827), who had been trained at Homerton, who took charge of the second Northampton Academy (1789–1798), and who, though not doctrinaire, remained in the middle way. A number of Belsham's manuscript lectures are extant.[134] Among these are some *Additional Lectures in Pneumatology*. They contain references to numerous authorities—especially to Locke, Clarke, Butler, Reid, Beattie, and Priestley (notably to his *Abridgment of Hartley*). Part I is a defence of the doctrine of necessity, in which such matters as personal identity, the passions and instincts, liberty and necessity, and the immateriality of the soul are discussed. The second Part concerns the being and attributes of God, and includes discussions of natural and moral evil, of Bonnet's *Essai analytique sur les facultés de l'âme* (1769), and references to Leibniz. There follow numerous blank pages, and then we come to lectures on sensation, ideas, vision, hearing, intellect—at which point the writer runs aground. Much of the material here treated appears in Belsham's major published philosophical work, *Elements of the Philosophy of the Human Mind* (1801); and further philosophical work appears in his manuscript lectures of

1805 and 1806 on *Evidences of Divine Revelation*. Among other things, he here offers answers to Hume's objections to miracles, among them this: 'The falsehood of Testimony in certain given circumstances is *impossible*: viz. when the witness is neither himself deceived nor desirous to deceive others.'[135] There are references to Paine, Price, Priestley, Paley, Hartley and others, and to numerous classical authors.

As for Horsey, there are extant lectures which he probably used,[136] and some of which he may have written;[137] but *Five Lectures on Government and thirteen on the British Constitution*[138] are definitely his, and in them his master is Locke. We have already noted the cloud of suspicion under which Horsey was forced to leave North-ampton Academy, and the circumstances in which he wrote his *Lectures to Young Persons*. He reports that when he delivered the lectures to the Castle Hill youths he did not attribute sources, for he sought an impartial hearing. In fact, however, Farmer, Price and Priestley were 'among those to whom my obligations are the greatest'. It may be that the tell-tale classical tutor, David Saville, had some ground for his allegation of Socinianism in Horsey's teaching. Be that as it may, Horsey hopes that his young friends will 'be chiefly disposed to consider, not *who* it is that advances an opinion of any kind upon any subject, but *what* it is, with the evidence adduced in support of it; and that as the individual himself states it, not as interpreted, or perhaps misinterpreted, by another'.[139] So the course proceeds, and Horsey is revealed as an associationist, and as one who regards miracles as 'deviations from the laws of nature', the purpose of which is to confirm the truth of the doctrines attested by them.[140]

We may draw our account to a close by noting those alumni of eighteenth-century Dissenting academies who wrote on philosoph-ical subjects, who remained within Dissent,[141] but who did not themselves become tutors. Three only need detain us: Isaac Watts (1674–1748), who had been a pupil of Thomas Rowe at Newington Green Academy, and who was a moderate (even, on occasion, an ambivalent) Calvinist, though of the most temperate kind; Samuel Chandler (1693–1776), who had studied under the open-minded Samuel Jones of the Gloucester/Tewkesbury Academy, where he was a contemporary of Butler and Secker, and who came to lean in an Arian direction; and James Foster (1697–1755), who had studied under Joseph Hallett at Exeter, was more liberal still, and who

adopted believer baptist views on reading John Gale, by whom he
was baptized.

Let us first very briefly sample Watts.[142] Alive to the intellectual
challenges of the day, Watts contends that neither atheism nor
deism, for all their vaunted reasonableness, can ensure that the
virtuous course is known to the bulk of mankind, and pursued.
Divine revelation alone makes plain the path, provides the power,
and inclines the will.[143] This is a theme to which Watts returns time
and again, not least in his *Logic*, that staple in the curriculum of
academies from most conservative to most liberal. On occasion he
has recourse to dialogue form.[144] As to the question of 'The Freedom
of the Will in God and in Creatures', Watts is concerned to uphold
freewill, otherwise rewards and punishments, praise and blame, are
beside the point. He concludes that 'though the will is left to its own
free agency and self-determining power, yet the light in which God
sets the gospel before the eyes of the mind is so great, as will finally
and certainly persuade the will, though not necessarily impel or
constrain it.' God foreknows that the Gospel will certainly, though
not necessarily, incline the individual's free will towards virtue.[145]
Here, it must be said, is a conclusion which seems merely to restate
the problem. Though he learned much from Locke, notably toler-
ance,[146] Watts was not with him at all points. Thus, against Locke on
thinking matter, he observes, 'Now though I never was, nor could
persuade myself to be a disciple of *Des Cartes* in his doctrine of the
nature of matter . . . and I have some years ago given up his opinions
as to the chief phaenomena of the corporeal world, yet I have never
seen sufficient ground to abandon all his scheme of sentiments of the
nature of mind or *spirit*, because I could not find a better in the room
of it, that should be free from objections and difficulties.'[147] Nevertheless, Locke is regularly described as 'Great' and 'judicious'
though this did not prevent Watts from having certain anxieties as to
Locke's eternal state. Thus in his lyric poem 'On Mr. Lock's
Annotations upon several Parts of the New Testament, left behind
him at his Death' the fourth stanza is as follows:

> Sister of faith, fair charity,
> Shew me the wondrous man on high,
> Tell me how he sees the godhead Three in One;
> The bright conviction fills his eye,
> His noblest powers in deep prostration lie
> At the mysterious throne.

'Forgive, he cries, ye saints below,
The wav'ring and the cold assent
I gave to themes divinely true;
Can you admit the blessed to repent?
Eternal darkness veil the lines
Of that unhappy book,
Where glimmering reason with false lustre shines,
Where the mere mortal pen mistook
What the celestial meant!'

In a footnote Watts explains, 'I invoke charity, that by her help I may find him out in heaven, since his Notes on 2 Cor. v ult. and some other places, give me reason to believe he was no Socinian, though he has darkened the glory of the gospel, and debased christianity in the book which he calls The Reasonableness of it, and in some of his other works.'[148]

Among the works of Samuel Chandler we may simply note his *Vindication of the Christian Religion* (1725, 1728) against the views expressed by the deist Anthony Collins in his *Discourse of the Grounds and Reasons of the Christian Religion* (1724), and his work, *Plain Reasons for being a Christian*, (1730). James Foster also took a deist, Matthew Tindal, to task in his book, *The Usefulness, Truth and Excellency of the Christian Revelation defended against the Objections contain'd in a late Book, intitled, Christianity as old as the Creation.* Foster readily grants that Christians themselves have encouraged prejudice against the faith by 'corruptions in doctrine, and gross superstitions in worship'.[149] He proceeds to explain that as between himself and Tindal, 'the dispute between us is not all about the *supreme* and *immutable excellency* of the *religion* of *nature*, nor whether this, which is by far the *greatest* and *best* part of *Christianity*, be as *old as the creation*, and *as extensive as human nature*; it is not, whether it be the *chief* design of *revelation*, to explain and restore this *primitive religion* in its original purity and perfection, and to assist and promote the regular and universal practice of it; nor whether *reason* be our *ultimate rule* in all our religious enquiries, a *rule* by which *revelation itself* must be judged; for the affirmative in all these questions is admitted.'[150] Some felt that all this being conceded, there was little left to argue about; and following the publication of Foster's *Discourses on all the Principal Branches of Natural Religion and Social Virtue* (1744 ff), the high Calvinist

Baptist, John Brine, countered with a forthright *Vindication of some Truths of Natural and Revealed Religion* (1746).

III

By the middle of the nineteenth century, and despite the fact that Nonconformists were not to be accorded the right to enrol at the universities of Oxford and Cambridge until 1871, many of the Dissenting academies had closed. After 1800 their endowments dwindled, and their efforts were dissipated by theological and ecclesiastical strife. The fate suffered by John Horsey was suffered by others too. Even William Parry of the conservative Wymondley Academy was charged with Socinianism—an accusation he strenuously denied.[151] However, by now there was, for the purposes of general higher education, the 'godless' institution, the University (later University College) of London (1826), which numbered such prominent Dissenters as Robert Vaughan and Henry Rogers among its teachers; and the Scottish universities continued to receive Nonconformist students. It remained necessary to supply theological education and ministerial training. Thus some of the older academies flowed into modern Nonconformist theological colleges, while a few became public schools.

Into the question how the academies at large are to be judged *vis à vis* the universities of Oxford and Cambridge we cannot here enter— not least because our concern has been the restricted one of investigating the philosophical contribution of the academies, and because we have not adduced evidence from the universities' side. It may not be entirely inappropriate, however, to say that our own investigations support the opinion of some more recent scholars, namely, that the view of such older historians as Irene Parker that where modern studies are concerned the Dissenting academies left the English universities standing, requires modification.[152] For example, while such better endowed and relatively well-staffed academies as Warrington could afford the luxury of scientific teaching (Dalton, Priestley) and apparatus, many could not.[153] Again, as we have seen, curriculum innovation was not a primary concern of the conservative academies, and some of them resisted it.

Where philosophy as such is concerned we have passed in review a considerable amount of material, some of it elusive. We find that philosophy was taught (though not always with distinction) in most of the eighteenth-century Dissenting academies, albeit in token fashion only in some of those established in the wake of the Evangelical Revival. Whereas many of the philosophical tutors and the vast majority of the alumni left no philosophical works at all, a few made contributions of lasting interest. Among these Price is supreme; Watts deserves more attention than he ordinarily receives, and Leslie Stephen's description of his philosophy as 'a crude amalgam'[154] is unduly biased; Grove is by no means uninteresting; and Priestley and Belsham are irrepressibly provocative. Nor are the activities of such philosophical journeymen as Foskett, Doddridge and Aikin to be despised. In the light of our findings we may not tempt Providence or distort the truth by declaring that all the eighteenth-century philosophical activity in the academies outshone all such activity under the auspices of Oxford and Cambridge universities. Nevertheless even without discussing the philosophical record of the latter during the eighteenth century[155] we make bold to venture the opinion that the Dissenting academies which, despite their faults, produced a Price and gave a Butler his grounding, boast philosophical alumni who were scarcely equalled and not surpassed in that century by any from the two English universities.

Two general remarks will bring our study to a conclusion. First, if the fate of the more liberal academies suggests that victory is not necessarily with those who pay excessive heed to reason, the relative absence of philosophy from the more evangelical academies makes one more than a little concerned—if not for faith itself, at least for the competence of ministers to offer viable defences of the faith when it is intellectually challenged.

Secondly, at the outset I recalled the positivistic embargo which was operative against metaphysics in the middle years of this century. It is interesting to note that in the penultimate year of the eighteenth century, David Daggett delivered a Fourth of July oration at New Haven engagingly entitled, *Sunbeams may be extracted from cucumbers, but the process is tedious.* He here opposes 'the credulity of the present age', which has become 'truly astonishing'. For example, 'It is believed that Socrates, and Plato, and Seneca-Bacon, Newton and Locke, and all who lived and died prior to the commencement of the French Revolution, were either fools or slaves'.[156] Those disturbed by embargoes should take comfort from the fact that it is easier to tranquillize ideas than to kill them. It is in any case heartening that there are signs that once again we are catching up with Richard Baxter who, as so often, presented both sides of the coin, without which there is no coin at all. He asked, 'What more can be done to the disgrace and ruine of Christianity, then to make the World believe that we have no reason for it?'[157] But he also wrote, 'What delights . . . there are at God's right hand, where we shall know in a moment all that is to be known.'[158] Perhaps such moderate academies as the line from Doddridge's Northampton, or Bristol Baptist Academy up to Caleb Evans's time, came closest to holding the two sides together. We may suspect that according to their success or failure in this matter theological colleges and seminaries may, to this day, properly be judged.

The United Theological College
Aberystwyth
Dyfed
Wales SY23 2LT

REFERENCES

1. An abbreviated version of this paper was presented at the conference of the British Society for the History of Philosophy held at Magdalen College, Oxford, on 11 April 1991. This piece of research was funded by The Social Sciences and Humanities Research Council of Canada.
2. See John Medway, *Memoirs of the Life and Writings of John Pye Smith, DD, LL.D.* (London, 1853), 75–76.
3. By 1810, however, the following complaint could be voiced: 'The grand error in almost every dissenting academy, has been the attempts to teach and to learn too much.' See *The Monthly Repository*, V (1810), 560.
4. Thomas Barnes, *A Discourse delivered at the Commencement of the Manchester Academy, September Fourteenth, One Thousand Seven Hundred and Eighty Six* (Warrington, [1786]), 14.
5. For the texts of these Acts see Henry Gee and William John Hardy, *Documents Illustrative of English Church History* (London 1896). For a recent study of Dissenting life under the adverse legislation, for the patchy way in which the laws were enforced, and for the sufferings of the Dissenters see Alan P. F. Sell, 'Through Suffering to Liberty: 1689

in the English and Vaudois Experience,' in *Dall' Europa Alle Valli Valdese*, ed. Albert De Lange (Turin, 1990), 215–236.

6. For a convenient summary of the statutes see H. Hale Bellot, *University College London 1826–1926* (London, 1929), 5–6.
7. See Alan P. F. Sell, *Church Planting. A Study of Westmorland Nonconformity* (Worthing, 1986), 27 and refs.; [T. G. Crippen], 'Richard Frankland and his Academy', *Congregational Historical Society Transactions*, II (1905–1906), 242–249.
8. For the circumstances surrounding the Toleration Act see Sell, 'Through Suffering to Liberty'.
9. J. Taylor, *A Narrative of Mr. Joseph Rawson's Case*, 2nd edn. (1742), 9. See further Alan P. F. Sell, 'Presbyterianism in England in the Eighteenth Century: the Doctrinal Dimension', *Journal of the United Reformed Church History Society*, IV (1990), 352–386; reprinted in idem, *Dissenting Thought and the Life of the Churches. Studies in an English Tradition* (Lewiston, NY, 1990), ch. V.
10. So Giles Hester, *Attercliffe as a Seat of Learning and Ministerial Education* (London, 1893), 31.
11. Quoted in DNB.
12. See further Walter D. Jeremy, *The Presbyterian Fund* (London, 1885); Geoffrey F. Nuttall, 'Welsh Students at Bristol Baptist College, 1720–1797', *Transactions of the Honourable Society of Cymmrodorion* (1978), especially 181 and appendix.
13. Joseph Priestley, *Memoirs of Dr. Priestley* (London, 1805), 16.
14. Quoted in J. Taylor, *A Scheme of Scripture Divinity* (London, 1762), preface, vi–vii. See further Alan P. F. Sell, 'A Little Friendly Light: The Candour of Bourn, Taylor and Towgood', in idem, *Dissenting Thought and the Life of the Churches*, ch. VII. For Warrington Academy see William Turner, *The Warrington Academy*, articles reprinted from *The Monthly Repository*, vols. VIII, IX, X, 1813–1815 (Warrington, 1957); P. O'Brien, *Warrington Academy (1757–86), Its Predecessors and Successors* (Wigan, 1989).
15. J. Priestley, *Memoirs*, 18.
16. The financial consequences of undue theological variety within a given institution could be severe, as when 'The Independents almost entirely deserted the [Carmarthen] Academy from 1759 to 1779, because of the theological views of the tutors.' See H. P. Roberts, 'The History of the Presbyterian Academy Brynllywarch-Carmarthen', *Transactions of the Unitarian Historical Society*, IV: 4 (October, 1930), 345.
17. For the earliest academies see, in addition to the standard works noted elsewhere, the series, 'Early Nonconformist Academies', *Congregational Historical Society Transactions*, VI (1915).
18. On this point he was opposed by William Parry (1754–1819) who, from 1799 until his death, served as principal tutor at the conservative Wymondley Academy. See his *A Vindication of Public and Social*

Worship, containing an Examination of the Evidence concerning it in the New Testament, and of Mr. Wakefield's Enquiry into its Propriety and Expediency (London, 1792).

19. Quoted by H. McLachlan, 'The Old Hackney College, 1786–1896', *Transactions of the Unitarian Historical Society*, III: 3 (October, 1925), 193; and idem, *English Education Under the Test Acts* (Manchester, 1931), 34.

20. *Memoirs of the Life of Gilbert Wakefield*, by himself (London, 1792), 353.

21. Ibid., 355.

22. In view of Thomas Barnes's statement at n. 4 above, it is strange that it should have been said of him that he questioned the value of philosophy for ministers of religion (see *The Monthly Repository*, V, 410) – the more so since he taught it to ordinands and lay students alike. See *A Discourse at the commencement of the Manchester Academy*, app. II, 7–8.

23. See further Donald K. McKim, *Ramism in William Perkins' Theology* (New York, 1987). For the general intellectual background see Olive M. Griffiths, *Religion and Liberty* (Cambridge, 1935), ch. III.

24. Irene Parker, *The Dissenting Academies of England*, ([1914], reprinted New York, 1969), 75–76.

25. *Extracts from the Diary and Autobiography of the Rev. James Clegg*, ed. Henry Kirke (Buxton, 1899), 21.

26. See *Lancashire and Cheshire Wills and Inventories at Chester*, ed. J. P. Earwarker (Chetham Society, N.S. vol. 3; 1884), 192–193. In Tetlaw's list of authors the less familiar are Franco Burgersdyck (1590–1635) the Protestant scholastic of Leiden, whose text books were used for more than two hundred years; Eustachius de Saint-Paul (1573–1640), whose *Ethica* was published at Cambridge in 1654; Andreas Froman, whose dissertation response, *De anima in genere*, was published in Jena in 1620; Thomas Goveanus, whose *Logica Elenctica* was published in Dublin in 1683; Adrian Heerebroord (1614–1661), the Leiden logician and ethicist; and Martinus Smiglecki (d. 1619?), the Pole, whose *Logica* appeared in 1618. Dr. Laurence Brockliss suggests that the reference to Colbert may be to a philosophy manual published by the French minister's tutor Jean Baptiste Du Hamel (1624–1706), Secretary to the French Academy of Sciences.

27. J. Toulmin, *An Historical View of the State of the Protestant Dissenters in England* (Bath, 1814), 225–230.

28. 'An Account of the Dissenting Academies from the Restoration of Charles the Second,' Dr. Williams's Library, London. MS, 24.59.25.

29. See Samuel Palmer (Ker's pupil), *A Defence of the Dissenters Education in their Private Academies* (London, 1703), 4–6. Palmer was replying to Samuel Wesley's *A Letter from a Country Divine, concerning the Education of Dissenters in their private Academies*

(London 1703). Wesley, who conformed in 1688, had been a student under Charles Morton at the Independent Academy at Newington Green.

30. For the fluctuating eighteenth-century fortunes of Locke in one Oxford college see E. G. W. Bill, *Education at Christ Church, Oxford 1660–1800* (Oxford 1988), 300.

31. Thomas Amory in his Preface to Henry Grove's *Posthumous Works* (London, 1745), xiv.

32. Toulmin, *An Historical View*, 230 ff.

33. 'An Account of the Dissenting Academies', 33.

34. *Cambridge History of English Literature, IX: From Steele and Addison to Pope and Swift* (Cambridge, 1912), 393. For high praise of Jollie's 'divine enthusiasm', see the remarks of his pupil, Benjamin Grosvenor in G. Hester, *Attercliffe*, 34–35. See further Derek Linkens, 'Timothy Jollie and the Attercliffe Academy', *The Banner of Truth*, 173 (February, 1978), 22–28.

35. Not 'at Kibworth', as stated by McLachlan, *English Education*, 213.

36. See H. McLachlan, *Essays and Addresses* (Manchester, 1950), 169–171.

37. See further H. M. B. Reid, *The Divinity Professors in the University of Glasgow* (Glasgow, 1923), ch. VI; Henry F. Henderson, *The Religious Controversies of Scotland* (Edinburgh, 1905), ch. I.

38. For the Scottish philosophical heritage see John Veitch, 'Philosophy in the Scottish Universities', *Mind* II (1877), 74–91 and 207–234. See also the admirable article by Martin Fitzpatrick, 'Varieties of Candour: Scottish and English Style', *Enlightenment and Dissent* VII (1988), 35–56.

39. For Leechman see Reid, *Divinity Professors*, ch. VIII.

40. So William Turner, *Lives of Eminent Unitarians* (1840), I, 364. See further Alan P. F. Sell, *Church Planting*, 39–41 and refs.

41. See the New College MS L185 at Dr Williams's Library, London. This is a notebook which contains (pp. 101–105) 'A Catalogue of Books given to the Academical Library [at Daventry/Northampton] with the Names of the Donors'. The list contains Watts's *Logic*, but nothing by Locke. See further Geoffrey F. Nuttall, 'The New College, London, Library', in his *New College, London and its Library* (London, 1977).

42. See Alexander Gordon, *Addresses Biographical and Historical* (London, 1922), 80.

43. For T. Dixon and Whitehaven see H. McLachlan, *Essays and Addresses*, 131–146.

44. For E. Latham and Findern see ibid., 147–166.

45. The complete programme is in *The Baptist Quarterly*, N.S. II (1924–1925), 249–252. Samuel Pufendorf (1632–1694), following Grotius, developed a doctrine of natural rights grounded in reason (as opposed

to rights grounded in the God-given Decalogue) in his *De jure naturae et gentium*, 1672 etc.

46. See Stephen A. Swaine, *Faithful Men; or, Memorials of Bristol Baptist College, and some of its most Distinguished Alumni*, (London, 1884), 78, 124. See also Norman S. Moon, *Education for Ministry. Bristol Baptist College 1679–1979* (Bristol, 1979).

47. Quoted ibid., 129–133.

48. See the extracts from Thomas Gibbons's diary in *Congregational Historical Society Transactions*, I, 328, 384, 380. Beware of McLachlan's broken quotation and reference at n. 6 on p. 177 of *English Education*. He here misquotes our third quotation, conflates it with our first, incorrectly places both in 1755, and wrongly locates both on p. 328. Gibbons's diary is in the Congregational Library at Dr. Williams's Library, London.

49. See Gareth Davies, 'Trevecka (1806–1964),' *Brycheiniog*, XIV (1971), 46. See further Geoffrey F. Nuttall, *The Significance of Trevecca College 1768–91*, (London, 1969).

50. [A. C. H. Seymour], *The Life and Times of Selina, Countess of Huntingdon*, II, (London, 1840), 102.

51. *The Monthly Repository*, XIII (1818), 66.

52. So DNB.

53. John Newton, *Works*, (6 vols., London, 1808), V.59–100. Newton's *Plan*, dated 14 May 1782, was first printed in 1784.

54. Josiah Bull, *Memorials of the Rev. William Bull* (London, 1864), 102. Our italics.

55. J. W. Ashley Smith, *The Birth of Modern Education. The Contribution of the Dissenting Academies 1600–1800*, (London, 1954), 231.

56. Letter of December 1786, *Memorials*, 162.

57. In fairness, it must be noted that the prescribed reading for the theological parts of the course was diverse, mystics and hyper-Calvinists alike being studied (and corrected as necessary).

58. See further, Alan P. F. Sell, 'Presbyterianism in England in the Eighteenth Century: the Doctrinal Dimension.'

59. D. Elwyn Davies, 'Education and Radical Dissent in Wales in the Eighteenth and Nineteenth Centuries', *Transactions of the Unitarian Historical Society*, XIX 2 (April, 1988), 96.

60. See art. 'Samuel Thomas', in *The Dictionary of Welsh Biography*, (London, 1959).

61. See further Alan P. F. Sell, 'Retirement Denied: The Life and Ministry of Noah Jones (1725–1785),' *Transactions of the Unitarian Historical Society*, XVIII: 2, (1984), 91–105; reprinted in idem, *Dissenting Thought and the Life of the Churches*, ch. XII.

62. For Hoxton Academy see, in addition to general works, Arthur D. Morris, *Hoxton Square and the Hoxton Academies* (privately printed, 1957).

63. The quotations are from Secker's letter, reprinted in Thomas Gibbons, *Memoirs of the Rev. Dr. Isaac Watts, D.D.* (London, 1780), 351, 348–349.

64. See further William Davies, *The Tewkesbury Academy* (Tewkesbury, [c. 1905]).

65. Letter of Philip Doddridge to Samuel Clark, [22] September 1722. See Geoffrey F. Nuttall, *Calendar of the Correspondence of Philip Doddridge DD (1702–1751)* (London, 1979), no. 35. The nineteenth-century Congregational historian John Waddington cites this sentence to show that 'The instruction [Doddridge] received at [Kibworth] was diversified, but not calculated to form a sound theologian or an efficient minister.' See his *Congregational History 1700–1800* (London, 1876), 273. As so often the moral is that one person's openness is another person's indecisiveness.

66. Dr. Williams's Library MSS 24.179.4 (copy); cf. G.F. Nuttall, *Calendar*, no. 190.

67. See further A. Victor Murray, 'Doddridge and education', in *Philip Doddridge 1702–51, His Contribution to English Religion,* ed. Geoffrey F. Nuttall (London, 1951).

68. See Doddridge's shorthand MS., 'An Abstract of the References in our Lectures of LOGICK', New College, London, MS L95, at Dr Williams's Library, London.

69. Job Orton, *Memoirs of the late Reverend Dr. Philip Doddridge* (Shrewsbury, 1766), 89ff. Cf. Doddridge's *Works*, (10 vols., Leeds 1802–1805), IV. 253–254.

70. Quoted by Ashley Smith, *The Birth of Modern Education*, 138; cf. 139.

71. J. Orton, *Memoirs* 101.

72. J. Williams, *Memoirs of the late Reverend Thomas Belsham* (1833), 78.

73. *The Monthly Repository* X (1815), 186.

74. Quoted by McLachlan, *English Education*, 158. The Kenrick Letters are at Dr Williams's Library, London, and are reprinted in *Transactions of the Unitarian Historical Society* III, IV (1923–1926 and 1927–1930).

75. See Williams, *Memoirs* 224–225.

76. So J. Drummond and C. B. Upton, *Life and Letters of James Martineau* (London, 1902), II. 258 (not 252 as given by McLachlan, *English Education*, 162).

77. J. Horsey's inaugural address was delivered on 8 January 1790.

78. R. L. Carpenter, *Memoirs of the Life of the Rev. Lant Carpenter, LL.D.,* (Bristol, 1842), 26, 25.

79. See further McLachlan, *English Education*, 167–168.

80. John Horsey, *Lectures to Young Persons on the Intellectual and Moral Powers of Man; the Existence, Character and Government of God; and the Evidences of Christianity,* (London, 1828), xiii-xiv. The *Lectures*

118 *History of Universities*

were written for the young people of Horsey's only pastorate: Castle Hill, Northampton, where he served from 1777 until his death in 1827.

81. Toulmin, *An Historical View*, 228. On the other side of the Atlantic, at Yale, the recitation of memorized material constituted a prominent classroom activity, and was prescribed in regulations of 1720 and 1726. See G. Stanley Hall, 'On the history of American College Text-Books and Teaching in Logic, Ethics, Psychology and Allied Subjects,' *Proceedings of the American Antiquarian Society*, N.S. IX (1894), 144. There are clear resemblances between the teaching method employed in the earlier academies and the old Scottish system of regenting; on which see John Veitch, 'Philosophy in the Scottish universities', 82–85. Veitch finds regenting a deficient method where philosophy is concerned: 'The teaching of Philosophy by means of approved books is better than none; but it is not a good arrangement. Its tendency is to make little demand either on the research or the power of active thought of the teacher, and thus to repress originality.' (83). Hence also the philosophical barrenness of the English universities, whose burgeoning [in 1877] philosophical life is not owing to native influences, but to foreign inspiration and individual force. (84 and note).

82. *Protestant Dissenter's Magazine*, III (1796), 83.
83. See e.g. *The Monthly Repository*, VIII (1813), 168.
84. [Strickland Gough], *Enquiry into the Causes of the Decay of the Dissenting Interest* (London, 1730), 43.
85. John Rippon, 'Essay on Bristol Academy', in his *The Baptist Annual Register*, I (1793) 345–351.
86. For this possibility, not mentioned in Gordon's DNB article on Oldfield, see Alexander Gordon, *Freedom After Ejection* (Manchester, 1917), 322.
87. So Jeremy, *The Presbyterian Fund*, 104.
88. J. Oldfield, *An Essay towards the Improvement of Reason*, (London, 1707), Introduction, para. 11; i.i;.ii.ix, para. 7.
89. Henry Grove, *Works*, (4 vols., London 1747), iii. 203.
90. Ibid., 230–231.
91. H. Grove, *A System of Moral Philosophy*. (2 vols; London, 1749), i. 198, 199.
92. From the Preface to Grove's sermon on the occasion of the ordination of Thomas Amory, his nephew and successor, and William Cornish, on 7 October 1730. See *Works*, i. 470–471.
93. See further Alan P. F. Sell, 'Henry Grove: A Dissenter at the Parting of the Ways', *Enlightenment and Dissent*, IV (1985), 53–63; reprinted in idem, *Dissenting Thought and the Life of the Churches*, ch. VI.
94. See John Ball, *Some Remarks on a New Way of Preaching* (London, 1736); and art. at n.93 above.

95. Quoted by Hall, 'On the History of American College Text-Books', 147.
96. J. Taylor, *A Sketch of Moral Philosophy*, (London, 1760), 101.
97. Idem, *An Examination of the Scheme of Morality, advanced by Dr. Hutcheson* (London, 1759), 47.
98. See further Alan P. F. Sell, 'A little friendly light'.
99. Alexander Gordon in DNB, art. 'Amory, Thomas'.
100. Thomas Amory, A *Sermon preached at Lewin's-Mead, Bristol, at the Ordination of the Reverend Mr. William Richards, May the 22d. 1751* (London, [1751]), 12.
101. Idem, *Christ the Light of the World . . . a Sermon preached at the Young Men's Lecture at Exon, Thursday, September 11, 1735* (London, 1735), iii.
102. Idem, *Twenty-two Sermons* (London, 1766), 39 n.
103. John Yates, *A Funeral Discourse, occasioned by the death of the Rev. Dr. Barnes, preached at Cross-Street Meeting-House in Manchester on Sunday, 15th July 1810* (Liverpool, 1810), 43.
104. William Enfield, *A Funeral Sermon, occasioned by the death of the late Rev. John Aikin, D.D., Professor* of *Divinity at the Academy in Warrington* (Warrington, 1781), 8–9, 12.
105. See D. O. Thomas, *The Honest Mind. The Thought and Work of Richard Price* (Oxford, 1977); and the present writer's review in *Philosophical Studies* (Dublin), XXVI (1979), 305–310.
106. This Samuel Jones (fl. 1715–1764) is not to be confused with two other Dissenting academy tutors of the same name: SJ of Brynllywarch (1628–1697) and SJ of Gloucester/Tewkesbury (1681?–1719).
107. McLachlan, 'The Old Hackney College', 190; and see refs. *ad loc.*
108. Andrew Kippis, *An Address delivered at the Interment of the late Rev. Dr. Richard Price on the twenty-sixth of April 1791* (London 1791), 8–9.
109. Joseph Priestley, *A Discourse on the occasion of the Death of Dr. Price: Delivered at Hackney, on Sunday, May 1, 1791* (London, 1791), 20.
110. See Alan P. F. Sell, 'Priestley's Polemic against Reid', *The Price-Priestley Newsletter*, III (1979), 41–52; reprinted in idem, *Dissenting Thought and the Life of the Churches*, ch. XV.
111. W. Jones in his *Life* of George Horne, D.D., prefixed to the latter's *Works* (London, 1809), 145, 148.
112. Thomas Ridgley, *A Body of Divinity* (London, 1731), iii.
113. Alexander Gordon in DNB, art. 'Ridgley, Thomas'.
114. Ridgley, *A Body of Divinity*, i. 110.
115. Ibid.
116. I am grateful to the Principal of Bristol Baptist College, the Reverend Dr. J. E. Morgan-Wynne, and to the Librarian, Stella Reed, for granting me access to the College's manuscript collection.
117. B. Foskett, MS on *Pneumatology*, 4.
118. Abraham Taylor, *An Introduction to Logick* (1739), 12.

119. Ibid., 33.
120. Ibid., 43–44.
121. For this episode see Waddington, *Congregational History, 1700–1800*, 266–267.
122. See Thomas Gibbons in *A Sermon preached at the Ordination of Mr. Thomas Gibbons, October 27, 1743. At Haberdashers' Hall, London. By John Guyse, D.D. Together with an Introductory Discourse by Richard Rawlin. Mr. Gibbons's Confession of Faith. And an exhortation to him by Thomas Hall* (London 1743), 17, 19.
123. Quoted by Swaine, *Faithful Men*, 123.
124. John Rippon, *A Brief Essay towards an History of the Baptist Academy at Bristol*, 1795; in idem, *The Baptist Annual Register*, II, 445.
125. Quoted by McLachlan, *English Education*, 242.
126. J. Locke, *Works*, ed. Bohn (2 vols.; London, 1854), ii. 457, 421.
127. Doddridge's two copies of Jennings's *Logica* (one interleaved and annotated) are in the New College, London, Library at Dr. Williams's Library. See further Nuttall, *New College, London and Its Library*, 34; idem, 'Philip Doddridge's Library', *Congregational Historical Society Transactions*, XVII: 1 (January 1952), 29–31.
128. Samuel Clark to Philip Doddridge, 3 October 1721, in J. D. Humphreys, *Correspondence and Diary of Philip Doddridge* (5 vols; London, 1829–1831), i. 39.
129. See Humphreys, *Correspondence*, i. 428.
130. P. Doddridge, *Works* (1804), v. 473.
131. Idem, *A Course of Lectures on the Principal Subjects of Pneumatology, Ethics, and Divinity: with reference to the most considerable Authors on each Subject* (London 1763), lect. 172.
132. Idem, *Works*, iv. 321–323, 341, 543.
133. Quoted by Waddington, *Congregational History 1700–1800*, 496.
134. I am grateful to Principal Ralph Waller of Manchester College, Oxford, and to Dr Joanna Parker, librarian of that institution, for granting me access to the Belsham and other manuscripts.
135. T. Belsham MS, 'Evidences of Divine Revelation', Lect. V, i.
136. 'Institutes of Moral Philosophy', DWL MSS 69.5.
137. 'Lectures Introductory to the Study of the New Testament', DWL, MSS, 69.16; and 'Thoughts concerning the Inspiration of Scripture', DWL, MSS, 69.2.
138. 'Dr Williams's Library, London.' MSS, 69.3.
139. Horsey, *Lectures to Young Persons*, xvii–xviii.
140. Ibid., 21, 137, 144.
141. Sadly, we thus exclude Joseph Butler, the most distinguished philosopher to emerge from a Dissenting academy.
142. On Watts's philosophy A.P. Davis, *Isaac Watts* (London, 1948), ch. VI, is entertaining but not definitive.
143. Isaac Watts, *Works* (7 vols.; Leeds, 1800), ii. 366 ff.

144. Ibid., iii, 'The strength and weakness of human reason argued in four conferences'.
145. Ibid., 575.
146. Ibid., v. 503.
147. Ibid., vi. 529. See also Watts's Essay XII in the same volume: 'Remarks on some Chapters of Mr. Locke's Essay on the Human Understanding'.
148. Ibid., vii. 262.
149. James Foster, *The Usefulness, Truth and Excellency of the Christian Revelation*, (London, 1731), iii.
150. Ibid., 4–5.
151. See *Evangelical Magazine* (1818), 172; McLachlan, *English Education*, 171–172.
152. See Parker, *The Dissenting Academies*, 132 ff. See further E. J. Price, 'The Dissenting Academies. A Neglected Chapter in the History of English Education', *Congregational Historical Society Transactions*, XI: 1 (April, 1930), 38–51; McLachlan, *English Education*, 26–27 and *passim*; Ashley Smith, *The Birth of Modern Education*, Ch. V. Among those who have sought to modify the claim is Nicolas Hans, *New Trends in Education in the Eighteenth Century* (London, 1951), 54–62.
153. This point is confirmed by O. Lewis in an unpublished M.Phil. dissertation, 'The Teaching of Science in English Dissenting Academies 1662–1800', The Open University, 1989. Lewis found that in almost half of the academies the teaching of science was absent from the curriculum. But, with reference to the brighter spots we may note John Gascoigne's admission that although Cambridge reigned supreme in mathematics during the eighteenth century, and although some Dissenting academies had little place for science, by the end of that century 'Dissenting academies with their close links with provincial society were generally more responsive to . . . changes in scientific interests than the universities.' See his *Cambridge in the Age of the Enlightenment. Science, Religion and Politics from the Restoration to the French Revolution* (Cambridge, 1989), 282; cf. 8. The Dissenters' influence upon and contribution to the learned life of provincial towns should not be overlooked where the fostering of scientific interests and the dissemination of scientific knowledge are concerned. See, for example, Diana Harding. 'Mathematics and Science Education in Eighteenth-Century Northamptonshire', *History of Education*, I: 2 (1972), 139–159. It is important to understand that where science was present in the curriculum of the academies it was not there simply or primarily for educational or utilitarian reasons. The undergirding motive was theological. God had supplied two 'books' – the Bible, and that of nature; and both were to be studied devoutly. Accordingly, the omnipresence of cosmological and teleological arguments for the existence of God throughout the century is not surprising. For an

account of another 'modern' subject see Yusef Azad, 'The Limits of University: The Study of Language in some British Universities and Academies 1750–1800', *History of Universities*, **VII** (1988), 117–147.

154. Leslie Stephen, *History of English Thought in the Eighteenth Century* (New York, 1927), ii. 386.

155. For the philosophical record of one Oxford college, see Bill, *Education at Christ Church Oxford*, 263–268; 297–307.

156. David Daggett, *Sunbeams may be extracted from cucumbers, but the process is tedious* (New Haven, Conn., 1799), 16; see Boston University Library, Bartman YE 289 D99.

157. R. Baxter, *The Saint's Everlasting Rest* (London, 1651), unpaginated preface to pt. II, dated 2 April 1651.

158. Ibid., pt. IV, 224.

Liberals or Libertines? Staff, Students, and Government Policy at the University of Padua, 1814–1835

David Laven

In thine halls the lamp of learning,
Padua, now no more is burning;
Like a meteor, whose wild way
Is lost over the grave of day,
It gleams betrayed and to betray:
Once remotest nations came
To adore that sacred flame,
When it lit not many a hearth:
On this cold and gloomy earth:
Now new fires from antique light,
Spring beneath the wide world's might;
But their spark lies dead in thee,
Trampled out by Tyranny.
Percy Bysshe Shelley, *Lines written among the Euganean Hills*[1]

In modern Europe the fate of universities following sudden changes in régime has usually been determined as part of the broader question of how far new governments have sought to accommodate or discard the institutions, practices and personnel of their predecessors. Yet within this context education has often retained a special significance because of the opportunities it offers for the development among the citizenry of values and opinions useful to the state. By the early nineteenth century universities had taken on a particular importance because of the role they played in many countries in the education of future public servants. In many states a rigorous control of universities was associated with a loyal and efficient administration. Establishing such control was perceived as a good means of securing future stability as well as easing the transition from one régime to another by limiting the intellectual legacy of the previous system. However, as centres of learning universities were dangerous: dangerous because they could be responsive to a far wider range of ideas than the narrow orthodoxies favoured by the state; and dangerous because, should new ideas take root, they could be transmitted rapidly to the future administrators of the régime, potentially creating an effective fifth column within the machinery of state itself.

It is this double-edged nature of universities which makes the case of Padua after the fall of Napoleon particularly interesting. The period 1790–1815, characterized by unprecedented revolutionary activity and almost unceasing war, witnessed the rapid development of two new ideologies—liberalism and nationalism—which the conservative rulers of Restoration Europe saw as both pernicious and extremely threatening. Of all European states, perhaps the most vulnerable was the Habsburg Empire, which by its very nature— deeply conservative and multinational—was imperilled by the spread of these new beliefs. Given the apparent growth of Italian nationalism that accompanied the revolutionary and Napoleonic era and the resentment that might have been expected among the Venetian population at their still recent loss of independence in 1797, it would have been surprising indeed if the Habsburg authorities had not expended considerable energy on securing the loyalty of both students and staff at Padua, the sole university of the former *Serenissima*. It is within this framework that the position of Padua after the Congress of Vienna must be examined.

Little good can be said of the Napoleonic administration of Venetia which collapsed in the face of Habsburg invasion in 1814. As with the rest of the so-called Kingdom of Italy (the French satellite state with its capital in Milan which coincided roughly in territorial terms with the post-Vienna Congress Austrian Kingdom of Lombardy-Venetia), the French emperor viewed it primarily as a source of conscripts and cash with which to furnish his armies. In Lombardy, however, he was at least prepared to countenance public expenditure with a view to securing popular affection. Venetia was simply bled dry through rapacious taxes, while public spending was kept to a bare minimum. This is nowhere clearer than in the realm of education. In the years 1806 to 1813 the puppet government in Milan spent a total of 2,358,609.54 *lire italiane* on *istruzione pubblica* in the Venetian *dipartimenti*. In the same period it spent well over twice as much (L.5,100,480.09) on education in the lands to the west of the river Mincio, even though the population of Lombardy was only fractionally greater.[2] In Venetia all levels of education were neglected from the primary schools through to the university.[3] Some gauge of the depths to which the university at Padua sank is afforded by student numbers: in the last five years of French rule these fluctuated between a low point of 215 and a miserable high of 375.[4]

The pathetic state of the educational system in Venetia was addressed swiftly by the provisionally established Habsburg authorities. This might appear surprising given that at the time the region was in the midst of famine, banditry was rife, and there was effectively no police force, not to mention the legion other problems connected with the change in régime. That there were immediate steps taken to begin remedying the lamentable state of education must be traced in large part to the characteristic commitment, shared by all Habsburg rulers since Maria Theresa, to the expansion of public instruction, a commitment based on the recognition of the useful role served by education as a tool of social and political control.[5] The prompt reform of the schools and university was to play a key part in the process of asserting central authority over Venetia and attaching the population more firmly to Habsburg rule. The expansion and rejuvenation of the university of Padua in the course of the next twenty years until the death of Francis I must be seen in this context: as Francis is alleged to have remarked, it was the aim of his education system to produce 'not savants but good honest citizens'.[6]

A fundamental problem for the provisionally established Austrian authorities in both Lombardy and Venetia following the collapse of the Kingdom of Italy was the extent to which public servants of the previous régime could be trusted.[7] This clearly extended to the staff of the two universities of Pavia and Padua. It was, after all, their primary role to educate future lawyers, priests, teachers and above all government officials. Obviously it was important that these should not be allowed to fall under the influence of enemies of the Austrian throne: it was absurd to allow the intellectual nurture of future generations of bureaucrats to be left in the hands of radicals or Bonapartists.[8] On the other hand, while it was necessary to cleanse the system of Napoleonic and revolutionary taint, there were severe practical limitations on implementing a wholesale purge.[9] As with other branches of the administration, to remove all those who had served the previous government risked the complete breakdown of the system: there was, after all, an acute shortage of academic staff (one report in the *Haus-, Hof- und Staatsarchiv* testifies to the fact that only twenty-five out of thirty-nine chairs at Padua were occupied[10]) and there were simply not the men of sufficient calibre to take their places. It was also widely recognised that purges would only alienate useful individuals who might well be reconcilable to rule from Vienna. In consequence the major task of educational reform when the Austrians took over the Veneto seems to have been one of reorganization and restructuring, rather than one of replacing teaching personnel. Open manifestations of sympathy for Napoleon could obviously not be tolerated, but an automatic purge was equally out of the question. For the time-being employees in the university of Padua, as in any other government job, were to be dismissed only if known to have committed a crime, to have been particularly ardent in their support of the previous régime, or to have actually fled before the advancing Austrian armies.[11] Yet at the same time as this moderate policy was being implemented, a policy of screening was introduced.[12]

It is scarcely surprising that the university of Padua was far from free of those falling within the categories considered suspicious under the new screening policy. The police president, von Hager, reported in August 1814 that a total of five professors had deserted Padua and that another five had remained who were nonetheless hostile to Austrian rule.[13] In fact, the number of those who allegedly fled was not five but six: Farini, Renier, Marsand, Francesconi, Gallina, and Collalto. It was soon established that the first three had been absent for perfectly legitimate reasons completely unconnected with the imminent arrival of the Austrian army and their petitions for reinstatement were readily accepted. Greater debate over the circumstances of the others' absence led the authorities to postpone any decision until further investigations could take place.[14] It was not long before the *Central-Organisierungs Hof Commission* also recognised that neither Collalto nor Gallina had abandoned his chair 'on the orders of the suppressed Italian government, as some prefects had done, but for reasons of their own'.[15] Having scotched accusations that he was guilty of 'philosophical materialism', Gallina was reinstated.[16] Collalto, was less fortunate. Despite having a perfectly good excuse for absence—he had been visiting his sick sister in Venice, in the middle of official holidays, when the city had been cut off by the allied blockade, making his return to Padua impossible[17]—he was not reappointed. This seems all the stranger given the acute shortage of teaching staff and the fact that he was generally acknowledged as an excellent mathematician.[18] Indeed, on two occasions in 1817 the most powerful body of the Austrian government in Venetia, the *Presidio di Governo*, supported him for a university post only to be turned down by the authorities in Vienna.[19] Some clue as to why a man of such unquestioned academic abilities with the open support of the Austrian authorities in Venice should have been reduced to eking out a meagre existence from private tuition lies perhaps in the fact that he was an ex-priest and as such unlikely to find favour under the fiercely Catholic, if not always pro-Papal Habsburg régime.[20] There is no such explanation for the fate of Francesconi, who, despite the active support of so influential a figure as Fieldmarshal Bellegarde, the acting viceroy of Lombardy-Venetia, seems to have been rejected out of hand by the C.O.H.C. In contrast to the fates of Collalto and Francesconi, the other four enjoyed much rosier futures. By 1821, Farini was *Decano* of the philosophy faculty and a member of the university's governing body, the *Senato accademico*; Marsand was a professor of law and had served a term as *Rettore magnifico*, the highest position in the entire institution; Renier and Gallina held chairs of physiology and natural history respectively.[21] If the C.O.H.C. seems sometimes to have been rather arbitrary it would appear from these cases not to have discriminated primarily on political grounds.

While flight in the face of the Austrian advance was seen as a likely indication of undesirable political sympathies, so too was membership of a masonic lodge. Among the first actions of the Habsburg administration on repossessing the Veneto was to forbid membership of the free masons to anyone in any branch of government service.[22] Freemasonry was not simply considered nefarious on account of its anti-Catholic connotations. It was also feared because of its intimate links with the previous régime. Lodges had flourished throughout the Kingdom of Italy and Napoleon's viceroy, Beauharnais, had numbered among the grandmasters.[23] It is, therefore, perhaps surprising that the tag of being a former mason does not seem to have handicapped Padua's professors in their subsequent careers. Of the staff holding office in 1821, six appear on an undated police list of thirty known members of the Paduan lodge.[24] Another two ex-professors also appear on the list, of whom one had moved to the Papal States and the other had possibly lost his position as his name does not appear on any list of university employees dating from after 1814. Of those who still held a post in 1821, two taught in the law faculty, three in medicine, and one in philosophy.[25]

The level of toleration shown by the authorities towards the academic staff of Padua is typical of the general restraint exercised by the Habsburgs on their repossession of Venetia. It is certainly true that many leading figures within the government and the police entertained grave misgivings about employing possible Napoleonic sympathisers, and many were happy to apply the label of *fanatico* (revolutionary) on the flimsiest of evidence. The general rule of thumb seems, however, to have been that adopted by Raab, the director of police, who was entrusted with vetting *all* government employees: 'an employee was not necessarily untrustworthy just because he had faithfully served the Napoleonic régime'.[26] Indeed, quite the contrary seems to have been true: the individual ready to serve one foreign master was likely to transfer his allegiance readily to another, and it soon became clear that many of those who had carefully cultivated reputations as stalwarts of the previous régime had done so out of crude careerism rather than genuine political conviction. Membership of the masons was certainly not any indication either of commitment to the principles of the organization or of deep attachment to the Kingdom of Italy; it would rather seem to have been an essentially cosmetic display of support for the Napoleonic status quo. When the French were driven from the Veneto, the lodges of both the *Dominante* and its *Terraferma* do not seem to have gone underground; they simply collapsed.[27] Although the emperor and Metternich sometimes displayed a hysterical fear of conspiracy, which threatened on occasion to slip into virtual paranoia, the authorities in Venice and Padua were, in practice, not unduly concerned with purging the system. They seem to have trusted that the desire to retain a safe government salary would guarantee the loyalty of Padua's academic staff.[28] This explains why so many apparently loyal servants of the Kingdom of Italy continued in office long after its fall: of the twelve senior staff in the *facoltà filosofico-matematica* in 1831 only three had not been in some form of government service under Napoleonic rule.[29]

It is instructive to compare the situation of Padua with that of its sister university across the Mincio. According to the research of Irene Ciprandi,[30] Habsburg policy towards Pavia seems to have been similarly mild. There would appear to have been very few genuine sympathisers for the system imposed by Napoleon. However, most of Pavia's academic staff were deeply conservative and were prepared to be reconciled to the Kingdom of Italy if only because it offered order and stability after a period of revolutionary upheaval. Napoleon had sought to consolidate support through concession of privileges which seem to have gone at least some way to compensate for the total want of freedom permitted by his system.[31] The bulk of Pavese academics seem to have openly welcomed the Austrian takeover. As Ciprandi writes:

In 1814 the adherence to the new régime on the part of the academic body at Pavia was almost unanimous: either they were simply tired and disillusioned with the old Napoleonic system or instead they backed renewed Habsburg rule with conviction; the Pavese professors welcomed the return of the Austrians with optimism and sometimes with a genuine sense of relief.[32]

The absence of purges at Padua does not mean that there were not rigorous efforts to make sure that the education system should be adapted as swiftly as possible to the ends desired by the emperor. Two basic themes ran through the educational reforms introduced in the early years of renewed Habsburg rule. The first, extended to schools as well as the university itself, was the straightforward intention of increasing educational facilities in general to make education more widely available. The second was that, as far as possible, the system was to be brought into line with the rest of the empire: a hierarchy of supervision and control was to be developed to guarantee a high level of uniformity with a view to fashioning future generations of useful, loyal and Christian subjects. Some indication of the readiness of the Austrian government to foster education generally can be derived from the increased spending witnessed in this field. Between 1814 and 1821 there was some L.6,204,654 spent on *istruzione pubblica* in Venetia in contrast with the paltry sums spent by the Kingdom of Italy. As a percentage of total public spending on services (justice, religion, education, health, charity, and communications) it also rose from the 8.27% it had been under the French to 11.08%.[33]

One of the first moves of the provisional government in the Veneto was to restore the prominent role of the Church at all levels of education. This had a dual advantage. Most students would be indoctrinated with a Catholic morality likely to foster virtuous and submissive behaviour, serving as an antidote to any revolutionary or radical beliefs that might still have had some currency as legacies of the Napoleonic era. The authority of the state was also bolstered. Francis's essentially Josephist stance, which severely limited Papal control over the Church within Habsburg frontiers, meant that he was able to maintain very extensive control over the clergy in his Italian territories.[34] The authority of the Church was thus appropriated for the benefit of the Habsburg state in education as well as in other fields. As Ciprandi remarks, Francis 'recognised in the Catholic religion the most secure bulwark against the diffusion of principles dangerous to the security of state and society'.[35]

The most immediate effect on the university of Padua was that rapid steps were taken to re-establish the theology faculty which had been closed under the previous régime. Since no similar steps were taken to open a theology faculty at Pavia—Lombardy was to await the foundation of a separate seminary in Milan—Padua automatically took on a much more clerical nature through the dramatic expansion of the number and influence of priests within the university and its various governing bodies.[36] Clerics, of course, were not confined to the teaching of theology alone. By 1821 ten out of thirteen law professors and nine out of thirteen philosophy staff were clergy,[37] although it should, of course, be remembered that many of these had also held positions under the Kingdom of Italy and that by no means all were automatically sympathetic to Habsburg rule, disliking the subservient role afforded to the Church by Francis's perception of the alliance of throne and altar.[38]

Perhaps more significant than the increasingly clerical nature of Padua's personnel, was the growing emphasis on religious instruction within the syllabus itself. In order to study in the faculties of theology, law or medicine, or to pursue one of the 'mathematical' disciplines with a view to obtaining a qualification as a surveyor, engineer or architect, every student had first to finish at a secondary school (*ginnasio*) and then to complete a course of so-called philosophical study. This could be pursued either in a *liceo*—of which there existed four in the Veneto at Verona, Vicenza, Udine and Venice—or in the *facoltà filosofico-matematica* of the university. Whether studied in a *liceo* or at Padua, the syllabus was wellnigh identical and contained two hours of religious instruction each week. Pupils at a *liceo* were also obliged to attend 'una esortazione spirituale' on Sundays.[39] It was expected, therefore, that students at

Padua would have been exposed to a fairly rigorous religious education from elementary school until at least their late teens, even if they subsequently went on to study law or medicine. Besides the prominent position of religious instruction, the curriculum for students preparing to study for a degree at Padua underwent other significant changes. The scientific and legal training offered by some *licei* under the Napoleonic system was rapidly jettisoned in favour of a much more traditional concentration on the classics, mathematics and philosophy bringing it into line not only with the university but with other institutions elsewhere in the empire.[40] In both *licei* and the preparatory courses of the philosophy faculty a significant section of the timetable was also given over to the study of history, and most especially the history of the Habsburg empire, thus providing ample scope for pro-Austrian propaganda.[41] History, however, was obviously a dangerous subject and its teaching was not to be left to the whims of masters who might exploit it for their own political ends. When it came to the selection of candidates for posts, the questions put to them seem to have been designed to test their political persuasion as much as their intellectual and academic abilities. Hence, while a surgeon might be asked about the appropriate equipment for an operation, or candidates for a chair in aesthetics about the differences between 'poesia' and 'eloquenza', the questions directed at prospective history teachers were rather more loaded: What did Alexander the Great use to keep the different people of his vast and heterodox empire in harmony? What was the political state of Europe at the time of Charles V? What merits had Italy in comparison with the rest of Europe in recent times, and what circumstances helped favour the development of arts and sciences in the peninsula? The intent of these questions, put to all candidates for history posts in Venetian *licei* in 1818, was none too veiled. The comparison between the great multinational, polyglot empires of Alexander and Francis is self-evident. The question about Charles V, the first Habsburg emperor to pursue large-scale territorial ambitions in Italy with success, offered a chance to gauge the candidate's feelings towards the ruling house. The third question hinted at others about national consciousness in Metternich's 'geographical expression'. What is evident now was also doubtless evident in 1818, at least judging from the anodyne responses offered by candidates.[42]

Both the *Repristino dell'università di Padova e fissazione del corso de' suoi studj* of 12 September 1815 and the *Sovrana risoluzione sull'organizzazione delle università di Pavia e di Padova* of 7 January 1817 underlined strongly that the syllabus of all faculties should be as near possible that followed in universities elsewhere in the Austrian monarchy.[43] This policy of uniformity had some immediate and unfortunate consequences for Padua including the closure of its veterinary school, apparently for no other reason beyond consistency. The measure appears all the more shortsighted given that, in order to attain a *laurea* as a physician or surgeon, students were still required to study a certain amount of veterinary medicine, and that, to compensate for the closure of Padua's *scuola veterinaria*, an *Istituto veterinario* had to be opened in Milan.[44]

In one area, at least, the principle of uniformity with the system current to the north of the Brenner was sacrificed. The language of instruction was, of course, Italian (or in a few cases Latin) and not German: to use German would have been clearly absurd. Anyway, both Francis and the C.O.H.C. approved of the study of 'native languages' and to this extent the notion of Germanization which lay behind many reforms was abandoned.[45]

The study of German itself seems to have been very half-hearted in both schools and university. There was certainly much less effort than during the previous régime to teach the language of the foreign ruler. Under Napoleonic rule, French had been a compulsory subject; while the Austrians wasted little time in depriving it of this status, no attempt was made to place the study of German in similarly privileged position:[46] in the schools and university alike it became a *studio non obbligato*—like drawing—and was considered essential only for those students who contemplated continuing their studies in a 'German' institution in the Hereditary Lands of the empire.[47] This is especially significant since in order to reach the higher echelons of the police or army bilingualism was essential. The poor provision for German teaching by the state almost certainly acted as a major block on the upward mobility of Venetians in other areas of government service, although in fairness to their Habsburg rulers it should also be recognised that, in the early decades of the *seconda dominazione austriaca*, there was apparently remarkably little ambition for *high* office among the Venetian élites. Even when German was taught it was usually at a woefully inadequate level, even at the highest levels of the profession: according to a report of

1821 the Abate Ridolfi, who held the chair in German at Padua, could apparently speak the language only 'stentatamente' (haltingly) and with very poor pronunciation;[48] he was later moved to the newly created chair of *pedagogia* to avoid embarrassment.[49]

Of all the faculties of Padua the one that felt the impact of the Habsburg takeover most forcefully was almost certainly the *facoltà politico-legale*. Tight control of the study of law was especially significant because a law degree was generally considered the prerequisite for attaining any but the most lowly jobs in the administration.[50] The authorities were certainly anxious that a steady supply of *licenziati* should be maintained with a view to filling government offices.[51] With this in mind it was especially important that legal studies should be kept in line with those elsewhere in the empire, so that future functionaries should be properly equipped for their work: it is no surprise, therefore, that there was a very heavy emphasis on Austrian law, although Roman law also retained a prominent place within the curriculum.[52] However, while growing numbers of young Venetians began to study law at Padua, in the late 1810s and early 1820s there still seems to have been some anxiety on the part of the authorities that these were insufficient to provide for the available positions both within the bureaucracy and the legal profession itself.[53] If such problems existed, they were to diminish as the university expanded over the next decade, although this growth was in turn to bring difficulties of its own.

As has been stressed, Francis saw the main aim of education as the provision of useful citizens and much of the curriculum was designed to this end. However tightly regulated the curriculum, for the system to function, the students had to be kept within it. Any loophole which might bring them into contact with ideas or ideologies possibly threatening to the status quo had to be blocked. Consequently, study outside the empire was strictly forbidden[54] and numerous restrictions were imposed on private tuition with a view to maintaining a virtual state monopoly on education.

Prior to 1825 and after 1834 private teaching of the *studio filosofico* was entirely forbidden. Since the course was necessary for anyone wishing to attend university this meant that all young men intending to progress beyond the *studio ginnasiale* had to undergo at least some training at the hands of the state. Even in the intervening decade the scope offered to those teaching privately was minimal:

both student and teacher had to register with the university or the nearest *liceo*, and the regular attendance of public examinations was compulsory. There was no greater leeway for private tuition in the *studio ginnasiale* and the *studio politico-legale*, although in neither of these was it ever completely outlawed: the private student was obliged to follow the same course as his peers in secondary school or the law faculty and to use identical texts; public examination and registration was compulsory.[55]

Besides keeping students within the state system, it was also necessary to ensure that the teaching staff did not abuse their positions to propound views other than the orthodoxies sanctioned by the state. To ensure this end they were allowed almost no flexibility. At all levels of education great care was taken to impede attempts at innovation or initiative on the part of the teaching staff. Not only was the syllabus laid down by government decree but so too were the texts from which the academics were to teach. It was stressed in the notes appended to the 1817 *Sovrana risoluzione* that it was the duty of all professors to work from the 'libro scolastico determinato'. They were also obliged to ensure completion of the course within the permitted period.[56] As such there was scarcely any opportunity to depart from the carefully formulated syllabus. Moreover, a rigid system of supervision was established whereby each faculty was placed under a *direttore degli studj*, usually selected from among *emeritus* professors or local dignitaries. It was the task of these *direttori* to make sure that good order was maintained. The director was supposed to attend classes on a regular basis to make sure that lecturers did not depart from prescribed texts and teaching methods; he was to collect regular reports from other members of the faculty on the students and to keep an eye open for any sign of moral lassitude or political radicalism. Any transgression was to be reported promptly to the police and as well as to any other interested government department. Besides this rather repressive role, the *direttore* also served as faculty representative on the *Senato accademico*, and in the capacity of adviser to the government on new appointments.[57]

As with most other posts within the educational system, the directors of faculties were usually selected from a short-list of three, known as the *terna*. This was prepared by the member of the Venetian *Governo* responsible for *istruzione pubblica*, in consultation with the *delegato provinciale* (provincial prefect) for the Padovano, the police and the university itself. Usually the system seems to have functioned reasonably smoothly, although problems could arise in finding an appropriate candidate. In 1818 an embarrassing situation arose when the octogenarian, half-senile, partially-paralysed Count Ascanio Fenicio was given the post of director of the law faculty. Not surprisingly he had to be replaced prematurely, both because he was unable to perform his duties and because he was becoming an object of universal derision among the undergraduates.[58] The problem was compounded by regular post-prandial drinking bouts. As a rule, however, the *direttori* seem to have provided a valuable link between the Austrian administration and the university, providing a useful source of information and tool for imposing the will of government.

Given the care taken to erect educational machinery designed to produce model subjects, it must be asked how successful it really was. Without embarking on a vast prosopographical survey it would be impossible to establish its overall effectiveness. Some indication can, however, be gained from examining the activities of the student population itself. From the sources available in the *Archivio di stato* in Venice a vivid picture can be drawn of student life in Padua in the first twenty years of Austrian rule. This reveals the frequently unruly and unpleasant behaviour of 'la scolaresca', but at the same time suggests that, while the student body caused almost constant anxiety for the police, government and educational authorities alike, this anxiety was only very rarely of a political nature.[59]

In February 1817, the provincial delegate for the Padovano wrote to the Venetian governor describing a typical incident. A group of students, who had been drinking heavily in a bar beyond the city limits, over-turned a table standing outside an *osteria* and proceeded to trade insults and then blows with its occupants, before chasing the unfortunate *padrone* into a neighbouring house. The same students later returned and assaulted a customer (whom in their inebriated state they mistook for the owner), whom they dragged off to the police to demand his arrest. The police promptly released the students' victim, described in the records as 'a peasant' ('un villico').[60] The perpetrators of this outrage were themselves later brought to justice: their ringleader being expelled from the university and spending a fortnight in gaol.[61]

Despite making examples of student malefactors, town-gown clashes of varying degrees of seriousness were a more-or-less constant characteristic of life in Padua during the restoration era. Students were by no means always the culprits, but the sort of arrogant treatment meted out to the bar-owner and his customers seems to have been fairly common. Sometimes it was of a relatively mild nature, as in January 1827, when a large number of students gathered in the *Piazza dei Signori* to pelt passers-by with snowballs.[62] Frequently it took a much nastier turn. On the night of 30/31 January 1834, a group of eight students, 'presi fortemente dal vino', took up the suggestion of one of their number, a Lombard, to repeat a prank ('burla') he had played the previous year while studying at Pavia by forcing anyone they met on their way through the streets to jump or dance around. It seems that most of those who suffered the indignity were not of a mind to report it, but a cooper and a waiter, who initially resisted and got beaten up, did go to the police. The authorities, despite the lowly social status of the victims, went to considerable pains to catch the guilty parties who were kept in gaol while the matter was investigated and were then punished with fines, expulsion from the university and restriction to their home towns.[63]

On the whole the authorities seem to have shown a laudable intolerance for students who maltreated members of less-privileged social groups. Shortly before Christmas 1832, nine drunken students, all Lombards attached to the medical faculty, attacked four coachmen who were quietly drinking coffee; all the students were promptly arrested and the ringleader was gaoled as an example.[64] Similarly, when a group of undergraduates were badly wounded by a group of *operaj* erecting an inscribed stone on the *Ponte Molin*, the workmen received protection from high-ranking officials on the grounds that the students had simply got their just deserts. The first response of the police chief, Amberg, had been to have the workmen arrested, frightened lest students might seek to exact revenge. Later, however, he was overruled from Venice on the grounds the students had been beaten with good cause: they had blatantly ignored a policeman who had told them the Ponte Molin was closed, scaled a barrier blocking the bridge and provocatively interrupted the men's work.[65]

As well as clashes with the civilian population of Padua, there was a good deal of tension between the *corpo goliardico* and the local garrison. At first glance hostility to the army might seem to indicate a more general antipathy to Austrian rule, the presence of Habsburg regiments considered provocative and soldiers as legitimate targets for attack. A closer inspection of individual cases, coupled with the apparent deep political apathy of the student population would tend to undermine this explanation. Relations between barracks and university were certainly often strained, but this seems to have been the predictable mutual enmity of two readily definable groups of young men, each with its own corporate identity. Moreover, whatever the underlying causes for hostility, many incidents seem to have had more personal immediate causes, with apparently petty disputes sometimes escalating into more serious tit-for-tat feuds. The sort of clashes that occurred can be seen from those recorded in a single *fascicolo* covering the period 1830–34.[66] This carries reports on various incidents including the following: a fight ('una zuffa') between a student and a sergeant from the Luxen regiment, in which the latter was stabbed for trying to gatecrash a party;[67] another wounding of a soldier over an alleged debt of four *lire austriache*;[68] and a scuffle over the right of way through a narrow *sottoportico* between a captain of dragoons and two students.[69] The last of these is particularly interesting since the officer in question was not immediately recognisable, being in civilian clothes at the time. The British traveller J. D. Sinclair remarked that Austrian officers tended not to sport their uniforms when off duty, a policy he considered wise 'as it makes people less shy of their masters'.[70] The *Delegato provinciale*, De Pauli, however, was at pains to stress that there was 'nissun malumore tra scolari e militari'—possibly rather an exaggeration.[71] He was probably more accurate when, in a report on student disorders in the period 1826–7, he wrote of the undergraduates that 'among the *majority* there is not even the slightest hint of opposition to the law or of opposition or hostility towards the military'.[72] Interestingly, while the authorities often took the side of townsfolk when they came into conflict with students, they also seem to have been generally willing to side with students against soldiers, even in the not infrequent cases when the latter were officers.[73]

It would of course be a mistake to suppose that student aggression was directed solely at the army and the civilian population. Students were perfectly happy to fight among themselves. In July 1831, for example, the *Rettore magnifico* was obliged to report a brawl that had broken out in the course of a lecture to the *Presidio di Governo*.[74] In a more serious incident the following year a group of Lombard and Tyrolese students fought in a bar after arguing over the respective merits of wines from their home regions, two of the Tyrolese receiving head wounds inflicted with an iron bar.[75] One clue to the cause of violence within the undergraduate community itself was the large numbers of students from different areas. Traditionally *campanilismo* was strong in the Veneto and the presence of a large contingent of Lombards and Tyrolese provided even greater scope for rivalry and antagonism. In the academic year 1830–31 there were 930 students from the Veneto and 335 *stranieri*, of whom 163 came from Lombardy and 89 were Tyrolese.[76] Yet, although student violence may have arisen in part from regional antipathy, it was never organized as it was in Germany. Admittedly, by the 1840s, students were forming into regionally-based *brigate* which used to frequent specific bars, but these seem to have been later and looser organizations and scarcely comparable with the *Landsmannschaften* to the north of the Brenner.[77] Moreover, if violence was a constant problem, it would seem to have been limited to only a minority of the rowdiest students and duelling (whether for real or in ritualized form) was never institutionalized as it was in German student clubs.[78]

Behind the vast majority of student transgressions lay alcohol. Heavy drinking was extremely common among at least a substantial minority of Padua's undergraduates. The problem had got so out of hand by 1824 that the provincial vice-delegate, Roner, urged the introduction of much tighter laws controlling coffee shops and bars to prevent riotous and immoral behaviour among students. His proposals were stymied because licence fees and the *dazio di consumo* on wine provided a valuable source of revenue and because the authorities had no desire to alienate the city's numerous and vocal bar-owners.[79] The following year, the chief of police, Kübeck, was forced to counsel an increase in patrols of *satellizio* (night-watchmen), both to deter and apprehend undergraduate malefactors.[80]

Heavier policing was not the answer to student crime, not least because the police force in the Veneto was singularly inadequate at the best of times. It was not unreasonable, therefore, that many of those in authority still believed that the best means of dealing with the problem lay in preventing the 'excessive abuse of taverns' ('il soverchio abuso dell'osterie'). To put an end to it was not, however, the easy task imagined by Niccolò Da Rio, director of the philosophy faculty for 1828, when he simply advocated stricter control of opening hours.[81] The problem lay partially with the opposition such a measure would arouse among the people of Padua in general and publicans in particular, but it was in large part the consequence of the organization of the university itself. Padua had long ceased to have *collegi* offering accommodation to undergraduates. This meant that almost all students were obliged to take cheap lodgings in the city's numerous *trattorie, osterie* and *locande,* many of which were dependent almost entirely on their custom: Padua's students not only caroused and brawled in taverns, but ate, slept and studied in them too.

Problems of student accommodation were further aggravated by the steady growth in numbers studying at Padua. In the final lustrum of the Napoleonic era the student population hovered around 300. By the late 1810s it had risen to 800,[82] and by 1830 it reached 1355, of whom only 214 (16.8%) were native Paduans likely to live with their families.[83] All the rest had to find lodgings, mostly in taverns. In 1824 this state of affairs led the *Rettore magnifico* to lament the demise of the *collegi,* the re-establishment of which he considered one of the best means of reasserting control over an increasingly wayward student body.[84] Four years later, the police chief, Amberg, remarked that with almost 1500 students it was impossible to prevent disorders and excesses, 'however much surveillance and care one might wish to employ'.[85]

The worries about student accommodation and drinking were not limited to Padua. Across the Mincio, Padua's sister university, Pavia, was experiencing similar difficulties. The *Senato accademico* in 1830 expressed its anxiety at the 'danno notabile' done to undergraduates by frequenting taverns, holding that such surroundings were unsuitable for students, not only because they led to lax morals and deteriorating academic performance, but because they also resulted in the development of plebian manners through bringing students into contact with people 'di infima classe'. This lifestyle had a thoroughly detrimental effect on students, 'from whom sovereign and state expect good magistrates and useful citizens'. In order to safeguard the 'moral rectitude' ('morigeratezza') of the students, that they might mature into the sort of staid and reliable citizens and bureaucrats the government and university wanted to produce, an announcement was made in July 1830, exhorting parents to have their sons lodge in the houses of 'upright' ('probe') families, rather than leaving them to their own devices in rented rooms.[86]

Even before Pavia's announcement triggered renewed debate over the student accommodation, matters were coming to a head in Padua. In April 1830 the Bishop of Padua had written to the *Presidio di Governo* of the growing impiety and immorality of students and their open contempt ('spregio') for the Church and religion[87]—obviously the years of religious instruction were proving counter-productive. The *delegato provinciale*, however, had been disinclined to agree with the bishop, suggesting that he lacked evidence for his assertions and claiming that the previous year had actually been rather free of trouble, marred only by the suicide of a first-year student. Nevertheless, he was prepared to admit that perhaps half the students were tainted with 'depraved and licentious habits' ('costumi corrotti licenziosi'), even if the cause of this stemmed not from time spent in bars but from

... the neglect of good manners in the parental house, the parents sometimes being no better themselves; the rebellion which already takes place in the *ginnasi* and *licei*; the sloth and slight application tolerated by university.[88]

The university authorities, however, did not agree with De Pauli but shared the views of their colleagues in Pavia. When the latter announced their proposals for checking dissolute habits among the students, the Venetian governor told the Paduan *Senato accademico* to examine the possibility of adopting similar measures. In the *seduta* of the senate of 12 December 1830, six main advantages were identified: there would be less contact between students and the vulgar, uneducated classes; opportunities for drunkenness would be greatly reduced; students would become more industrious; there would be fewer friendships between students, so less likelihood of bad behaviour; there would be fewer distractions from study; and, finally, there would be fewer public scandals resulting from otherwise well-behaved young men being seen to break fast ('a mangiar di grasso nei giorni di viglia').

But despite these apparent advantages, the *Senato* acknowledged drawbacks. The major stumbling block was that there were simply not enough suitable families for nearly 1300 students to find lodgings. Even if there had been enough, there were other complications. To prevent students lodging in taverns was feasible, but to stop them drinking in them was virtually impossible. It was predicted too that many *bettolieri* would close their establishments, currently dependent on student trade, and simply reopen them under the guise of lodging houses. Moreover many taverns provided food at a far cheaper rate than could families taking in only a handful of lodgers, and the higher prices could well prove prohibitive. There was even the danger that the timetable of family meals would probably not fit in with that of lectures and lessons. It was necessary to legislate because a simple statement of advice like that made by Pavia was simply inadequate, yet to make it obligatory to lodge with families was an unreasonable imposition on the freedom of students and their parents.

To resolve the debate, a three man commission was appointed to examine the accommodation issue. The commission's findings were predictable. If any benefit were to be derived from placing students with families, then the families had to be 'probe ed educate'. There would be no point in transferring undergraduates from taverns to the houses of people belonging to 'le classi inferiori'. On the other hand it was self-evident that the well-to-do ('persone facoltose') would not be prepared to provide rooms for the small remuneration students could offer. If households with unmarried daughters were also ruled out, it would perhaps be possible to find places for 400 students, or under a third of the total, at a cost of around half as much again as that currently paid in *osterie*. The commission stated, therefore, that the idea of accommodating students in this fashion was neither desirable, because higher costs would prove prohibitive for many, nor realistic, because of insufficient appropriate households. It did, however, suggest that, wherever possible, students should be placed *a dozzina* with families, and that in future a sterner eye should be kept on those left to fend for themselves. Finally it stressed that students found to be pursuing a dissolute or immoral existence should be promptly expelled. It was also urged that the restoration of *collegi* be given renewed consideration[89] Most of these decisions were summarised in the *avviso* which appeared in the *Gazzetta privilegiata di Venezia* almost eight months later. They were only recommendations, no stronger than those made at Pavia the previous year. Moreover, no provision was made for the creation of *collegi* which alone might have solved the problem of providing the correct environment for developing the studious, law-abiding qualities required of a good Habsburg subject.[90]

Why though was there no attempt to establish some form of hall of residence? One obvious reason was the expense involved in such a project. It also seems as if the authorities had their reservations about large concentrations of students for reasons of security and public order. In 1830, the Bishop of Padua, worried as usual at the irreligious nature of the undergraduates, suggested that they should all be obliged to attend compulsory mass at the *Chiesa di Santa Sofia.* The response of the police chiefs, Lorio and Amberg, was one of complete horror: the assembly of so large a body, far from reaching the 'ostensible goal' ('lo scopo specioso') of instilling virtuous behaviour, was bound to result in disorder. The students would resent the disruption of their Sunday mornings and, even if the service passed off without incident, disturbances were sure to arise as they congregated in the streets before and after mass.[91]

The misgivings expressed by Lorio and Amberg were understandable, particularly given the widespread unrest elsewhere in the Italian peninsula during the early 1830s. Evidence for Padua's student population espousing anti-Austrian, liberal or radical political views is, however, hard to come by. Unlike Pavia, the events of 1820–21 seem to have passed off virtually without echo in Padua.[92] This may seem strange given the large numbers of Lombards who studied at Padua, and the apparent strength of support shown by their fellows at Pavia. It is less surprising, however, when the particular conditions of Pavia and Padua are taken into account. Of the Lombards studying at Padua a very large percentage were probably Brescians (certainly by the early 1830s this was the case)[93] who traditionally maintained close ties with the Veneto. Pavia's student population, however, included 128 students from across the Ticino and Po who would obviously entertain a lively interest in the events taking place in their homelands. Almost all the rest of Pavia's students were Lombards (Venetians do not seem to have been attracted), many from the border regions which always had close economic and cultural links with Sardinia-Piedmont. Many students at Pavia had relations across the Ticino and some were from families which held land there. There were also strong economic arguments for Lombardy looking westward which did not apply to Venetia.[94] According to Sorigà's figures, of the 84 students who excitedly rushed into Sardinian territory most were Lombards and many probably did entertain genuine liberal or nationalist sentiment. The inevitable excitement of the Piedmontese at Pavia was bound too to have affected them. Above all Pavia's geographical location and close links with the lands ruled by the House of Savoy, sparked an interest which could scarcely be kindled in Padua.[95]

The early 1830s witnessed renewed revolutionary stirrings in many parts of Italy, especially in those areas of the Papal states which bordered on the Veneto. Once more the political outlook of the Paduan students seems to have been characterized above all by apathy. It is the case that in 1831, Spaur, the Venetian governor advised Metternich that troops be left in Vicenza and Padua, rather than rushed to the border of the Papal States, on account of the alleged conspiracies in the first and the 'numerous rash youth' of the latter.[96] His fears seem to have been misplaced. In a search of the files of the Venetian *Presidio di Governo* including those of the *Geheim* section, it has been difficult to discover examples of political opposition, and certainly there seems to be *no* record of political unrest in the lists of students expelled from the university in the 1820s and 1830s.

The apparently passive nature of Padua may, of course, be attributable to preventive measures on the part of the authorities. Troops were constantly on hand, and the police maintained a continuous and vigilant watch for trouble-makers. But comparable measures existed elsewhere in Italy—indeed, throughout Europe—yet did not prevent organized political activity. In Germany especially students were widely politicized and, although fears were sometimes deliberately exaggerated in order to guarantee the acceptance of repressive legislation, it would be foolish to deny the existence of a broad hostility towards the existing régimes. In Padua such sentiments were extremely rare. Though it is true that in most European universities of the same era there was a fair degree of immorality and debauchery, in Padua the problems posed by student behaviour were *always* more likely to stem from a propensity for *macao* or other prohibited games,[97] leaving the city without proper permission,[98] or being found with a prostitute[99] than from politics. Even when the police did discover a club with the suspicious-sounding name of the *Società inglese* it was soon revealed to be dedicated solely to carousing and womanizing.[100] Padua's problems lay with libertines not liberals.[101]

There were occasional incidents which did seem to hint at possible revolutionary sentiment among Padua's student population. One such involved the trip made to Bologna in March 1831 by two undergraduates, Maiset and Lion, when that other ancient university city was in 'open rebellion against its own legitimate government'.[102] When the two were apprehended crossing back into the Veneto, they were found to be in possession both of tricolour cockades and of a revolutionary paper, *Il Precursore*. Investigations lasted a month, during which time the young men were held under arrest, before it was decided that their motives were not political and that they had been guilty neither of 'criminal deceits' ('criminosi raggiri') nor of 'evil designs' ('rei disegni'). Nonetheless, 'thoughtlessness and folly' ('leggerezza e follia') had led them to transgress both university and police regulations, and, though no criminal punishment was imposed, they were expelled from Padua and kept under police surveillance.[103] It had, after all, been their own fault that they had missed a term while under arrest; it made sense that they should miss at least one academic year.[104] Lion, who already enjoyed a reputation for indolence, must have antagonized his faculty for on its advice he was barred from any further studies.[105] In the short term Maiset fared little better: two petitions for his readmittance were rejected that same year.[106]

The activities of Lion and Maiset clearly never posed any threat. An alleged conspiracy against Habsburg rule, centred on a second-year law student from a noble family of Bassano, seemed rather more serious. When Virgilio Brocchi[107] drew attention to himself through his occasionally outspoken comments and frequent travels, he was placed under investigation.[108] One of his acquaintances turned police informer and he was arrested for high treason.[109] Allegedly a plot existed with supporters in Padua, Verona, Vicenza and Milan as well as some 500 heavily armed men in the *Sette comuni*.[110] In fact, the police seem to have been misinformed and over-reacted. The worst charges that could be levelled against the twenty-four students implicated out of the total of 139 individuals under suspicion were seditious shouting, the distribution of cockades, vague offers of monetary support and the inscription of graffiti.[111] The overall picture that emerges from the secret reports on this conspiracy is one of a group of romantic youths, for the most part resentful of Austrian rule, but singularly unprepared to make genuine sacrifices to overthrow it. That numerous arrests were made reinforces the traditional picture of Habsburg readiness to suspect conspiracy among any group of educated men remotely critical of the status quo. A good deal of moderation was also displayed on the part of the authorities. Brocchi's trial was untainted by any of the harshness sometimes evident in the earlier *Carbonari* witch-hunts. Despite two years under arrest in Milan, Brocchi was acquitted for lack of evidence and allowed to return to Bassano. That he was not readmitted to the law faculty was not, however, because of political qualms. On returning to Bassano he had married beneath him and squandered his fortune: it was inappropriate for such an individual to have access to a university education and the careers a degree might offer. Morals and decency rather than politics seem to have been the main concern.[112]

The extreme political passivity of Padua during the reign of Francis I should not necessarily be seen as an indication of the success of the Habsburg system of what Rath described as 'education for citizenship'. It is clear that as far as the morality of the students was concerned the system did not work from the outset: drunkenness, dissipation, whoring, gaming and fighting were integral parts of student life to many undergraduates, and no amount of religious instruction could guarantee piety. Political indoctrination seems also to have had its limitations even if there were few signs of opposition before 1835. Although notorious for their conservatism, the academic staff grew tired of the restrictions imposed on them by Vienna and even before the revolution of 1848 many were prepared to voice their opposition to the existence of stifling censorship. The students themselves certainly grew more militant. In stark comparison to their behaviour in the early 1820s and 1830s, in 1848 Padua's undergraduates were at the forefront of patriotic insurrection and involved in some of the earliest fighting against Austrian whitecoats.[113]

Why then did the system appear to work so smoothly between 1814 and 1835 but break down by the 1840s? In part the answer to this question has little to do with the university itself. If Padua's staff and students were prepared to tolerate, even support, the restoration of Austrian rule, this had much to do with the general loathing in the Veneto for the excesses of the old Napoleonic system and the absence of any viable alternative to Habsburg government; as memories of Napoleon's excesses diminished and as the international balance of power altered, Venetians of all social classes were more likely to look critically at Austrian domination.[114] It is also important to distinguish between the nature of Austrian government in the period up to Francis's death (when the albeit clumsy Habsburg bureaucracy functioned reasonably well) and that of Ferdinand's rule after 1835 (when the government in Vienna was crippled by infighting and inertia). There is, however, another consideration which applies more specifically to the university: the availability of employment. When the Austrians occupied the Veneto there was a tendency to give government jobs to non-Venetians, but the relative scarcity of graduates meant that the majority of Padua's students still stood a good chance of attaining some form of professional or government employment if they so desired. In the course of the 1820s and 1830s the numbers of students studying at Padua increased steadily before levelling off in the 1840s. At the same time the percentage of government jobs held by Venetians also increased slightly, but inadequately to absorb the far larger numbers of students. Hence, despite the far greater readiness to give top positions to Venetians, a degree, which had never *guaranteed* employment in a government office or even as a doctor or lawyer, became increasingly worthless on the labour market:[115] as in many other areas of Europe, Venetia was suffering from an excess of educated men.[116] The Austrian authorities were aware of this and began to consider the introduction of a *numero chiuso*, higher fees or tougher examinations to restrict student access. One of the reasons for the far greater militancy of Padua's students after 1835 was almost certainly the disenchantment that arose from the realization that a university degree was of little use when seeking well-paid and secure employment. More detailed research on the student body in the years after the death of Francis I is, however, necessary before any firm conclusions can be drawn.

In his *Lines written among the Euganean Hills* quoted at the head of this article, Shelley, fiercely anti-Austrian and noisily radical, was perhaps a touch unfair. The university had undoubtedly often fared much worse than under Habsburg rule—indeed in the early eighteenth century it was rumoured that degrees were being awarded to local farm animals in mistake for students,[117] and under Napoleonic rule it had sunk to insignificance. Nor does Shelley's allegation of tyranny really stick as the reasonable treatment of Brocchi indicates. On the other hand Habsburg notions of education as little more than a tool for social engineering did little for scholarship or creativity: if Padua's lamp of learning was not extinguished, it certainly burnt with little vigour in the twenty years after the fall of Bonaparte.

Department of History
University of Keele
Newcastle-under-Lyme
Staffs. ST5 5BG

REFERENCES

1. The poem was written in Oct. 1818. See Thomas Hutchinson (ed.), *The Complete Works of Percy Bysshe Shelley*, (Oxford, 1940), pp. 550–4.
2. For statistics on government expenditure in Lombardy and Venetia for the periods 1806–13 and 1814–21 see Reviczky's long report dated Verona, 8 Dec. 1822 in *karton* 72, *Kaiser Franz Akten* (henceforth K.F.A.) in the Haus-, Hof- und Staatsarchiv, Vienna (henceforth H.H.S.W.). See especially the table entitled *Prospetto di confronto tra le spese sostenute negli anni corsi dal 1805 al 1813 dal cessato Governo Italiano pei Dipartimenti formanti ora il Regno Lombardo-Veneto riferibilmente ai rami di pubblica amministrazione di sotto indicati, e le spese sostenute per gli uguali titoli dall'I. R. Governo Austriaco negli anni corsi dal 1814 al 1821*. For information on the population of Lombardy and Venetia see Reuben John Rath, *The Provisional Austrian Régime in Lombardy-Venetia, 1814–1815* (Austin, Tex., 1969), pp. 5–6.
3. Even a historian as grudging in his praise of the Austrians as Augusto Sandonà was obliged to admit that their education policy was a vast improvement on that of the Napoleonic régime. See Augusto Sandonà, *Il Regno Lombardo-Veneto 1814–1859. La costituzione e l'amministrazione. Studi di storia e diritto; con la scorta degli atti ufficiali dei dicasteri centrali di Vienna*, (Milan, 1912), p. 143.
4. Ibid., p. 167. See also the long report of the Austrian governor of Venetia, Goëss, dated Venice, 3 January 1819, H.H.S.W., K.F.A., 71, for statistics on student numbers. On Padua university under the Kingdom of Italy see Maria Cecilia Ghetti, 'Struttura e organizzazione dell'università di Padova dal 1798 al 1817', *Quaderni per la Storia dell'università di Padova*, 16 (1984), pp. 135–82. The picture painted by Ghetti of reforms under the French is in some senses quite favourable, at least with respect to the French policy of creating 'un'università di stampa moderna'. However, increased state control, modernization

and the abolition of various mediaeval and increasingly anachronistic practices and customs were of little value given the pitifully poor attendance by students.

5. The use of education as a form of social control has long been seen as standard in early modern Italy as well as in the post-Theresian Habsburg Empire. For a recent attack on the thesis that seventeenth and eighteenth-century Italian universities were primarily institutions of social control see Brendan Dooley, 'Social Control and the Italian Universities from Renaissance to Illuminismo', *The Journal of Modern History*, 61 (1989), pp. 205–39.

6. Francis allegedly made this remark to a group of teachers from the *Gymnasium* at Laibach in 1821. The only record that he actually made it is a newspaper article, but it was certainly referred to frequently during his lifetime. The full text reads: 'I do not need savants but good honest citizens. Your task is to bring young men up to be this. He who serves me must teach what I order him. If anyone cannot do this or comes up with new ideas, he can go or I will remove him.' See C. A. Macartney, *The Habsburg Empire, 1790–1918*, (London, 1969), p. 212. The stress on education as a means of fashioning loyal and subservient citizens is made clear in R. J. Rath, 'Training for Citizenship in the Austrian Elementary Schools during the Reign of Francis I', *Journal of Central European Affairs*, 4 (1944), pp. 147–67. With more specific regard to Lombardy-Venetia it is unnecessary to go further than the *Regolamento per le scuole elementari nel Regno Lombardo-Veneto* of 1821, that specified the role of the school teacher was 'to instil in the hearts of his students love for their sovereign and fatherland, obedience to law and respect for public servants'. Cited in Giampietro Berti, *Censura e circolazione delle idee nel Veneto della restaurazione* (Venezia, 1989), p. 471. See also the remarks made by Luisa Gasparini, 'I libri di testo delle scuole austriache', *Rassegna storica del Risorgimento*, 22 (1935), pp. 203–47. On the Austrian use of education as a means of creating good citizens after the death of Francis I see the remarks made by the British traveller Peter E. Turnbull in *Austria* (2 vols.; London, 1840), ii. 124–5 and 154–5. In the first of these two passages Turnbull wrote that the aim of Habsburg policy throughout the Empire was to view education as 'a mighty engine to mould the public mind; to cement it together in a bond of cordial union with her existing institutions; to excite and regulate its energies, so that it shall be neither a drag on the state machine by its ignorance and grossness, nor a spur to unsafe speed by its crude theoretical fancies . . . [It] strives at the creation of a happy, not a brilliant people'. In the latter the role of education is identified as developing 'a formation of mind . . . which will render . . . [Habsburg subjects] contented and useful in their respective states and will repel the ambition of rising above them'.

7. For the best discussions of the change from Napoleonic to Habsburg government see Rath, *The Provisional Austrian Régime*, and Marco Meriggi, *Amministrazione e classi sociali nel Lombardo-Veneto (1814–1848)* (Bologna, 1983).

8. The fear that the universities might corrupt a whole generation of future public servants was certainly not limited to Lombardy-Venetia. The Austrian chancellor Metternich seems to have considered the German universities the single biggest threat to the stability of the Confederation. Writing to Prince Wittgenstein in November 1818 he warned of a sinister strategy of indoctrination that lay behind the teaching of many liberally-inclined professors. This was all the more dangerous because, as the presidential preamble to the notorious Carlsbad Decrees stressed, 'in Germany the education for public services and for official life is entirely left to the universities'. See Prince Richard Metternich (ed.), *Memoirs of Prince Metternich 1815–1829*, trans. Mrs. Alexander Napier, (8 vols.; London, 1881), iii. 206 and 316–7.

9. It is interesting by way of comparison to look at the way in which the Austrians and French had viewed the university of Padua in the years 1796–1813 during which there were frequent changes in régime. In 1797 Padua had briefly been under the control of the French and their sympathisers. After the Treaty of Campo Formio it had passed to Austrian rule which was to last until December 1805. From January 1806 until 1813 it was under Napoleonic rule, except for a brief spell in 1809 when the Austrians once again re-established control. Although occasional members of staff were sometimes sacked by both French and Austrians because of their political opinions and although under the Kingdom of Italy some reforms were implemented (most radically the abolition of both the theology faculty and the old Venetian division of studies into the so-called *Università legista* and the *Università artista*) on the whole the period was remarkable for the degree of continuity between different régimes. This, however, should not be attributed so much to a desire shared by different governments for some degree of continuity as to a sense that there was little point wasting time in instituting reforms in an area of so unpredictable a political future. Constant shortages of funds also impeded any spirit of reform. See Ghetti, 'Struttura e organizzazione' (1984), *passim*.

10. *Charakteristik der Beamten in der Lombardie und Venedig*, H.H.S.W., K.F.A., 12. Unfortunately the document is undated but it must be from before 1818, the year in which the *Central Organisierungs Hof Commission*, to which it was submitted, was disbanded. The C.O.H.C. was the committee established in Vienna to deal with the reincorporation of the Italian and so-called Illyrian provinces into the empire.

11. Rath, *The Provisional Régime*, p. 18.

12. Ibid., p. 42.

13. Ibid., p. 51. Rath cites the report from Hager of 24 April 1814 in the H.H.S.W., *Kabinets-Akten* 1814, no. 103. See also the *Elenco degli signori professori della Imp.* *Regia Università di Padova*, dated 14 June 1814 that is reproduced in Lelio Ottolenghi, *Padova e il dipartimento del Brenta dal 1813 al 1815*, (Padova, 1909), pp. 403–6. This list divided all the university staff into those of sound political persuasion and those of 'cattiva' or 'pessima condotta politica'. This report gives a far more sinister picture of the views of the teaching staff, seventeen of whom were placed in one of the latter two categories, compared to sixteen adjudged trustworthy. It would seem from subsequent events that this was an absurdly over cautious assessment. Certainly the authorities did not act on the information provided. Ottolenghi's assertion that almost all the academic staff were 'macchiati di partigiana indicazione alle nuove idee, importate in Italia dai francesi . . .', (ibid., p. 172) might have been shared by some Austrian officials, but if so they were very tolerant of past conduct.

14. Sussani to *I. R. Governo*, Venice, 7 Nov. 1815, *Archivio di Stato, Venezia* (henceforth A.S.V.), *Presidio di Governo* (henceforth P. di G.), (1815–19) xx 4/2. See also Ottolenghi, *Padova ed il dipartimento del Brenta*, p. 170 and Ghetti, 'Struttura e organizzazione', (1984) p. 168.

15. Francheschini, 7 March 1815 and C.O.H.C. to *Presidio di Governo*, Vienna, 25 March 1816, A.S.V., P. di G., (1815–19) xx 4/2. The original Italian reads: '. . . non abbiano abbandonato le loro cattedre per comando del soppresso governo italiano, come alcuni prefetti, ma per proprio impulso.' On the treatment of the absent professors see also Giuseppe Solitro, 'Maestri e scolari dell'università di Padova nell'ultima dominazione austriaca (1813–1866)', *Archivio Veneto-Tridentino*, 1 (1922), 114–5.

16. Goëss to Lazansky (president of the C.O.H.C.), A.S.V., P. di G., (1815–19) xx 4/2.

17. Goëss to Lazansky, Venice, 22 May 1816, A.S.V., P. di G., (1815–19) xx 4/2.

18. Goëss to Lazansky, Venice, 24 Nov. 1815, A.S.V., P. di G., (1815–19) xx 4/2.

19. Pontani to C.O.H.C, Venice, 10 Jan. 1817 and Passy to C.O.H.C., Venice, 20 May 1817 (countersigned by Goëss, 23 May), A.S.V., P. di G., (1815–19) xx 4/2.

20. For the best examination of Habsburg attitudes to the Church during the Restoration period see Alan J. Reinerman, *Austria and the Papacy in the Age of Metternich* (2 vols.; Washington, D.C., 1979–89).

21. *Almanacco per le provincie venete* (1821), p. 382. For Marsand's appointment as *Rettore magnifico* ahead of Luigi Lanfranchi, known as a keen supporter of the Habsburg government, see Roner to *Presidio di Governo*, Padua, 27 Oct. 1818 and Passy to Marsand, Venice, 30 Oct. 1818, A.S.V., P. di G., (1815–19) xx 4/6.

22. Alexander von Helfert, *Zur Geschichte des lombardo-venetianischen Königsreichs*, (Vienna, 1908), p. 1 and Rath, *The Provisional Austrian Régime*, p. 43.
23. Alexander Helfert, *Kaiser Franz von Oesterreich und die Stiftung des lombardo-venetianischen Königsreichs*, (Innsbruck, 1901), p. 128.
24. See the list of members of the Masonic lodges of the Veneto in H.H.S.W., *Staatskanzlei, Provinzen: Lombardei-Venedig* (henceforth St. k Prov., L.-V.), 35.
25. The professors were: Abate dott. Giacomo Giulliani, professore ordinario di scienze pubbliche, leggi politiche austriache e spiegazione del codice penale sulle gravi trasgressioni di polizia; Cavaliere Luigi dott. Mabil, professore provvisorio d'introduzione enciclopedica allo studio politico legale e diritto naturale privato e pubblico e diritto criminale; dott. Valeriano Luigi Brera, consigliere di governo e professore ordinario di terapia speciale e di clinica medica; dott. Franco Fanango, professore ordinario di polizia medica e medicina legale; dott. Girolamo Melandri, professore ordinario di chimica generale animale, farmaceutica, and Abate Salvatore Dal Negro, professore ordinario di fisica. See *Almanacco* (1821) for the posts.
26. Rath, *The Provisional Austrian Régime*, p. 44.
27. Raab's words, cited by Helfert, were '... daß seit dem Sturz der vorigen Regierung in Venedig keine Freimaurer-Versammlung stattgehabt habe'. *Kaiser Franz*, p. 263. The one area of the *Terraferma* where the Masons may have remained a force was the Polesine. On the Freemasons of the Veneto generally, see Angela Mariutti, *Organismo ed azione delle società segrete nel Veneto durante la seconda dominazione austriaca (1814–1847)* (Padova, 1930), pp. 17–47. Police lists of suspected Masons dating from 1824 and 1832 suggest that there may later have been some resurgence.
28. It should be noted that academic salaries were by no means vast and that in Padua's sister university, Pavia, there were certainly intermittent complaints. See Irene Ciprandi, 'L'Università di Pavia nell'età della Restaurazione', in *Problemi scolastici ed educativi nella Lombardia del primo ottocento*, Vol. II, *L'istruzione superiore* (Milano, 1978), pp. 247–9. On the other hand, academic salaries could provide a comfortable living. In the 1820s at the top end of the scale they compared with those of a *Segretario di governo* or a *Vice-delegato* at around 2,000 *fiorini*. The starting salary in law or medicine was 1,500. The junior staff of the philosophy faculty, however, received a mere 600 *fiorini* and in the theology faculty, admittedly staffed only by priests who might have been expected to have been less mercenary than their lay colleagues, the highest salary was a mere 1,000. Ugo Tucci, 'Stipendi e pensioni dei pubblici impiegati nel Lombardo-Veneto dal 1824 al 1866', *Archivio economico dell'unificazione italiana*, 10 (1964), 62–3. It should be noted that, according to Ciprandi, even in Pavia there was a

general readiness among professorial staff to accept the Austrian régime simply to safeguard livelihood and careers. 'L'Università di Pavia', p. 265.

29. *Tabella dimostrante lo stato personale della facoltà filosofico-matematica dell'I. R. Università di Padova per l'anno 1830–31*, A.S.V., *I. R. Governo* (hereafter I.R.G.), (1830–34) xv 48/4. Some officials were, of course, more energetic in their opposition to servants of the former régime than others. In 1816, for example, Tornieri, the *delegato provinciale* for Padua, criticised four professors with provisional contracts for their past politics. Yet, despite police testimony that they were guilty of past political 'fanaticism', they were all felt by this stage to be acting with political prudence and allowed to keep their jobs. Those identified by the *delegato* were professors Dall' Oste, Girolamo Molin, Menghelli and Mabil. Tornieri to *I. R. Governo*, Padua, 14 Dec. 1816, A.S.V., *P. di G.*, (1815–19) xx 10/1. There were good grounds for suspicion of Luigi Mabil who had been an open supporter of both the French and 'Jacobinism' in 1797. He had been persecuted by the Austrians for his political beliefs after 1798, but had been reinstated under the Kingdom of Italy in 1805. Ghetti, 'Struttura e organizzazione', (1984) p. 149.

30. Ciprandi, 'L'Università di Pavia', *passim*.

31. Ibid. See especially pp. 197–201.

32. Ibid., p. 261.

33. Education expenditure in the Veneto also represented part of a general process of creating more equality with Lombardy in the provision of government services. For the statistics on government expenditure see *Prospetto di confronto tra le spese . . .* Reviczky, Verona, 8 Dec. 1822, H.H.S.W, K.F.A., 72. For Austrian education policy in the Veneto generally (which admittedly sometimes looked more impressive on paper than in reality) see N. Mangini, 'La politica scolastica dell'Austria nel Veneto dal 1814 al 1848', *Rassegna storica del Risorgimento*, 44 (1957), 769–83, and Claudia Salmini, 'L'Istruzione pubblica dal Regno italico all'unità', in *Storia della cultura veneta dall'età napoleonica alla prima guerra mondiale* (Vicenza, 1986), pp. 59–79. Also useful is A. Filipuzzi, 'L'Istruzione pubblica', in *I problemi dell'amministrazione austriaca nel Lombardo-Veneto. Atti Convegno, Conegliano 20–23 settembre 1979*, (Conegliano, 1981). For a brief analysis of the Austrian *politica scolastica* in the Veneto see also Mirella Chiaranda Zanchetta, 'Educazione e coscienza civile nell'"Istitutore" di Giovanni Codemo', in Giorgio Chiosso (ed.), *Scuola e stampa nel Risorgimento. Giornali e riviste per l'educazione prima dell'Unità*, (Milano, 1989), pp. 90–95.

34. On Francis's attitude to the Church see Rath, *The Provisional Austrian Régime*, p. 50 and p. 84. It should, of course, be noted that Francis,

unlike his reforming uncle, does seem to have been a genuinely committed Catholic.
35. Ciprandi, 'L'Università di Pavia', p. 215. Turnbull, *Austria*, ii. 125, states that the Austrian education system was governed by two fundamental principles: 'that the state alone shall direct the education of all its subjects' and 'the connexion of all education with religion'. It should of course be remembered that there was nothing especially unusual about the prominent role afforded by the Habsburg system to religious education. See for example the influence wielded over education by the Church in France while the Comte de Frayssinous was director of the *Université* between 1822 and 1828. See A. Garnier, *Frayssinous. Son rôle dans l'Université sous la Restauration (1822–1828)* (Paris, 1925), *passim*.
36. In a report of 31 Nov. 1815, Goëss wrote of the establishment of 'die gänzlich abgängig gewesene theologische Fakultät', H.H.S.W., K.F.A., 12. The *Sovrana notificazione* of 12 Sept. 1815 aimed to put the faculty on a firmer footing. See *Collezione di leggi e regolamenti pubblicati dall'imp. regio Governo delle provincie venete* (Venezia, 1815–48), Vol. II/2, esp. pp. 72–82. Until the establishment of a seminary to serve Lombardy, Padua trained all those seeking to become priests for both regions. See 'Sovrana risoluzione sull'organizzazione delle università di Pavia e Padova', in *Collezione*, Vol. IV/1, pp. 81–2. On the status of theological studies in Padua during the late eighteenth century see Maria Cecilia Ghetti, 'Struttura e organizzazione dell'Università di Padova dall metà del '700 al 1797', *Quaderni per la storia dell'Università di Padova*, 16 (1983), 76, and on the re-establishment of the theology faculty by the Austrians see Ghetti, 'Struttura e organizzazione', (1984), p. 170.
37. *Almanacco* (1821), pp. 382–5.
38. Salmini, 'L'Istruzione', p. 72 and G. Biadego, *La dominazione austriaca e il sentimento pubblico a Verona dal 1814 al 1847* (Roma, 1899), pp. 41–2. Clergy employed in educational establishments were also vetted for political and moral reasons in exactly the same way as other public servants. See, for example, correspondence in A.S.V., P. di G., (1815–19) xx 14/2 and (1824) xx 2/1.
39. For the obligatory attendance at a *ginnasio* before beginning the philosophy course see the additional notes appended to the 'Sovrana risoluzione sull'organizzazione delle università di Pavia e Padova', *Collezione*, Vol. IV/2, p. 95. Other documents of relevance, see 'Repristino dell'università di Padova e fissazione del corso de' suoi studj', in *Collezione*, Vol. II/2, pp. 66–81 and 'Circolare governativa alle delegazioni relativa all'organizzazione dei licei nelle Provincie venete', in *Collezione*, Vol. I, 'Appendice 1813–1818', pp. 69–84. This latter states: 'Gli studj di filosofia saranno organizzati nei loro rispettivi rami uniformi in tutti i licei, e nel modo medesimo, come li

prescrivo per la facoltà di filosofia in ambedue le università italiane'.
Besides teaching the two year 'philosophy' course, the *facoltà filoso-fico-matematica* offered a two year diploma in surveying (the *corso per i periti agrimensori*) or a *licenza* after three years. It also offered the *Corso degli studj per gl'ingegneri architetti* which conferred the title of *baccelliere* after one year's study and that of *licenziato* after three. The bachelor's degree must have been of very limited value given that it was confined to mineralogy and purely theoretical mathematics and physics. See 'Repristino', p. 69–70. The decision to allow the pursuit of the philosophy course at the *licei* as well as the universities of Padua and Pavia seems to have arisen from the desire to keep students under parental control and supervision for as long as possible. Study at a local *liceo* made it much easier for the student to live at home. Ciprandi, 'L'università di Pavia', p. 212. It is noteworthy that this measure had already been effectively adopted under the Venetian Republic as early as 1786. Ghetti, 'Struttura e organizzazione' (1983), p. 80. The study of vocational 'mathematical' disciplines (surveying, engineering and architecture) was somewhat unusual in early-nineteenth century European universities. The retention of such courses at Padua reveals an interesting continuity with the eighteenth century when a number of Italian universities introduced chairs in new practical sciences. In Padua, for example, a chair of *agricoltura sperimentale* was set up in 1761 and one in *architettura civile* was established in 1771. Ibid., p. 78 and Dooley, 'Social Control and the Italian Universities', p. 238.

40. 'Circolare governativa . . . relativa alla organizzazione dei licei', p. 70.
'Hanno a cessare tutte le altre cattedre sin adesso esistenti in alcuni licei, gli altri scientifici rami d'istruzione, come sarebbe a dire, la scienza legale, la chimica, la botanica, l'agricoltura, etc., etc.'

41. See 'Repristino', p. 67–8 and 'Circolare relativa . . . alla organizzazione dei licei', p. 73–4. Study of history in the third year of the *liceo* was only a *studio obbligato* for those going on to read law.

42. See reports of Giuseppe Antonio Bonato of 4 April 1818, A.S.V., I.R.G., (1820) xxii 26/28; Angelo Ridolfi, 25 May 1818, I.R.G., (1820) xxii 26/29; A. Maurogato, 16 April 1818 and Giacomo Bonvicini, Vicenza, 10 July 1818, I.R.G., (1820) xxii 26/27.

43. See for example 'Repristino', p. 66 and 'Sovrana risoluzione sull'organizzazione delle università . . .', p. 82, p. 84, p. 86.

44. Sandonà, *Il Lombardo-Veneto*, p. 164. For the compulsory element of veterinary studies in the *corso degli studj per i medici* and for the *corso degli studj per i chirughi di laurea* see 'Repristino', p. 71 and p. 73. In both cases veterinary science was studied for two or three hours a week in the fourth year of the course. The closure of the veterinary school should not be seen as indicative of any Habsburg hostility to veterinary studies *per se*. Indeed, as Ghetti points out, since the mid-eighteenth

century veterinary studies had been actively encouraged in the Habsburg Empire. 'Struttura e organizzazione', (1984), pp. 172–3. See also Helmut Engelbrecht, *Geschichte des österreichischen Bildungswesens.* *Erzeihung und Unterricht auf dem Boden Österreichs. Band 3. Von der Aufklärung bis zum Vormärz*, (Wien, 1984), p. 280.

45. That Germanization was perceived not in linguistic but administrative terms is clear even from the fact that the dictum 'il faut germaniser' was invariably expressed in French. On the support for the study of 'native languages' and the establishment of chairs in 'Illyrian', Czech and Polish at Laibach, Prague and Lemberg respectively see Arthur Haas, *Metternich, Reorganisation and Reform, 1813–1818* (Wiesbaden, 1963), pp. 95–6. It should be noted that in the eighteenth century the standard language of instruction had remained Latin despite the fact that most students had a thoroughly inadequate knowledge of the tongue. Study in Latin had been effectively abolished in most subjects by the French in 1806, although it was reintroduced for a few courses in 1808. See Ghetti, 'Struttura e organizzazione' (1983), p. 74 and (1984), pp. 151–4.

46. Goëss, Venice, 21 November 1815, H.H.S.W., K.F.A., 12.

47. 'Circolare governativa . . . relativa alla organizzazione dei licei . . .', p. 69 and 74. On the study of German at a lower level see also 'Sovrana risoluzione sulla sistemazione de'ginnasi', in *Collezione*, Vol. IV/1, pp. 95–6 and Salmini, 'L'Istruzione pubblica', p. 61.

48. Despite poor spoken German, Ridolfi was a respected scholar and could admittedly read and write the language with some fluency. *Schiarimenti sopra i 23 quesiti portati dal presidiale decreto, relativi ai disordini che si ritengono sussistere dalla superiorità nell'I. R. università di Padova*, Venice, 20 October 1821, A.S.V., P. di G., (1820–23) x 2/8. For examples of poor German teaching at lower levels see reports from the directors of *licei* in A.S.V., P. di G., (1820–23) xx 27/15. On Ridolfi's ability as a scholar see Melan, Padua, 23 December 1819, A.S.V., I.R.G., (1820) xxii 26/31.

49. For Ridolfi's transfer see Goëss to *I. R. Commissione aulica degli studj*, Vienna, 21 July 1820, A.S.V., I.R.G., (1820) xxii 26/31.

50. Meriggi, *Amministrazione e classi sociali*, p. 256 and 'Aspetti dell'impiego di concetto in Lombardia durante la restaurazione (1816–48)', in Nicola Picardi and Alessandro Giuliani (eds.), *L'Educazione giuridica. IV. Il pubblico funzionario: modelli storici e comparativi. Tomo II – l'età moderna* (Perugia, 1981), p. 334.

51. Marino Berengo, 'Il numero chiuso all'università di Padova. Un dibattito della restaurazione', *Quaderni per la storia dell'università di Padova*, 14, (1981), 41–53. See esp. p. 46.

52. 'Sovrana risoluzione sull'organizzazione delle università di Padova', p. 84 and 'Repristino', pp. 76–8. The significance of Roman Law in legal studies within the Habsburg Empire was, of course, less than it

had been before the abolition of the Holy Roman Empire. Jacob
Probst, *Geschichte der Universität in Innsbruck seit ihrer Enstehung bis
zum Jahre 1860*, (Innsbruck, 1869), p. 317.

53. Berengo, 'Il numero chiuso', pp. 46–8. This view was not held
    universally. Even as early as 1819 the Venetian Governor, Goëss, was
    warning of the danger that the Lombardo-Venetian administrative
    structure was not able to respond to the demand for employment from
    the young *laureati* of Pavia and Padua. Meriggi generally paints a
    much gloomier picture of prospects for employment during the 1810s
    and 1820s than does Berengo. *Amministrazione e classi sociali*, pp. 291–
    302. For Goëss's remarks see p. 294.

54. 'Divieto della gioventù d'ambo i sessi di frequentare gl'istituti di
    educazione dell'estero', in *Collezione*, Vol. IV/2, pp. 110–11. Students
    from north of the Brenner were not allowed to study outside the
    empire either. Indeed, by the early 1830s it was almost impossible for
    young men from anywhere in the empire even to travel abroad without
    parental escort and official (sometimes even imperial) sanction. Probst,
    Geschichte der Universität in Innsbruck, p. 331. There was nothing
    innovatory about states imposing restrictions on studying abroad.
    However, the climate of 'academic protectionism', which according to
    Brendan Dooley was characteristic of early modern Italy, would seem
    to have had rather different origins. The tendency of Italian states from
    the seventeenth century onwards to impose prohibitions on foreign
    study and to refuse to recognise degrees awarded by foreign institu-
    tions arose from a desire to avoid 'competition from other universities
    in Italy and transalpine Europe'. The nineteenth-century Habsburg
    authorities were worried less by foreign competition than by the fear
    that students might come in contact with pernicious ideologies through
    studying in foreign universities. On early modern Italy see Dooley,
    'Social Control and the Italian Universities', p. 217.

55. On restrictions on private tuition see Mangini, 'La politica scolastica',
    pp. 776–87. See also the 'Circolare governativa', and the 'Aulico
    dispaccio', in *Collezione*, Vol. VII/2, pp. 180–2 and Mittrovsky,
    Studienhofcommission, to *I. R. Governo*, Vienna, 28 August 1834,
    A.S.V., I.R.G., (1830–34) xv 1/52. On restrictions on private study in
    other parts of the Empire see Probst, *Geschichte der Universität in
    Innsbruck*, p. 330.

56. 'Sovrana risoluzione sull'organizzazione della università di Pavia e di
    Padova', p. 93. See also, for example, the texts listed in *Prospetto degli
    Studj dell'Imperial Reg. Università di Padova per il corrente anno
    scolastico cioè dai xv ottobre MDCCCXVII al xv agosto
    MDCCCXVIII*, (Padova, 1818).

57. 'Istruzioni generali sull'ufficio dei direttori degli studi dell'università',
    in *Collezione*, Vol. III/1, pp. 7–23. For the relationship between the
    direttori and the government see esp. pp. 2–3, and for the control of

teaching methods and texts see p. 13, where it is stated that they were supposed to make sure that 'gli istruttori si attengano precisamente ai libri elementari a loro prescritti, non essendo in loro facoltà il deviare dai principj adottati, e molto meno poi di prevalersi di altri libri in luogo di quelli che sono già prescritti, o di usare delle loro particolari confutazioni.' For their advisory role to the government over appointments etc. see p. 9. The position of *direttore* was nothing new in the Habsburg university system having emerged in the mid-eighteenth century from reforms undertaken initially by Maria Theresa's physician and key adviser on education, Gerhard van Zwieten. Essentially the post developed from that originally created in the medical faculty of the Vienna University, the role of which was described by van Zwieten in a famous memorandum of 1749: 'Avant tout il faut que Sa Majesté nomme une personne, qui de son part, et sans aucune dependence de la faculté a le droit d'assister a tous les examens, elections du Doyen, promotions publiques, visitations des apothécaires, avec le droit d'y présider, pour faire observer avec toute exactitude ce qu'il plaira à Sa Majesté d'ordonner, devant estre responsable de tous les abus s'y pourront glisser contre l'intention de Sa Majesté. A cette personne on doit donner une instruction bien détaillée pour éviter toutes les chicanes.' Cited in Rudolf Kink, *Geschichte der kaiserlichen Universität zu Wien*, (2 vols; Vienna. 1854), ii. 254. The idea of placing a faculty under a responsible official, independent of other academic staff was soon extended from the Vienna medical faculty to other universities and other faculties. On the introduction and the development of the *Directoren der Facultäten* or *Studien-Direktoren* in the Hereditary Lands of the Habsburg Empire see, for example, Engelbrecht, *Geschichte des österreichischen Bildungswesen*, iii. 189; Probst, *Geschichte der Universität in Innsbruck*, p. 198; Wenzel Wladiwoj Tomek, *Geschichte der Prager Universität* (Prag, 1849), pp. 324–5. On their supervisory role in the nineteenth century, see Engelbrecht, *Geschichte des österreichischen Bildungswesens*, iii. 283.

58. For Fenicio's dismissal from office, see Tornieri to *Presidio di Governo*, Padua, 16 Dec. 1818, A.S.V., P. di G., (1815–19) xx 4/5.

59. However ill-behaved the undergraduate population of Padua in the early nineteenth century, it never again reached the depths of depravity and lawlessness experienced in the late seventeenth and early eighteenth centuries when students frequently indulged in mugging and highway robbery. Piero Dal Negro, 'L'università', in Girolamo Arnaldi and Manlio Pastore Stocchi, eds., *Storia della cultura veneta*; Vol. 5/1, *Il settecento* (Vicenza, 1986), pp. 47–8.

60. Tornieri to Goëss, Padua, 28 February 1817, A.S.V., P. di G., (1815–19) xx 5/1.

61. Goëss to Tornieri, 2 March 1817, A.S.V., P. di G., (1815–19) xx 5/1.

62. Uhrer, Padua, 1 Feb. 1827, A.S.V., P. di G., (1825–29) xiv 3/1. See also Fanzago, *Direttore della facoltà medica*, to *I. R. Governo*, Padua, 28 Nov. 1828, A.S.V., I.R.G., (1830–34) xv 63/35.

63. De Pauli to *Presidio di Governo*, Padua, 18 Feb. 1834, A.S.V., P. di G., (1830–34) xiv 2/6.

64. See report made by Cattanei, *I. R. Direzione generale di polizia*, Venice, 24 Dec. 1832 and De Pauli to *Presidio di Governo*, Padua, 29 Dec. 1832, A.S.V., P. di G., (1830–34) xiv 2/6.

65. Amberg to *Presidio di Governo*, Venice, 2 July 1831; Pascotini to *Direzione generale di polizia*, Venice, 4 July 1831; A.S.V., P. di G., (1830–34) xiv 2/6. The students included one Luigi Zambetti who was later cleared of an apparently unprovoked attack on a soldier on the grounds of insufficient evidence. See De Pauli to *Presidio di Governo*, Padua, 9 July 1831, ibid.

66. The *fascicolo* in question is A.S.V., P. di G., (1830–34) xiv 2/6.

67. De Pauli to *Presidio di Governo*, Padua, 31 May 1831.

68. Cattanei to *Presidio di Governo*, Venice, 16 Dec. 1832.

69. De Pauli to *Presidio di Governo*, Padua, 9 March 1833.

70. J. D. Sinclair, *Autumn in Italy* (Edinburgh, 1829), p. 44.

71. De Pauli to *Presidio di Governo*, Padua, 9 March 1833.

72. De Pauli to *Presidio di Governo*, Padua, 26 Nov. 1828, A.S.V., I.R.G., (1830–34) xv 63/35. The original Italian reads: '. . . nella *moltitudine* non vi entrò neppure la menoma scintilla di opposizione alle leggi o di opposizione ossia odio verso il militare'. The emphasis is mine. The situation in Padua stands in marked contrast with that in Pavia where relations with the garrison were awful, with several cases of students being killed by troops. Kübeck to *Presidio di Governo*, Venice 1 July 1825, A.S.V., P. di G., (1830–34) 2/6.

73. In none of the cases cited above do the students appear to have been punished.

74. Capellari, *Rettore magnifico*, to *Presidio di Governo*, 30 July 1831, A.S.V., P. di G., (1830–34) xiv 2/6.

75. Cattanei, 24 Dec. 1832 and Lorio, *Commissario superiore*, to *I. R. Direzione generale di polizia*, Padua, 28 Nov. 1832, A.S.V., P. di G., (1830–34) xiv 2/6. Three of the Lombards involved in this fight were also later involved in the attack on the coachmen mentioned above.

76. *Stato numerico dei giovani studenti che ottenero la rasta [?] di permanenza dall'I. R. Commissariato Superiore di Polizia in Padova per l'anno scolastico 1830–31 divisi per provincia*. Signed by De Pauli. A.S.V., P. di G., (1830–34) xiv 9/7. Of the Lombards, the vast majority came either from Brescia (79) or Mantua (44). Of those who came from outside the Tyrol and the Kingdom of Lombardy-Venetia, 16 came from the 'Illyrian' provinces, 53 from Istria and Dalmatia and 14 from the Hereditary Lands of the empire.

77. According to Solitro by the 1840s the Venetians and Polesini drank in the *Posta*, the Veronesi and Vicentini in the *Tomba d'Antenore*, the Friulani and the Bellunesi at the *Commercio*, the Istrians and Dalmatians at the *San Daniele*, the Trentini and 'Germans' at the *Svizzero* and the aristocrats, for the most part Paduan, at the *Pedrocchi*. The *habitués* of the famous *Caffè Pedrocchi* were known as *Pedrocchini*. Solitro, 'Maestri e scolari', pp. 159–60. It is, of course, hardly surprising that young men from the same region should have been drawn together.

78. On German student clubs see Konrad H. Jarausch, 'Sources of German student unrest, 1815–1848', in Lawrence Stone ed., *The University and Society*, (2 vols.; London, 1975), Vol. II, *passim*. For a contemporary, if rather idealised account of the clubs in Germany, see William Howitt, *The Student-Life of Germany from the Unpublished Manuscript of Dr. Cornelius* (London, 1841). Much German duelling was between friends.

79. Roner to *Presidio di Governo*, Padua, 8 Dec. 1824, A.S.V., P. di G., (1824) xiv 2/1.

80. Kübeck to *Presidio di Governo*, Venice, 11 May 1825, A.S.V., P. di G., (1825–29) xiv 3/1.

81. Da Rio to *I. R. Governo*, Padua, 19 Nov. 1828, A.S.V., P. di G., (1830–34) xv 63/35.

82. Goëss, Venice, 3 Jan. 1819, H.H.S.W., K.F.A., 71.

83. *Stato numerico dei giovani studenti . . . in Padova per l'anno scolastico 1830–31 divisi per provincia.* Signed by De Pauli. A.S.V., P. di G., (1830–34) xiv 9/7. Padua's numbers compare interestingly with those of other European universities in the same period. Vienna in the academic year 1835–6 had 5,420 students and Paris over 6,200 in law and medicine alone. Berlin by contrast had fewer than 2,000. See Laurence Brockliss, 'The European University in the Age of Revolution, 1789–1850', in M. G. Brock and M. C. Curthoys (eds.), *Nineteenth-Century Oxford* Pt. i (forthcoming).

84. Fanzago to *Presidio di Governo*, Padua, 9 Jan. 1824, A.S.V., P. di G., (1824) xx 2/1. 'O, quanto desiderabile, che anche in Padova, come in tante altre università, esistessero dei collegj, in cui raccolti fossero almeno gli studenti della facoltà filosofica [. . .]! Ne' tempi addietro esistevano anco da noi utili collegj, in cui custodivasi un gran numero di studenti della università'. On the *collegi* at Padua during the eighteenth century see Ghetti, 'Struttura e organizzazione', (1983), p. 79, and also G. Gullino, 'Una riforma settecentesca della Serenissima: il collegio di S. Marco', *Studi veneziani*, 13 (1971), 515–86. On the institution of *collegi* in an earlier period of Italian history see P. Denley, 'The Collegiate Movement in Italian Universities in the Late Middle Ages', *History of Universities*, 10 (1991), 29–91, esp. pp. 82–6.

85. Amberg to *I. R. Governo*, Venice, 17 Dec. 1828, A.S.V., I.R.G., (1830–34) xv 63/35.

86. Announcement of 27 July 1830 printed in the *Gazzetta privilegiata di Milano*, 14 Aug. 1830, A.S.V., P. di G., (1830–34) xiv 2/10. The original Italian of the piece quoted reads: '[la scolaresca] . . . dalla quale il munificente sovrano e lo stato attendono buoni magistrati ed utili cittadini'. One English traveller had described the students of Pavia as looking like troops on half-pay. Lady Morgan, *L'Italie* (Paris, 1821), ii. 21. An Italian historian writing in the Fascist era tried to suggest that this was because they had a hardened, manly air in response to the plight of their country [see Renato Sorigà, 'Gli studenti dell'università di Pavia e i moti del '21', *Bollettino della società pavese di storia patria*, 23 (1923), 177–84]. Probably the style cultivated by the students had more to do with loutishness or, perhaps, romantic posturing.

87. Bishop of Padua to *Presidio di Governo*, Padua, 20 April 1830, A.S.V., P. di G., (1830–34) xiv 2/10.

88. De Pauli to *Presidio di Governo*, Padua, 24 April 1830, A.S.V., P. di G., (1830–34) xiv 2/10. 'Di questo malcostume io credo la causa – la negletta educazione in casa paterna, non essendo talvolta migliori i genitori; – la sedizione che già nei ginnasj e i licei prende piede – ed in Padova, l'ozio e poca applicazione tollerata dall'università'. The delegate's claim that things were not actually getting any worse echoes his reports on the years 1826–28, in which he stated that the greater part of student population was quieter and more disciplined than in previous years (è più docile, più subordinata in pubblico la scolaresca, di quello che fu negli anni antecedenti'), continuing, 'Ad ognuno che dimora in Padova apparebbe veramente strano l'asserto che l'ultimo biennio, e specialmente l'ultimo anno, ancora più tranquillo dall'altro, abbia maggior motivi ad inquietudine che gli anni anteriori, essendo appunto l'opposto la realtà . . .', Padua, 26 Nov. 1828, A.S.V., I.R.G., (1830–34) xv 63/35.

89. *Processo verbale della seduta dell'inclito Senato Accademico dell'I. R. Università*, Padua, 12 Dec. 1830, A.S.V., P. di G., (1830–34) xiv 2/10. Expulsion was obviously not a new idea having always been the standard punishment for student misdemeanours.

90. Capellari to *Presidio di Governo*, Padua, 11 Aug. 1831, A.S.V., P. di G., (1830–34) xiv 2/10.

91. Lorio to *I. R. Direzione di polizia*, Padua 27 Oct. 1830 and Amberg to *Presidio di Governo*, Venice, 29 Oct. 1830, A.S.V., P. di G., (1830–35) *Geheim*, 34.

92. Solitro, 'Maestri e scolar', p. 131, points to a few patriotic proclamations which circulated in student circles early in 1821, but the evidence for support for either the Neapolitan or the Piedmontese rising is minimal. See also, *Carte segrete ed atti ufficiali della polizia austriaca in Italia dal 4 giugno 1814 al 22 marzo 1848*, (4 vols.; Capolago, 1851), i.,

255, for a report that the Pavese students were seeking to stir up anti-Austrian feeling among their Paduan fellows. Berengo, 'Il numero chiuso', p. 42 mentions violent clashes between students and police at the *Teatro Nuovo* in 1820, but this predates the Neapolitan risings by two months. Moreover, the theatre was frequently the scene of student outrages and violence. See, for example, the reports of students kidnapping a *prima ballerina* and fighting with officers of the Esterhazy regiment in A.S.V., P.di G., (1825–29) xiv 3/1, or the disturbances at the *Teatro di Santa Lucia* in 1832. Cattanei to *Presidio di Governo*, Venice, 7 Dec. 1832, A.S.V., P. di G., (1830–34) xiv 2/6.

93. *Stato numerico dei giovani studenti . . . in Padova per l'anno scolastico 1830–31 divisi per provincia.* Signed by De Pauli. A.S.V., P. di G. (1830–34) xiv 9/7.

94. Sorigà, 'Gli studenti dell'università di Pavia', p. 178 and the same author's *Le società segrete, l'emigrazione politica e i primi moti per l'independenza,* (Modena, 1942), p. 210. See also Ciprandi, 'L'università di Pavia', pp. 304–5.

95. There were 892 undergraduates at Pavia in 1821. Those who slipped across the border in twos and threes on the outbreak of the insurrection mostly gathered at Voghera where they were armed and assigned to the 'Battaglione della Minerva o dei Veliti italiani' along with students from Turin. See Ciprandi, 'L'università di Pavia', pp. 303–5 and Sorigà, 'Voghera e la rivoluzione piemontese del 1821', *Bollettino della società pavese per la storia patria,* 21 (1921), 79–80. Many returned to continue their studies subsequently, although a few did feel the wrath of the imperial authorities. Pietro Vaccari, *Storia dell'università di Pavia,* (Pavia, 1948), p. 138–9. For the trials and sentences of implicated students from Pavia, see Alfredo Grandi, *Processi politici del Lombardo-Veneto, 1815–1851,* (Roma, 1976), p. 77. As a consequence of the revolts of 1821, a *risoluzione sovrana* of 4 April 1822 forbade Piedmontese students to study in Pavia. This was not limited merely to the university, but extended to include the *ginnasio* which drew a fair proportion of its pupils from across the border. The director of the school, Sartirana, appealed against this decision, on the grounds that his students were too young to pose any serious threat, and the *Delegazione provinciale* agreed to readmit those students already studying there before the rebellion took place. In fact, from November of the academic year 1822–23, Piedmontese subjects were once again admitted, although they were kept under special surveillance. G. Marabelli, 'Cenni sulle vicende dell'istruzione classica in Pavia e in particolare del R. Liceo-Ginnasio "Ugo Foscolo"', *Bollettino della società pavese per la storia patria,* 24 (1924), 148–219. See esp. 169–70.

96. Spaur to Metternich, Venice, 9 Feb. 1831, H.H.S.W., St. K., Prov. L-V., 15. Some indication of the seriousness with which the Austrian

authorities took the threat of revolutionary contagion spreading across the frontiers of the Habsburg Empire is to be seen in their readiness to take precautionary measures even in provinces north of the Brenner. In March 1831, following the suppression of insurrections by Austrian troops in the states of Parma and Modena, Italian students were forbidden to study in universities in the Hereditary Lands of the Empire. Franz von Krones, *Geschichte der Karl Franzens-Universität in Graz. Festgabe zur Feier ihres dreihundertjährigen Bestandes*, (Graz, 1886), p. 148.

97. Amberg to Spaur, Venice, 25 May and De Pauli to *Presidio di Governo*, Padua, 10 Jan. 1832, A.S.V., P. di G., (1830–34) xiv 2/6.

98. Amberg to Spaur, Venice, 26 Feb. 1832, A.S.V., P. di G., (1830–34) xiv 2/6.

99. De Pauli to *Presidio di Governo*, Padua, 14 Jan. 1832, A.S.V., P. di G., (1830–32) xiv 2/6.

100. Inzaghj to *Presidio di Governo*, Venice, 7 Jan. 1824, A.S.V., P. di G., (1824) xx 2/1.

101. Examples of political opposition in other educational institutions seem equally rare. One ridiculous case reveals the over-sensitivity of the Habsburg authorities to criticism, but can scarcely be seen as a symptom of dissatisfaction with the régime. In 1831, a brief note was sent to the governor, stating that 'non vi è più giustizia' and that 'tutti i superiori sono ladri, principalmente il governatore di Venezia'. It eventually emerged that the authors of this biting political attack were two pupils of the *scuola elementare maschile*, in Rovigo, aged twelve and thirteen, who had written it in the hope of implicating a 'compagno di scuola' against whom they bore a grudge. The boys were scolded and received an admonitory forty-eight hours in gaol, which seems harsh and unnecessary, if a long way from tyrannical. See correspondence in A.S.V., P. di G., (1830–34) xiv 9/16, esp. Brusoni, *Commissario superiore di polizia*, Rovigo, 12 Aug. 1831.

102. Pascotini to Ranier (the Austrian viceroy and emperor's brother), Venice, 27 June 1831, A.S.V., P. di G., (1830–34) xiv 9/15. '. . . allora in piena rivoluzione contro il proprio legittimo governo.'

103. Maiset and Lion had gone to Bologna to visit the latter's sweetheart. The cockades were purchased to gain easier access to revolutionary Bologna (which had in fact been occupied by Austrian forces by the time they arrived) and the papers as souvenirs. Amberg to *Presidio di Governo*, Venice, 18 April 1831, A.S.V., P. di G., (1831–35) *Geheim*, 24.

104. Pascotini to Ranier, 27 June 1831, A.S.V., P. di G., (1830–34) xiv 9/15.

105. Anon. (name illegible) to De Pauli, Venice, 24 April 1831, A.S.V., P. di G., (1831–35) *Geheim*, 24.

106. Pascotini to Ranier, Venice, 27 June 1831, A.S.V., P. di G., (1830–34) xiv 9/15.

107. Franco Della Peruta, *Mazzini e i rivoluzionari italiani: Il 'partito d'azione'*, *1830–45* (Milan, 1974), pp. 54–5 gives Brocchi's name incorrectly as Virginio. See also Mariutti, *Organismo ed azione*, p. 63. For the discovery of graffiti which first raised suspicions see Lorio to *Direzione di polizia*, Padua, 28 Jan. 1831 and Capellari to *Presidio di Governo*, 2 March 1831 in A.S.V., P. di G., (1831–35), *Geheim*, 24.
108. Amberg to Spaur (the Venetian governor), Venice, 18 May 1831, A.S.V., P. di G., (1831–35), *Geheim*, 24. '. . . hatte sich durch seine Äusserungen und öftere Reisen in höherm Grade verdächtig gemacht.'
109. Sedlnitzky (chief of police in Vienna) to Spaur, Vienna, 19 Nov. 1831, A.S.V., P. di G., (1831–35) *Geheim*, 24.
110. Ibid.
111. *Elenco di tutti gli individui indicati nel processo contro Virgilio Brocchi come sospetti di azione contro la sicurezza dello stato*, A.S.V., P. di G., (1831–35), *Geheim*, 24.
112. Cattanei to Spaur, 28 Nov. 1835, A.S.V., P. di G. (1831–34), *Geheim*, 24.
113. On resistance to censorship among academic staff at Padua see George Macaulay Trevelyan, *Manin and the Venetian revolution of 1848*, (London, 1923), pp. 63–4 and Solitro, 'Maestri e scolari', p. 165. For the student in the early stages of the 1848 revolution see Paul Ginsborg, *Daniele Manin and the Venetian revolution of 1848–9* (Cambridge, 1979), p. 77. It is worth noting that Padua does not seem to have been the only Habsburg university to experience politicization in the course of the 1840s. Probst, writing of Innsbruck, points to the political activity among students and staff in 1848 as of marked contrast to the remarkable passivity of the preceding decades. *Geschichte der Universität in Innsbruck*, p. 326 and pp. 341–3. In Graz, like Padua, protest seems to have crystallized in the early stages around the issue of censorship: in mid-March 1848 a petition was signed by over 600 students, professors and *Studien-Directoren* and sent to the Emperor demanding an end to the activity of the *Censur* and greater freedom in the field of instruction. Von Krones, *Geschichte der Karl Franzens-Universität*, p. 162 and pp. 537–40. The part played in the Vienna revolution by the so-called Academic Legion (by no means drawn exclusively from students but including large numbers) is also extremely well-documented.
114. The key change in the international situation was the overthrow of the Bourbons in France and the creation of the July Monarchy. Henceforth the Habsburgs would be unable to take their Italian hegemony for granted.
115. On the trend towards employing more Venetians see Meriggi, *Amministrazione e classi sociali*, pp. 201–47. On the issues of expanding student numbers and the availability of jobs, see Berengo, 'Il numero chiuso', *passim*, and Meriggi, *Amministrazione e classi sociali*, pp. 291–

323. Although Meriggi argues that graduates found difficulty in finding government employment from the earliest years of Austrian rule, he is basically in accord with Berengo's thesis that the problem had reached crisis proportions by the 1840s, some indication of this being the ever-growing percentage of graduates who were prepared to take work as an unsalaried *alunno i concetto* in the hope of one day receiving a permanent, salaried post. For example, in 1828 in the *amministrazione di giustizia* there were 48 unpaid *alunni* for 1,741 salaried officials (i.e. 2.6% of the total); by 1847 the figures had risen to 601 and 1,852 respectively (i.e 24.9% of the total). See p. 296. It is difficult to tell to what extent the growing scarcity of opportunities for government employment were offset by growing opportunities in the professions. Figures for the whole of the Veneto for *avvocati abilitati* (advocates operating with a licence) show a massive increase from 139 in 1822 to 414 seven years later. However, even in 1829 there were vacancies for a further eighteen to practise under government licence, albeit for the most part in small and doubtless unappealing villages where business was probably rather slack. A similar, although less dramatic increase occurred amongst physicians. In 1822 there were 650 *medici*, 347 *chirurghi* and 616 *farmacisti* practising in Venice and the *terraferma*. By 1829 the figures stood at 711, 602 and 731 respectively, an overall increase from 1,613 to 2,044. The growth in numbers might in part have been the result of a growth in demand, but it is unlikely that such an increase in demand would have been sustainable or that it would have kept pace with the ever-greater numbers of graduates available on the labour market. For statistics on licensed professionals see *Almanacco per le provincie dell'i.r. Governo di Venezia per l'anno 1822* (Venezia, ?1822), pp. 579–98 and *Almanacco per le provincie dell'i.r. Governo di Venezia per l'anno 1829* (Venezia, ?1829), pp. 287–96 and pp. 547–76.

116. The best general discussion of the over-production of university graduates and its political consequences is Lenore O'Boyle, 'The Problem of an Excess of Educated Men in Western Europe, 1800–1850', *Journal of Modern History*, 42 (1970), pp. 471–95. See also Pamela M. Pilbeam, *The Middle Classes in Europe, 1789–1914. France, Germany, Italy and Russia*, (London, 1990), p. 116.

117. Brenden Dooley, 'Science Teaching as a Career at Padua University in the Early Eighteenth Century: the Case of Giovanni Poleni', *History of Universities*, 4 (1984), 113. The laconic and damning phrase used was, 'Si dottorono i bo'.

University and Multinational Society in the Habsburg Monarchy: Students from Slovene Countries at the University of Graz, 1884–1914

Harald Heppner

This article will consider an aspect of the theme of 'University and Society' which has rarely been investigated: the national origins of students in a multinational state. States composed of several ethnic groups develop in different ways from those which are ethnically homogeneous, not least because their basis is more complex. They are obliged to have regard to their ethnic heterogeneity.

One such multinational state was the Habsburg Monarchy, populated by Germans, Hungarians, Czechs, Slovaks, Poles, Ukrainians, Rumanians, Serbians, Croatians, Slovenians, Italians, and others. There the relation between university and society had a national dimension.

The matriculation records which have existed since the foundation of universities in the Habsburg Monarchy give no direct indications of national student origin; such conclusions have to be inferred from the data about geographical origin, or from names and religion. Since the end of the eighteenth century in addition to the matriculation records there have been the so called 'catalogues'. These university sources are filed in faculties, years, and subjects of study, and supply information about the geographical and social origin of students as well as the progress of their studies. But these data shed no more light on the national origin of students than the matriculation records. It was not until the 1880s that a new category of source—the so called 'Nationale'-data—was introduced.

These 'Nationale'-data were the result of the struggle for greater equality of national rights within the Austro-Hungarian Empire. It became a matter of concern to the authorities to know the national origin of students. These data were filled in by the students themselves and not by university officials. They give information about the students (name, age, religion, birthplace and country, occupation and place of residence of the father or guardian, school origin and scholarship) and also mention their mother tongue (in German 'Muttersprache'). These sources have a considerable advantage, for the data about the mother tongue gives a more precise indication of national origins than data about the 'Umgangssprache' (the language used in public, which was demanded by the censuses of 1880, 1890, 1900, and 1910). Furthermore it becomes possible to obtain better information about the role of the universities for each nationality.

This study does not attempt to investigate the questions of student origin affecting all Austro-Hungarian universities, but tries to present one typical example—the university of Graz and the students from one ethnically heterogeneous area: the so called 'Slovenian countries'.

These Slovenian countries (see map) at that time were neither political nor cultural entities.[1] What they all had in common was that Slovenian-speakers (who belonged to the linguistic group of Southern Slavs) made up the majority of the population. Nevertheless, there were pockets too, where German- or Italian-speakers preponderated. For practical reasons, the provinces Carniola, Gorizia-Gradisca, Trieste and that part of Styria that until recently formed part of Yugoslavia (ancient Lower Styria or Slovenian Styria), have been taken into consideration for this research. The choice is based on the fact that the majority of Slovenes lived in these areas and that these areas were clearly defined.

The university of Graz was founded in 1585.[2] In the second half of the nineteenth century, after becoming a fully acknowledged university with all scientific branches, its significance increased due to its huge catchment area to the southeast, both at home and abroad, from the Adriatic to Galicia, from the Alps to the Balkans. It was not so important as Vienna or Prague, yet there were no rival universities in the near southeast.[3] Within the period from 1884 when the 'Nationale'-data[4] was introduced in Graz till the outbreak of World War I 3322 students (including 152 women) coming from Slovenian countries studied in Graz. Those thirty years comprised a period of great change within the Habsburg Monarchy, changes in population density, educational system, economy and transport. Access to the university broadened in this period, to include children not only from the upper classes, but also those from middle and

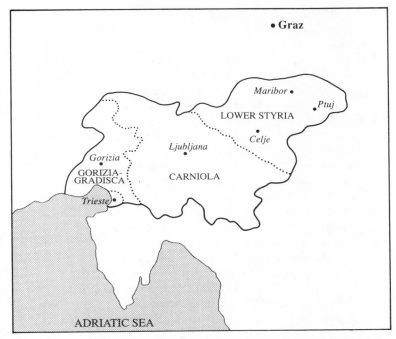

lower social strata. The results were already evident before 1914, but particularly marked after the collapse of the Austro-Hungarian Empire in 1918.

Geographical aspects

The major part of Lower Styria is hilly and thus subdivided into small areas. It had comparatively well developed transport facilities. With the exception of three areas of concentration (Maribor, Celje and Ptuj) these regions were predominantly agricultural, comprising arable-farming and wine-growing in the lowland and, in the mountains, cattle-breeding and forestry. Although there was no major industry, several small centres and the rail connection between Vienna and Trieste were of no little importance.[5]

Carniola, a province adjoining Styria in the southwest, differs considerably from the Slovenian part of Styria with its large mountain areas. In Carniola there was only one centre, the capital Ljubljana, and a few built-up areas. The prevalence of a rural economy was even larger in scale in Carniola than in Styria, which was to some extent due to bad transport facilities and a relatively scattered population. Further to the west, towards the Adriatic, there are Gorizia-Gradisca and Trieste. This region was influenced by the sea and contained strong contrasts. Along the coast there were dense settlements of population with good communications whereas the mountain area in the north was poorly developed and isolated. About one third of the whole population of the region lived in Trieste, a seaport (with about 150,000 inhabitants in 1900).

These geographical factors affected the numbers of students.[6] The ratio between the number of inhabitants and that of students shows that comparatively more students came from Styria and Trieste than from the other two provinces (see table 1). These differences are attributable to Trieste's position as a large town and the advantages which the Slovenian part of Styria (Lower Styria) enjoyed from having a well developed infrastructure and of being situated close to Graz. This conclusion can be drawn by locating places of student origin on a map and classifying them into three categories (town = more than 2500 inhabitants; small town = between 1000–2500 inhabitants; village = less than 1000 inhabitants). The results show that in Styria barely a half of the students came from 'urban' areas (towns, small towns), whereas in Carniola (60.78%) and in Gorizia-Gradica (72.03%) students from 'urban' areas were in a majority. Styria had relatively the largest share of students from villages, not because it was more agricultural but rather because most students from the other provinces originated from urban areas. The predominance of Styrian representation is not so much due to shorter distance but rather to structural framework, i.e. a higher population density, better communications and a better developed school-network.

Table 1. Geographical origin of students at Graz, 1884–1914

Province	Students
Lower Styria	1343
Carniola	798
Gorizia-Gradisca	398
Trieste	783

An important question is, to what extent the students from the villages were able to compete with fellow students from urban centres. Indeed, one would wish to know if rural students were already attending Graz at the beginning of this period. Spot checks reveal that the students from the villages participated early, but their number increased only after 1900.

National aspects

The question of the national origin of students is important because the population in Slovenian countries was not homogeneous, but rather a mixture of different nationalities.[7] The results show to what extent the national proportions of the students corresponded to those of the population as a whole.

In rural areas of the Slovenian part of Styria Slovenes were in the majority, whereas the German-speaking element ('Germans') predominated in towns and small towns. In Carniola the Slovenian majority was even larger; the German-speaking population on the whole was confined to the capital, Ljubljana, and to a language island in the south-west. The province of Gorizia-Gradisca was subdivided into western and eastern parts according to nationalities; Italian-speakers ('Italians') predominated in the capital and along the coast, whereas in the remaining mountainous area Slovenes were in the majority. In the town of Gorizia there was a small German-speaking minority. In Trieste 'Italians' were in majority, Slovenes making up only one third of the population (census 1900). The percentage of German-speakers was higher in Trieste than in Gorizia.

Quite a different picture results from data on the national proportions amongst the students at the university of Graz (see table 2).[8] About three-quarters of the students from Trieste were Italian-speakers (584 persons). In the remaining quarter there were three times more German- than Slovenian-speakers. Two-thirds of students from the province of Gorizia-Gradisca were Italian- and one quarter Slovenian-speakers, the rest being German-speakers. In Carniola, which was a centre of Slovenian culture, little more than half of all students were Slovenes (52 per cent), the rest were Germans: the explanation for this lies in the high proportion of students coming from Carniola's capital, Ljubljana, which was partly a German-speaking town. More than half of the students from Lower Styria were German-speakers, coming almost exclusively from towns and small towns.

Table 2. National Origins of Students at Graz, 1884–1914 (Percentages)

Province	Slovene	Italian	German	Other
Lower Styria	41,48	——	56,51	1,63
Carniola	52,00	——	45,61	2,38
Gorizia-Gradisca	27,63	62,56	8,54	1,25
Trieste	5,61	74,58	16,73	3,06

The results show that Slovenes on the whole were not nearly so strongly represented amongst the student population as other nationalities, which were in fact minorities in Slovenian countries. Although national equality was, in principle, guaranteed by the state, there were factors which favoured particular nationalities: administration, urban economy, urban development, and education. Since towns in Slovenian countries were generally dominated by German or Italian majorities, while there were more German and Italian language grammar schools than Slovenian ones, these nationalities could produce more students than the Slovenes. These proportions are closely connected with the social structure. Nevertheless, it has to be pointed out that many Slovenes from the countryside were attracted and assimilated by non-Slovenian urban environments.

Social aspects

When examining the social origins of students two problems emerge (see table 3).[9] First, the data indicate the occupational group of a father, but not his status within it. Hence, only approximate conclusions can be drawn about the number of students coming from poor and rich families. Nevertheless, student grants made it possible for lower social classes, too, to enable their children to study. Secondly, about one fifth of students gave no information about their fathers' professions, for a variety of reasons (VIII). This may have been because their fathers were dead, or else students simply may not have filled in the forms completely. In spite of these problems a reasonably clear picture of the social origins of students from Slovenian countries can be obtained from the remaining 80 per cent of the data.

Table 3. Social Origins of Students at Graz, 1884–1914 (Percentages)

Social group	Lower St.	Carniola	Goriz.Gr.	Trieste
I. Professionals: Doctors, Lawyers	8,63	8,89	9,04	10,34
II. State Officials	30,37	33,83	28,39	34,86
III. Commerce and Finance: Managers	6,47	8,39	8,29	19,92
IV. Tradesmen and Craftsmen	6,99	3,88	12,56	5,61
V. Industrial: Owners and Employees	2,97	3,50	4,02	3,44
VI. Rural: Landowners and Peasants	21,66	17,04	17,33	——
VII. No Occupation: 'Private Persons'	2,97	4,88	3,51	6,76
VIII. Not known	19,88	19,54	16,83	19,02

There is a small group of professions (I) which was more or less equally represented in all parts of these provinces (9–10 per cent), professional people such as doctors, lawyers, apothecaries etc. These were people who had themselves studied and who further improved their social position by having their children study. The largest professional group (II)—producing about one third of the students on average—were civil servants in the broadest sense (executive, financial, justice, railway and general administration). The large proportion of students from these families was a result of the long tradition of bureaucracy in the Habsburg Monarchy, so that a civil servant had social prestige, even if he had a minor job. The second largest group (VI) consisted of children originating from the villages. This group was the largest in the Slovenian part of Styria and non-existent among the students from Trieste. It consists of two sub-groups that cannot be accurately quantified: peasants and land-owners who did not work themselves. When assessing these data, it becomes clear that one third of this rural group was likely to

History of Universities

comprise land owners and two-thirds were likely to be peasants. The occupational group 'commerce and financial management' (III) comprised only 6–8 per cent, with the exception of the seaport and trade centre Trieste, where the proportion was about 20 per cent. The trade and craft class (IV) showed a similar proportion to group (III), with the exception of the small town milieu of Gorizia-Gradisca, where the percentage (over 12 per cent) was somewhat higher. The industrial branch (V)—whether it was entrepreneurs' or workers' children—was poorly represented (only about 3 per cent). This was, firstly, because Slovenian countries were in general sparsely industrialized; and secondly, because only a small number of workers' children went to university; and finally, because quite a number of students coming from working class backgrounds were included in the public service category (railway). Finally, there is a small group of fathers described as private persons (VII). If some of the landowners included in group VIII are taken into this category, it would be around 10 per cent.

Conclusions

Four factors can be shown to determine these results: the national structure of the population in the above mentioned countries; the social structure of this population; the geographical characteristics of the regions studied; and finally, the random factor of chance which plays a part in those statistics which are based on very small data. Five aspects require closer attention.

The first concerns the classification of the Slovenian share of students at Graz.[10] The data show that the number of Slovenes arriving from urban environments (with the exception of Ljubljana) was rather small. It could be deduced from this that Slovenes represented the main share of students coming from rural areas. But the considerable number of Slovenian students coming from sub-urban areas should be taken into account. This can be seen when studying the data about conurbations like Maribor, Celje, Ptuj or Gorizia-Gradisca. But the share of Slovenian students from Trieste is remarkably small—only 44 students in Graz within thirty years, while the size of the Slovenian population in Trieste grew to one third of all inhabitants in this seaport. The relatively small number of town Slovenes among the students suggested that the Slovenes at

Graz were mainly peasants' children. This is wrong, if the data for the bigger towns are analysed by nationality. Of course it is true that Slovenian students coming from rural areas must be added to categories IV and VI. But the cases of Maribor, Celje, Ptuj, Ljubljana, Gorizia or Trieste show that the fathers of Slovenian students belonged to the upper classes and middle classes as well, including the independent professions and branches of the civil service (especially teachers). In Ljubljana they also came from the trading class or were in the financial administration.

The German share of students at university of Graz is of central interest. Table 2 shows that German-speaking students dominated the big urban settlements of Lower Styria and Carniola. There are two causes for this phenomenon. One of the causes was demographic. The results of the census show that the share of German-speaking population in towns and small towns of Lower Styria and also in Ljubljana was markedly high.[11] The other cause was that the German population socially and economically belonged mainly to the upper and middle classes. This becomes obvious when the data about the bigger towns are analysed from the point of view of national origin: it becomes apparent that category II (public services) mainly consisted of students whose mother tongue was German; category III (trades, banking) likewise shows a high percentage of German-speakers; and finally independent professions were also mainly constituted by these. These parental professions obviously encouraged university education in order to maintain the family's social position, or to gain social security as civil servants.

Italian-speaking students formed the third important national group.[12] As shown above they came mainly from Trieste and the province of Gorizia-Gradisca. The data on their social and national origin show that Italian students belonged to all social classes. They included children of urban upper class families, and also children of middle and lower class families from rural areas. The national percentages of the social categories I to VII in Trieste and Gorizia-Gradisca, show that public services, independent professions, commerce and financial management had a strong attraction for Italian-speakers, and those who had become Italian-speakers, and these went on to establish a connection with the university.

A further aspect results from the contrast between urban and rural student catchment areas. It is striking that the preponderance of students coming from urban environments over those from rural areas increased the further west, towards the coast, that they came from. Only Lower Styria produced a considerable number of students from rural areas. The upper classes in urban environments mainly comprised Germans or Italians. Until the outbreak of World War I Slovenes only partly managed to gain ground in the upper social classes. The relatively high number of Slovenian students coming from rural areas indicates that Slovenes were trying hard to make up for this disadvantage—an intention which was only successful after 1918. Of course, two motives have to be considered: first, the desire for individual social mobility and secondly the endeavour to achieve national emancipation, for a university graduate could expect to become part of the state elite. Moving into a town—either for occupational reasons or in order to attend a grammar school and afterwards university—involved one danger, the danger of national assimilation. Upward social mobility and the concomitant influence of urban life, or the creation of family ties to other national groups could lead to a change of national affiliation. This phenomenon comes to light in individual cases where there are contrasts between names and the actual national and social origins of students. The data about urban centres indicate that those who moved to towns inevitably became more closely connected with German or Italian cultural influences. Some examples illustrate this: 26 of 83 German-speaking students of Ptuj definitely had Slavic names; 65 of the 198 German-speaking students of Maribor definitely had Slavic names; 58 of 153 German-speakers of Ljubljana had Slavic names. Similar instances can be found in the coastal regions. Only 381 of 584 Italian-speakers of Trieste definitely had Italian names, there were 126 people with undoubtedly Slavic and 72 with German names (some of whom were Jewish). Only 63 of 122 Italian-speakers of Gorizia had Italian names, however 40 had Slavic and 19 German names. By contrast a rural occupation (civil service, schools) could lead to a closer affiliation to the Slovenian nationality.

The last aspect to be dealt with concerns the disproportionately low share of Slovenian students in relation to the structure of population. Legally the Slovenes were in no worse a position than the other nationalities in the Habsburg Monarchy since they had the same freedom of access to the university. There was undoubtedly an institutional disadvantage, since no Slovenian university existed in Ljubljana before 1918; a similar desire of the Italians for a university in Trieste was likewise not met. Although Slovenes had weaker ties to the upper classes than to the middle and lower classes, social discrimination is only partly significant in affecting their chances of university education. The fact that most of the Slovenian students came from rural areas, and the fact that there existed numerous scholarships, weaken the argument that, on the ground of nationality alone, they had worse chances. And there was the further consideration that those who did not link upward social mobility or national interest with university attendance, mostly did not need such an education for their professional life. Society at that time— whether German, Slovene or Italian—lacked not so much the opportunity as the demand for university education.

Institut für Geschichte
Mozartgasse 3
8010 Graz
Austria

REFERENCES

1. J. Pleterski, 'Die Slovenen', *Die Habsburgermonarchie 1848–1918* iii pt.II, eds. A. Wandruszka and P. Urbanitsch (Vienna 1980), 801–838.
2. W. Höflechner, 'Zur Geschichte der Universität Graz', *Tradition und Herausforderung. 400 Jahre Universität Graz*, eds. K. Freisitzer, W. Höflechner, H. L. Holzer, W. Mantl (Graz, 1985), 3–76.
3. H. Heppner, 'Die Rolle und Bedeutung der Grazer Universität für die Studentenschaft aus Südosteuropa 1867–1914', *Wegenetz europäischen Geistes*, eds. R. G. Plaschka and K. Mack (Vienna 1983), 286–293.
4. University archives Graz, Nationale 1884–1914.
5. T. Hočevar, *The Structure of the Slovenian Economy 1848–1963* (New York 1965), 15–50 also for the following.
6. H. Heppner, 'Die Studenten aus den slowenischen Ländern an der Universität Graz 1884–1914. Die geographische Herkunft', *Südost-europa-Fallstudien*, ed. H. Haselsteiner (Graz 1990), 23–48.
7. B. Bolognese-Leuchtenmüller, *Bevölkerungsentwicklung und Berufs-struktur. Gesundheits- und Fürsorgewesen in Österreich 1750–1918* (Vienna 1978), table 12.
8. H. Heppner, 'Die nationale und soziale Herkunft der Studenten aus den slowenischen Ländern an der Universität Graz 1884–1914', *Zeitschrift des Historischen Vereins für Steiermark* lxxxii (1991), 199–212.
9. Ibid.

10. Compare V. Melik and P. Vodopivec, 'Die slowenische Intelligenz und österreichische Hochschulen', *Wegenetz europäischen Geistes* ii, eds. R. G. Plaschka and K. Mack (Vienna 1987), 134–154.

11. Brix, E., 'Die zahlenmäßige Präsenz des Deutschtums in den südslawischen Kronländern Cisleithaniens 1848–1918', *Geschichte der Deutschen im Bereich des heutigen Slowenien 1848–1941* (Wien-München 1988), 43–62.

12. U. Corsini, 'Die Italiener', *Habsburgermonarchie 1848–1918* iii pt. II eds. A. Wandruszka and P. Urbanitsch (Vienna 1980), 839–879.

English Civic Universities and the Myth of Decline

Elizabeth J. Morse

I

In his article, 'Universities and Elites in Modern Britain',[1] R.D. Anderson argues persuasively in favour of new perspectives on the recent history of higher education in the British Isles. He warns against a too-trusting acceptance of the role of universities in the formation of professional elites and advocates an end to the assumption that all university development of any note took place along what has become known as the London-Oxford-Cambridge axis. In this piece, I shall argue that these perceptions are both a cause and a symptom of certain inequalities in the English system of higher education.

Significantly, the concept of a triangular locus of power, centred on the South of England and encompassing the two ancient universities originated with the sociologist Edward Shils in the 1950s, and it has been widely adapted since then to describe apparent cultural trends in England, especially those relating to the development of higher education.[2] Anderson argues that the too-ready adoption of this model leads to a 'parochially English approach' which distorts much recent historical writing, either by encouraging historians to ascribe their discoveries about the ancient universities to the system of higher education as a whole, or by assuming that those trends in university history that were atypical of Oxford and Cambridge were, therefore, aberrant. Although Anderson notes the existence of powerful forces for assimilation at work on the peripheral universities from the time of their inception, he is more inclined to stress the separate national identity of the non-English periphery, the universities of Scotland, Ireland and Wales.

The aim of this article is to expand on Anderson's critique of English university historiography (leaving to others the discussion of other British universities) and to suggest reasons why the majority of English universities have been neglected by historians in the past. To achieve this, reasons must first be found for the civics' failure, although they were more numerous and accessible to a far greater number of students than the ancient universities of Oxford and Cambridge, to compete with the Oxbridge-based idea of a university in the public mind. Although historians delight in obscure discoveries and recondite themes, in the case of university history it appears that scholarly attention has accurately mirrored public apathy in the recent past.

The practice of twentieth-century English social history has been skewed by this neglect, especially in the area of the 'decline of Britain' debate. The theory that the elitist English universities promoted anti-business values and catered not at all to the children of businessmen was propounded by the historian Martin Wiener in 1981, at a time when the political climate in Britain made the universities exceptionally vulnerable to charges of elitism, extravagance, and social uselessness.[3] Wiener provided ample anecdotal evidence to support this contention with respect to Oxford and Cambridge, but was able to avoid the powerful contradictory example of the civic universities only by ignoring them.[4] For instance, Wiener overlooked evidence that the majority of the civic universities not only catered to the children of merchants and businessmen, as well as to those of the artisanal and lower middle class, but aimed to send their graduates back into industry, when industry could be persuaded to accept university-trained engineers, scientists and managers.[5] It is arguable that Wiener's thesis that university education gentrified its recipients out of industrial careers found widespread acceptance partly because of the void in the historiography that allowed the common reader to assume that the two ancient universities were indeed typical of the English university system as a whole.

Five years ago, virtually nothing had been published on the history of civic or provincial universities, except for commemorative histories of individual institutions, written on the occasion of a centennial or other milestone in the institution's history. The limitations of this medium were such that none was able to offer a balanced view of the civic university in its social or historical setting. Apart from one very general history of the civic universities, the only work to discuss them in historical context was Michael Sanderson's definitive history of the universities' relationship with industry, which was, and remains the most perceptive study of the civic universities' role in the higher education system.[6] Since 1986, there have been reassuring indications that the vacuum is slowly being filled: doctoral research (especially in the United States, a geographic perspective of some importance,) publications and ongoing non-commemorative research by scholars at the civic universities promise a shift in perspective away from an exclusive concentration on the ancient universities.[7] This body of work evinces an interest in the civics on the part of historians of universities, and may be evidence of stirrings of public consciousness of the importance of provincial and non-elite forms of higher education. The challenge for the historian is to argue the case for the civic universities' uniqueness and to refrain from analysing them solely as separate but unequal colleagues of the ancient universities.[8] Having done this, some arguments can be advanced as to why the civic universities have suffered these 'invidious comparisons' for so long and why they themselves were unable or unwilling to find for themselves a more positive self-image.[9]

Such has been the subordinate role of the civic universities that no agreed-upon name for them has evolved. Although the terms 'civic,' 'provincial' and 'redbrick' have been used interchangeably in the past, I have preferred the term 'civic universities' as it was the name those institutions chose for themselves and because it is the only one of the three that carries no pejorative connotation. Although even this term is imperfect (it is questionable whether the universities of Durham or London can properly be called 'civic,' for example) it has the advantage of being both contemporary and neutral.

At the turn of the twentieth century, there were five English universities—Oxford, Cambridge, London, Durham and the Victoria University, the last a loose federation composed of the university colleges of Manchester, Liverpool and Leeds. By the end of the year 1900, they were joined by the fire-new University of Birmingham, the first 'unitary' civic university, which both taught and examined for its own degrees. By 1945, the English civic universities and the University of London numbered nine in all (including the three component colleges of the old Victoria university, now the Universities of Manchester, Liverpool and Leeds,) together with six university colleges that taught for the University of London degree examinations. Together they educated over three times as many students as the ancient universities.[10] Although most still recruited more students locally than nationally, by 1947 many recruited as many as half their students from outside their immediate area. This figure suggests that the civics drew at least a portion of their students by reputation, rather than sheer convenience, although no true national market would be possible before the 1950s, when a national system of grants offered the poor student a real alternative to living at home and attending the local university.[11]

Civic universities, then, were numerous and catered to a far higher proportion of the country's undergraduates than did the ancient universities, but how influential were they? Despite a profusion of evidence that the work of individual departments had reached international calibre, less can be said about the overall quality of civic university education, especially in the areas of social life and customs. This is the case in part because the ancient universities and their graduates have hitherto exercised indisputed control of standards for excellence in universities. Oxbridge has set the standard for the ideal forms of tuition, of student life, for the relationship of arts to sciences and the proper balance in which they should be held, and finally, for the 'idea of a university' itself. This last is of critical importance for understanding the apparent decline of the civic universities in the 1930s and 1940s, and the utter neglect of their unique attributes in the formation of a plan for university expansion in the 1950s and beyond.

At the birth of the civic universities, towards the end of the nineteenth century, two ideas of a university competed for dominance in England. The civic university idea was of comparatively recent currency, although there had been calls for regional universities as early as the seventeenth century, and Oliver Cromwell had briefly lent his support to a university for the north of England. It differed from the elite idea of a university in its openness to teaching new or vocational subjects, its cheapness, which implied mass instruction rather than the labour-intensive tutorial, together with non-residence, which also cut the costs of a university education. Nineteenth-century accretions to the idea decreed that it should be non-sectarian and that it should offer some instruction to women. It was by nature urban and geared towards the needs of the residents of the great industrial towns.

This idea of a university found supporters in two of the key figures in the civic university movement, Richard Haldane and Joseph

Chamberlain. Both were liberal imperialist in their politics and may have derived their interest in improved education for the governing classes from their political views. Chamberlain was concerned with both municipal reform and the improvement of regional education and presided, as Member of Parliament for Birmingham, over the transformation of Mason College into the first wholly autonomous civic university in 1900. Haldane, whose bias was in favour of national strategies for education, was less concerned with the development of a specific region and more interested in the provision of higher technical education in the German manner. First as barrister, then as Privy Councillor, and finally as a member of Sir Henry Campbell-Bannerman's cabinet, Haldane promoted regional and technical higher education on the German model in the English civic universities whose charter campaigns he supported from his position in government, as well as in the Welsh and Irish universities.[12] City councillors supported this idea of a university (though never unanimously), partly out of civic pride, from a desire to improve local industry through technical training, and partly from a sincere regard for the benefits of higher education, even in its non-vocational forms. Central government never had a plan for the expansion of higher education in this period, preferring cautious sponsorship of local initiative at small cost to the state.

Foremost among local motivations was a desire for the prestige a university conferred on its community.[13] Michael Sanderson has described the romantic impulse behind university-building and presented the civics' much-maligned Victorian exteriors as a hymn to civic pride:

... a kind of secular religiosity, the architectural expression of family and civic pride, the ideals of learning or the belief in material progress through science.... to observe these exterior forms of the old colleges is to appreciate that they could not have been conceived by their founders totally as the product of Victorian rational economic calculation.[14]

But did the public—parents, would-be students, city councillors accept the civic universities in this spirit? It appears that, after the initial enthusiasm of the 'foundation period,' they did not. Although the universities were welcomed by local parents, eager to find a cheap non-sectarian alternative to the ancient universities, they did not attract lasting public loyalty. Reasons for this failure, which

brought the civic universities into low repute and sometimes desper-
ate financial straits in the mid-twentieth century, include their
distaste for and inept conduct of publicity, their essentially regional
loyalties which prevented them from developing a national clientèle,
their inability to create for themselves an image that would appeal to
the paying public, but most of all the existence of an older, stronger
and more captivating 'idea of a university' based firmly and immut-
ably upon the ancient foundations at Cambridge and Oxford.
Perhaps it is the aura of broken romance that clings to the civic
universities, the sense that they belong to a state of mind now fallen
from fashion, once both innovative and utterly of their time, that
makes them such a fascinating but often melancholy subject for
historical inquiry.

The traditional idea of a university, based on observation and
experience of the ancient universities' collegiate organisation, their
face-to-face relationships between tutors and undergraduates, and
their atmosphere of privilege, has been thoroughly discussed so
frequently that it is not necessary to discuss it in more detail here. In
their 1971 study of the British academic profession, A.H. Halsey and
Martin Trow anatomised that idea and, through their analysis of
contemporary attitudes, demonstrated its continuing power. There
were, they argued, six defining characteristics that constituted the
English idea of a university: antiquity, cosmopolitanism (that is,
national, rather than local student recruitment), selectivity, 'education' rather than 'training' (emphasizing liberal, rather than vocational studies), domesticity (students residing in college), and intimacy (a high ratio of staff to students.)[15]

It would be inadequate to say that seven hundred years without
competition had been sufficient to root this 'Oxbridge' idea firmly in
the English mind, for it is only since the nineteenth century that
universities have impinged much on the public consciousness. Furthermore, there existed four Scottish universities of great antiquity,
offering a form of instruction and of corporate life much closer to
that of the civic than to that of the ancient universities. In the late
nineteenth and early twentieth century, widespread anxiety about
England's ability to compete as a world power led English observers
to study the higher education systems of industrial competitors,
especially Germany and the United States, and to make recommendations for better provision for advanced technical training.[16] The
civic universities were clearly in a position to provide such training

on the highest level, so there was no practical reason why their strength in science and engineering should not dovetail nicely with the newly-perceived national needs. They did so in practice, but never in theory, for the idea of higher education in applied science found no resonances in the public mind.

Could not a wealthy and powerful nation support two ideas of a university? The civic universities did not seek to replace the ancient institutions, nor even, in the early years, to achieve the same level of prestige.[17] Rather, they viewed their role as supplementary, to supply cheaply and efficiently the demand for unadorned technical, scientific and liberal education on a regional level.[18] Yet the story of the civic universities, for all their triumphs, is a sad one, for they never escaped the ancient idea of a university. Instead, they were ineluctably drawn into habits of emulation and undue deference, falling victim to a barrage of criticism in the 1930s and 1940s, which pointed to their failure to attain an ideal to which they had never aspired and for which they were fundamentally unsuited.

Before discussing the period of apparent decline, it will be useful to look in some detail at the kind of image a newly-established civic university was trying to achieve, at the ways in which pressure to emulate the ancient universities was exerted, the resistance and eventual yielding of the civic universities to this pressure, and the ways in which the resultant mixture of ancient and modern was received by the public. An episode in the early history of the University of Bristol illustrates all of these themes.

II

The University of Bristol, founded in 1909, was the last of the civic universities to receive its charter before the First World War. It had its roots in the university extension movement of the 1870s, by which members of the ancient universities sought to bring university education to provincial cities. Bristol's early patrons included the Master of Balliol College, Oxford, Benjamin Jowett. The university itself consisted of an uneasy alliance between two rival institutions, one of which was the old university college which had evolved from the informal extension classes. It emphasized liberal and medical studies and enjoyed the support of local Liberals. The second was the Merchant Venturers' Technical College, the recent creation of the powerful Society of Merchant Venturers, supported by local Tories and devoted to the study of practical subjects, especially engineering, then rarely seen as a university subject. The amalgamation of the two colleges produced a sometimes uneasy union. Although the number of students more than doubled between 1900 and 1913, the University was one of the smaller civic universities, with 375 students in the latter year.[19] Unlike the northern universities, Bristol owed the bulk of its endowment to one family, the Wills (manufacturers of Woodbine cigarettes) who relieved it of the necessity of attracting a broad spectrum of local financial support. Its history set it apart from the older, northern universities, for it incorporated two opposing political and educational views, providing a focus for community divisions to a degree unknown by the other civic universities.

This lack of a solid base of local support may have been the cause of apparent public apathy towards the University in its early years and may help to explain the young institution's uncommon ability to get itself into trouble with its public. Civic universities did not, in general, attract a great deal of public attention, but, when the public did become aware of their affairs, it displayed a number of assumptions about the nature and dignity of universities, together with an implicit hierarchical ranking of these institutions. Existing cases of civic universities' catching the public eye, therefore, are extremely suggestive of popular ideas of what a university should be. The Bristol degree scandal offers an unparalleled case study of such an incident.

In 1912, only three years after receiving its university charter, the University of Bristol became the centre of a national scandal. It started simply enough, with the installation of Lord Haldane, the civic universities' principal spokesman in government, as university Chancellor. On such ceremonial occasions it is usual for universities to award a handful of honorary degrees to men and women of academic distinction, and civic universities had adopted this custom, bestowing degrees sparingly and with care. On this occasion, however, the University of Bristol awarded seventy honorary degrees to a wide variety of individuals, many of whom appeared to be distinguished primarily by the material support they had given to the new university.

Whose idea was this magnificent, foolhardy gesture? In his memoirs, the Bristol physicist Arthur Tyndall blamed the Vice-Chancellor, Sir Isambard Owen for the excessive number of honours.[20] It was not the first time Owen's love of pageantry had led to tasteless excess; on one memorable occasion he overrode the recommendations of the committee appointed to choose a design for university gowns, replacing its chaste selection with a garish combination of red and salmon pink, intended to evoke the colours of the Avon Gorge after rain.[21] On the other hand, the inflated degrees list may have been the work of a committee, of whose members none was willing to offend friends of the university by deleting names and which abdicated responsibility by passing the list intact to Owen.

Although it is impossible to say for certain why such an inflated number of degrees was thought necessary, the list of names offers some clues to possible motives, suggesting that a well-defined agenda lay behind its composition. Many of the honours were conferred on persons of undoubted merit: the DLitt to the popular poet Henry Newbolt and the English scholar Sir Arthur Quiller-Couch, for instance, and the LLD to a number of university vice-chancellors, to the Lord Bishop of Bristol and, *in absentia*, to the Prime Minister. It is true that a number of local city councillors, aldermen and local notables were honoured, but so were the heads of local secondary schools, together with twenty-one past and present members of the university teaching staff. The composition of the list suggests no miscalculation, but rather a plan to establish the university's place among other universities and as the centre of the educational establishment in the West of England. It may also be suggested that the university's aim was to create a past for itself, to tighten its links with other educational institutions through a web of mutual obligation, to heighten its own status through the instant creation of a distinguished academic staff, and to enrich its own history by honouring the luminaries of its past. If this was the case, the attempt failed and instead exposed the proud young institution to ridicule.[22]

Two strands of opinion within the university itself first opened up the scandal to the public scrutiny. The students were the first to protest, (before the event there had been murmurs of dissent from Convocation, the representative body of former graduates, but no vocal objections.) The first public protest was a scathing editorial in the medical students' journal:

No university in the world, of any repute, would permit such an action for a moment, and we must conclude that our authorities here wish to vie with the tenth-rate American institutions, only they have not even the privilege of paying a few pounds for their honours![23]

Students and recent graduates of the new university would have had good cause to be concerned for the reputation of their *alma mater*, for the public's acceptance of and respect for the institution determined the value of their degrees on the employment market.

Second, the honorary degrees provided the focus for a bitter dispute between the university administration and staff, the latter accusing the former of arrogance, authoritarianism and bad government. Preferring to hang together, most members of staff kept their protests muted, but one professor, Maurice Gerothwohl, published his protest in the national press and, subsequently, was hanged separately. After the sacking of Gerothwohl, questions were asked in the House of Commons and the Privy Council contemplated an investigation. The University of Oxford representative on the University Court, the constitutional body responsible for upholding Bristol's public image, called for the intervention of the Visitor, as provided in the university's charter, but the Court defeated the motion, preferring to settle its affairs internally and privately.[24]

This public display of discord, with its implications of unplumbed depths of impropriety in university administration, probably did more than the original degree scandal itself to provoke a storm of critical comment by press and public. Indeed, even at the height of the scandal, most critics of the degrees were careful to avoid singling out any individual degree-holder as unworthy of that honour. Two local newspapers, the *Western Daily Press* and the *Bristol Guardian* voiced dissatisfaction with the granting of the MA to persons of no academic distinction but approved of rewarding the university's friends. They proposed a degree of Civic Merit, which would express gratitude without debasing the degree currency.[25]

As the university derived a portion of its income from the Bristol City Council, it could be threatened with financial consequences if its reputation sank low enough to bring shame to the city. There does not seem to have been a serious threat of financial sanctions, thanks to the support of the Lord Mayor in the council, but the affair raised questions, both in the City Council and in the press about the true extent and nature of the university's local service function. Critics asked whether the ordinary Bristolian was getting value for money from a university that educated a tiny minority of the population. Why, it was asked, did foreign faces appear among the students, and was it the city's place to subsidize them?[26] In this manner, the degree scandal called into question all of the civic university's functions, raised questions about its utility and internal affairs that had no bearing on the original controversy, and demonstrated the weakness of the tie that linked the university with its parent town.

Despite the new institution's undoubted practicality, the controversy arose because the idea of a civic university had not replaced the dominant ancient idea in the public mind. A local university might be asked to respond to local needs, cater to local students, and at the same time to conform to standards of excellence and selectivity (in the honours it conferred, if not in its admissions) set by the ancient universities. At the time of the degree scandal, *The Times* published an article entitled 'New Universities and Old Truths'. Although appreciative of the new institutions' local orientation and function, it contained a warning to them to stay within the established hierarchy:

While they have refused to hamper themselves with the fetters of medieval tradition, it is nevertheless to the example of Oxford and Cambridge that the younger universities turn for lessons in the art of building the fabric of a liberal education.[27]

The affair ended in anti-climax. The Privy Council declined to conduct an inquiry. A generous gift from a local benefactor enabled the university to embark on an ambitious building programme, which had the effect of shoring up both public confidence and the university's self-esteem.[28] Shortly thereafter, the outbreak of the first world war deflected public attention from university matters. The lesson had been truly learned, however, and the University of Bristol was careful not to offend against conformity again. Public opinion had left no doubt that, while the new university might experiment with brightly-coloured gowns if it chose to do so, in matters of more importance, it would be held to an exacting standard, upheld by the ancient universities and endorsed by the general public.

In his essay on Victorian institutions' attempt to establish legitimacy by the 'invention of tradition,' David Cannadine has pointed to a trend common to all new institutions of the period. To gain legitimacy, '. . . venerable and decayed ceremonials were revived, and new institutions were clothed with all the anachronistic allure of archaic but invented spectacle.' The civic universities were part of this trend, '. . . with their deliberately anachronistic styles of architecture, their aristocratic chancellors, their antique gowns and lavish degree ceremonies. . . .'[29] The evidence of the Bristol degree scandal suggests a modification of this argument. Civic universities conformed to the strict letter of the ancient idea of a university under compulsion, and the threat of public censure quickly brought an end to their attempt to free themselves in any important way from traditional customs. The failure of the new idea of a university was foreshadowed by these early events.

III

At the end of the first world war, the civic universities found themselves in serious financial trouble, partly as a result of the loss of student fees during the war and partly as a consequence of high levels of postwar inflation. In 1921, the government grant to universities was cut from £1,500,000 to £1,200,000, a temporary economy that reflected no dissatisfaction with the universities' performance but which was felt as a blow, coming as it did on top of the financial privations of wartime. In desperation, the universities launched public appeals for funds to offset their losses, an exercise in self-help warmly applauded by the new University Grants Committee.[30] In an unprecedented attempt to commercialize its product, Bristol University placed itself in the hands of a professional publicist, who produced a remarkable pamphlet designed to spur public giving by a combined appeal to the public's aesthetic and patriotic impulses.

The most striking feature of this pamphlet is its military tone and style, reminiscent of wartime recruitment propaganda, a similarity that cannot have escaped its readers. From its title, 'The First Line of National Defence,' the reader moves to its frontispiece, an illustration featuring a busy construction site. In the foreground of this picture stands a stern-visaged young man, arms crossed, chin raised, staring purposefully out from the page. This picture is captioned: 'In the mental training, guidance and development of our youth lies the wealth of the Empire.' Facing page one is a map of the West of England, drawn in a style familiar from wartime news reports, with Bristol at the centre and, radiating out from it the trade routes to Europe, the Americas and the Empire. The war, in which the public's alliance was sought was not of conquest, then, but of trade.[31]

The text is equally forceful: 'The destiny of the Empire rests upon the action of every citizen of Great Britain to-day . . . first of all upon the action of virile youth. Brains are our First Line of National Defence.'[32] The universities were characterised as 'power stations of mind,' whose function was to train: 'the forces of character and intellect, originality and knowledge, thought and judgement, vision and action, wisdom and enterprise.'[33] The list of qualities suggests a cunning blend of the traditional academic desiderata: force of intellect, knowledge, thought and wisdom, with those of the practical man: force of character, originality, judgement, action and enterprise. The university, it is implied, will produce neither cloistered academics nor philistine men of action, but a new breed combining the best features of both.

Next, an appeal is made to the competitive spirit, first nationally, in reference to the superior funding of higher education in the United States, then locally, in reference to the rise of the port of Liverpool to a position of dominance over the older port of Bristol in the nineteenth century, and to its new ability to outstrip Bristol in the quality of its higher education. The reader, whipped to a frenzy of patriotism and local pride, is quickly reassured as to the type of institution that seeks his help. In a section entitled 'The Modern Ideal University,' the idea of a civic university, situated in the heart of a great city, oriented toward the practical and the modern, is enunciated, together with a reassurance that the modern university can combine modernity with a respectful sense of the past.[34] There follows an attempt to invest the university with the city's antiquity, praising the distinction of its buildings, 'which for spaciousness, convenience and architectural merit are held to surpass anything else of the kind in England outside Oxford and Cambridge.'[35] The pamphlet then turns to Bristol's halls of residence, advocating residential life, for the formation of 'character and culture,' and for providing the vital elements of conversation and friendship integral to the intimate atmosphere of the elite university.[36] In this fashion, the pamphlet's authors attributed the ideas of antiquity and domesticity to the new universities in an effort to bestow legitimacy on institutions which were, by their own account, neither antique, nor elite, nor offering education at the expense of training. The appeal itself was couched in the frankest possible terms: 'There are none who do not benefit, and no sum is so small that it will not be welcome.'[37] In addition, county councils were reminded that they benefited from the university, both in its capacity as an educational institution and through the work of its agricultural research station. Detailed instructions were given on how to write one's cheque or devise a bequest to the university.

It is not known how the public reacted to these uncharacteristically bold merchandizing techniques, nor how many actually saw the pamphlet. Financially, the appeal was not a success. Arthur Tyndall recalled that the university staff recoiled in horror from the crude commercialization of the appeal, the publicist's 'vulgar propaganda methods, suitable for advertising a new face cream but not a University.'[38] When the university's principal donors, the Wills family, gave £100,000 to cover post-war building expenses incurred by the building programme they had funded, to everyone's horror the advertising agency claimed a cut of the donation. The Wills brothers (regular donors to the university who would not have regarded their donation to their own project as a response to the appeal) were affronted, and the University had quickly and quietly to buy off the advertising firm, abandoning the appeal in the process.[39]

This incident, small in itself, illustrates a dilemma common to all civic universities—how to advertise when advertisement is by definition an ungentlemanly thing to do. The ironic side of the incident is that the pamphlet was in fact a fair reflection of the university's real needs. Its appeal to civic pride and competition, its use of the pre-war national efficiency rhetoric were all in the best traditions of civic university fund-raising and what Americans would call boosterism. It was not, however, the pamphlet's contents that were held to be at fault, but rather the university's recourse to advertising techniques, and, for a major educational institution, reticence in this matter spelt hard times ahead as the century unfolded. Without advertising, the university would be limited in its ability to disseminate information about its services and its needs, but with advertising it would lay itself open to charges of vulgarity. In the case of the Bristol appeal, it was the university itself, rather than the public, that recoiled from the reality of fundraising tactics. Better to trust to luck and to the eventual restoration of the full government grant, it seemed to say, than to soil one's hands by extending them, palm upward, to the public. The transatlantic observer cannot help but notice the contrast with the American universities, with their shameless self-advertisement, willingness to court public favor, and their significantly higher levels of funding.

IV

It has been suggested that the study of the new English universities, their ideals, aims and attempts to find a place among established institutions, can often be undertaken profitably by outsiders, and this has been equally true of the American universities.[40] This section will examine some English views of American higher education in the pre-1940 period, revealing on the part of the observers a very much more relaxed attitude toward the diversity and occasional follies of these institutions. In part, the observers expected mediocrity. As the evidence of the University of Bristol's honorary degree scandal indicates, the presumed low quality of the American university was a readily-available image with which to beat those English counterparts which displayed excessive entrepreneurial spirit at the expense of quality. There were, however, English observers whose study of American institutions was sufficiently objective to allow them to make balanced and perceptive comments which provide the modern historian with valuable points of comparison.

In his study of late nineteenth-century American political and social institutions, *The American Commonwealth*, James Bryce devoted a chapter to the country's universities. In common with other English observers, Bryce noted that the majority of universities were not, in fact, doing university-level work, both because of their students' inadequate preparation at secondary school level and the universities' lack of adequate teaching staff.[41] He was, however, struck by the variety of the American institutions, by the infinite capacity of any given college to grow and to attain status, and by the popular appeal of even the humblest. Contrast his tolerant, even laudatory attitude towards the weak young American institutions with the expectations of excellence for the new English universities discussed above:

They light up in many a country town what is at first only a farthing rushlight, but which, when the town swells to a city, or when endowments flow in, or when some able teacher is placed in charge, becomes a lamp of growing flame, which may finally throw its rays over the whole State in which it stands.[42]

Bryce concluded that the multiplication of small universities caused no danger to educational standards but rather that excellence was promoted by the very number of colleges and universities in the country, which multiplied the chances that one would eventually produce a scholar of distinction.

In a frontier society, unfettered by long traditions and existing models, new universities very similar in spirit and conception to the English civic universities were able to expand and flourish, with no constraints upon their growth or their potential to achieve excellence. The absence of a well-established 'idea of a university' in American society allowed for a rich growth of institutions of all types and standards, from powerful state universities to tiny denominational colleges, to which a form of natural selection applied. Colleges and universities either throve or failed according to the fortunes of their host community, their ability to attract students and staff, and the entrepreneurial abilities of those who governed them.

The ability of American universities to be all things to all men was certainly not viewed by contemporaries as an entirely desirable trait, and attracted criticism at home and abroad. In the 1930s, the American academic Abraham Flexner excoriated both the American and the English civic universities for their ready acceptance of 'non-university' subjects designed to bring them profit but little academic recognition. Writing on English vice-chancellors, Flexner noted that: 'The English scorn—and very properly—the "advertiser" and "money-raiser" who have latterly emerged in America.'[43] He did not address the problem of how to attract funding without some sort of appeal to the public and adopted an entirely anti-vocational stance towards the university curriculum, deploring the existence of even such well-respected departments as Automobile Engineering at Bristol and Brewing at Birmingham.[44] At the same time, Flexner displayed some ambivalence toward the ancient idea of a university, to which he was powerfully attracted:

In all countries, history, traditions, vested interests hamper reconstruction. Obstacles are not always bad: a rich and beautiful past may interfere with reconstruction, while at the same time offering considerable compensation.[45]

Ultimately, it seemed, Flexner would have the civic universities resign themselves to their dependence on the ancient university ideal. Despite its freedom from a monolithic, all-controlling and detailed 'idea of a university,' America did have very definite ideas about what a university should be. Overarching assumptions about the function of a university linked institutions of widely-differing quality into something like a coherent whole. In the 1920s, Edward Fiddes (historian and Registrar of the University of Manchester) returned from a visit to America and reported his impressions in a lecture. In common with all English observers, he noted the high percentage of American youth in higher education, but, like Bryce, was quick to point out the elementary nature of much of that instruction.[46] As Bryce had done, he commented on the universities' wide appeal to all social strata and on the wealth of many of these institutions. Unlike Flexner, he was not dismayed by the universities' forays into non-academic or vocational teaching, because he perceived that their unifying principle, that which made them universities in American eyes, was not the dissemination of an agreed-upon body of knowledge but rather the transformation of immigrants and aliens into Americans. As long as the university performed this function, what did it matter if liberal and vocational education jostled within its portals, or if the latter sometimes appeared to dominate the curriculum? Fiddes quoted an unnamed American critic as having said:

It [the university] is the educational power station of the land, occupying itself to a most burdensome extent with even minor forms of the education that leads to prosperous and understanding American citizenship.[47]

It may be remembered that the University of Bristol was forced for very shame to withdraw its pamphlet characterizing British universities as 'power stations of mind.' To the average American reader, however, neither the metaphor, nor the universities' mixed agenda would have seemed incongruous.

V

To the English observer and critic at home, however, the issue of what a civic university was, or ought to be, too often became enmired in comparisons between the ancient and the modern, and it was the rare inside observer who could overcome the influence of the ancient idea of a university and give a clear picture of the civic university as it was, or as its founders intended it to be.

Between the two world wars, the civic universities adopted a new course, attempting to conform, insofar as they could, to what they felt to be the essentials of the traditional idea of a university. Lack of funds inhibited them from going the whole way; I know of no civic university that seriously considered adopting the tutorial system, for instance, or offering its staff residential rooms in college. Other areas, such as antiquity, were obviously intractable, although there were rather pathetic attempts to link the universities with anything ancient in their surroundings. The area most amenable to change proved to be that of student residence, and new building projects were put in hand in the inter-war period. Bristol, for instance, expressed the intention of becoming fully residential, although this was never realized.[48] Even at the time, it must have been obvious that full residence was a quixotic dream for these underfunded institutions. Bristol, with less than one third of its students living in halls in 1928, would have had an even better chance of achieving this ambition than the big northern universities, whose proportion of students living in halls was closer to one fifth.[49] Shortly after the first world war, Bristol's Vice-Chancellor referred to the halls of residence as 'residential college[s] on the lines of similar Colleges at Oxford and Cambridge', so it is clear that university administrators viewed residence as an area in which they could and should emulate the ancient universities.[50] Whether the proposed changes were insufficient, or whether critics perceived the fatal loss of focus implicit in such slavish copying, the promise of improved provision of residence was not enough to stem the tide of criticism, both from outside and from within, that was to swamp the civic universities in the inter-war years. By the 1930s, it was obvious that the roots of the dissatisfaction lay much deeper than wrangles over student residence, for instance, would seem to imply.

In this period, economic depression and high unemployment, together with fears for the future of liberal democracy combined to create widespread dissatisfaction with the guardians of liberal culture, including the universities. Eric Ashby has traced the increasing influence of the National Union of Students in this period to the twin issues of university reform and the growth of a student political consciousness.[51] More detailed study of this period suggests that, while students at the ancient universities became involved with politics, particularly on the Left, those at the civic universities were more profoundly affected by the scarcity of jobs, especially in the teaching profession.[52] Many of these were scholarship students, whose families had made sacrifices to allow them to continue their education, on the understanding that a professional qualification would lead to improved employment prospects. Although they felt the political currents of their day, they had too much invested in a university education to accept with equanimity the risk, however slim compared with that of other workers, of unemployment.[53]

There were other, perfectly genuine causes for complaint about the quality of the universities' service to the state; Michael Sanderson has called their lack of provision for the bright working-class child '... not only ... socially unjust but also economically bizarre.'[54] Paradoxically, this very real shortcoming seems to have attracted very little contemporary attention. Instead, universities in general and civic universities in particular were made to bear the blame for what were essentially social, economic and ultimately cultural limitations of their society. The civics' real loss of prestige occured when they began to be viewed as Victorian fossils, remnants of that proud provincial culture that had flourished in the nineteenth century and then declined to pitifully low levels in the twentieth.

A multiplicity of explanations exist for the decline of provincial culture. In his history of the English provinces, Donald Read cites, among other causes, 'centralisation *upon* London as the centre of government and standardisation *from* London as the arbiter of standards.'[55] Specific causes included the rise of pressure group politics, the growth of the professions and of professional organisations, decline in provincial interest in politics, the decline of the provincial great towns, including the phenomenon of 'moving out,' in which leading families deserted the centre of town for the suburbs and the consequent disappearance of networks of important local families. There were causes linked to technical innovations, such as improved communication and faster travel, the rise of a national press, followed by the influence of radio and television. Finally, Read blames the effects of standardisation in education, including the failure of the civic universities to make a local impact.[56] The last factor is hardly just. The civic universities were caught in a trap from which they could not escape: they were, like it or not, linked into a national system by their common indebtedness to the University Grants Committee, by participation in such organizations as the National Union of Students and the Association of University Teachers, by the national and international professional activities of their staff, and later by the national recruitment of students; at the same time they still paid lip service to an ideal of local service that had lost all power to command and only served to degrade them in the public eye. Among their other national affiliations, the civic universities were forced to accept allegiance to the elite idea of a university, following the collapse of more suitable and congenial local roles.

During the second world war, much serious critical thought was given to the post-war university, and it was commonly accepted that the universities, in particular the civics, had sunk to unacceptably low depths during the previous two decades. Paradoxically, even those who wrote with appreciation of the civic universities' unique role were forced into total negation of the idea of a civic university because they would have them conform to the impossible ideals of intimacy and domesticity. At the same time, critics frequently advocated a return to local service as the civic universities' best chance of rediscovering a role.

In 1949, Sir Walter Moberly, the Oxford-educated Vice-Chancellor of the University of Manchester, published a Christian tract advocating the rebirth of the university as a counter-poise to the evils of technocracy, totalitarianism, and secularism. He praised the alchemical transforming power of universities, but lamented that this effect was limited to Oxford and Cambridge, calling the non-residential civics, 'a bargain-counter, at which certain specific articles ... are purveyed.'[57] In his judgement, the civic university student was in great need of transformation:

The 'Redbrick' universities at least cater predominantly for a clientèle which is 'suburban,' without roots and without standards; and they have too much taken their colour from their environment.[58]

Although he suggested that they might be able to join in a spiritual reformation, Moberly utterly denied the civics' ability to effect transformation solely through the influence of place. The ancient universities were expected to wield this transfiguring power over their undergraduates and there were many who claimed to have experienced it. The civic universities had never aspired to such powers, now it was clear that these were necessary for survival but, for them, tantalizingly unattainable.

Moberly did not advocate simple-minded emulation of the ancient universities, regarding such copying as snobbish and unproductive. Rather, their proper role should be to play Martha to the ancient universities' Mary, and to this end they should, 'cultivate a somewhat greater austerity' than Oxford or Cambridge.[59] Even in the post-war world, their function was to serve the needs of the local community, not to aspire to a national role. Moberly realized that there was a price to be paid for this severe dedication to local service:

Instead of spacious and stately buildings, green lawns, and the glamour of a historic tradition splendidly embodied, you have buildings frequently dingy and cramped and sometimes sordid, set in an environment of smoke and slums.[60]

It was scarcely an inviting prospect, and not one to promote competition with the ancient universities for the most promising students. It could only work if the civics confined their aspirations to the second rank.

Surprisingly, in view of his description of their domestic life, Moberly concluded that the civic universities had not succumbed to a sense of inferiority, suggesting that they might yet become flagships of local education and culture by forging tighter links with their parent towns.[61] It was a hopeless prescription for institutions which, for almost half a century, had been part of an increasingly rigid, hierarchical university system, and whose localities had little use left for them.

The most famous, most devastating and, paradoxically, the most constructive criticism of the university system as a whole appeared during the war, misleadingly entitled *Red Brick University*. Its author, the Oxford-educated Edgar Allison Peers, professor of Modern Languages at the University of Liverpool, considered the work subversive enough to prefer the anonymity of the pseudonym Bruce Truscot, a cover which was only broken at his death.[62] His programme for university reform was sweeping and brutal in its treatment of the upper- or middle-class student idler and of the idle don. Although he made cutting remarks about the ancient universities' population of 'pass men,' tutorials empty of content and lectures delivered year by year from yellowing notes, it was towards the civic universities that he directed his most detailed recommendations. The civics' career as local service institutions must end, he wrote, if they were to take their place as potentially equal members of a university system. He proposed a vastly-increased government grant with a threefold purpose: to bring most students into halls of residence, to offer more open entrance scholarships (promoting national, rather than local student recruitment) and the development of specialised subjects within the universities.[63] In other words, the civic universities would adopt two features of the traditional idea of a university, residence and cosmopolitanism, while the ancient universities joined with them in a hitherto unimagined pastime, competition.

Bruce Truscot is better-known for painting the life of the civic university in its blackest hues. His imaginary industrial city 'Drabtown' with its dreary university buildings of red brick (a medium ineluctably associated in the public mind with asylums and board schools) left a far deeper impression on his numerous readers than his constructive program for reform. Even after history had left him behind (Truscot opposed any major increase in numbers, either of universities or of students) English readers continued to savour the Truscot duality for which their culture had prepared them: Oxbridge elegance *versus* Redbrick drabness.[64] Although Truscot offered a more realistic assessment of the university problem than did Moberly, the latter recognised a reality that Truscot was prepared to ignore: the civics could never be the equals of the ancient universities because to be an English university was to be Oxbridge. The 1960s saw the working out of this dilemma.

VI

At the time of the university expansion of the 1950s and 1960s, the civic idea of a university was more deeply discredited than at any time in its history. Planners of new universities bypassed them, even though the civics themselves were undergoing a period of expansion. The new universities were deliberately sited in cathedral towns, despite the lobbying of industrial towns for universities of their own. Their settings were pastoral, and, if they were ill-served by the fashionable architects of the day, they could often count on one ancient building to sustain the desired effect. Norwich offered the new University of East Anglia a site with an eighteenth-century house whose 'warm stucco walls and . . . miniature Tom tower . . . have already a fittingly collegiate flavour.'[65] Creative course planning did away with the perceived narrowness of the single-subject degree, while the group tutorial and semi-collegiate system created instant intimacy and domesticity. The simultaneous creation of a separate tier of technological universities, with limited arts sides, such as Aston and Salford which grew out of former Colleges of Advanced Technology (CATs), ensured that the new universities' commitment to liberal education, not training, remained untarnished. Of course there were exceptions and anomalies. Warwick University, for instance, combined a cathedral town setting with an industrial one, and suffered the odium of its staff and students when its connections with industry grew too intimate. Despite such variations in the model, it is clear that the new institutions answered to the traditional idea of a university, ascribing little if any spiritual ancestry to the civic universities.

This study has attempted to demonstrate why civic universities have received less than their share of attention from historians and why interest in them has been revived mainly by scholars outside Britain. The trends discussed above give some clues as to why this has been the case and to why it is beginning to change. The nature of the historical profession itself suggests some further answers. The generation of historians described by David Cannadine in his article, 'British History: Past, Present—and Future?,' who came up to university in this period of expansion preferred, as historians do, to study historical trends with implications for the future.[66] If they knew nothing else about universities, they knew their Truscot and they had learned from him that the civics were worthy but dull.

Historians prefer continuities: Oxbridge begat the new universities, Redbrick begat nothing. Nothing except the Commonwealth universities, where the federal principle was to find its fullest expression, the ex-CATs, and the first round of polytechnics to attain university status. No inconsiderable legacy, thinks the outsider.

If historians have now decided to remedy this situation, as the recent body of historical writing suggests, and to put the civic universities back in their place as pioneers of popular, meritocratic university education in England, some caution must be exercised. Little will be accomplished if we imagine them as dingy, utilitarian utopias, in which leisure, aesthetics, friendship and the transforming power of place have been discarded as expensive, elitist frills, unnecessary beautification of the grim face of learning. To do this is to cast our lot with the elitists, to imagine that the civic universities contributed nothing to the pleasures of the mind and spirit. No one who has set foot inside a civic university could imagine such a thing, and that is where we should begin.

Center for Studies in Higher Education
University of California,
Berkeley
Ca 94720
USA

REFERENCES

1. R. D. Anderson, 'Universities and Elites in Modern Britain', *History of Universities* x (1991).
2. Edward Shils. 'British Intellectuals in the Mid-Twentieth Century,' in *The Intellectuals and the Powers and Other Essays.* (Chicago and London, 1972), 135–153.
3. Martin J. Wiener. *English Culture and the Decline of the Industrial Spirit, 1850–1980* (Cambridge 1981), 22–24.
4. Michael Sanderson. 'The English Civic Universities and the "Industrial Spirit", 1870–1914.' *Historical Research* 61 (1988), 90–104.
5. Michael Sanderson. *The Universities and British Industry 1850–1970* (London, 1972), 95–101.
6. Ibid. See also, W. H. G. Armytage. *Civic Universities: Aspects of a British Tradition* (London, 1955).

7. See for instance, Julie Sims Gibert. 'Women at the English Civic Universities: 1880–1920,' (Unpublished doctoral dissertation, University of North Carolina, Chapel Hill, 1988); Elizabeth Jean Morse. 'The Changing Idea of a University: The Universities of Bristol and Manchester, 1900–1940,' (Unpublished doctoral dissertation, University of California, Berkeley, 1990). I would like to thank Sarah Barnes of Northwestern University for sharing her research for a dissertation on the comparative histories of Northwestern and the University of Manchester. For recent published works on the civic universities, see David R. Jones, *The Origins of Civic Universities: Manchester, Leeds and Liverpool* (London, 1988), and Peter R. H. Slee, *Learning and a Liberal Education: The Study of Modern History in the Universities of Oxford, Cambridge and Manchester 1800–1914* (Manchester, 1986). Jones's book is based on his Yale University doctoral dissertation. For articles relating to the civic universities by established scholars of English culture, see Thomas William Heyck, 'The Idea of a University in Britain, 1870–1970.' *History of European Ideas* 8 (1987), 205–219, and Sheldon Rothblatt, 'Historical and Comparative Remarks on the Federal Principle in Higher Education.' *History of Education* 16 (1987), 151–180. A recent grant to the University of Birmingham extends the promise of a major scholarly history of that institution in the near future: see 'Research in Progress', below.

8. Writers inside the civic universities have had the utmost difficulty in doing this. In his study of the post-war university novel, Ian Carter coins the term 'not-Oxbridge' to describe the attitude of both Oxbridge writers to the periphery and the attitude of civic university writers towards their own institutions. Ian Carter, *Ancient Cultures of Conceit: British University Fiction in the Post-War Years* (London, 1990).

9. For further thoughts on this subject, see A. H. Halsey. 'Invidious Comparisons: Oxford and the British Universities 1914–1970,' in B. H. Harrison (ed.), *The History of the University of Oxford*, vol. 8 (forthcoming). I am grateful to Professor Halsey for letting me read his draft version of this piece.

10. University Grants Committee. *Returns from Universities and University Colleges in Receipt of Treasury Grant, Academic Year 1947–48* (London, 1949), 5.

11. Ibid. 9.

12. Eric Ashby and Mary Anderson, *Portrait of Haldane at Work on Education* (London, 1974).

13. For a fuller discussion of the varied motivations of civic university founders see Morse. *op. cit.*, 1–2.

14. Sanderson, *The Universities and British Industry*, 81.

15. A. H. Halsey and M. A. Trow, *The British Academics* (London, 1971), 67–83.

16. See C. R. Searle, *The Quest for National Efficiency* (Oxford, 1971), 75–76.
17. For the opposing point of view, see Roy Lowe. 'Structural Change in English Higher Education, 1870–1920,' in Detlef K. Müller *et al. The Rise of the Modern Educational System: Structural Change and Social Reproduction 1870–1920* (Cambridge, 1987), 164. I do agree with Lowe's companion point, that the civic universities were eager to strengthen their arts side and to avoid the stigma of providing only technical training. For further evidence of the civics' desire to become a new kind of university, see below.
18. Morse, *op.cit.*, ch.2.
19. For student numbers, see Sanderson. *The Universities and British Industry*, 96. Note that this figure excludes students in the Faculty of Medicine.
20. A. M. Tyndall, 'Sixty Years of Academic Life in Bristol,' from a slidetalk to the Forum of the S.C.R., Bristol University, March 10, 1958, p.18. University of Bristol Archives (UBA), DM219 Box 2.
21. Don Carleton, *A University for Bristol* (Bristol, 1984), 28.
22. For a complete list of the honorary degrees, see *The Nonesuch* ii (Dec. 1912), 23–4.
23. *Stethoscope* 15 (Aug. 1912), 23.
24. Carleton, 29; *Bristol Times and Mirror* 11 April, 1913, 5 in UBA DM 526; Public Record Office PC 8/760, Folder 111190, June 1913. Handwritten notes on the cover and inner cover.
25. *Western Daily Press* 10 Sept., 1912. *Bristol Guardian* 14 Sept. 1912. UBA DM 526.
26. *Bristol Guardian* 23 Nov., 1912, and *Bristol Times and Mirror* 12 Mar., 1913. UBA DM 526.
27. *The Times* 18 Oct. 1912. UBA DM 526.
28. Tyndall, 'Sixty Years', 19–20.
29. David Cannadine, 'The Context, Performance and Meaning of Ritual: The British Monarchy and the "Invention of Tradition"', c. 1820–1977,' in Eric Hobsbawm and Terence Ranger (eds) *The Invention of Tradition* (Cambridge, 1983), 138.
30. Carleton, 37, and University Grants Committee, *Report of the University Grants Committee, 3rd February 1921.* (London, 1921), 4.
31. *The First Line of National Defence* (London, nd[1921]).
32. Ibid., 1.
33. Ibid., 2.
34. Ibid., 6.
35. Ibid., 7.
36. Ibid., 12.
37. Ibid., 16–17.
38. MS note by A. M. Tyndall dated December 1949, thought to relate to the pamphlet (DM 363:23). It is ironic that Tyndall of all people should

react so violently to the publicist's tactics, as he himself enjoyed a reputation as one of the most entrepreneurial academics of his generation. His reaction in this case suggests that he had a shrewd idea of the public's likely reaction to the use of advertising techniques by an institution of higher learning. For a further discussion of Tyndall's methods for promoting physics at Bristol, see S. T. Keith, 'Scientists as Entrepreneurs: Arthur Tyndall and the Rise of Bristol Physics.' *Annals of Science* 41(1984), 335–357.

39. Tyndall, MS note.
40. For an excellent example of the comparative perspective, see Martin Trow, 'The Robbins Trap: British Attitudes and the Limits of Expansion' (University of California, Berkeley. Center for Studies in Higher Education, Occasional Paper no. 63, June 1988).
41. James Bryce, *The American Commonwealth* (2nd edn, 2 vols London and New York, 1889), ii. 545–546.
42. Ibid., 568.
43. Abraham Flexner, *Universities: American, English, German* (New York, 1930), 250.
44. Ibid., 255–256.
45. Ibid., 35.
46. Edward Fiddes, *American Universities. A lecture delivered at the University of Manchester on 16th November, 1925* (Manchester, 1926), 11–14.
47. Ibid., 32.
48. A. M. Tyndall, 'The University of Bristol' (typescript n.d.), UBA DM 363:81.
49. University Grants Committee. *Report including Returns from Universities and University Colleges in Receipt of Treasury Grant, Academic Year 1928–29* (London, 1930), 57. The comparative figures for Bristol are from Manchester and Birmingham.
50. 'Draft Memorandum for issue to L.E.A.'s etc in the West of England. Sub-Committee on Closer Relationship between the University and Western Counties', Mar. 1919, p. 2, UBA DM883. For further discussion of the use of residence to emulate the ancient universities, see Morse, ch. 3.
51. Eric Ashby and Mary Anderson, *The Rise of the Student Estate in Britain* (London, 1970), 69–70.
52. For a fuller discussion of these themes, see Morse, ch. 7. For the point that the ancient universities and London were the locations of the bulk of student political activity in the 1930s, see Brian Simon, 'The Student Movement in England and Wales During the 1930s', *History of Education* 16(1987), 189–203, 191.
53. For a survey of the extent of graduate unemployment, see *The New University*. n.s. (Dec. 1934), 11. On the comparatively privileged position of the university graduate in the job market, see Armytage, 269.
54. Sanderson, *The Universities and British Industry*, 278.

55. Donald Read, *The English Provinces c. 1760–1960: A Study in Influence* (London 1964), 207.
56. Ibid. ch. 5.
57. Walter Moberly, *The Crisis in the University* (London, 1949), 24.
58. Ibid. 25.
59. Ibid., 305.
60. Ibid., 243.
61. Ibid., 246–248.
62. For an account of the revelation of Truscot's true identity, see Peter Searby's review of Thomas Kelly, *For Advancement of Learning. The University of Liverpool 1881–1981* in *History of Universities* iv (1984), 218–20.
63. Bruce Truscot, *Red Brick University* (Harmondsworth, 1951), 54–61.
64. For his views on expansion, see Truscot, 266–73.
65. *The Times Educational Supplement* 6 Feb. 1959, 218.
66. David Cannadine, 'British History: Past, Present – and Future?' *Past and Present* no. 116 (Aug. 1987), 169–91.

Curricular and Structural Developments at the Hebrew University, 1928–1948*

Yaacov Iram

Preface

The idea of establishing a Jewish University in Palestine[1] was proposed systematically from 1882. However, the corner-stone for the Hebrew University in Jerusalem was laid in 1918, and it opened formally in 1925.

The Hebrew University played a unique role in contemporary Jewish history. It was intended to fulfil a threefold purpose: 1) to help generate Jewish national revival at the turn of the nineteenth century by providing a centre for research in Judaic studies and in the arts and sciences; 2) to respond to practical needs of an emerging Jewish community in Palestine; and 3) to make provisions of higher learning for Jewish students whose admission to universities in some European countries was restricted by a notorious *numerus clausus*.

Indeed, the higher learning enterprise of the developing Jewish community in Palestine, both the Hebrew University and the *Technikum* (renamed later as the Technion—Israel Institute of Technology in Haifa), was conceived from its inception as a responsibility of the Jewish people throughout the world. This explains some of the characteristics, the debates, and the international and sometimes conflicting influences on the development of these two institutions.

Differences of opinion focused on the relation of research to instruction and also on the relative importance of the university's roles in serving the needs of the developing Jewish community in Palestine and in alleviating the plight of many Jewish students who were denied an opportunity of higher education in some European

countries. The debates reflected different traditions in higher education in addition to ideological differences within the Jewish national
movement, namely between cultural and political Zionism.

The aim of this study is an interpretive exposition and analysis of
the influence of different higher-education traditions and the effects
of ideological, geo-political, demographic, and socio-economic developments in Palestine, and later in Israel, on curricular and
structural developments at the Hebrew University in its initial
stages.

Before we turn to discuss the development of the Hebrew University it is worthwhile to outline briefly the course of events leading to
the establishment of higher education foundations in the Arab/
Middle-East world in the later part of the nineteenth and the first
half of the twentieth centuries. This will enable us to observe both
similarities and differences between the two systems.

Higher education institutions among Arabs and Jews date back to
the Middle Ages. These were the Jewish Rabbinical Academies
(*Yeshivot*)[2] and the Islamic college-mosques (*Madrasahs*)[3] . These
institutions were devoted exclusively to the interpretation and
propagation of the religious literature, its values and way of life, and
to the training of the religious and spiritual leadership. Philosophical, natural, and practical knowledge were pursued in the Arab
world for their religious and instrumental value in special institutions outside the *Madrasah*, in institutions such as *Beit al-Hikmah*
(house of wisdom), hospitals, and libraries. However, the rise of
modern, secular, Western-type higher education in the Middle East
occurred in the later part of the nineteenth century. In its early stages
this development was in the form of professional schools of medicine, pharmacy, law and the like. The first modern-type university in
the Arab World was the Syrian Protestant College, founded in
Beirut in 1866 by American missionaries, which from 1920 became
known as the American University of Beirut.[4] The French Jesuit
Order founded in 1875 the *Université St. Joseph*, also in Beirut.[5] As
of 1859 the French government founded in Algeria professional
schools which formed together in 1909 the University of Algeria.
Although higher-education institutions were established in Egypt
throughout the nineteenth century these were professional schools.
The first university in Egypt was the private Egyptian University
founded in 1908 in Cairo.[6] In 1919 the American Protestant mission
in Egypt founded the American University of Cairo. The first

national university in the Arab world was the Syrian University founded in 1923 comprising existing professional schools. The second national university was founded in Egypt in 1925 by annexing the private Egyptian University as its faculty of arts. By 1939 eight universities existed in the Arab countries, half of them were private institutions affiliated with foreign organizations. More state universities were founded after World War Two following the independence of Arab countries in the Middle East and North Africa.[7] It is therefore right to assert that 'modern higher education was not a continuation of the old Arab-Islamic system, but an import from the West'.[8] The main models influencing modern Arab Universities were the French, the American, the British, and later the Egyptian universities.[9] Indeed, some of the most influential characteristics of Arab higher education from the mid-nineteenth century to the 1950s stemmed from foreign initiative and influence. These included instruction through a foreign language; governmental and political intervention, leading to continuous conflicts on academic freedom; teaching faculties or separate, semi-independent colleges or schools; and a utilitarian approach oriented toward degree-granting and employment. While higher education in both the Arab world and in Israel was not a continuation but a departure from their traditional patterns in structure, content and aims, nevertheless in the initial stages of the development of their modern universities they differed in almost every aspect. Thus, the Hebrew University, although initiated by individual scholars and educators, was a national endeavour employing the national language, Hebrew; it was initially a research institute and remained research-oriented throughout its development; it was a unified system and enjoyed academic independence, as will be seen in the following analysis.

The Hebrew University—Historical Background

In order to understand the development of the Hebrew University we need to review briefly the socio-historical background and major events which led to its establishment and affected the changes in its structure. Although *Yeshivot*, traditional Jewish Rabbinical Academies date back to the Middle Ages, they were devoted exclusively to the study of the *Talmud*.[10] The first proposal to establish a Jewish university in the western sense dates back to the fifteenth century. In 1466 the Jewish community in Sicily petitioned King John II to grant them rights to establish a Jewish university.[11] Another attempt to establish a 'Community House of Knowledge' was made in 1564 by Rabbi David Provencal and his physician son, Abraham Provencal of Mantua, Italy.[12] They envisioned a combination of a *Yeshiva* and a faculty of medicine and sciences. The idea of a Jewish university continued to be raised occasionally. A famous proposer of such an idea was Jean-Jacques Rousseau who thought that a Jewish university would be an essential component of a Jewish state and wrote in *Emile* (1762): 'I shall never believe that I have seriously heard the arguments of the Jews until they have a free state, schools, and universities, where they can speak and dispute without risk. Only then will we be able to know what they have to say.'[13]

However, systematic steps for the establishment of a Hebrew university in Palestine and especially in Jerusalem are linked to Jewish national revival toward the end of the nineteenth century. At this stage the initiative called for the establishment of a secular Jewish higher-education institution which would include all branches of knowledge. The initiator of this idea was Hermann Zevi Schapira, Professor of Mathematics at the University of Heidelberg.[14] During 1882–84 he published a detailed plan on higher learning in Palestine in a series of articles in a central Hebrew periodical. In these articles he dealt with issues of funding, the language of instruction (German at the beginning and later Hebrew), textbooks, and faculty. The envisioned university was to consist of three faculties: theology (for the training of teachers and enlightened Rabbis), theoretical sciences (to train mathematicians, philosophers, historians, etc.), and practical sciences (to train chemists, agriculturalists, engineers, and architects).[15] He also presented his ideas at the *Hovevei Zion* ('Lovers of Zion') conference in 1884[16] and to the First World Zionist Congress in 1897. He even expressed his willingness to resign his post at Heidelberg and to accept an appointment as lecturer at the future Hebrew University. Schapira's idea of a Jewish University in Palestine was deemed by the Jewish public and the Zionist movement as premature and unpractical. But he did not give up his dream and he signed his last article published *post mortem*: 'A prisoner of Zion whose daily prayer is the wish to teach his people, with the help of the Almighty, in the temple dedicated to science and wisdom which may be granted to us to erect.'[17]

Although Schapira's initiative did not gain the support of the public and the Zionist leadership, it nevertheless enlisted the support of young scholars and students active in the Democratic Faction within the Zionist movement. They were headed by Martin Buber, a philosopher at that time in Vienna;[18] Chaim Weizmann, a chemist from Geneva and later in Manchester[19]; and Berthold Feiwel, a journalist from Berlin.[20] They proposed that the Fifth Zionist Congress in 1901 adopt a resolution of opening a Hebrew University in Jerusalem, as part of the Zionist movement's programme of Jewish national revival and of its colonization activity in Palestine. In July 1902 Buber, Feiwel, and Weizmann published their detailed programme in a pamphlet, *Eine jüdische Hochschule*, which might be viewed as the founding document of the Hebrew University.[21] They used as a motto the words of Rabbi Yochanan Ben Zakkai, spoken to the Roman emperor, Vespasian at a time of severe crisis for the Jewish people, the siege of Jerusalem: 'Give me Jabneh and her wise men.'[22] Thereby they expressed their faith that a university in Palestine 'would promote the revival of the national language, become the focus of Jewish literary, artistic, and scientific work . . ., and be the cultural centre which will radiate his spirit in all directions.'[23] On the practical side, such a university would not only obviate the necessity of students in Palestine to go abroad for further education but also attract potential immigrants to Palestine by advancing the cultural and scientific development of its Jewish community. Therefore they argued that the establishment of a university was complementary to the political and practical actions of Jewish settlement in Palestine. Being aware that the Jewish population in Palestine at that time was only about 50,000, the authors of the pamphlet supported the argument with statistical data in order to convince their readers and the Jewish leadership that their proposal was not a utopian vision but a viable one. They devoted a special section to the justification of a Hebrew University as a response to *numerus-clausus* and other regulations which restricted the admission of Jews in universities in some European countries and also in American universities.[24] Although the authors also used ideological arguments about the contribution of Jewish studies to national revival, in order to convince the Zionist leadership, their emphasis was primarily on the practical, technological, and scientific importance of the proposed institution, for building the Jewish homeland in Palestine.

The comprehensive approach of the initiators of this proposal explains why their initiative gained permanence on the Zionist Movement's agenda and found supporters among its members both in Western and Eastern Europe as well as in the United States. It gained support also among non-Zionist Jewish intellectuals like the Anglo-Jewish scholar Dr. Israel Abrahams of Cambridge,[25] who published in 1908 a detailed proposal in the London *Jewish Chronicle* arguing that 'if a Jewish University is at all desirable, there is no more suitable centre for it than Jerusalem',[26] and that the language of instruction must be Hebrew. These two elements, Jerusalem and Hebrew, became thenceforth essential features of the proposed university.

The programme was brought before the Eleventh Zionist Congress in Vienna in 1913, which adopted a resolution to take preparatory steps to establish a Hebrew University in Jerusalem. This was the first time that the Zionist congress took practical steps by appointing a committee to solicit the support of Jewish philanthropists, and scholars throughout the world for the realization of a Hebrew University. Among the committee members were Prof. Otto Warburg of Berlin,[27] a botanist and president of the Zionist organization at that time, Baron Edmond de Rothschild and his son James de Rothschild,[28] Prof. Paul Ehrlich,[29] Prof. Edmund Landau, a mathematician of Berlin,[30] the Jewish American philanthropist, Nathan Strauss,[31] Russian Zionist leaders, and Dr. Judah Magnes of the United States who became the first chancellor of the university.[32]

The outbreak of World War I halted all preparatory steps for establishing the university. British occupation of Palestine and the 'Balfour Declaration' of November 1917, in which the British government expressed 'sympathy with Jewish Zionist aspirations' and viewed with favour 'the establishment in Palestine of a national home for the Jewish people', added a new momentum to the Jewish settlement of Palestine, and revived the plan for the establishment of the Hebrew University.[33] Indeed, in April 1918 a Zionist Commission headed by Weizmann and composed of delegates from the Allied countries came to Palestine to represent Jewish interests to the British military authorities. A few months later on July 24, 1918, while the war was still raging, the foundation-stones of the Hebrew University were laid on Mount Scopus, a site which was purchased in 1916 through the generosity of Isaac Leib Goldberg, a Russian Jewish philanthropist, and the *Hovevei Zion* Committee in Odessa.[34] Although the plans for opening the university were still in their initial phase there were immediately differences of opinion over the nature and policy of the future university. The question was whether it should be a research institute or engage primarily in instruction and training. A decision was reached to establish research institutes rather than faculties devoted mainly to teaching.[35] During the coming seven years (1918-1925) practical steps were taken towards the implementation of the idea. Three committees were formed, in London, New York and Jerusalem, each of them charged with specific responsibilities. All were co-ordinated by the Hebrew University Advisory Committee organized in London in 1920.[36] The aim of the Hebrew University Committee in London was to establish an institute of chemistry. The American Jewish Physicians' Committee,[37] organized in 1921 during the visit of Weizmann and Albert Einstein to the United States, became responsible for raising funds for the establishment of a microbiological institute as an initial unit for a future medical faculty, whereas the Jerusalem Committee organized in 1922 initiated the establishment of an institute of Jewish studies as part of a future institute for the humanities. The efforts to open the university gained further momentum because of a proposal in 1922 by the British Governor of Jerusalem, Sir Ronald Storrs,[38] to establish an English-speaking, British-controlled university in Jerusalem which was to include a Hebrew department. It was feared that an English university would compete with and even endanger the proposed opening of the Hebrew University.

After the first three institutes (chemistry, microbiology, and Jewish studies) had been established, the Hebrew University was formally opened on 1 April 1925.[39] These events which led to the formal opening of the Hebrew University are essential to understand the course of its developments and its future curricular and structural reforms.

Administration—Structural Reforms 1928–1935

The formal opening of the Hebrew University required the reorganization of its administration. During the preparatory phase the Zionist Organization alone had been responsible for planning, finance, and the appointment of academic and administrative staff through the 'Hebrew University Advisory Committee' and various sub-committees. On 12 April 1925 a provisional Board of Governors was convened by the Zionist Organization. On behalf of the Zionist organization its President, Weizmann, transferred the property of the University and all rights to the Board of Governors which was organized as a self-governing and independent body. At a meeting held in Munich on 23 September 1925, the Board of Governors was enlarged and given a juridical status. Weizmann became President of the Board and Magnes was appointed Chancellor of the University. From its outset the Board of Governors as well as other administrative bodies represented a spectrum of Jewish groups within and outside Palestine: The Zionist Organization, whose leaders had initiated the founding of the University; the Jewish community in Palestine; major Jewish communities in various countries, which were represented by prominent wealthy individuals instrumental in providing financial support to the university; and eminent Jewish scholars throughout the world, whose co-operation and advice was essential both for maintaining high academic standards and for recruiting competent scholars for the university.[40] The Board of Governors delegated in 1925 the administration of the University to an Executive Council consisting of the Chancellor, his Deputy, the Registrar and co-opted advisory members.[41]

An international Academic Council was formed to guide the Board of Governors in academic matters. It was headed in succession by Prof. Albert Einstein, Dr Chaim Weizmann and Prof. Leonard Ornstein of Utrecht University.[42] The Academic Council was composed of the Professors of the Hebrew University and scholars from many countries. Its function was to supervise the academic development of the university, and to recommend to the Board of Governors the appointment of professors.[43] Between 1925 and 1934 the real representative of the academic staff was the University Council in Jerusalem which was composed of the professors on the staff. However, it was too small to exercise real academic self-government.

While the academic model for the Hebrew University was the Humboldtian German university, as will be discussed later in this article, its organizational model was the private university in the United States. Although the Hebrew University was a public institution during its various preparatory phases, under the responsibility of the Zionist Organization, it became soon after its formal opening in April 1925 a private institution supported mainly by private donors. Therefore, the pattern of a corporation run by a president appointed by a board of governors with responsibility for the operation of the corporation was chosen as the initial form of government.[44] Indeed, in 1925 the Board of Governors appointed Dr Judah L. Magnes as the university's chancellor, but with the authority and power of an American university president, responsible for academic organization, planning, raising funds, and day-to-day administration.[45] However, Chancellor Magnes' attempt to govern the university in an autocratic fashion typical of American university presidents in the early 1920s was opposed by faculty members accustomed to the continental European tradition of academic self-government. They were supported in this opposition to Magnes' administration by eminent academic members of the Board of Governors, especially Albert Einstein, Weizmann and the British members on the Board.

Thus, the nature of the academic administration of the Hebrew University became a dominant and divisive issue during the first decade of its existence. Attention focused on the authority of the office of the Chancellor whose administrative power and influence on academic matters increased with the years, and also on his personality and qualifications. In August 1926, the Board of Governors appointed a 'Sub-Committee on Research and Instruction and Academic Administration'. It was chaired by Prof. Selig Brodetsky[46] of the University of Leeds, Dr Cyrus Adler,[47] President of the Dropsie College in Philadelphia and the Jewish Theological Seminary of America, Prof. Joseph Horowitz[48] of the University of Frankfurt am Main, and Prof. Leonard S. Ornstein of the University of Utrecht.[49]

Einstein became the chief advocate for the separation of the academic administration from the Chancellor's office and for the appointment of an Academic Head of the University who would be both an established academic and have substantial experience in university administration. In a letter to Weizmann dated May 29, 1928 Einstein stated: 'I consider the appointment of a competent Academic Head as the Alpha and Omega of any sort of development of the University. If this cannot be pushed through at this time it would be much better, I think, "to shut up shop" '[50] . Einstein considered the issue as a test case for his future association with the University and stated his position clearly in the same letter: 'As far as I am concerned it is a *conditio sine qua non* for my further continuance on the Board of Governors that an Academic Head be appointed now, and indeed at once, and that his functions be clearly defined'. In a letter to the Academic Council and the Board of Governors, Einstein specified the desired qualifications of a proposed Academic Head. Such a person would be '. . . an inventive academic and executive agent who will unite in himself expert skill and insight into the problems of a university in general and personal knowledge of the intellectual climate of the University and Palestine . . .'[51] At the same time Einstein explained what the role of the Academic Head would be:

Among the various types of organs that perform this function it seems to me, for our university as an autonomous corporation, *the English model of an academic Vice-Chancellor is best suited*; this is even more vital at this time while we, in Jerusalem, have no representative academic Senate,[52] and especially as the University is still in the process of development. I firmly emphasize that the aforementioned Academic Head must not simply be an honorary president of the faculty similar to the German Rector who serves for one year, he must rather be a working functionary of the university, appointed to serve for a long period of time, who should direct the academic expansion of the University with the consent of the University Executive in Jerusalem, and in accordance with the decision of the Board of Governors . . . He certainly should not be merely an honorary head of the University . . . On the contrary, he should be the central, responsible leading authority in the academic hierarchy of the university, appointed by the Board of Governors and responsible only to it and to the Academic Senate . . . He must be completely independent of the University administration; at the same time, it must naturally be his duty to keep an eye on its administrative affairs—with the exception of the finances.[53]

Weizmann who was at that time the head of the Zionist Organization and President of the University's Board of Governors, appreciated Magnes' value in securing financial support among his friends in America. However, as a scientist familiar with the tradition of English universities, he sympathized with Einstein's demand for an Academic Head. He was joined by the English academic members on the Board who were familiar with and were in favour of Einstein's model of the Vice-Chancellor in the British Universities.

Also, Weizmann and the majority of the Board members believed that Einstein's academic prestige made his association with the Hebrew University invaluable. Weizmann made his position known to Magnes emphasizing the need 'to find a solution which would enable him [Einstein] to remain connected with the University, a connection which . . . is to me of unrivaled importance. Should I not succeed then, my own connection with the University, as I told you last year, would also become intenable'.[54] Weizmann and members of the Board hoped to persuade Einstein to work, at least periodically, in Jerusalem, thus enhancing significantly the status of the Hebrew University and attracting competent scholars to join the new University. Moreover, Magnes' political stand on the Arab-Jewish problem (he favoured the idea of a bi-national community in Palestine, a position opposed to the official policy of the Zionist Organization), might have had also a negative effect on his personal relations with Weizmann, and harmed their co-operation on behalf of the University.[55]

Brodetsky's committee submitted its report to the joint-meeting of the Board of Governors and the Academic Council in London on 3–5 June 1928. The committee recommended two measures to make the academic management of the university more effective: 1) to appoint a small standing committee composed of members of the Academic Council that should meet often and be in constant contact with the Chancellor and the University Council; 2) to appoint an Academic Head with a distinguished career and intimate experience of university life and administration in Europe or America.[56] The debate on the proposals revealed the deep controversy over the issue of academic administration and therefore no final decision was reached except the appointment of a special committee 'to consider the academic administration of the Hebrew University and submit its report in good time for the next meeting of the Board of Governors'.[57] This decision was not implemented and the controversy continued. Einstein did resign from the Board of Governors but without making it public in order to minimize the possible damage to the university's reputation. He reduced his involvement to occasional addresses at fund-raising meetings of the Hebrew University on behalf of Jewish scholars and scientists, who were excluded from German universities by the Nazis, and were willing to resume their scientific activity at the Hebrew University.[58] He had refused an offer of a professorship at the Hebrew University 'because of longstanding differences with the University administration', but asserted, however, that he would be 'ready in principle to assume the directorship of Mathematics and Physics' at the Hebrew University once the required reforms were implemented.[59]

Einstein's persistent pressure for a reform of the academic administration and the appointment of an Academic Head resulted in an appointment of a 'Survey Committee' by the Board of Governors in October 1933. The Committee consisted of three distinguished academicians: Sir Philip Hartog, a chemist, formerly Registrar of London University and Vice-Chancellor of the University of Dacca, India;[60] Dr. Redcliffe N. Salaman, Director of the Institute of Virus Diseases at Cambridge University;[61] and Prof. Louis Ginzberg, a Talmudic Scholar of the Jewish Theological Seminary of America.[62] The Survey Committee was authorized 'to inquire generally into affairs of the Hebrew University with a view of such reforms as may be found desirable to the framing of plans for the development of the University and especially to strengthening the University by inclusion of a suitable number of teachers excluded from German universities under the present regime'.[63] The committee submitted its voluminous Report in April 1934.

Although the report was critical of almost every aspect of the University's activity its most severe and far reaching recommendations were in regard to the academic administration.[64] The report was particularly critical of the Chancellor in that he had assumed too many powers, including those of the President of the Board of Governors and of the Board itself. Thus, the Committee's constitutional recommendations proposed to increase the size and the power of the Executive Council by turning its advisory role into an executive authority, and to replace the University Council with an enlarged Senate which would 'exercise general academic control'. The Committee proposed also that the title of the Administrative Head of the University should be 'Provost with wide experience in university administration' instead of Chancellor since that title has been associated in the University with excessive authority.[65] Magnes defended his administration in a voluminous 'Reply' that he submitted to the Board of Governors by the end of July 1934.[66]

Following a series of successive board meetings which were held between May and August 1934 in New York, Zurich, London, and Jerusalem, a new Executive Council was appointed. It was composed of eleven members: four academicians elected by the Senate;

four lay Governors, residents of Palestine; a Treasurer, the chief authority in financial matters; a Technical Advisor; and the Chancellor as Chairman. The Executive Council became indeed the executive arm of the Board of Governors' in Palestine with broad authority in academic and administrative matters. Another constitutional change transformed the University Council into a Senate with jurisdiction over all academic matters. The original international Academic Council was abolished; thus the Senate became the supreme self-governing body of the faculties, departments, chairs, and institutes.

During the 1935 Board of Governors meeting,[67] the University's organizational design was changed by a constitutional amendment: the post of the Chancellor was 'suspended' and Dr Magnes became President with very little executive power; Weizmann continued heading the Board of Governors but without the title of 'President'; his title was Chairman. The Treasurer, Salman Schocken,[68] was appointed as Chairman of the Executive Council, and vested with the authority and functions formerly performed by the Chancellor. The administration of academic affairs was given to each of the extant and future faculties. Each of the extant faculties (humanities and sciences) was to elect its own dean to serve two years, and the new Senate was to elect its own chairman with the title of rector, as the Academic Head of the University. This scheme of organization was approved by the Board of Governors on 9 September 1935. Thus the Hartog Committee had led to important constitutional revisions in the academic and administrative organization of the Hebrew University. The 1935 revised constitution became a permanent feature of the University.

Out of the constitutional debates over academic administration during the first decade—1925–1935—The Hebrew University emerged as a private presidential university whose president's authority was, however, chiefly limited to fund raising. The president had some influence, but no authority, on academic matters. Thus, although the title of the head of the Hebrew University was, as of 1935, 'President', his authority and functions resembled those of a German university *Kurator*, rather than those of an American university president. Another result of the reform in academic administration of 1935 was that while the academic head of the University held the title of Rector as in Germany where this was a position of honour, the authority of the Rector at the Hebrew

University was similar to that of the British universities' Vice-Chancellor, who actively participated in the academic administration of the university. As for academic self-government, this was more comprehensive at the Hebrew University than in Germany, where the universities were under the jurisdiction of directors of higher education in the different federal states who regulated and even restricted sometimes institutional autonomy. Indeed, academic autonomy at the Hebrew University bore greater resemblance to the English than to the German system of higher education.[69]

Research and Teaching

One of the most important questions which engaged all those involved with founding or reforming universities from the mid-nineteenth century was the relationship between research and teaching and their relative importance in the universities' activities. The foundation of the University of Berlin in 1810 through the initiative of Wilhelm von Humboldt[70] had established a new type of university, one which soon became synonymous with the idea of the German University, as well as with the idea (one might say the ideal) of a university in general. Humboldt's idea of a university was based on the following principles: education through scholarship (*Bildung durch Wissenschaft*); institutional autonomy and academic freedom of its members vis-à-vis the state (*Universitäts autonomie*); the harmonious unity and universality of all sciences (*Universalität der Wissenschaft*); and the unity of research and teaching (*Einheit von Forschung und Lehre*).[71] The University of Berlin became an example not only to other German universities but also to universities in central and eastern Europe, and inspired higher education in England and France, the Graduate School in the United States,[72] and universities in Japan[73]. Albeit the admiration and emulation of the German model was rather selective. Indeed, Harold Perkin, in summarizing the implementation of the German model by its followers in different parts of the world pointed out that 'they [the Japanese] were doing much the same as the British and the Americans ... the French, the Scandinavians, the Russians, and many other bemused admirers who emulated the German style, in adapting to their own situation and needs what they took, usually mistakenly, to be the most important features of the German success story'.[74] The German model was also known to advocates of the establishment of a Hebrew University. Some of them were graduates of German and other central European universities and others were engaged in teaching and research in European higher-education institutions. No wonder that the proposed character of the future Hebrew university and particularly the question of research and teaching became a central issue to all those involved in the various stages of its planning.

Although the idea of founding a Hebrew University in Jerusalem was welcomed by the leadership of the Zionist movement, it brought to light their different conceptions of what a university is for or what it could and should be. They differed among themselves over the question whether the university should be primarily a research institute, or should focus on teaching in order to qualify its graduates for liberal-arts degrees and the professions. This question was not peculiar to the founders of the Hebrew University; it was an issue with which universities, new and old, had always struggled.[75] However, to the academic considerations were added ideological and political differences within the Zionist movement and its leadership. Throughout the debate two distinct views were evident in the Zionist movement. The first, advocated by Vladimir Ze'ev Jabotinsky, founder of the activist Zionist Revisionist Movement, demanded the building of a 'normal' university, which would include in addition to research, also instruction and training for the professions.[76] The second approach, led by Weizmann and the Zionist philosopher Ahad Ha'am, a proponent of cultural Zionism,[77] opposed Jabotinsky's plan. They stressed the primacy of research in the university and proposed the establishment of small research institutes of high standard, rather than a comprehensive university.

It is important to stress Ahad Ha'am's view because of his influence on the founders. As early as 1902 Ahad Ha'am expressed a wish 'to make Palestine a permanent and freely developing centre of our national culture, of our science and scholarship, our art and literature ... [by the] establishment of a single great school of learning or art in Palestine, or of a single Academy of language and literature'.[78] Ahad Ha'am argued that since the Hebrew University would not be able to recruit scientists in the humanities and natural sciences, it should focus on Judaic Studies in which it could attain a world-wide reputation. Ahad Ha'am's dream was to build in Jerusalem a national Hebrew academy with a library, and national museum. Here, a staff of about twenty scholars would lecture on their research, compose a Hebrew dictionary, publish scientific editions of Hebrew literature, and publish a scientific journal. Describing the cultural significance and national mission of such an academy, Ahad Ha'am concluded: 'Such an institution could even now become a source of new inspiration to the Jewish people as a whole and bring about a true revival of Judaism and Jewish culture'.[79] Sixteen years later, on 12 August 1918, following the laying of the corner-stone of the Hebrew University, Ahad Ha'am wrote to Weizmann restating his position:

We do not know what the future has in store for us, but this we know: that the brighter the prospects for the re-establishment of our national home in Palestine, the more urgent is the need for laying the spiritual foundation of that home on a corresponding scale, which can only be conceived in the form of a Hebrew University. By this I mean—and so, I am sure, do you— not a mere imitation of a European University, with Hebrew as the dominant language, but a university which, from the very beginning, will endeavour to become the true embodiment of the Hebrew spirit of old, and so shake off the mental and moral servitude to which our people has been so long subjected in the diaspora. Only so can we be justified in our ambitious hopes as to the future universal influence of the 'Teaching' that will go forth out of Zion.[80]

In this congratulatory letter Ahad Ha'am alluded to Weizmann's reference to this issue in his address during the ceremony of laying the corner-stone: 'No teaching can be fruitful nowadays unless it is strengthened by a spirit of inquiry and research; and a modern university must not only produce highly trained professional men, but give ample opportunity to those capable and ready to devote themselves to scientific research.'[81] Indeed, Weizmann opposed the establishment of a university whose main function would be the training of an 'intellectual proletariat'. For this reason he advocated the establishment of research institutes rather than teaching faculties and departments.[82] Ahad Ha'am and Weizmann shared the view that the University should engage only in fields of research in which it could excel scientifically or contribute to Jewish national revival in Palestine spiritually or materially.

Jabotinsky opposed the approach of Ahad Ha'am and Weizmann, both in principal and in practice. He was concerned with the plight of Jewish students in Europe in gaining admission to universities there. In Russian and Rumanian universities Jewish admission was limited to five per cent of the student body. Therefore he preferred instead of a research institute the establishment of a small university which would see instruction and training as its main task; it should include professional schools such as medicine, education, and public administration, and teaching faculties in the humanities, sciences and Judaica. Jabotinsky introduced his concept of the university to the eleventh Zionist Congress in Vienna in 1913 and proposed to announce the opening of the university in 1917.[83] Jabotinsky's disagreement with Weizmann over the policy of the future university was viewed by many also as a dissent over priorities: while Weizmann and Ahad Ha'am were concerned with the advancement of Jewish scholarship and cultural renaissance, Jabotinsky worried over the plight of Jewish scholars and students. He gave priority to the forthcoming needs of skilled manpower in the process of nation building.[84] This issue also reflected political differences over major issues in Zionist policy before and after World war I. It caused Jabotinsky to resign from the Zionist executive in 1921 and the forming of a Revisionist Zionist party which challenged Weizmann's leadership in the Zionist Organization and favoured a more activist policy.[85]

The views of Ahad Ha'am and Weizmann prevailed and guided university policy in its initial stages of development. Before the official opening of the Hebrew University on 1 April 1925, research institutes were established in chemistry and microbiology, along with an institute of Jewish studies. The Jewish studies institute was engaged in teaching from the beginning, but this was within a free, non-structured framework. During 1925/26, research institutes were added in Oriental studies; Palestine natural history; hygiene; and a department of mathematics bearing the name of Einstein.[86] Weizmann emphasized this research orientation in his address at the inauguration ceremonies of the university:

We have made no attempt to extemporise a pretentious replica of one of the great teaching universities of the West. We have made up our minds to . . . build up its reputation by the distinctive value of its contributions to the common stock of knowledge. We have begun with a group of institutes for advanced research in those branches of science and learning for which Palestine offers peculiarly congenial soil.[87]

It seems quite clear that both Ahad Ha'am and particularly Weizmann were familiar with the Humboldtian idea of the role of universities in advancing scholarship and contributing thereby to the intellectual and cultural progress of society. They also subscribed to its organizational implications: the replacement of teaching universities by universities characterized by non-utilitarian scholarly endeavour. Such scholarship was expected also to make a practical contribution to the society and the nation not only by the results of research but also through the spirit and methods of scholarly enquiry.[88] Ahad Ha'am and Weizmann equally accepted the distinction between the theoretical and practical components of professional education common to the German-type university. According to the Humboldtian model: 'It was to be the university's task to carry out the theoretical part of professional education. Professional practice should be learned outside the university.'[89] Thus applied science and technology were relegated to *Technische Hochschulen* and *Gewerbe Instituten*. Guided by this concept the initiators of higher education in Eretz-Israel planned simultaneously the establishment of a *Technikum* devoted to technological needs, primarily engineers and architects. This institute was finally opened in 1924 in Haifa and became known as the Technion—Israel Institute of Technology.

Both institutions emulated the German model as well because this model was best known to the initiators and the teachers recruited to teach in them. The German influence can also be seen in the intentions of the initiators of the Technion to use German as the language of instruction. The idea to make German the medium of instruction caused a controversy in 1913, delaying the opening of the Technion, and was finally abandoned in favour of Hebrew.[90]

This policy of research institutes rather than teaching departments was defended not only as academically sound, but also for practical reasons. It was maintained that the findings of the scientific research to be conducted in these institutes might assist in solving some of the practical problems of the country. It was also anticipated that the scientific institutes and the Jewish Studies Institute would function together as the cultural centre of the Jewish people. It was further pointed out that the teachers, recruited from among Jewish scholars abroad in most cases, knew little Hebrew, and that the language itself lacked a scientific terminology. It was hoped therefore that while engaged in research the teachers might master the language and also develop scientific terminology in Hebrew.[91] It should be added of course that meagre financial resources made it more practical to start with small research institutes rather than with a fully-fledged university.

However, there were persistent pressures from the *Yishuv*, the Jewish Community in Palestine, and from Jewish communities in Eastern Europe for the introduction of undergraduate instruction leading to degrees and diplomas. School teachers and graduates of the expanding high-school system in Palestine in particular requested that academic training be provided by the Hebrew University so that they would not have to go to universities abroad as in the past. As a result of such pressures the University Council representing the academic staff recommended that provision be made for systematic instruction and for conferring degrees. The university administration began to plan for the introduction of a teaching curriculum a year after the opening of the university.[92] Thus already in August 1926, Brodetsky's international 'Sub-Committee on Research and Instruction and Academic Administration' examined the issue and recommended the commencement of instruction 'without damage to research'. Teaching was to be given only in those subjects which attained high academic standards and degrees should be granted only in subjects for which a professor assisted by competent academic staff members was available. To safeguard these desiderata, the report proposed a preparatory period of two years for the humanities and five years for the sciences during which qualified teachers could be recruited and laboratories equipped, prior to opening masters' and doctoral courses. Following this decision the university formed a faculty of humanities comprising the Institutes of Jewish Studies, Oriental Studies and courses in humanities.[93] In spite of the committee's strict guidelines for the introduction of teaching the decision of the Board of Governors and the Academic Council was not unanimous. Einstein, unable to attend the meetings of the Board of Governors due to illness, and aware that 'at the centre of your discussions will surely be the problem of teaching and research at the University' wrote a letter to the Academic Council and the Board in favour of the committee's proposals: 'In spite of my initial doubt, I have become convinced that a gradual transition to teaching is not incompatible with the principles which we laid down for the development of the University'.[94] Weizmann opposed the proposal as premature. He argued that it was vital to lay foundations for high-quality research from which teaching might evolve later gradually and organically. He urged the Board 'not allow itself to be stampeded by external or internal pressure to a course for which the University is not yet ready ... The Chancellor should announce that the Board is fully conscious of the urgency of the question but is not yet ready to introduce undergraduate teaching'.[95] However, the majority of the Board members and of the Academic Council supported the recommendation whether for practical reasons (Magnes)[96] or academic considerations (Landau)[97]. Magnes also announced that the University Council in Jerusalem was in favour of the committee's recommendation to introduce teaching and planned its implementation without lowering the standards of research, sharing the view that research was a necessary and primary condition for instruction. The Board's decision was soon implemented. The University inaugurated instruction leading to the degree of 'Master of Arts' in the newly established Faculty of Humanities. A Master of Science programme was instituted in the Faculty of Sciences in 1931.[98]

An analysis of the Hebrew University's response to the demands to introduce instruction shows that it was a compromise between two schools of thought in regard to the primary role of the Institution. Thus, teaching was to take place at the level of master's degrees and doctorates but not the undergraduate bachelor's level. Students were required to specialize in one major field of study and in two minor fields. The specialization was intended to insure that the university's decision to introduce instruction and grant degrees would not be at the expense of research. Moreover, the university's goal was to equip its students with a scientific-research orientation throughout all stages of study, rather than with a general education or professional training. Evidently, in matters of the structure and content of the curriculum, the dominant influence was that of the German-university model, where research was emphasized at all levels.[99] American higher education affirmed the importance of general education at the bachelor's level, a degree not even offered at that time at the Hebrew University, and relegated specialization and research to graduate programmes.[100] In contrast, the German universities, and those European institutions which followed the

German model, prescribed a course of study of four years. Upon its completion they granted a diploma which was recognized as evidence of the mastery of specific scientific knowledge, sufficient for a professional, academic, or research career without additional formal study. Thus, German universities offered a single-degree curriculum in all disciplines. The doctorate and the advanced thesis, the *Habilitationsschrift*, were achieved through one's own work, private study, or course work, but these were not formal requirements.[101] The single-degree curriculum was adopted also by the Hebrew university, while American universities elaborated a three-tiered, formal curriculum and degree structure.[102] The Hebrew University's exclusion of technology, engineering, business administration, and all of the 'practical professions' from its programmes, as well as its academic structure and authority of the professors and their chairs, reflected again the influence of the German model of higher education rather than the American.

Controversies concerning the place of research, instruction, and training for the professions continued unabated at the Hebrew University surfacing whenever new fields of study were proposed. Typical was the controversy over the establishment of the Department of Education during the 1930s and its gaining academic recognition.[103] The deliberations preceding the introduction of educational studies reflected the dilemma of new disciplines, especially in the social sciences, anxious to gain academic respectability at the university.[104] It revealed differences between two approaches to higher education. On the one hand were the supporters of flexibility in the university curriculum, who favoured the inclusion of new fields of study and the broadening of the university's role in professional training and service to the public, in imitation of American institutions. Indeed, the supporters of the inclusion of educational studies and teacher training at the Hebrew University were persons educated in American higher-education institutions, or familiar with the American system and in favour of its adoption.[105] On the other side were those in favour of the traditional classical and scientific curriculum. The latter believed that the mission of the university should be to extend knowledge through research and scholarship and to transmit it to elite students. They were in favour of the German-type university, which excluded practical subjects and avoided professional training such as engineering, agriculture, commerce, and social work. University professional training was only acceptable for law and medicine and 'learned' professions, i.e. 'occupations with a clear disciplinary basis'.[106]

These opposing traditions in higher education collided whenever major curricular changes were suggested, such as the plans to introduce an undergraduate programme at the Hebrew University ('the Reform') during the 1940s. The arguments of those involved in the discussions over this proposal and their decisions were rooted in the different higher-education traditions, mainly that of Germany, England and the United States.[107]

Curricular Reform—Undergraduate Studies

The 1930's witnessed changing political, economic and demographic conditions in Palestine. There was large-scale Jewish immigration from Germany and central Europe which brought to the country more professionals than the small country and its economy could absorb.[108] Thus, the training of professionals was not considered an important function of the university. Moreover, any additional professionals could have made worse the poor employment situation.[109] Therefore, research was regarded not only in principle but also in practice as the main function of the University. Until 1949, the curriculum of the Hebrew University was structured around an aim of training students for research in the arts and sciences. Indeed, the Hebrew University offered only a Masters Degree requiring examinations in one major and two minor subjects and submission of a thesis on a level equivalent to a German university doctorate. In spite of its financial weakness, small size (164 students in 1924/25; 250 in 1928/29; 417 in 1934/35; and 1041 in 1939/40), and peripheral location, the University attracted a few scholars and scientists of great eminence and international reputation especially after the rise to power of Hitler in 1933.[110] Their presence gave credibility to the emphasis on research. The student population included a large percentage of young immigrants from central Europe (about 30 per cent in the late 1930s), graduates of excellent gymnasiums who had genuine interest in science and scholarship,[111] and because employment opportunities were poor, students accepted the university's research emphasis. Indeed, Ben-David was right in observing that: 'Due to this circumstance, the Hebrew University in about 1940 probably adhered to the Humboldtian idea of unity of research and teaching more than had any university anywhere in the world (including Germany) before'.[112]

Plans for the introduction of undergraduate studies at the Hebrew University were initially discussed shortly after the university assumed the role of instruction leading to master's degrees in 1928. The proponents of this major curricular reform were individuals such as Chancellor Magnes and Prof. Alexander M. Dushkin,[113] who were familiar with the tradition of American higher education, and faculty members like Prof. Leon Roth[114] and Prof. Ben-Zion Dinur,[115] who knew also the English higher-education system and were close to the educational problems in Palestine. They became also in time the main implementors of the reform. Magnes, Dushkin, Roth, Dinur and others were dissatisfied with the present state of the university that provided the best education for the serious, scholarly-oriented students while almost ignoring the rest. They were also discontented with the narrow and specialized disciplinary education of the existing curriculum which did not cater for different types of students and did not provide a general education in the humanities, sciences and Jewish culture. They believed that the university should be responsible for the education of all its students providing not only specialized disciplinary instruction but also general education. It was proposed therefore to form a Hebrew version of a liberal-arts programme, conferring a first degree with less specialization than the existing master's degree, with no requirements of independent research and with considerable components of general education.

Roth played a decisive role in the eventual introduction of undergraduate studies. While serving as Rector, the academic head of the university during 1940–43, he not only espoused the idea, but worked toward its realization. In 1943 he submitted to the Executive Council a detailed memorandum on undergraduate instruction in which he stressed the university's responsibility to care for both the general and Jewish education of its students in addition to their 'scientific specialization'. Thus, he expressed the wish 'to build the university from start', restructuring it around three levels or 'stages'. The first stage should be modelled after an American college of Arts and Sciences. It would admit everyone and provide cultural foundations of higher education. The second stage would include broad liberal arts studies with initial specialization for qualified graduates (i.e. those who had completed their bachelor's course with at least the grade 'good'.). The third stage would be aimed at specialization in a particular field.[116] Roth's idea was to adopt the American three-level degree structure of bachelor's, master's, and doctorate with certain modifications and adaptations. He was interested in particular in introducing the American bachelor of arts degree conferred after three years of study, but also in adopting the British characteristics of undergraduate studies. Thus he stressed the importance of personal development and character-formation through disciplinary study and particularly through the interaction between teacher and student, similar to the British tutorial system.[117]

The University appointed a special committee headed by Dinur which submitted its findings to the Senate and the Executive Council in 1947. In 1948 the programme was approved by the Faculty of Humanities but because of the 1948/49 War of Independence it was put into effect only in the 1949/50 academic year.[118] An analysis of the structure of the undergraduate programme shows that it was a compromise. The supporters of the 'reform' demanded that students be given at the first stage of study a general education similar to undergraduate studies in the United States, adding to it elements of Jewish culture. Their opponents believed in scientific specialization from the beginning through all the stages, similar to the German model. The adopted undergraduate programme was a synthesis of the American and German traditions and also had British features. It incorporated elements of a liberal education and scientific specialization and aimed also at character—formation of the young student. The uniqueness of this synthesis was reflected in the double structure of the undergraduate programme, with an attempt to integrate both general education and specialization. The programme was divided into two nearly equal parts: 1) 'Basic Studies'—this section included 'general education' which comprised courses in the liberal arts, Judaica, Hebrew language and literature, and foreign language and literature, and was intended for the first and second years of study; 2) 'Professional Studies'—in this section students were required to specialize in one major subject and one minor, during their second and third years of study. It was assumed that students would complete the programme toward the BA degree in three years.[119]

The intentions of the initiators of this reform became evident also in the appointment of Prof. Alexander M. Dushkin, an American–Jewish educator, to become the first Director of Undergraduate

Studies. The reasoning behind Dushkin's appointment was recounted by Nathan Rotenstreich, the associate director of the programme and later the Rector of the university: 'since the department of Undergraduate Studies had a built-in educational conception, the University wanted as its director an experienced educator. Since the direction of Undergraduate Studies was conceived ... more on the lines of American than British, let alone, European colleges, it was natural to look for an educator in the United States'.[120]

The American influence on the reform, and specifically the spirit that was expressed in the contemporary 'Report of the Harvard Committee' on 'General Education in a Free Society',[121] was evident in encouraging the supporters of the new structure of studies at the Hebrew University in the direction of a democratization of higher learning, and in the desire to impart both a liberal education and the national culture.

An explicit expression of this influence was stated by Dushkin; the first director of Undergraduate Studies:

This phenomenon of the establishment of an undergraduate school is quite a radical revolution in [the Hebrew] University thinking. For a long time the Continent served as the example of higher academic education ... It [the Hebrew University] was an institution primarily for the intellectually elite, for research, for scientific work, rather than an institution which also made possible *general education in a free society* ... It [Undergraduate Studies] is accepted not in the imitation of American models, but as an adaptation of American ideas.[122]

The introduction of undergraduate studies expanded the Hebrew University's activity. Thus, for example, the experience gained during the teaching of certain subject-areas in the 'Basic Studies' section of the undergraduate programme induced the establishment of new disciplinary departments. The reform also advanced the foundation of schools, offering professional training, within the university, a trend which coincided with the growing manpower needs of the developing economy and the expanding civil service and educational system of the newly established state of Israel.

The new BA degree made possible the admission of a steadily increasing number of students, which would not be possible had the research-oriented master's degree been the only curriculum at the

University. Indeed, the number of first-degree students grew rapidly from 1635 students in the 1948/49 academic year to 3022 in 1950/51 and to 5514 in 1954/55.[123]
The Reform had a catalytic effect on the university's continual concern for change and innovation in existing programmes both in their curricular and structural aspects. It was also instrumental in the introduction of new subjects, fields of study, and professional training, to meet the needs of its growing student population and the development of Israeli Society.

The Pinchas Churgin School of Education
Bar Ilan University
Ramat Gan 52900
Israel

REFERENCES

*This research was supported by the Schnitzer Foundation for Research on the Israeli Economy and Society.

1. The term Palestine is used throughout this article to designate the formal name of the land of Israel (Eretz Israel – in Hebrew) during the Ottman empire's rule and the British Mandate, prior to the proclaimed independence of the state of Israel on 14 May 1948.
2. *Yeshivot* – Institutions for the study of the Oral Law as expounded in the *Talmud*, its commentaries and its super-commentaries. On the history and development of the *Yeshivot* and bibliographic references, see: *Encyclopaedia Judaica* (Jerusalem, 1971), xvi. 762–73; *The Encyclopedia of the Jewish Religion*, eds. R. J. Z. Werblowsky and G. Wigoder, (New York, 1966), pp. 8–10, 409.
3. The most famous and prestigious Arab-Islamic university-mosques were al-Zaytounah in Tunis, founded in the eighth century, al-Qarawiyin in Fez Morocoo, founded in 859, and al-Azhar in Cairo, founded in 970. On the *madrasahs* and their role in the development of higher education in the Arab world, see: B. Dodge, *Muslim Education in Medieval Times* (Washington D.C., 1962). For a detailed discussion on traditional Islamic-Arab higher education, see: M. Akrawi, 'The University Tradition in the Middle East', in *The University and the Man of Tomorrow*, ed. F. Sarruf (Beirut, 1969), pp. 97–125.
4. On the American University of Beirut, see: Akrawi, 'The University Tradition'; Id., 'Changing Patterns in Higher Education in the Middle East', in [American University of Beirut], *The Liberal Arts and the*

Future of Higher Education in the Middle East (Beirut, 1979), pp. 39–67.
 5. For a comparative study of these first two universities in Beirut, see: M. A. Bashshur, 'The Role of Two Western Universities in the National Life of Lebanon and the Middle-East: A Comparative Study of the American University of Beirut and the University of Saint-Joseph', Unpublished Ph.D. dissertation (Chicago, 1964).
 6. On the development of higher education in Egypt, see: H. Erlich, *Students and University in 20th Century Egyptian Politics* (London, 1989); G. Hyde, *Education in Modern Egypt* (New York, 1983).
 7. For a detailed description of the expansion of universities in the Arab world, see: Akrawi, 'Changing Patterns', pp. 44–46.
 8. Ibid., p. 43.
 9. For a detailed discussion on the influence of foreign higher-education traditions on the university curriculum in various Arab universities, see: Ibid., pp. 50–52.
10. *Talmud* (lit. study or learning) – The interpretation and elaboration of the *Mishnah*, the Oral Law. Since the study of the *Mishnah* was pursued in two centres: Eretz Israel and Babylon, two distinct *Talmuds* emerged: the *Jerusalem Talmud* and the *Babylonian Talmud*. On their scope, content and methods of study, see: *Encyclopaedia Judaica*, xii. 93–109; xv. 750, 755–67, 772–79; *The Encyclopedia of the Jewish Religion*, pp. 373–75.
11. On the proposal and programme of the Jews of Sicily in 1466, see: M. Güdemann, *Geschichte des Erziehungswesens und der Cultur der abendländischen Juden während des Mittelalters* (Vienna, 1884), vol. 2, chap. 9. The Jews were granted the permission to establish a university to train doctors, jurists and others. But it never materialized because a few years later all Jews were expelled from Sicily. On the background for this plan, see: C. Roth, *The Jews in The Renaissance* (New York, 1959); Id., *The Jewish Contribution to Civilization* (New York, 1940); M. A. Shulvass, *The Jew in the World of the Renaissance*, trans. E. I. Kose, (Leiden, 1973).
12. David Ben Abraham Provencal was born in 1506. He served as Rabbi of Mantua, preacher and linguist. For the text of the proposal, see: S. Asaf (ed.), *Sources for the History of Education in Israel* (4 Vols. in 2; Tel-Aviv, 1930–1954), ii. 115–20. (Hebrew). The fulfilment of this programme was hindered by the growing intolerance of the Catholic Church towards Jews in the era of the Italian Counter-Reformation, see: J. R. Marcus, *The Jew in the Medieval World: A Source Book 315–1791* (Cincinnati, Ohio, 1938); Shulvass, *Jew*; Roth, *Jews in the Renaissance*; Roth, *The Jewish Contribution*. Roth rightly notes that the incentive for both proposals, namely the need for formal training, particularly in medicine, by Jews who were excluded from Christian universities, together with fears of assimilation, are similar to the

considerations which motivated the nineteenth- and twentieth-century proposals for establishing the Hebrew University.

13. J.-J. Rousseau, *Emile or On Education*, intro., trans., and notes A. Bloom (New York, 1979), p. 304.

14. Schapira, Hermann (Zevi-Hirsch) (1840–1898)—Rabbi and later Professor of Mathematics at Heidelberg University. One of the founders of *Hovevei Zion* in Odessa in 1883: see note 16 below. He was the initiator of the Jewish National Fund for the acquisition of land for Jewish settlement in Palestine, while the establishment of a Jewish University was meant to provide a spiritual basis for the Jewish people. See his collected writings in: Z. H. Schapira, *Zionist Writings* ed. B. Dinaburg (Jerusalem, 1925) (Hebrew); M. Hurwitz, 'The Father of the National Fund', in *Eretz Israel: Jubilee Volume of the Jewish National Fund* (New York, 1932); L. Jaffe, *The Life of Hermann Schapira* (Jerusalem, 1939); I. Klausner, *Soil and Spirit – Life and Deeds of Prof. Z.H. Schapira* (Jerusalem, 1966) (Hebrew).

15. *Ha'melitz* – 1882, nos. 22, 26–27, 29, 33, 37; 1884, no. 19. More on Schapira's ideas and its effects, see: J. Klausner, *Our University* (Tel-Aviv, 1932), pp. 8–12. (Hebrew).

16. *Hovevei Zion* (Lovers of Zion) – a widespread movement in the mid-19th century among the Jews in Russia and Romania advocating the return of Jews to Eretz-Israel, large scale settlement of the land, and attaining recognition of the major powers for this purpose. Joined political Zionism in 1897. *Encyclopaedia Judaica*, viii. 463.

17. *Ha'zevi* [Heb. periodical], 1898, Vol. 27; Schapira, *Zionist Writings*, 61–63.

18. Martin Buber (1878–1965) – philosopher, theologian, Zionist thinker and leader. He emphasized that Zionists should concentrate on cultural rather than political activity and expressed his views at Zionist congresses as well as in his capacity as editor of *Die Welt*, the central weekly organ of the Zionist movement. In 1938 after being expelled from Germany he was appointed as professor of Social Philosophy at the Hebrew University. For an analysis of Buber's philosophy and comprehensive bibliography, see: P. A. Schilpp and M. Friedman, (eds.), *The Philosophy of Martin Buber* (Lasalle, 1967); M. Friedman, *Martin Buber's Life and Work*, (3 vols.; New York, 1981–83).

19. Chaim Weizmann (1874–1952) – chemist, Zionist leader, President of the World Zionist Organization and later first President of the State of Israel (1948–1952). The intensity of Weizmann's continued involvement with the Hebrew University is revealed in the vast collection of his personal and official correspondence. *The Letters and Papers of Chaim Weizmann*, ed. M. Weisgal, (7 vols.; London and Jerusalem, 1968–1975). On Weizmann's attitude toward the Hebrew University, see his autobiography: *Trial and Error* (London, 1949), ch. 21.

20. Berthold Feiwel (1875–1937) – Zionist leader and poet. Associate of Herzl the founder of the Zionist movement in 1897.
21. *Eine jüdische Hochschule* (Berlin, Jüdischer Verlag, 1902).
22. Babylonian Talmud, Tractate *Gittin*, p. 56, a-b. Shortly before the destruction of the Second Temple in Jerusalem, Jabneh became a centre of Torah. The town made peace with Vespasian. After the fall of Jerusalem Jabneh became *the* religious centre with a Torah academy, and the new seat of the Jewish self-governing administration in place of destroyed Jerusalem.
23. *Eine jüdische Hochschule*, p. 22.
24. On the history of restrictions on the admission of Jews to institutions of higher learning in various countries during the 19th and 20th centuries, see: *Encyclopaedia Judaica*, xii. 1263–70.
25. Israel Abrahams (1858–1924)—Scholar of Rabbinic and Talmudic literature at Cambridge University. On his support for the establishment of the Hebrew University, see: H. Sacher, *A Hebrew University for Jerusalem*, 2nd ed. (London, 1918), p. 4. See also: A. M. Hyamson *Israel Abrahams: a Memoir* (London, 1940).
26. *Jewish Chronicle*, 28 Feb. 1908.
27. Otto Warburg (1859–1938)—The third president of the World Zionist Organization. He favoured large scale Jewish agricultural settlement in Palestine. *Encyclopaedia Judaica*, xvi. 286–88. On Warburg's role in establishing both the Technion and the Hebrew University, see: S. I. Troen, 'Israeli Universities: Higher Education and the Development of the State', paper presented at the Second International Symposium on the Role of Universities in Developing Areas, 26–29 Dec. 1989, Ben-Gurion University, Israel.
28. Baron Edmond James de Rothschild (1845–1934); James Armand de Rothschild (1878–1957) – Family of financiers and philanthropists, patrons of the arts and sciences, and contributors to Jewish causes. Baron Edmond and his son James were associated with early Jewish settlements in Eretz-Israel from the 1880s and founded in 1923 the Palestine Jewish Association (PICA) headed by James which continued settlement activity. For a detailed presentation of the Rothschilds' enterprise in Palestine, see: D. Druck, *Baron Edmond de Rothschild* (New York, 1928); I. Naiditich, *Edmond de Rothschild* (Washington, D.C., 1945); *Encyclopaedia Judaica*, xiv. 342–3; 346–7.
29. Paul Ehrlich (1854–1915) – German Jewish chemist and Nobel Prize winner for Medicine in 1908. He was active in Jewish affairs. *Encyclopaedia Judaica*, vi. 514–15.
30. Edmund Landau (1877–1938)—Professor of Mathematics at Göttingen from 1909 to his forced resignation by the Nazi regime in 1933, member of the academies of Berlin, Göttingen, Halle, Leningrad, and Rome. In 1927–28 he was a visiting Professor of Mathematics at the Hebrew University in Jerusalem and became thereafter involved in the

development of the university's Institute of Mathematics. *Encyclopaedia Judaica*, x. 1387.

31. Nathan Straus (1848–1931). American Jewish merchant and philanthropist. His lifelong interest in public health was evident in his establishing health and welfare centres in New York and in Palestine. *Encyclopaedia Judaica*, xv. 430.

32. Judah L. Magnes (1877–1948)—an American Reform Rabbi, President of the *kehillah*, the organized Jewish community in New York city 1908–1922, served also as secretary of the American Zionist Federation (1905–1908). N. Bentwich, *For Zion's Sake. A Biography of Judah L. Magnes* (Philadelphia, Pa., 1954). W. Brinner and M. Rischin (eds.), *Like All the Nations?* (New York, 1987). J. L. Magnes, *Addresses by the Chancellor of the Hebrew University* (Jerusalem, 1936). These addresses of Magnes from 1925 to 1935 depict the development and the problems of the Hebrew University. A. A. Goren, (ed.), *Dissent in Zion: From the Writings of Judah L. Magnes* (Cambridge, 1982).

33. On the background to the Balfour Declaration and its impact on Zionist activities in Palestine, see: L. J. Stein, 'The Balfour Declaration', in *History of the Land of Israel from 1880 – Israel Pocket Library Series* (Jerusalem, 1973), ch. 3; W. Laquer, *A History of Zionism* (New York, 1976), pp. 181–205.

34. Isaac Leib Goldberg (1860–1935) – Zionist leader and philanthropist in Russia. He settled in Palestine in 1919. J. Klausner, 'Before the University was Opened', in *The Hebrew University of Jerusalem 1925–1950* (Jerusalem, 1950), pp. 35–36; S. Eisenstadt, *Isaac Leib Goldberg* (Tel-Aviv, 1945) (Hebrew).

35. On the dispute over the issue of the future course of the university vis-à-vis research instruction, see: Klausner, 'Before the University was Opened', pp. 32–41; Y. Iram, 'Higher Education Traditions of Germany, England, The U.S.A. and Israel: A Historical Perspective', *Paedagogica Historica*, XXII (1982), 93–118. The issue will be discussed later in this article.

36. On the co-ordinating role of the London Advisory Committee, see: N. Bentwich, 'The Friends of the Hebrew University, 1926–1951', in *Hebrew University Garland*, ed. N. Bentwich (London, 1952), pp. 126–33.

37. The American Jewish Physicians' Committee (AJPC) was organized in 1921 to establish a Medical School. It financed the Microbiology and Chemistry Institutes of the Hebrew University. The committee was semi-autonomous because it existed and functioned before the Board of Governors was established. Klausner, 'Before the University was Opened', pp. 32–41.

38. Sir Ronald Storrs (1881–1955) was the Governor of Jerusalem (1917–26), later governor of Cyprus and Professor at Cambridge University. See his memoirs: *Orientations* (London, 1937). On the reactions to the

proposal to open a British university in Jerusalem, see: Klausner, 'Before the University was Opened', pp. 37–39.

39. The speeches and ceremonies at the inauguration of the university are recorded in: [The Hebrew University in Jerusalem], *Inauguration April 1, 1925* (Jerusalem, 1925) (Hebrew and English edition).

40. On the composition of the administrative bodies of the Hebrew University, and their functions, see: 'Organization and Administration', in *The Hebrew University Jerusalem: Its History and Development* (Jerusalem, 1942), pp. 6–8, 19–20. S. Brodetsky, 'Development of the Hebrew University', in Bentwich (ed.) *Hebrew University Garland*, pp. 118–125; Bentwich, 'The Friends of the Hebrew University, 1926–1951', pp. 126–133; B. Cherrick, 'Friends of the Hebrew University', in *The Hebrew University of Jerusalem, 1925–1950*, pp. 177–181.

41. 'Organization and Administration', in *The Hebrew University Jerusalem*; L. Kohn, 'The Hebrew University, 1925–1935', in *The Hebrew University 1925–1950*, pp. 42–9. The Hebrew University's constitution was adopted during the third annual meeting of its Board of Governors in London, 1–3 August 1926. It was in effect until 1935. Minutes of this meeting are found in the Hebrew University Archives, File 26.

42. Leonard Salomon Ornstein (1880–1941) – Dutch Zionist and physicist. Professor of mathematical and experimental physics at Utrecht University; member of the Netherlands Academy of Sciences. From 1925 to 1940 he was a member of the Board of Governors of the Hebrew University. *The Universal Jewish Encyclopedia* (New York, 1945), viii. 328; *Encyclopaedia Judaica*, xii. 1475.

43. On the Academic Council, see: Kohn, 'The Hebrew University', p. 43; *The Hebrew University Jerusalem*, p. 7.

44. J. Ben-David, 'Universities in Israel; Dilemmas of Growth, Diversification, and Administration', *Studies in Higher Education*, 11 (1986), 109.

45. Ibid. On the role of the American university president, see for example; J. Ben-David, *American Higher Education* (New York, 1972); M. D. Cohen, and J. G. March, *Leadership and Ambiguity: The American College President* (New York, 1974).

46. Selig Brodetsky (1888–1954)—Professor of Mathematics at the University of Leeds from 1920 to 1949. Fellow of the Royal Societies of Astronomy and of Aeronautics. Zionist leader, President of the Board of Deputies of British Jews (1939–1949) and President of the British Zionist Federation. In 1949 he was nominated as the second President of the Hebrew University. See: S. Brodetsky, *Memoirs, From the Ghetto to Israel* (London, 1960).

47. Cyrus Adler (1863–1940)—Professor of Semitics and Assyriology at Johns Hopkins University and the Smithsonian Institution, founder and president of the American Jewish Historical Society. President of the Dropsie College in Philadelphia since 1908 and of the Jewish

Theological Seminary of America in New York since 1915. C. Adler, *I Have Considered the Days* (Philadelphia, Pa., 1941); Id., *Lectures, Selected Papers, Addresses* (Philadelphia, Pa; 1933); H. Parzen, *Architects of Conservative Judaism* (New York, 1964), pp. 79–127.

48. Joseph Horovitz (1874–1931)—German Jewish Orientalist. A graduate of the University of Berlin. Taught Arabic at the University of Berlin from 1902, in India (1907–1914) and at the University of Frankfurt from 1914 to his death. He was a member of the Board of Trustees of the Hebrew University from its inception, and established its department of Oriental Studies. W.J. Fischel, and S. D. Goitein, *Joseph Horovitz 1874–1931* (Jerusalem, 1932); J.L. Magnes, 'In Memory of Joseph Horovitz', (in Magnes, *Addresses*, pp. 293–96.

49. See note 42 above.

50. Einstein to Weizmann in a 'personal and confidential' letter from Berlin, 29 May 1928. The letter is published as a supplement in H. Parzen, 'The Magnes-Weizmann-Einstein Controversy', *Jewish Social Studies*, 32 (1970), 201–202.

51. Letter of Einstein to the Academic Council. Berlin, 29 May 1928. Cited in Parzen, 'The Magnes . . . Controversy', p. 203.

52. The University Council, consisting of all professors of the Hebrew University and representatives of the junior staff became in 1935 the Senate.

53. Einstein's letter of 29.5.1928 to the Academic Council of the Hebrew University, in Parzen, 'The Magnes . . . Controversy', pp. 203–4.

54. Letter of Weizmann to Magnes, 8 Oct 1928, in Parzen, 'The Magnes . . . Controversy', p. 206.

55. Magnes was among the founders of *Brith-Shalom* (Heb.: Alliance for Peace) whose members were Jewish intellectuals in Palestine favouring a bi-national-Jewish-Arab community in Palestine. See: Bentwich, *For Zion's Sake*, p. 185ff.

56. Minutes of the fourth meeting of the Board of Governors in London 1928, Hebrew University Archives, File 26.

57. Ibid.

58. J. L. Magnes, *Reply to the Report of the Survey Committee of the Hebrew University of Jerusalem* (Jerusalem, 1934), p. 141. Hereafter referred to as *Magnes' Reply*.

59. *The Palestine Post*, 19 April 1933. *Jewish Chronicle*, 28 April 1933. *Magnes' Reply*, pp. 142, 149–150.

60. Sir Philip Joseph Hartog (1864–1947) was known as an authority on academic administration. He served on British Royal Commissions of Inquiry of two universities. *The Jewish Year-Book* (London, 1939). Brodetsky, *Memoirs*, pp. 195–96, 213. *Encyclopaedia Judaica*, vii. 1363–4.

61. Redcliffe Nathan Salaman (1874–1955) – In addition to his scientific work in pathology and genetics he was involved in Jewish and Zionist

affairs in England. He served also as president of the Jewish Historical Society of England. *Encyclopaedia Judaica*, xiv. 670–71; *The Jewish Year-Book* (London, 1939), p. 442.

62. Louis Ginzberg (1873–1953) – Parzen, *Architects of Conservative Judaism*, pp. 128–54.
63. *Report of the Survey Committee of the Hebrew University* (Jerusalem, 1934), p. 1. Hereafter referred to as *Report*.
64. *Report*, pp. 211–22. *Magnes' Reply*, pp. 11–23.
65. *Report*, p. 120.
66. *Magnes' Reply* (above, n. 58).
67. Minutes of the Meeting of Board of Governors, Lucerne, 8–9 Sept. 1935. Hebrew University Archives. File 26.
68. Salman Schocken (1877–1959) – publisher and philanthropist from Berlin. He was active in Zionist affairs and served as director of the Jewish National Fund. Emigrated to Palestine in 1933. From 1934 to 1945 he served as chairman of the Hebrew University Executive Council. *Encyclopaedia Judaica*, pp. 986–7.
69. Ben-David, 'Universities in Israel.'
70. There is a vast literature on Humboldt and his idea of a university. See for example: M. Cowen, (ed. and trans.), *Humanist without Portfolio: An Anthology of the Writings of Wilhelm von Humboldt* (Detroit, Mich., 1963); D. F. S. Scott, *Wilhelm von Humboldt and the Idea of a University* (Durham, 1960). For an English translation of Humboldt's programmatic memorandum, see: W. V. Humboldt, 'On the Spirit and the Organizational Framework of Intellectual Institutions in Berlin', *Minerva*, 8 (1970), 242–50.
71. This formulation is based on E. Leitner, 'On the Relationship of Idea and Reality in German Higher Education at the End of the 19th Century', in *Higher Education and Society – Historical Perspectives* (Salamanca, 1985), ii. 405–415. For a slightly different formulation, see: W.R. Muir, 'The Elusive Influence of the German Model on Higher Education in Canada', in C. Gellert, E. Leitner, and J. Schramm, (eds.), *Research and Teaching at Universities – International and Comparative Perspectives* (Frankfurt a/M, 1990), pp. 7–27.
72. J. Ben-David, *Centers of Learning: Britain, France, Germany, United States* (New York, 1977), pp. 21–24; 93–126. A. Flexner, *Universities: American, English, German* (New York, 1930).
73. J. R. Bartholomew, 'Japanese Modernization and the Imperial Universities, 1876–1920', *Journal of Asian Studies*, 37 (1978), 251–71; M. Nagai, *Higher Education in Japan* (Tokyo, 1971). The Humboldtian transformation of German higher education and its effects outside Germany is discussed comparatively by H. Perkin, 'The Historical Perspective'. in B. R. Clark, (ed.) *Perspectives on Higher Education* (Berkeley, Calif., 1984), pp. 33–41.

74. Perkin, 'The Historical Perspective', p. 41.
75. For a clear but simplified formulation of this issue, see: Flexner, *Universities*, pp. 3–36. For a more recent interpretation of the concept, see: Clark, *Perspectives*; L. Elton, 'Research and Teaching: Symbiosis or Conflict', *Higher Education* 15 (1986), 299–304; Gellert *et al. Research*, particularly Schramm's article.
76. Vladimir Ze'ev Jabotinsky (1880–1940). On Jabotinsky's views concerning the policy of the Hebrew University, see: Klausner 'Before the University was Opened'; N. Bentwich, 'Beginnings', in *The Hebrew University of Jerusalem 1925–1950*, pp. 67–70; and J. B. Schechtman, *The Vladimir Ze'ev Jabotinsky Story*, (2 vols.; New York, 1956), vol. i, ch. 10.
77. Ahad Ha'am (in Hebrew – One of the People) – Penname of Asher Ginzberg (1856–1927), an influential thinker of Jewish nationalism. He was in favour of 'Cultural Zionism', namely cultural revival, rather than 'Political Zionism'. Asher Ginzberg, *Essays, Letters, Memoirs*, trans. and ed. L. Simon, (Oxford, 1946); L. Simon, *Ahad Ha-am – Asher Ginzberg: A Biography* (New York, 1960).
78. *The Hebrew University of Jerusalem, 1925–1950*, p. 15 (cited in an extract from Ahad Ha'am's address to the Russian Zionists' Conference, 1902). Ginzberg, *Essays*, p. 97.
79. Ibid., p. 98.
80. Ibid., p. 295.
81. *Chaim Weizmann Addresses on The Hebrew University* (Jerusalem, n.d.), p. 26 (Hebrew).
82. Ibid., pp. 31–32.
83. On Jabotinsky's position, see: Klausner, Bentwich, and Schechtman (above, n. 76).
84. On Jabotinsky's continuous struggle to transform the Hebrew University into a 'school for students and not a laboratory for scholars', see: J. B. Schechtman and Y. Benari, *History of the Revisionist Movement – Volume One, 1925–1930* (Tel-Aviv, 1970), pp. 162–64.
85. On Revisionist Zionism, led by Jabotinsky, see: A. Hertzberg, 'Introduction', in A. Hertzberg, (ed.) *The Zionist Idea: A Historical Analysis and Reorder* (New York, 1959), pp. 14–100; W. A. Laquer, *A History of Zionism* (New York, 1976), pp. 338–383.
86. Kohn, 'The Hebrew University, 1925–1935', pp. 42–49.
87. *Inauguration*, p. 23.
88. Ben-David, *Centers of Learning*, pp. 97–100. S. Schwartzman, 'The Focus on Scientific Activity', in Clark, *Perspectives on Higher Education*, pp. 199–207.
89. E. Leitner, 'Scholarship and Professional Education', in Gellert *et al.*, *Research*, p. 75.
90. On the history of the Technion, see; C. Alpert, *Technion: The Story of Israel's Institute of Technology* (New York, 1982). Weizmann alluded

to the issue of the language of instruction in his inaugural address: 'But we feel in our innermost being that if this University is to express us ... it must be through the medium of Hebrew', *Inauguration*, pp. 24–5.

91. Kohn, 'The Hebrew University, 1925–1935', p. 45.
92. Magnes, *Addresses*, pp. 20–26. *The Hebrew University in Jerusalem Yearbook – 1942*, pp. 5–6.
93. Kohn, 'The Hebrew University, 1925–1935', p. 46. The deliberations about the report during the London meeting of the Board of Governors 3–5 June 1928 are found in The Hebrew University Archives; File 26.
94. Einstein in a letter to the Academic Council and the Board of Governors of the Hebrew University, Berlin, 29 May 1928 (quoted in Parzen, 'The Magnes ... Controversy', p. 202). Einstein stipulated in his letter three conditions made by the committee. These regarded the quality of research, the admission of students capable of participating in research in order to insure that 'mass production of academic degrees will be absolutely prevented', and the restriction of teaching to 'those departments which have professors and lecturers of university caliber on their staff'.
95. Minutes of the Board's meetings. The Hebrew University Archives; File 26.
96. Magnes assured that 'the instruction which the University Council at Jerusalem wished to see introduced would in no way be derogatory to research'. He also argued that it would be difficult to raise funds in the future if the University continued to be an exclusive research institution. The Hebrew University Archives; File 26.
97. On Landau, see above, n. 30. Landau defended the University's decision, based on his experience during his stay as a visiting Professor at the Hebrew University to organize its department of Mathematics.
98. The developments in degree granting by the university are recorded in *The Hebrew University Yearbooks 1928–1931*.
99. For a comparative analysis of various traditions in higher education, see: Ben-David, *Centres of Learning*. On the impact of the German higher-education tradition on the Hebrew University, see: Iram, 'Higher-Education Traditions'.
100. On the American model of higher education, see for example: J. Ben-David, *American Higher Education* (New York, 1972). The influence of the American model on the Hebrew University is discussed by Iram, 'Higher-Education Traditions'.
101. E. Ashby, 'The Future of the Nineteenth-Century Idea of the University', *Minerva*, 6 (1967), 3–17; J. Ben-David, 'The Universities and the Growth of Science in Germany and the United States', *Minerva*, 7 (1968/69), 1–35.

102. F. Rudolph, *The American College and University: A History* (New York, 1962). L. Veysey, *The Emergence of the American University* (Chicago, Ill., 1965).
103. On the discussions leading to the introduction of educational studies at the Hebrew University, see: Y. Iram, 'Higher Education in Transition – The Case of Israel – A Comparative Study', *Higher Education*, 9 (1980), 81–95.
104. On the struggle of new fields of research and of new sub-specialities of traditional disciplines to gain academic status, see: J. Ben-David, 'The Universities and the Growth of Science in Germany and the United States'; A. Oberschall, *Empirical Social Research in Germany, 1868–1914* (Paris and the Hague, 1965), pp. 1–5, 137–45; F.K. Ringer, *The Decline of the German Mandarins* (Cambridge, Mass., 1969), pp. 102–13, 227–41.
105. The supporters of educational studies were the Chancellor, Dr Magnes; the Vice-Chancellor, Prof. Max Schlessinger; Prof. J. Kliegler; and the educationalists – Dr I. B. Berkson, E. Rieger, and Dr A. M. Dushkin; all of them were associated with American Universities. For more details, see Iram, 'Higher Education Traditions'; Ben-David, 'Universities in Israel'.
106. Ben-David, *Centers of Learning*, p. 47. On the issue of professional training in universities, see; Ben-David, 'The Universities and the Growth of Science'; K. H. Jarausch, (ed.) *The Transformation of Higher Learning 1860–1930. Expansion, Diversification, Social Opening and Professionalization in England, Germany, Russia and the United States* (Stuttgart, 1983).
107. For recent discussions on the role and functions of universities from both historical and comparative perspectives, see: Gellert, *et al.*, *Research*; H. Perkin, 'History of Universities', in P. G. Altbach, (ed.), *International Higher Education—An Encyclopedia*, (2 vols., New York & London, 1991), i. 169–204.
108. On the size and characteristic of Jewish immigration to Palestine in the years 1924–31 and 1932–39, see: A. Bein, *The Return to the Soil: A History of Jewish Settlement in Israel*, I. Schen, trans. (New York, 1952), pp. 330–495; *Immigration and Settlement—Israel Pocket Library Series* (Jerusalem, 1973), pp. 27–34.
109. D. Gurevich, A. Gertz and R. Bachi, *The Jewish Population of Palestine: Immigration, Demographic Structure, and National Growth* (Jerusalem, 1944). According to Table 28 in this book about 12 per cent of the Jewish immigrants in 1932–42 belonged to liberal professions – a relatively high percentage by the standards of those years.
110. Among the scholars of international eminance at the Hebrew University were Saul Adler, Martin Buber, Ladislau Farkas, Michael Fekete, Abraham Fraenkel, Richard Koebner, Joel Racah, Yitzhak Baer, Gershom Scholem. See; *The Hebrew University Year-books, 1928–42.*

111. *The Hebrew University Year-book, 1942*, p. 74.
112. Ben-David, 'Universities in Israel', p. 109.
113. Alexander M. Dushkin (1890–1976), an educationalist. Received a Ph.D. from Columbia University in 1918. Held administrative and academic positions in education in the United States and in Palestine alternatively. See his autobiography: *Living Bridges: Memoirs of an Educator* (Jerusalem, 1975); *Jewish Education—Selected Writings*, ed. A. P. Gannes (Jerusalem, 1980).
114. Leon Chaim Yehuda Roth (1896–1963)—Professor of Philosophy at Manchester University (1923–27), at the Hebrew University (1928–1953), Rector of the Hebrew University (1940–43) and Dean of its Faculty of Humanities (1949–51), a graduate of Oxford and Fellow of the British Academy.
115. Ben-Zion Dinur (Dinaburg) (1884–1972) – Professor of Jewish history, Principal of the Hebrew Teacher College in Jerusalem, member of Israel's first *Knesset* (Parliament) and Minister of Education and Culture from 1951 to 1955.
116. Ch. Y. Roth, 'Revising the structure of studies in the university' – memorandum to the Executive Council of the University, May 1943 (Hebrew). It was published later in his book of addresses: *Higher Learning and Contemporary Education* (Hebrew) (Tel-Aviv, 1944), pp. 111–21.
117. On these characteristics of British higher education, see: Ben-David, *Centers of Learning*; id., *American Higher Education*; Ashby, 'Future of the University'; C. Gellert, 'Academic Inquiry and Advanced Training', in Gellert *et al.*, *Research*, pp. 28–64.
118. 'Curriculum for undergraduate degrees in the Faculty of Humanities'. 17 February 1948. Hebrew University Archives, Dushkin Files. (mimeograph, Hebrew).
119. Ibid., and *The Hebrew University Year-books 1949/50 – 1950/51*.
120. N. Rotenstreich, 'Professor Dushkin and the Undergraduate Studies at The Hebrew University', *Jewish Education*, 41 (1971), 99.
121. *General Education in a Free Society* (Cambridge, Mass., 1945).
122. 'Statement by Dr. Alexander M. Dushkin at Press Conference', 28 March 1949. Dushkin Files, Hebrew University Archives (mimeograph).
123. Anon., 'Students', in *The Hebrew University 1925–1950*, pp. 79–83; [Council for Higher Education], *Higher Education in Israel—Statistical Abstracts 1983/84* (Jerusalem, 1985), p. 2.

Research in Progress

Higher Education and Society, 1880–1980: The Leverhulme Trust Project at the University of Birmingham

E.W. Ives

By any standard, the expansion in English higher education at the start of the twentieth century was unprecedented. Where previously only London and a small collegiate venture at Durham had challenged the centuries-old dominance of Oxford and Cambridge, in less than a decade the country became possessed of six new universities, each of them in a great provincial city.[1] Furthermore, since the 1914–18 war and the ensuing recession put the brake on creating independent universities, the original civics were left to dominate the non-collegiate sector of higher education until well after the Second World War. Even now the historic civics accept one in six of all university students studying in England.

Given the part which these universities have played in the history of British universities and, by extension, their contribution to the impact of higher education on English society overall, the research which has been devoted to them has been piecemeal and limited in quantity. The University of Birmingham has, therefore, secured major support from the Leverhulme Trust for a research project into the overall role of the civic university in higher education and society in the period 1880 to 1980, which will be based on its own archive. Work began in July 1991, for four years in the first instance.

The venture obviously has a local relevance, given that the University will celebrate the centenary of its charter in the year 2000. On the other hand, the project is in no way conceived of as domestic hagiography, unlike the official history of 1947, or as popular reminiscence, in the style of *Mirror to a Mermaid* published in 1975.[2] The impending centenary is an opportunity to arouse interest and support for an investigation into the past of the University of Birmingham, which is neatly congruent with the conclusion that if the historical connection between higher education and society is to be explored successfully, then the appropriate method is a case study of a specific institution.

At one level, opting for case-study is a surrender to the realities of the data and the extreme difficulty in conducting a comparative study of several institutions that has any hope of being at all comprehensive. Every university has its own idiosyncratic systems and ambiences, and the documents it produces follow in kind. Universities also differ in the way records are handled and kept, while the level of cataloguing and arrangement is very variable— indeed, a comprehensive list of the Birmingham archive was only completed in 1990 as a necessary preliminary to the *Higher Education and Society* Project.[3]

However, more important in producing the decision for case-study than such technical constraints is the recognition that a project of this kind ought to adopt a holistic approach. A university is an organism and can only fully be understood as such. The familiar categorisations—academic, administrative, estate, curriculum, teaching, research and the rest—are functional, not fundamental; parts cannot be understood in isolation from the whole. The holistic emphasis is especially necessary given the danger in the 'issue-centred' approach so often adopted—by historians of university history as much as any other—in an effort to produce results. 'Source-mining'—the pursuit of specific questions in order to discover 'significant' answers—all too often sacrifices the original significances to the anachronistic priorities of later historians and achieves apparent clarity by suppressing lateral considerations.

The adoption of a holistic approach is, it is true, not without problems. It is unlikely to be wholly achievable in practice, and from time to time the project will have to have recourse to the alternative of analysis by topics. This will certainly be necessary if concentration on a single institution is not to inhibit the drawing of wider conclusions. For generalisation to be possible, other civics will have to be used as controls, and the practicalities of this dictate that comparative testing will have to be on a topic basis. However this does not mean that holism ought to have been rejected in favour of an approach by topics overall. Though certainly more manageable and possibly suited to the study of other institutions, in the case of a tightly integrated civic such as Birmingham, the topic method would encourage myopia—too much concern with the individual tree and too little attention to its place in the wood.

Though detailed articles may appear from time to time during the project, the decision for the holistic approach carries with it an implication about the form in which the final research will be published. This will be as a single text, not as a series of monographs, and will attempt to give an overall and sequential picture of civic university development, as at Birmingham. There may well be more than one volume and it is possible that a chronological subdivision will be necessary—for example to 1914, covering the origins and the problems of the foundation, 1914–63, the years of constraint, and finally the Robbins expansion from 1963 and its aftermath, or alternatively divisions to 1900, from 1900 to 1945 and since 1945. But none of that is by any means settled and a number of concerns would certainly cut across either division, notably how to handle the story of the University's research. With the project not due to be completed until June 1995 and with publication lying beyond that, a good deal of thinking and rethinking is to be expected.[4]

Basing a study of the civic university on the example of the University of Birmingham has a particular appropriateness in that Birmingham was the earliest of them and appears to have been something of a catalyst. Like the other civics, it had its roots in the nineteenth-century move to set up colleges in major towns to disseminate higher education locally—in Birmingham's case, a medical school, opened in 1828, and the Mason Science College (later Mason University College), founded in 1880 by a successful local industrialist and philanthropist, Sir Josiah Mason.[5] What made Birmingham distinct, however, was its decision in 1899 to petition for a royal charter and so become the first independent degree-awarding civic university.

Birmingham's decision to go for independence may turn out to have been the move which effectively settled for six decades one of the enduring issues which face higher education: 'Is a university a mechanism for awarding degrees, or is it a community of scholars?' The University College at Manchester, which as Owen's College antedated Mason by thirty years, had achieved its access to degrees by joining with colleges in Liverpool and Leeds in 1880 to set up the 'Victoria University' on a federal basis. A strong body of local opinion urged that Birmingham should enter the consortium also, or, perhaps, co-operate with university colleges at Nottingham and Bristol to set up a new federation.

One argument was the saving of cost, but a powerful group of Mason College professors in science and medicine were clearly driven by a preference for a minimalist university, a shell without access to funds, with no independent authority and no role in teaching, which would leave them to run things as they wished. They had no love for the alternative of becoming part of and directly accountable to a university which held real power and, in addition, was answerable to the local community. But the broader concept carried the day; Birmingham's charter was drawn accordingly, and from that point the mechanistic alternative seems to have withered—at least until the advent of the CNAA, CAT and the latest White Paper. Manchester and Liverpool became full universities in their own right in 1903 and Leeds in 1904, while Sheffield followed in 1905, and Bristol in 1909.

The reason why Birmingham, a relative late-comer, took the initiative in this way was undoubtedly the involvement from 1881 in the city's educational scene, of Joseph Chamberlain, politician and cabinet minister and erstwhile reforming mayor of Birmingham. By 1893 he had caught the vision of an independent university and he had the clout to raise the money locally and the influence with government and the privy council to get a charter in the terms he wanted. It is certainly one of the advantages of the *Higher Education and Society* project in discussing what seems to be the vital breakthrough in the battle over the nature of a university, that the Chamberlain papers are housed in the University Library and can augment the copious material from local repositories and the University's own archive.

The project at Birmingham has a management forum which represents a wide spectrum of the interest which has been aroused. It includes historians from a variety of backgrounds and with a variety of skills (with Dr. Leonard Schwarz responsible for the computerisation which plays a major part in the programme), educationalists, geographers, medics, librarians and the University Archivist, Miss C. L. Penney. The directors of the project are Dr. Roy Lowe and

Professor E. W. Ives, and the leader of the research team is Dr. Diana Drummond.[6] Dr. Lowe's role as editor of *History of Education* and a member of the executive of ISCHE provides the links with scholars outside Birmingham. The University of Birmingham archive is a substantial one. It consists of sixteen library bays of bound material, 32,000 boxed documents and 70,000 student records, plus a hundred and more volumes of the official minutes of committees back to 1880 and a vast collection of plans and drawings covering estates and buildings. Such size and richness certainly undergirds the project, but it also presented an initial problem of some magnitude. Little progress was possible until the bulk, variety and articulation of the collection had been elucidated and made accessible. The first task, therefore, was to produce an archival topography. This sets out the contents of, and establishes the relationships between the thirty-three archive classes, and proved to be so substantial an undertaking that in order to facilitate subsequent use, a customised file/disc system in MSDOS is being developed.

Of the material itself, the most valuable is the record card, containing the personal and educational details of each student which was raised at initial registration and added to during his or her subsequent university career. This record class thus contains the raw material from which to make a comprehensive analysis of the student body both at specific points in time and also as it changed through the century. This analysis can include examination of the local origin of students, school background, gender, social class, discipline chosen, and sometimes post-university career. In order to make such analysis possible, the project provides for these student records to be entered on computer using a specially adapted software program. Analysis waits on the completion of this data entry which is consequently identified as the principal goal of the first year of the project.

Computerising a record class of this size inevitably raises problems of method. Tests established that it would not, on economic grounds, be possible in the case of every student to put on disc the number of fields necessary to allow for the manipulations which are proposed; complete coverage was only possible at minimum input. It was decided, therefore, to retain the range of the data entered but to restrict the cohort computerised. As a result, all records will be computerised for students who registered in the early years of the university when total numbers remain manageable, but thereafter coverage will be selective, according to a standard sampling technique.[7]

Concurrent with the process of data entry, the project has moved on a second of its objectives, the taking of oral evidence. A member of staff with expertise in oral history has been recruited and a significant number of interviews already completed; after use, it is intended that these will become part of the University archive. One complication which has arisen with this aspect of the project has been its success. Even a limited request for help produced far more possible interviewees than was anticipated or could be handled, and with, not surprisingly, an uneven spread between students, academics and administrative staff, with the weighting towards the last. The project is, therefore, having to introduce a two stage procedure, with a written questionnaire to reach a wider and more representative audience, particularly alumni, which can then be followed up by direct interviews on a selective basis.

While the data entry and the collection of oral material are proceeding, a systematic study of the archives has been begun. Among the themes which are beginning to emerge, are many which have been already identified in related projects in other institutions. Scholars, particularly in Glasgow and Aberdeen, have been notably generous with advice, experience and assistance, and there are clearly excellent prospects for comparative work in a number of areas. One such is the motivation behind the founding of a particular university and its relation with the local community. Birmingham certainly was established as the educational equivalent of the City's water supply, a facility which was essential in order to support the economy and the population of the City and the West Midlands. When and how did this transmute into an institution of national and international relevance?

Another obvious area for comparative work is the development of teaching and curricula. Here the University of Birmingham possesses a collection of regulations, syllabi, examination papers etc. which is extensive and effectively complete. An overall study of this is clearly impracticable and the plan of the project is to concentrate detailed investigation on selected disciplines. Student life is a further issue of general reference. The Birmingham archives include material for its Guild of Students back, without a break, to the Mason College of 1880.

Along with comparison goes contrast. In university government, Birmingham seems to have been distinctive in operating, from a date and for reasons which have yet to be explored, a bifurcated administrative structure.[8] The registrar and the secretary were each supreme in his own realm with staffs which were distinct and which served and serviced separate areas of activity. It may, indeed, not be too misleading to talk of trifurcation, for the independent initiative exercised by the estates officer was considerable. As for academic management where the story at each university is certain to be different, the position in Birmingham is so far opaque. Folklore tells of a golden age of Faculty autonomy but in the early days it was the Senate which was effectively the deciding body and oral evidence already collected suggests that at least in the post-War expansion it was Deans rather than the Boards of their Faculties which took decisions.

Birmingham is certainly distinctive in another respect, as the first English university to be campus-built on a green-field site. The twenty-five acres donated in 1900 in Edgbaston, three miles from the City Centre, have now become 170, with a further 105 for student residences. The buildings of the Edgbaston campus are a physical archive of the development of English university architecture in the twentieth century—from the walled academic city of the original plan, and its modified execution in archetypal redbrick, Byzantine style, to the post-Robbins high-rise and non-humane concrete and glass.

The growth of the campus also chronicles the elaboration and sophistication of British university education and, as well, exemplifies the particular character of Birmingham—what other university built a Great Hall in preference to laboratories for organic chemistry?[9] Then there is the story of the creation of a campus community—with the gains, and with the losses which followed from a weakening of contact with the community outside. Particular attention here attaches to the fifty-five year long division of the University, between engineering on the Edgbaston campus, later joined by science and the faculty of medicine, and the remainder of the university left in the heart of the City in the decaying late-Victorian buildings of Mason College.[10] For many students and staff there were two universities, and very rarely did the twain meet.

A particular concern of the project is to follow the development of the University as a producer of research. Research had been a major objective of Chamberlain and his co-founders from the very beginning, but the story of how the base for it was built up and how it was funded has yet to be told. There is also the challenge to assess what it achieved. The historic 'firsts' are easy to document, whether the synthesising of vitamins, the magnetron which made microwave radar possible or the theoretical physics which demonstrated the feasibility of an atomic bomb and the work in chemistry which helped to make it a reality.[11] But whether these were merely triangulation points on a consistently high plateau or whether they were peaks standing alone, remains to be seen—and also the reason for whichever turns out to have been the case. Then, too, there is the university's designated role as the generator of technical advance for West Midland industry. Does Joseph Chamberlain sleep in his grave satisfied?

Over and beyond these, the immediate issues which the project is coming or has plans to come to grips with, there are the successively broadening dimensions of the original consideration which provoked it—the relationship between the history of British society in the century before Mrs Thatcher and the development of higher education as exemplified by the civic universities. Attempts at such general assessment lie, of course, some way in the future, at the point where research moves into publication, but already possibilities are beginning to emerge.

At one level the issue is professionalisation. Even a small example makes the point. The University war memorials carry the names of scores of former students. They died like other men, did they serve like them? At another level the issue is social mobility. Was the most significant development at Birmingham the opening of its first purpose-built hall of residence in 1908—and for women at that?[12] Then there is the supposed and periodically trumpeted connection between higher education and national economic success—the 'white heat of the technological revolution', the concern with 'value for money in research' and the current emphasis on the economic utilitarianism of 'training'.

Above all else, however, there is the matter of identity. What was 'a university' in 1900, what is it today, and the unspoken question: what should it be tomorrow? If the book which comes out of the project goes even a modest way towards an answer to that question, success will be beyond doubt.

University of Birmingham
Edgbaston
Birmingham B15 2TT

REFERENCES

1. Bristol, Birmingham, Leeds, Liverpool, Manchester, Sheffield.
2. E. W. Vincent and P. Hinton, *The University of Birmingham, its History and Significance* (Birmingham 1947); M. Cheesewright, *Mirror to a Mermaid, Pictorial Reminiscences of Mason College and the University of Birmingham, 1875–1975* (Birmingham 1975). The latter commemorated the centenary of the laying of the foundation stone of Mason College, opened 1880.
3. See E. W. Ives and C. L. Penney, 'The University of Birmingham and its Archives', in *Archives* xx (1992).
4. As well as the projected *History of the University*, it is intended to publish a catalogue of the University archives. In addition, a popular illustrated history is proposed for the celebrations in 2000 AD.
5. The medical school ('Queen's College') introduced courses in other subjects and in 1868 amalgamated with a rival medical school ('Sydenham College', founded 1851). In 1892 the scientific and medical courses were transferred to Mason College, leaving Queen's teaching only theology. It later became an Anglican theological college; the University's Department of Theology developed separately.
6. The Leverhulme Project, The Library, University of Birmingham, Edgbaston, Birmingham B15 2TT (021:414:5934).
7. The precise parameters have yet to be settled.
8. This was ended in 1987.
9. E. W. Ives, *Image of a University: the Great Hall at Edgbaston, 1900–1909* (Birmingham 1988), 4.
10. Mason College was vacated by the University in 1960 and demolished in 1963.
11. Ascorbic acid synthesised by Haworth and Stacey, 1932; the resonent cavity magnetron valve, invented by Boot, Randall and Sayers, 1940; atomic bomb: physics – Frisch and Peierls; chemistry – Wilkinson, Haworth and Stacey.
12. University House. The first warden was Margery Fry, later Principal of Somerville.

Conference Reports

The Quality of Citizenship: Utrecht, 20–22 March 1991

This conference on the theme of citizenship, organized by the Faculty of Social Sciences of Utrecht University, included a section on 'The cultural range of citizenship' which attracted a number of university historians. The programme was arranged by Brita Rang and Jan Rupp, who have now edited a book containing most of the papers (*The Cultural Range of Citizenship: Citizenship and Education in England, Scotland, Germany, the United States and the Netherlands*: Utrecht, Faculty of Social Sciences, 1991).

The special interest of the conference lay in the need to place university history in the wider context of educational systems and to relate it to the theme of citizenship. Three main approaches were discernible. While access to higher education might be seen as one of the rights of citizenship created by the growth of modern democracy, the restriction of this right by the hierarchical structuring of education was stressed by Brian Simon, Fritz Ringer and Detlef Müller. Simon pointed out the limitation of opportunity in England through the privileged position of independent secondary schools, and explored the historical origins of this structure. Ringer ranged widely over the nature of modern educational systems, and gave a foretaste of his forthcoming work on French higher education before the First World War. Müller discussed the fate of the concept of *Bildung* in modern times, a theme reinforced by a paper from Adalbert Rang on the relation between *Bildung* and citizenship in the thought of Wilhelm von Humboldt. Also in this group may be placed the paper by Jan Rupp which sought to elaborate an analytical framework for comparing the social 'inclusiveness' of national educational systems, with special reference to the U.S.A. and the Netherlands.

The historical development of citizenship in the Netherlands was the theme of Brita Rang's paper, which formed an interesting comparison with Donald Withrington's on the national educational system in Scotland. In both countries, a concept of citizenship expressed through wide participation in education could be traced back to the early modern period, and seems to have been related in complex ways both to the assertion of national identity and to community ideals expressed through the churches. The third theme was the deliberate use of education for the forming of citizens. Sheldon Rothblatt distinguished between the different traditions of national citizenship which developed in the United States, and discussed the contemporary crisis caused by the rise of cultural pluralism. This was nicely complemented by Wilna Meijer's paper on current controversies in the Netherlands about 'cultural literacy' and 'basic' education. This topic stimulated much discussion, enlivened by the presence of scholars from Poland, and was perhaps the closest to the general themes of the conference – the future of the welfare state and participatory democracy, and the problematic nature of citizenship, historically a product of the strong nation-state, in an *Europe des régions* with multiple focuses of loyalty.

These intimate sectional discussions were only part of a very large conference which was impressive for its efficient organization and for the support of the public authorities, both national and local. For British participants, the speech at the opening session in Utrecht Cathedral of Mrs Hedy d'Ancona, the Netherlands minister of Culture, formed a painful contrast with the level of political discourse at home.

Robert Anderson
Department of History
University of Edinburgh
Edinburgh EH8 9JY

Le Collège de Riom et l'enseignement de la Congrégation de l'Oratoire en France au 18ᵉ siècle: Maison Antoine Pandu, Riom, 28–30 March 1991.

The colloquium was organized by the Société des Amis du Centre de Recherches Révolutionnaires et Romantiques in collaboration with the Centre de Recherches Révolutionnaires et Romantiques (Université Blaise Pascal, Clermont-Ferrand).

The colloquium had the merit of bringing together researchers and teachers of different disciplines and intermeshing global perspectives and locally-based studies. Thereby it became possible to know in detail the present state of our knowledge of one of the great French teaching orders. Willem Frijhoff (Rotterdam) and Dominique Julia (Florence), beginning from the register of entrants to the Oratory and the precise indications which these furnish of the educational history of future Oratorians, reconstituted for twenty-five year periods from 1665 to the French Revolution, the respective importance of different types of college in the entrants' formation. Points raised by this study included the role played by the diverse teaching orders (especially the Jesuits) and secular priests, the place of *pensionnats*, the sheer diversity of the school network, and the decreasing influence of the Oratorian colleges as the eighteenth century advanced.

Etienne Broglie (Université de Paris-Sorbonne) compared the respective recruitment to the Royal Academy of Juilly and to the college of the town of Riom by using the surviving matriculation registers of these two institutions. He was able to show the filter-effect (not just in terms of numbers and the geographical and social background of students, but also in respect to pedagogy and scholarly performance) that a *pensionnat* as elitist as the Juilly Academy could exercise on a municipal college, even one whose importance was not negligible in the eighteenth century. Olivier Paradis by plunging into the accounts-registers of the Ecole Militaire at Effiat and using the catalogue of *pensionnaires* and the collection of public exercises which survive for the school traced the scholarly life of the institution from 1776 to the Revolution. He examined the length of time students stayed in the college, evidence of retaking courses, the rhythm of studies, the composition of the classes, the educational framework, and the role of emulation in learning. Pascal Piera (Clermont-Ferrand), both in the course of a visit to the site of the old college and in her paper, revealed the vicissitudes undergone by the buildings of the Riom college in the course of their history.

An entire afternoon was given over to the study of libraries. Jean Ehrard (Université de Clermont-Ferrand) compared the information in the catalogue of the Riom library drawn up in 1822 with the results of a systematic survey of the 'ex libris' in a collection of works of the Oratorians which still survive (some 500 titles, two-thirds belonging to the Oratorians of Riom, a third coming from Effiat). He was thereby able to underline the need for methodological caution when analysing a library catalogue drawn up after the event. The catalogue of 1822 only gives a very incomplete idea of the Oratorian collection, and the negligence of the administrators of the Riom district, who in the Year III drew up an inventory of books that they had collected without indicating their origin, is not completely reparable. Lucette Perol (Université de Clermont-Ferrand) has been able to reconstitute the library of the Ecole Militaire at Effiat not only by using two inventories (one dating from 1784, the other from 1793), but also by using account-books which reveal the purchases made over the years. In this way she was able to distinguish legitimately between what she called 'active' books (i.e those really used) and 'dead' books (i.e those eaten by rats or declared of little value). At the same time she was able to explore the scientific content of the library (using the term broadly) and show to what extent the library was open to recent literature, foreign books, or to contemporary events (there were eleven subscriptions to various journals). In addition, she pointed out that the place afforded translations in the library was an indication of the type of teaching at Effiat.

John Renwick (University of Edinburgh) expanded the discussion by analysing the catalogues of the libraries of the Oratorian college of Pézenas (there are catalogues from 1830 and 1874) and the Jesuit college of Rennes (there is a catalogue from 1762). At Pézenas, where the Oratorians at the same time directed a minor seminary until 1745, theological works represented more than three-quarters of the collection (77.6%). The 'secular' works in the library were divided between the mass of classical literature which forms the canon of the authors recommended in the *Ratio Studiorum*, a wide variety of historical works, and French literature. Books in foreign languages were totally absent. While there was a notable presence of polemical literature concerning Jansenism and the Bull *Unigenitus*, there was an equally remarkable absence of books on the dangers of *encyclopédisme* and philosophical unbelief. The Oratorians subscribed to the *Journal encyclopédique* and the presence of mathematical works (some twenty in total) was connected to the foundation of a chair of mathematics. The Jesuit library at Rennes was the more important (containing more than 2000 titles and nearly 4500 volumes), but the religious section was proportionately much reduced (65 per cent, equivalent to the figure at Riom of 61 per cent). John Renwick surmised that the college deliberately ignored modern thought for there was no Bacon, Descartes, Leibniz, or Locke, and a clear emphasis on Aristotelianism and Thomism. The library's richest period of acquisitions was the decade 1690–1700. From 1740 the only purchases were books which denounced the modern philosophy and waxed indignant at the development of incredulity; apologetics had become the staple diet. Alain Collet, in classifying the old collection of the library of the Société de la Diana at Montbrison, has been able to discover 932 titles (nearly 1,500 volumes) which carry an ex-libris of the Oratorians of the town; this is probably 30 per cent of the Congregation's collection in 1790. About a third of the books (*c.* 500 volumes) also bear the arms of Gilbert d'Hostun (died 1732), who bequeathed his library to the Oratorians, and thus must be dealt with separately. The majority of the titles that are datable come from the eighteenth century (more than two-thirds). The religious section of the library continually grew, so that in the eighteenth century 63 per cent of the titles can be thus classified. Of notable importance were the works of religious polemic (11.5 per cent on Jansenism), of theology (12 per cent), and of piety and the pulpit (10.7 per cent). In contrast there were hardly any works of mathematics (1.4 per cent).

Agnès Cornevin (Paris) presented an analysis of the *Traité des études* of Père Charles François Houbigant (1694–1783). This manual, compiled about 1720, was destined for the young *confrères* of the Congregation as a teaching aid in their initial introduction to the classroom. It provided a series of instructions according to the subject and author treated and offered recommendations on the method of teaching and the books to be used either in class or by the teacher to perfect his knowledge. Bruno Belhoste (Institut National de Recherche Pédagogique, Paris) presented an account of mathematics teaching in the Congregation, taking as his starting-point a collection of forty *affiches* or booklets of public exercises in mathematics from 1744 to 1791. Before 1776 the surviving exercises (sustained by pupils studying physics) displayed a very great variation in content and standard, some covering every aspect of the mathematical manuals studied, others being much more restrained. After 1776, on the other hand, there was a definite tendency towards uniformity in both content and form, and an apprenticeship in mathematics was not only reserved for students of physics. The pupils were grouped according to the level attained and in the large *pensionnats* the course was clearly inspired by the hefty manuals of Bezout or the *abbé* Bossut. Charles Pérol (Université Blaise Pascal, Clermont-Ferrand) continued this theme by analysing an almost complete collection of public exercises from the Ecole Militaire at Effiat between 1777 and 1791 (only the exercises for 1786 and 1790 are missing). From 1777 to 1785 the teaching of mathematics at Effiat never ceased to progress with the inclusion of spherical trigonometry, algebraic geometry, Cartesian geometry, and differential and integral calculus, the emphasis being placed not only on the knowledge of theorems but the resolution of problems. Catherine Larrère (Université de Bordeux III) concentrated on explaining what the philosophy theses sustained at the Collège de Riom can tell us about philosophy teaching in the eighteenth century. At Riom, it would seem, a course in philosophy remained largely scholastic, with only a very limited opening to elements of modernity (such as the controversy between Arnauld and Malebranche over the vision of God). In contrast, the public exercises at the Ecole Militaire at Effiat, as far as can be ascertained through the source, suggest that the course there was influenced strongly by Condillac and that the connection between logic and metaphysics had been dissolved.

The focus of interest of Mr Bellot-Anthony and Mme D. Hadjaj (Clermont-Ferrand) was the language curriculum at Riom and Effiat. The comparison between a municipal college and an *école militaire* underlined the evident modernity of the teaching of the *école militaire*. Effiat provided systematic teaching in the French language and foreign languages (English and German), gave a fundamental role to translation in teaching Latin (Latin prose or verse composition and the Latin *thema* had entirely disappeared), and placed an important emphasis on translation throughout.

André Chervel (Institut National de Recherche Pédagogique) gave an account of the essential features of language-teaching in the colleges of the ancien régime and emphasized some fundamental methodological pitfalls: it is wrong to consider the stipulated texts as an expression of the teaching actually provided, just as it is unwise to conclude that the teaching provided reveals what the student takes in; also, it is dangerous to overestimate the degree of coherence in the instruction given even within the same teaching order, as in the case of the Oratory important differences can be found between colleges, *pères* (priests) and *confrères* (laymen). Furthermore, the contrast established in the historiography of the end of the nineteenth and the beginning of the twentieth century between the Jesuits and the Oratorians is probably quite artificial. Perhaps Oratorian colleges were closer than others in anticipating the curriculum of the French faculties of arts in the nineteenth century, but the Oratorians were not really more modern than the Jesuits: the last course of rhetoric in Latin was given in 1790 and was delivered by an Oratorian professor at Nantes. Peter France (University of Edinburgh), in examining specifically the rhetoric courses given in the Oratorian colleges of the eighteenth century and the public exercises sustained there, came to much the same conclusion. There was not such a great pedagogical contrast between the Jesuits and the Oratorians as people have thought, for they used the same manuals. What was manifest about the development of a course in the eighteenth century was its evolution towards a course in *belles-lettres* where the study of elocution formed the lion's share. A course in rhetoric became a preparation for life in society; it formed good taste, a prerequisite in an age which valued polite sociability above pedantry. It was a question of learning the everyday art of social intercourse wherein lay the charm of the salons. Jean Ehrard and Mme Volpihac Auger finally analysed the teaching of history at the Collège de Riom, not only by using public exercises but also the surviving course notes of a pupil called Archon in 1789, 1790, and 1791. It thus becomes possible to see how an Oratorian professor constructed his course taking as his starting-point Mably, the *abbé* Millot or the *abbé* Vertot, and especially to see how through a history course news of the most recent events could penetrate the walls of a provincial college. The intellectual ferment at the moment of the summoning of the Estates General led to inaccuracies in the professor's text. While reliant on Mably, he forgot, for instance, to point out the role played by the nobility in the assemblies of the Germans.

In sum, the colloquium proved an excellent opportunity to return to the sources and to banish the historiographical image which dates from Epinal and the Third Republic of a Jesuit order ultramontane and absolutist opposed by an Oratorian Congregation Gallican and sympathetic to the Revolution. The historical reality is more complex and less one-dimensional, and the colloquium has been able to ask a series of new questions which it will be necessary to attempt to resolve in the coming years.

Dominique Julia
Département d'histoire et civilisation
Institut Universitaire Européen
Florence   (*translated by Laurence Brockliss*)

Università e Scienza Nationale tra Otto e Novecento: Certosa di Pontignano, Siena, 4–6 April 1991

The celebration of the 750th anniversary of the inauguration of the Università di Siena gave the Dipartimento di Storia the opportunity to organize a conference: Università e Scienza Nazionale tra Otto e Novecento (Italian Universities and science as a national factor in 19th and 20th century).

During three days four general themes were discussed: Università e potere politico, in which the speakers were Luigi Berlinguer, Simonetta Soldani, Luciano Pazzaglia, Ilaria Porciani; Modelli europei – Pierangelo Schiera, Rüdiger vom Bruch, Victor Karady, Christophe Charle; Università e Scienza nazionale – Claudio Cesa, Antonio La Penna, Giulio Cianferotti, Antonio Cardini, Roberto Maiocchi; Università e professioni – Mario Mirri, Aldo Mazzacane, Marino Raicich, Mauro Moretti, Annalucia Forti Messina.

The history of Italian universities during these years is not very well known. There was much discussion of reform, of adapting to French or German models, of changing the hierarchy of sciences, of better teaching, of the role and status of professors and teaching personnel. Italy had particular problems with small universities, some of which had only two faculties or only some sciences. Reformed universities were seen by some as an impetus for national unity. The group of younger scholars at the conference intend to do more research on all these subjects. The papers will be published.

The 'segreteria scientifica' was Ilaria Porciani, Dipartimento di Storia, Via Roma, 76, I 53100 Siena.

Notker Hammerstein
University of Frankfurt

The History of Philosophy Teaching in Universities: Magdalen College, Oxford, 9–11 April 1991

This conference was sponsored by the British Society for the History of Philosophy, in association with *History of Universities* and Magdalen

College. It was well attended and offered a very full programme, albeit one which could only sample the rich field of philosophy teaching through the ages. Most of those attending probably came with the common assumption that the history of the early universities *is* the history of philosophy teaching. Their illusions were entertainingly dispelled in an opening paper on the medieval curriculum by John Fletcher. Many medieval institutions had little or no significant arts teaching, he argued; and where they had, many students did not stay for any philosophical instruction beyond logic.

Through accidents of membership, BSHP has tended to specialize in the past on topics close to the mainstream of 17th and 18th-century philosophy – which has meant that it has already heard a good deal recently about the Oxford of Hobbes and Locke, and the Cambridge of Henry More. There was a deliberate and very welcome attempt on this occasion to range more widely than usual. Two contributors on the Renaissance and Reformation periods dealt with developments in ideas of the soul, as Aristotle's *De anima* came to be reinterpreted and assessed in the light of new cultural and theological developments, Emily Michael discussed the controversy at Padua between Zabarella and Piccolomini over the Averroist interpretation of Aristotle on the substantial nature of the agent mind. Sachiko Kusukawa showed how a holistic view of Aristotelian man was restored at Wittenberg under Melanchthon. Both speakers discussed their topics against a rich contextual background.

Padua also figured in the discussions by Leonidas Bargeliotes and Athanasia Leontsini of the transmission of philosophy among the Greeks from the Byzantine period to the Ottoman Empire. Although the universities of present-day Greece are modern foundations, there was a long tradition of church-related academies which kept alive the traditions of Greek philosophy and science, while expatriate Greek professors were widely dispersed across Italy and the Balkans. By the time of the European Enlightenment the Greek church's influence was largely repressive – as late as the 1790s, for example, they still rejected Copernicus. But secular and commercial interests encouraged the new learning, and texts in Greek were prepared in the west for shipment back to the Greek world. Locke, Condillac, the French *philosophes*, and Herder had the strongest impact.

Roger Ariew and Jean-Paul Pittion discussed the considerable diversity between the Aristotelian traditions in the seventeenth-century Jesuit colleges, the University of Paris, and the French Huguenot colleges, and Wolfgang Rother used textbooks and dissertations to trace the shift in seventeenth-century Zürich from Aristotelian to Cartesian philosophy. Constance Blackwell also analysed textbooks – primarily those of the German protestants in the eighteenth century – to show how the changes in philosophy from the Renaissance and the decline of scholasticism, to the rise of the new philosophy and the revival of some of the non-Aristotelian

traditions, were variously (and sometimes alarmingly) perceived and classified by the heirs of those changes.

British institutions of the eighteenth century were explored by Alan Sell
and R.G. Frey, who both spoke on the Dissenting academies and their
curricula, and by Paul Wood, who added a new instalment to his continuing
work on the development of Philosophy teaching at Aberdeen. Sell provided
a lively overview of both the liberal and conservative institutions – their
philosophical ambience and leading personalities. His hero was the Welsh-
man Richard Price; whereas Frey's was Joseph Butler, one of a group of
Tewkesbury students who later conformed to the Church of England and
collectively gave it such scanty intellectual leadership as it could muster at
this period. Frey tentatively documented the influence of the Leiden
curriculum on Tewkesbury, and the influence of the writing of a 17th-
century Fleming, Sarasa, on Leiden. Wood showed that there is no single
'common-sense' tradition in Scottish philosophy, and that the diversity of
the tradition is already apparent by the mid-century, before the rise of Reid.

Nineteenth-century France and Germany were represented by Patrice
Vermeren and Ulrich Johannes Schneider. Vermeren discussed the political
context of French developments in the first half of the century. Schneider
provided a statistical analysis of shifts in the German curriculum, and some
reflections on the use to be made of such analyses. The whole programme
was enough to whet the appetite for a follow-up conference before too long.
Among the significant topics one might hope to explore on another occasion
would be the early development of philosophy in the institutions of eastern
Europe, the rise of the discipline in America, the role of Dutch, German and
French universities in disseminating philosophy to other parts of Europe,
the impact of the new secular foundations on English philosophy in the
nineteenth century, the influence of World War and Cold War politics on
the teaching of the subject in twentieth-century Europe, and the changing
role of the journal in the development of institutional philosophy since the
seventeenth century.

Fuller abstracts of most of the papers mentioned above are being
published in the Autumn 1991 issue of the BSHP *Newsletter*. Further
information on the Society is obtainable from the Secretary, Dr Tom Sorell,
Philosophy Department, The Open University.

M. A. Stewart
Department of Philosophy
University of Lancaster
Lancaster LA1 4YG

The Jesuits and Philosophy in Renaissance Europe (sixteenth and seventeenth centuries): Paris, 10 June 1991.

This day-long session was the second of four colloquia organized by an international research network based in Paris studying the Jesuits as producers and circulators of knowledge in Renaissance Europe (sixteenth and seventeenth centuries). The six papers and discussion focused on the emergence of philosophy in the Jesuit curriculum in the sixteenth century and on Jesuit contributions to selected topics in the history of philosophy and of science into the early seventeenth century.

Pierre-Antoine Fabre (Ecole des Hautes Etudes en Sciences Sociales, Paris) traced the emergence of philosophy as a zone of mediation between the trivium and theology during the first twenty years of the Company, citing the objections and directives concerning its teaching. Luce Giard (CNRS, Paris) highlighted the unquestioned importance of philosophy in the first and second versions of the *ratio studiorum* (1586 and 1599) which advocated disputations as appropriate training exercises and also outlined the significance of mathematics. The discussion which ensued raised the question of the specificity of Jesuit teaching, in particular as compared with the programme of Johannes Sturm, which would be worth further study.

In the second part of the colloquium the paper by Charles Lohr (University of Freiburg i.B., Germany) stressed the multiplicity of Renaissance Aristotelianisms and in particular the latitude allowed Jesuits to develop philosophy in the service of Catholic theology without being bound to the defence of any medieval master from the order. Jenny Ashworth (University of Waterloo, Canada) presented a fine technical analysis of the doctrine of analogy among Jesuit logicians, especially Francisco Toledo, as compared with the doctrines of Boethius and Cajetan.

Edward Grant (Indiana University) and William Graham Randles (Ecole des Hautes Etudes en Sciences Sociales) discussed the evolution of Jesuit cosmology through the first half of the seventeenth century. Grant showed how the Jesuits were unanimous in rejecting the Copernican hypothesis of a mobile earth, but reached a variety of conclusions on the questions of the fluidity and incorruptibility of the heavens where they were not constrained by biblical interpretation. Randles followed in closer detail the evolution of Jesuit commentaries on Genesis and Aristotle's *de caelo* before and after 1630, to consider the question of the fluid heavens in the new light of interpretations of the empyrean sphere.

The conference was remarkable for its interdisciplinarity and congenial size. Bringing together scholars with different backgrounds and approaches, it fostered discussions which will surely extend beyond the grant funding these particular sessions. The proceedings of this meeting are expected to be published with those of the first colloquium (on Jesuits and education). Two further one-day colloquia are planned for October 1991 and May 1992, treating Jesuit mathematics and politico-theology respectively. Inquiries should be directed to Luce Giard, 9 rue Eugène-Gibez, 75015 Paris.

Ann Blair
Dept. of History of Science
Harvard University
Cambridge MA 02138
USA

Les Jésuites et la civilisation du baroque (1540–1640): Centre culturel Les Fontaines, Chantilly, 17–20 June 1991.

The conference opened with a half-day dedicated to the founding texts of the Company. Adrien Demoustier (SJ Centre Sèvres, Paris) showed how the *Spiritual Exercises* of Ignatius Loyola drew on the past: certain passages were clearly inspired by previous developments in meditation. Meditation in the hands of Ludolph the Carthusian had become an autonomous mental activity distinct from vocal spirituality (said prayers and Bible-reading), while the practice of mental prayer had been stimulated by Garcia de Cisneros, abbot of Monserrat. Loyola's originality lay in the deliberate choice of an *indirect* style. The *Exercises* was a book destined to be read by a master, who would then address orally a third person and propound the way of doing the exercises. Luce Giard (CNRS Paris) underlined the slow genesis of the Constitutions of the Company which only gained their definitive form in 1594. She also stressed the devolved nature of responsibility they permitted at each stage of the Company's hierarchy (temporal coadjutor, spiritual coadjutor, *profès des quatre voeux*) and the unity of the Company produced by its manner of acting, itself the product of the linkage of the complementary values of obedience and free-will. Decisions in the interior of the Company never stopped circulating through the pyramid of functions. Louis Marin (EHESS Paris) analysed from a narratological angle the *Récit du pèlerin*, the 'testamentary' text dictated by Ignatius to Louis Gonzaluez da Camara, where the voice of the founder is transformed into a third person singular 'he', which signifies that the subject is absent. The account of this singular life was intended at the same time to be an example for Ignatius's companions and successors. By appropriating this account in which it was related how God formed Ignatius from the time of his conversion, each companion could also read his own vocation in a sort of eucharistic communion with the text.

Jean-Claude Margolin (Université François Rabelais de Tours) next evoked the successive images of Erasmus in the contradictory readings of his work from the Age of the Enlightenment to the Second Vatican Council. François Laplanche (CNRS Paris) showed how in the early days theological polemic gained its violence from the mortal combat in which the partisans of the old Church and the supporters of innovation were engaged. Each side wanted to be certain of possessing the authentic original: the Catholic church claimed the privilege of authenticity according to the principle that 'novelty' is synonymous with error; Protestants claimed the rights of truth on the grounds of individual conscience or reason. Later on, theological controversy evolved from the mutual impact of each side's arguments. Jesuit controversialists (such as Maldonat) attempted to determine the literal sense of Scripture and the quality of their exegesis was recognized by the Protestants themselves. Thereby a common language of philologists was formed. Nevertheless, the weight of tradition obliged the Jesuit theologians to outline the rudiments of a history of the faith, and encouraged Catholic apologetics to become directed towards history, a field in which Protestant erudition was particularly brilliant at the turn of the sixteenth and seventeenth centuries (Scaliger, Casaubon, Blondel, Daillé). In the decade of the 1620s there was paradoxically a reversal of positions. The Protestants insisted more and more that they were not innovators but on the contrary the true 'ancients'. Jesuit theologians, on the other hand, increasingly made an appeal to the decisions of the post-Tridentine Church in order to resolve the thorny problem of the discontinuities of history and from then on appeared to be the 'moderns'. Marc Venard (Université de Paris X, Nanterre) underlined the role of the bishops in the introduction of the Jesuits to France and equally showed the resistance that the Company encountered at the very heart of the episcopate. The situation changed considerably at the turn of the sixteenth and seventeenth centuries.

Dominique Julia (Institut Universitaire Européen de Florence) traced the genesis of the text of the *Ratio Studiorum*, using as his supporting source the publication, *Monumenta Paedagogica* of Father Ladislaus Lukacs. How far, he inquired, did the transformation in the general architecture of the *Ratio* between the text of 1586 and that of 1591 echo the crisis caused by the growth of the Company in the course of the sixteenth century and the problem that became central in consequence, the search for a good form of collegiate government, rather than just the growing precision of the curriculum and rules relating to piety and morals? Jean-Marie Valentin (Université de Paris IV Sorbonne) concentrated on analysing the functions of Jesuit theatre. Doubtless this was one of the key components of the pedagogical machinery of the Company and it corresponded in its functioning and purpose to the ideals of rhetoric. But beyond this well-known aspect, it was at the same time a creative representation of emotions, it almost monopolized dramatic entertainment in numerous regions, and it contributed in diverse ways to the definition of an aesthetic of the theatre. Louis Châtellier

(Université de Nancy II) provided a definition of the Marial congregations which emanated from the Jesuit residences and colleges. These were schools of spiritual formation and they were perfectly adapted to the social structure of the age, taking on a different guise according to their social composition (nobles, judicial officers, merchants, master-artisans or journeymen), according to the age of members (married or celibate), and according to their 'national' location (as in the Flemish and French-speaking parts of the Low Countries). The congregations especially played a social, cultural, and even political role, aiming at nothing less than the establishment of an ideal Christian society. This was the model adopted in Bavaria, Lorraine, and the Habsburg territories, where the prince, by placing himself at the head of the premier congregation and taking upon himself the task of constructing a Christian society, reinforced his authority. In France, on the other hand, Gallican traditions such as the recognition of the existence of Protestants after the Edict of Nantes prevented the Most Christian King from following suit.

Bernard Dompnier (Université de Clermont) showed how the figure of the Jesuit missionary slowly emerged as a form of apostleship which gained an individual identity from the end of the sixteenth century. The general Acquaviva underlined the necessity of missionary activity in a climate of eschatological struggle against heresy. The Company of Jesus was the army of the Lord, and the Jesuits were to go and search out souls by journeying as apostles throughout the world. The Indies thus became the heart of Europe and almost at the outskirts of Rome. In the course of this first period of the Company, the struggle for the conversion of souls was internalized by the Jesuits as the right way of founding their own relationship with God.

Father Robert Bireley SJ (Loyola University of Chicago) analysed the relations between the growth of the modern state and Jesuit spirituality which insisted on the fact that the Christian life must be lived in the world. Beginning from the works of four 'anti-Machiavellian' Jesuits (Pedro de Ribadaneira, *El principe christiano*, 1595; Juan de Mariana, *De rege et regis institutione*, 1599; Adam Contzen, *Politicorum libri decem*, 1621; and Carlo Scribani, *Politico-Christianus*, 1624), Bireley analysed the major traits of the political programme proposed. These were the search for popular support, economic development and taxation, the creation of a powerful armed force, and zeal for the advancement of religion, that is Catholicism. In their desire to present the advantages that religion could bring to the state, the Jesuits in fact prepared the way for the identification of the Church with state power which characterized the ancien régime. Jean-François Courtin (Université de Paris X, Nanterre) attempted to understand the consequences that the axioms of the moral theology of the Jesuit Francesco Suarez had on his theory of politics. Suarez envisaged the idea of a state of pure nature where man in virtue of the perfection of his metaphysical nature would have been created solely for natural happiness: here he confronts us with a humanity congenitally enclosed in a profane organic circle. At the same time, the civil power of the legislator, according to Suarez, has as its end the natural happiness of the perfect human community: citizens must live in peace and the common good is discovered on a purely earthly plane, completely divorced from any question of the supernatural. For Suarez there was no longer a theological politics. In addition, the binding-force of law no longer comes from its rationality vis-à-vis the common good, but from the imperative character of the will, from a coercive force emanating from a sovereign body: the authority of natural law has become external to the authority of positive law. With Suarez therefore, albeit under the cover of safeguarding tradition, a new concept of sovereignty emerged which prepared the way for the idea of a contract and popular sovereignty. In analysing *La Doctrine curieuse des beaux esprits de ce temps* (1623) of the French Jesuit Garasse (1584–1631), Christian Jouhaud (CNRS, Centre de recherches historiques de l'EHESS) aimed to reveal, through reference to the ways of reading open to contemporaries, the author's strategy of composition. In this weighty in-folio tome which could not be read from beginning to end, Garasse utilized the classification devices most familiar to preachers and controversialists in an unfamiliar intellectual setting. In the struggle against the libertines, what was needed were active examples of an effective rhetoric.

Joao Francisco Marques underlined the role of Jesuit confessors at the Portuguese court in the sixteenth and seventeenth centuries. In directing the conscience of kings, they participated in major policy decisions for the kingdom but were also exposed to their consequences. Thus, after the loss of independence (1580) they became the heralds of an unorthodox Sebastianism founded on a messianic nationalism.

Marc Fumaroli (Collège de France) provided an analysis of the commemorative work produced by the Company's Franco–Belgian province for the Society's first centenary: the *Imago Primi Saeculi Societatis Jesus* (Antwerp, 1640), illustrated by pupils of Rubens, was a great moment in neo-Latin poetry where the Society offered its readers a sort of unveiling of its *arcana*. As a kind of mirror on the past or theatre of memory it summed up a genre (*topica*) peculiar to the Society. Evonne Levy (American Academy in Rome) presented an iconographical analysis of the altar of the Jesuit church at Rome, which has just been restored. Pierre Antoine Fabre (EHESS) raised the question of whether or not imaginative contemplation according to Loyola's *Spiritual Exercises* could 'naturally' derive sustenance from the support of material images. How could image and text be reconciled and what is the meaning of illustrated *Exercises*? Michale Kiene (University of Wuppertal) analysed the architectural work of Bartolmeo Ammanti (1551–1592) and demonstrated through reference to buildings still standing, plans, sketches and letters, how the conception of the Jesuit college differed both from traditional monasteries and from Italian university colleges. It was a question of a new synthesis between monastic and university architecture. Finally, Irving Lavine (Princeton University Institute for Advanced Studies) showed how Bernini in his statues of Francis 1 d'Este and Louis XIV developed a new model for the Christian prince, that of the heroic prince.

In sum, the colloquium on the Jesuits and Baroque civilization opened up numerous avenues of research in bringing together different disciplinary approaches, by returning to the sources and the founding texts, and in shifting the foci of enquiry. There can be no doubt that it will be the point of departure for new research in the years to come.

Dominique Julia
Département d'histoire et civilisation
Institut Universitaire Européen
Florence   (*translated by Laurence Brockliss*)

Universities and the Sciences. Historical and Contemporary Perspectives: Bologna, 18–20 September 1991.

The conference brought together historians of higher education, historians of science and educational sociologists from Europe and America. The first day was devoted to the examination of the different national traditions of university science; the second and third days to the history of science in the university from the middle ages to the present. Particular attention was paid to the developments in the relationship between science and the university since 1945. The conference was organized by the International Centre for the History of Universities and Science at the University of Bologna (CIS), Via Zamboni 31, 40126 Bologna, Italy. The centre was founded in December 1990 with the aim of promoting research in the history of universities, of science and technology, and of institutions of higher learning. Its present director is Giuliano Pancaldi, Professor of the History of Science at Bologna. In September 1991 the Centre published the first number of its Newsletter, *Universitas* (12 pp.), which contained information about the aims and organization of the Centre and details about current projects on the history of science and of higher education, especially in Italy. The Newsletter is intended to be an occasional publication with at least two issues per year. Anyone seeking further information about the Newsletter or the conference should contact Giuliano Pancaldi.

L. W. B. Brockliss
Magdalen College
Oxford

The Universities in the Age of Western Expansion. The Colonial Factor in Research and Higher Education: Leiden, 27–29 September 1991.

Participants in the third Biannual Conference of Historians of Universities from the British Isles, Belgium and the Netherlands were welcomed by Harm Beukers, deputizing for Prof. Wesseling, who noted that meetings were to be held in the houses of two former Leiden scholars active in the fields of medicine and oriental studies.

C. Fasseur opened the proceedings with a lively and humorous examination of the Delft college to train administrators for the Dutch East Indies. Established in 1843 as a response to fears that the French were about to expand provision in this field, the college had a limited success but did anticipate the more academic provision eventually made at Leiden. Mgr. Luc Gillon, first rector of the university of Lovanium, then gave a personal and graphic account of his experiences at the foundation of this institution. Further descriptions of the spread of education in the Belgian Congo were given by Marc de Paepe, who discussed the missionary contribution, and by Zana Etambala, who described the experiences of Congolese students abroad not only in Belgium but also in Colwyn Bay, north Wales! The work, especially that of the female members, of the protestant Dublin University Missionary Society in India was described by Oenagh Walsh; a serious attempt to reach Indian women was greatly hindered by local customs and by male resistance. M. Algera-van der Schaaf presented a very interesting introduction to the rise and fall of quinine cultivation in the Dutch East Indies: in the early years of this century the Dutch controlled around 97 per cent of the world's quinine production. Bruce Lenman contributed a valuable insight into the work of Scottish-trained medical doctors in the southern states of north America. He showed how their education encouraged them to undertake a wide variety of scientific enterprises including the exploitation of local iron ore deposits by slave labour on a massive scale. The problem of whether European institutes for the study of tropical medicine should be established at home or overseas was discussed by Harm Beukers. Paul van der Velde gave a general survey of the career of the somewhat eccentric but liberal scholar P. J. Veth, who wrote much on the Dutch East Indies without ever visiting that area! Military affairs were treated by J. A. de Moor who showed how slowly the Dutch Royal Military Academy at Breda responded to the need to train its recruits to understand colonial conditions, officers were to find their position by reference to church towers! Finally, the English experience was introduced by Mark Harrison who described the early development of the Indian medical services and by Ravi Rajan who showed how much the establishment of the

Oxford Imperial Forestry Institute was dependent on experience of administration in India.

The papers were received with enthusiasm and provoked much discussion. It is expected that the proceedings will be published. The conference for 1993 will be held in Leuven, Belgium. For further details contact the British organizer, Dr. John M. Fletcher, Department of Modern Languages, Aston University, Aston Triangle, Birmingham B4 7ET.

John M. Fletcher

The Universities in the Middle Ages and in the Early Modern Period. The Form and Limitations of a Successful Institution: Tübingen, 21–24 November 1991.

This conference was organized by the Section for the Study of the Philosophical Basis of Theology of the University of Tübingen, under the direction of Georg Wieland. Fifteen papers from representatives of five countries presented for consideration research and new attitudes relating to university history. An opportunity for discussion was provided between each paper and at the conclusion of each day's proceedings.

In his opening lecture Wolfgang Kluxen (Bonn) emphasized that the universities did not develop from the monastic or cathedral schools; therefore from the beginnings they intended to offer no set cultural or social style of argument. As completely unique and spontaneous developments they would first take up their positions later from their experience of society and their requirements. The papers on the following days were concerned with the relationship between the character of university organization and the type of work produced there. As Jakob Hans Josef Schneider (Tübingen) demonstrated, from the thirteenth century there was developed a division of learning into 'scientia sermocinalis' (the study of language) and 'scientia realis' (the study of things) without this separation of material having institutional consequences. Mechthild Dreyer (Bonn) discussed the form of the *Theoremata* as a remaining feature of science '*more geometrico*'. The 'theorematical', 'axiomatical' and 'deductive' texts of the Middle Ages sprang not from forms used in the teaching of the schools but from the inner needs of scientific methodology. Olga Weijers (The Hague) next described to the participants the rules for examinations in the medieval universities. How the teaching activities of the faculty of arts of Cologne university moved increasingly into the large, privately financed and organized burses was portrayed by Erich Meuthen (Cologne). To end the first day, Claude Lafleur (Quebec) presented an examination of introductions to philosophy in the faculty of arts of the thirteenth-century university of Paris.

The third day considered the theme of the university's existence between the professional classes and the general public. In connexion with a short presentation of the conflict with the mendicants, the director, Georg Wieland, developed his thesis that the more theology moved towards a professional, 'objective' science, the more clerical it became, the more belief gained greater weight as the subjective personal responsibility of the theologian. Alain de Libera (Paris) showed how influential was Albert the Great on German mysticism, which grew up mainly outside the universities. This mysticism developed from a considerable philosophical and intellectual basis, especially from that received through Averroes. Early proposals for a planned historical-philosophical research project were presented by Maarten J. F. M. Hoenen (Nijmegen). He intends to show the previously much disputed philosophical relevance of the mystic, Johannes Tauler, and investigate traces of the extensive reception of Tauler's work in the Netherlands. Ruedi Imbach (Freiburg, Switzerland) in his contribution suggested a stronger interest from the philosophical culture of the public in a partial compromise with scholastic university philosophy. Associated with the names of Dante and Nicolaus Oresme, a growing appreciation of the vulgar tongue as the language of learning produced an alteration in the philosophy of the schools and its unique character. The relation between the university and the world as seen in the example of the historical impact of the widespread German and Latin versions of the Compendium theologicae veritatis of Hugo of Strasbourg, was discussed by Georg Steer (Eichstätt). In the discussion following, participants considered the stagnation in university theological and philosophical studies; as with other disciplines philosophy, especially in the early modern period, received its real dynamism from outside the university.

The last day's session, devoted to an examination of the schools of philosophy and theology, was opened by Ludger Honnefelder (Bonn) with a paper on the teaching and controversies within the fourteenth-century schools. Scotist innovators did not attack only the Thomists but also on occasions members of their own party, for both the nominalist tendencies of William of Almwick and the platonic tendencies of Francisus Mayronis were to be found in Duns Scotus himself. Scholastic conflicts also appeared at this Tübingen conference! Olaf Pluta (Bochum) attracted some criticism, mainly over his interpretation and methodology, when he described in his presentation the development of a medieval Alexanderism, whose materialistic supporters, amongst them Johannes Buridanus, defended arguments for the mortality of the soul. While the 'radical' Buridanists supported this view, the 'conservative' Buridanists attempted to 'catholicize' Alexander of Aphrodisias. Zdzislaw Kuksewicz (Warsaw) discussed the development of Latin Averroism from the thirteenth to the fifteenth century. The two first Averroist schools in Paris from 1260, which soon collapsed, obtained a following in Bologna in the first half of the fourteenth century and later in Erfurt. A completely new and less restrictive type of Averroism was received in the Italian renaissance, especially by Paul of Venice. The final paper was given by Zenon Kaluza (Paris). He described the debates of realists and nominalists at Paris from 1473–1482 and showed that the process of education in the schools at that period was not only the result of internal intellectual movements but was also strongly controlled by external, political influences. In the following discussion, participants were agreed that because there never was an accepted single nominalist standpoint, the nominalist 'school' in the fifteenth century was so diffuse that its associations can hardly be recognized.

At the farewell ceremony Georg Wieland pointed out some gaps and omissions in the range of the Tübingen conference by which the organizers of a later conference in two or three years time might be sufficiently motivated. The contributions to this first conference will be published as collected papers.

Bernward Loheide
Section for the study of the Philosophical Basis of Theology
Tübingen (*translated by John M. Fletcher*)

Essay Review

Hilde de Ridder-Symoens (ed.), *A History of the University in Europe. 1. Universities in the Middle Ages.* Cambridge: Cambridge University Press. 1992. xxviii + 506 pp.

It would seem a recipe for certain disaster to invite twelve of the leading historians of the medieval universities to come together and express their combined views of the origins and development of these complex institutions. The Standing Conference of Rectors, Presidents and Vice-Chancellors of the European Universities has sponsored such an invitation and now sees the publication of the first of what is intended to be a four-volume history of the European university from its origins to the present. Its bold and welcome initiative deserves our serious and careful evaluation.

First, a comment on the appearance of the volume. It is attractively produced and, for such a large volume, lies easily open. There are signs, however, that the contributions of some of the non-native English speakers have not been properly served by translators or advisors. What is 'the cluster of two' (p. 213) as a group attending the university? Luckily the German word is given also and it seems that 'peer group' is intended. There is some confusion, again with the German, when reference to 'loans' made annually to college fellows (p. 238) appears to be a mistranslation of 'Lohn', a payment or salary. The Latin of the Freiburg Collegium Sapientiae statutes 'ne sordes animos molescent' is translated (p. 228) as 'so that the dirts is not a burden to the soul', which seems both poor English and a poor version. We must suspect also a mistranslation when we are told that parts of Duke Humfrey's collection 'now form the basis' of the Bodleian Library (p. 463). Students 'audit' courses on the Bible (p. 418); the beadle carries a 'verge' (p. 127) where surely the more usual 'mace' would have been better. A selective trial of the Indexes suggests that they cannot be completely trusted.

Turning next to the contents in general, there are several astonishing howlers, some serious some amusing. Chaucer was not born in 1440 (p. 224); the King's Hall College (so named here) and New College were not 'the first colleges to admit undergraduate students' (p. 117). In 1483 students leave Paris for 'the German universities of Prague, Vienna, Heidelberg, Erfurt and Cologne' (p. 289) despite the fact that two of them had not yet been founded! On two occasions (pp. 115, 284) we are told that the river

Trent divided the Oxford nations, but A. B. Emden disproved this in 1964.
Alfred, king of Wessex 849–99, is identified by the Index and text as a visitor
to Toledo in the twelfth and thirteenth centuries (p. 297). With such
longevity and travel experience he certainly deserves his title! Alfredus
Anglicus, indexed elsewhere, is, of course, intended here. Your reviewer is
saddened by the fact that his friends and colleagues of long standing are not
aware of his initials nor consistent in their use of them (pp. 3, 133, 320). And
shame on the CUP for confusing the Queen's College, Oxford, with the
Queens' College, Cambridge (p. 215)!

There is also a disturbing tendency by many contributors to assert the
doubtful with an authority that is alarming. Perhaps this is a failing of
'homines computerissimi'. We are told that there is an 'absence of clearly
defined boundaries between universities and schools' (p. 175), that 'the vast
majority of new entrants to the university were of this age' (fourteen or
fifteen) (p. 183), that students were required to avoid 'contact with women
of all kinds' (mothers and sisters also?) (p. 225), that 'between 1348 and
1505, there were 200,000 German university students' (not one more or
less?) (p. 270), and that 'only 2 per cent of the students at Oxford and
Cambridge came from the Continent' (p. 296). These are a selection of many
examples and this reader would respond with 'prove it', and 'how do we
know?' Generalization in this wide ranging work cannot be avoided, but
surely some qualifying words could be introduced to show, in so many
cases, the inadequacy of the evidence. We have no idea of how many
students there were in the medieval German universities or then at Oxford,
and we should not deceive readers by claiming more than informed
guess-work!

Finally, to consider individual contributions before attempting an assessment of the volume as a whole, we begin with a general introduction by
Walter Rüegg on 'Themes'. He has a difficult task, but performs it
admirably. We detect as elsewhere an understandable readiness to concentrate too much on the great archetypal universities of Bologna and Paris,
but here is a stimulating and thoughtful contribution. Jacques Verger
follows with a sound and complete survey of 'Patterns' which complements
well the preceding chapter. Part two of the volume examines 'Structures'
and commences with a study by Paolo Nardi of 'Relations with Authority'.
He gives us an excellent survey of papal policy towards the universities, but
notes also the experiments of secular control initiated in Naples by
Frederick II and revived by Charles I. He discusses the use of trained
graduates in local courts in Italy and shows how their experiences helped to
build up the concept of a *corpus* of legal privileges that properly belonged to
a university. This *corpus* received a clear endorsement by the Pope at the
establishment of the *studium* in Rome in 1303. The movement from papal-
inspired foundations to 'princely institutions' is well traced, although it is a

pity here that the unusual example of the role of ecclesiastics in the Scottish experience is not discussed. This is an extremely valuable section. Aleksander Gieysztor next provides a chapter on 'Management and Resources'. Sadly, here his extremely busy life in international historical affairs and perhaps his difficulties in obtaining in Poland recent specialist studies certainly shows. Surely students were not usually forbidden 'to marry' (p. 109), especially as examples are given of university statutes protecting their wives and children (p. 120). The nations at Oxford were not abolished in 1274; the university of Aberdeen was not founded in 1494 (Jacques Verger has the revised date correct on p. 64). This is a disappointing piece. For his second essay, Jacques Verger considers 'Teachers'. Here we see beginning to emerge what is to become a major problem for later contributors: the difficulty of making generalizations to cover so many different universities at different times. The discussion of 'examinations', for example, is of little value except on a most elementary level, and surely not every student was 'a virtually silent listener' before obtaining the BA degree. Several universities organized exercises which required the participation of these students. Also it would appear doubtful if 'year after year the students used to follow the same courses given by the same teacher'. Masters came and went; books were redistributed amongst the teaching staff often on an annual basis. However, within the limitations of space this is a gallant attempt to cover the ground.

Part three, 'Students', opens up for examination an expansive and complicated theme. Rainer Schwinges begins with a study of 'Admission' and 'Student Education. Student Life'. One does not envy him his task! Here the difficulties of generalization become serious. 'It is not even certain . . . that all those attending university could . . . read and write' (p. 174). Professor Schwinges should know very well that such references, including that at Perpignan he quotes, speak of schoolboys. Of course, they were legally part of the university, but so were many others, servants, carriers and so on, who probably also could not read and write. His comment is misleading and unnecessary. 'It would be anachronistic to expect . . . [there to be an] hierarchically ordered educational system' (p. 175). What about the well organized pattern of Winchester–New College and Eton–King's College? 'The vast majority (of students) were satisfied to attend and belong'. Surely they had no choice, for many, as we know, simply could not afford to take expensive degrees. The author deserves credit for stimulating such a response in the informed reader but it would appear dangerous to leave the non-specialist with the impression given by these and similar sentences. Professor Schwinges writes that 'all the larger English colleges were founded by bishops who were or had been lord chancellor of England' (p. 215). The statement certainly made this reviewer start as he at once thought of The King's Hall and King's College, Cambridge; he then traced the error to a misquotation from Rashdall (Vol. 3, p. 229) that 'all the greater medieval colleges at *Oxford* were founded by bishops who were also chancellors'. More serious is the tone of the few pages devoted to 'learning'. Apart from the fact that there are here many dubious statements and quarter-truths, clearly Professor Schwinges has no sympathy with this aspect of the medieval university. He writes of 'formalistic nonsense–events' (public disputations) and even resurrects the 'how many angels . . . on the point of a needle' legend. He has a point of view, but is rather dated and certainly exaggerated. This section should not have been allowed to pass. Peter Moraw in his chapter on 'Careers of Graduates' sees the emergence of graduates as an important social group first in Italy; he notes that successful graduates elsewhere usually had the advantage of higher birth. He sees the popularity of an ecclesiastical career and the willingness of the church to recruit university trained personnel as stronger in England than elsewhere. He suggests that it was usually the student with a variety of advantages – education, birth, social and local contacts – who best made his way in late medieval society. This is a thought-provoking and well-presented section.

The editor concludes Part three with an essay on 'Mobility', a subject which she has made her own over the past years. She combines an excellent use of detailed case-studies with general analysis. Some statements must be based on a misunderstanding of common usage in English: how can fifteenth-century universities be described as 'predominantly aristocratic institutions' (p. 286)? She sees special factors, the movement of the papacy to Avignon, for example, as shaping temporary mobility, but strangely does not mention the role of the marriage of Anne of Bohemia to Richard II as encouraging an important movement of Bohemian scholars to Oxford. She points out the role of the Orders in sending members to foreign convents in often distant universities. Migration, she suggests, slowed down in the fifteenth century with the growth of the 'territorial' university.

Part four examines learning, with essays on 'The Trivium and the Three Philosophies' by Gordon Leff and on 'The Quadrivium' by John North. This division of the faculty of arts seems rather forced especially as the trivium and quadrivium generally formed the studies for the lower and the three philosophies those for the higher degree. Gordon Leff gives a useful if somewhat pedestrian description of early studies, suggesting that Paris masters looked to metaphysics while those of Oxford looked to the natural sciences for inspiration. He is clearly not at ease with later developments which he covers speedily and superficially: there were not *two* separate arts faculties in the German universities that accepted both philosophical *viae* but *one* that was divided internally. John North's brief survey often degenerates into lists of names, but he has much of interest to say, especially on the role of astrology, and, unusually in this volume, emphasizes how little we know of certain fields of enquiry. Nancy Siraisi surveys 'The

Faculty of Medicine'. She emphasizes the dominance throughout the medieval period of a few great centres of medieval study, but warns us not to forget that a small faculty in a small university could still be important to a local court which then had a qualified medical advisor at hand. This is an excellent short summary. Antonio García y García in his examination of 'The Faculties of Law' provides a very useful glossary of the terms used by lawyers. He sees law studies as providing much of the basis for the modern discussion of the nature of authority, of papal power, and of the state. But surely he is not correct in stating that it was to theology rather than to law that the majority of students at Paris, Oxford, and in the Empire was drawn (p. 401). His figures for Oxford on the same page would appear to indicate the reverse. Monika Asztalos contributes an examination of 'The Faculty of Theology'. She sees Paris refusing to accept the integration of philosophical and theological concepts whereas the reverse is true at Oxford. From this she derives the Parisian claim to be the guardian of 'pure' theological doctrine so important at the time of the Conciliar Movement. Her discussion of the late medieval situation is brief and inadequate, for instance on the role of *viae* controversy within the faculties of *theology*.

In an Epilogue, Walter Rüegg turns to 'The Rise of Humanism'. In a short chapter dealing with a vast subject, he urges us to see the humanists as well-paid scholars, appreciated by courts and aristocrats, but whose wide interests brought them to dabble in a variety of subjects. The Italian lawyers, as a body, were particularly incensed at their 'meddling' and criticisms. This is a careful and well-thought-out concluding chapter. Walter Rüegg views the humanists as feeling themselves 'nearly overwhelmed by [the medieval imprint] and [they] found it difficult to go their own way' – a very sensible comment about a much-debated situation.

To turn again to a consideration of the volume as a whole, how far has it achieved its aims, how far does it give a new or different approach to the subject and what lessons has its appearance for us? We are informed that the readership intended will be both general and specialist, although how ready a general reader will be prepared to pay so much for a long volume written by specialists is perhaps doubtful. Nevertheless, with varying degrees of success, the contributors can claim to have surveyed a large field, usually including references to recent changes of opinion and often insinuating, for good or ill, their own particular approach. We could not demand more of them. Certainly, all essays stress the social role of the university, as required by the editorial board and this is a welcome approach. Whether this represents already a 'dated' view of the university supported by scholars of a disappearing generation remains to be seen. Will our successors find this concentration on careers, social origins, numbers and figures as equally distracting as we found an earlier concentration on origins and constitutions? Finally what does this volume tell us about the present and future state of research into universities in the Middle Ages? Here one can present only a personal view. Let us hope that this will be the last of such attempts to write the complete history of these universities. As we see the contributors to this volume struggling to encompass so much different material in a few pages, attempting to compare like with unlike, forced to generalize where generalizations have little or no meaning, we must surely realize that this must come soon to an end. May I make one simple suggestion? We should recognize that the cultural division of Europe between, broadly, the countries of the north and east and those of south France and the Mediterranean imposes on us a duty to treat the universities of both areas separately. Of course, comparisons can be made here and there, but not over the entire field. We need, if a similar project is ever undertaken in the future, *two* histories of medieval universities, one for the northern, arts and theology area, one for the southern, legal region. That this need is clear is a tribute to this always stimulating volume. Let us hope, that after careful rereading and correction, a cheaper, revised paperback version will make its conclusions available to a wider audience.

John M. Fletcher
University of Aston

Book Reviews

Jacques Verger (ed.), *Histoire des universités en France*. Bibliothèque historique Privat. Toulouse: Privat, 1986. 432 pp.

Ever since the publication of the general history of the French (and foreign) universities by St. d'Irsay in 1933–35, research in French university history has been restricted in time or space and has privileged a limited number of themes, varying according to the period under review. At present, the medieval universities are much better known than their successors. It might well be our comprehensive knowledge of the universities in this period that makes them virtually appear as 'greedy institutions', much more at any rate than the early modern university. Recent research on the French universities in the early modern period has been mostly concerned with the social and intellectual aspects of recruitment and teaching, whereas the contemporary university is largely approached in political terms, as an instrument of state-making in the hands of the central authorities, or sociologically, as an institution which is completely dependent on the demands of the society at large. With the exception of the medieval period, the internal dynamics of the university system and of individual universities, prominent in the older university historiography, has not been able to resist the confrontation with the socio-cultural approach that has prevailed during the last decades. University history has exploded. Instead of presenting us an uninterrupted journey across the time, university historians now distinguish four or five profoundly different periods with their distinctive dynamics founded upon particular forms of relationship between the university institution and the society or the state, regulating even the intellectual life of the period.

As Jacques Verger puts it in his short and vigorous introduction to this new history of the universities in France, previous historical writing started from the principle of an essential continuity of the integral university system between the different periods. In spite of all the historical differences in the forms and functions of university life, its core was naïvely supposed to have remained unaltered through the eight or nine centuries of university existence. The ultimate proof of this basic historical identity was the continuity of rites and symbols: the ceremonies of student life, the gown, graduation, etc. But are we allowed to postulate a common identity where the historian only discovers formal similarities or continuities? In short, what is the historical balance between the internal history of the university institution and its relation to the surrounding society? Has the medieval university, apart from its name, anything in common with its contemporary counterpart?

The principal merit of this book is to ask explicitly this central question and propose a clear answer. Clear but necessarily unsatisfactory. In fact, the editor and the five other authors (L. W. B. Brockliss, D. Julia, V. Karady, J.-Cl. Passeron and Ch. Vulliez) adopt a middle position between the previous essentialist approach and a purely environmentalist view of the university. On the one hand the self-definition of educational institutions as 'universities' is taken for granted; on the other hand university-level institutions bearing another name and formally excluded from the university in the narrower sense of the word (colleges, seminaries, professional schools, *grandes écoles*, etc.) are taken into consideration and confronted with the universities themselves.

Yet the major consequence of this pragmatic choice is the absence of a unifying principle able to interconnect the different periods and to show how they proceed from each other through the interplay of internal and external factors. Hence the scattered treatment of the central issues, continuously present in university life but handled as if the different periods (medieval, early modern, modern, contemporary) were self-sufficient. Each of the authors gives a masterly assessment of the results of recent research in his particular field, and some chapters present for a particular period perceptive analyses of the role of the university in society and in intellectual life, but virtually no attempt is made to achieve a general picture of the history of the French universities through the eight centuries of their existence or to identify in the long run the real particularities of the French university system. As Jacques Verger puts it in his introduction, this volume is a provisional balance-sheet of current research, without trying to reach a synthetic image. As such, the predominance of the social perspective is as striking as is the absence of an economic or an anthropological approach.

Is it possible to imagine another solution? Such a solution would not start by defining formal university structures or functions, or even 'essential' rites or symbols, but by identifying the central issues that constitute the identity of the university system both through its self-perception and the way its partners look at it in the society at large. Wouldn't the central issue of the self-consciousness of the educational institutions have procured a first guideline? The question whether a new, rival institution claiming university status could or could not be admitted to the select range of university level institutions appears as a central item in all periods. The same applies to the introduction of new teaching matters, always sharply discussed. Or to the reflection on the tasks, duties and functions of university teaching and research. Isn't it through such recurrent debates that the university not only defends but also defines itself and realizes its 'identity'?

The final conception of any long-term synthesis in university history depends on the answer given to the basic problem whether the continuity of the university system and of academic teaching bears a formal, a functional, or a symbolic character. In this particular volume, however, a thorough and well-informed treatment of particular aspects of single periods, not always consistent between each other, is preferred to a long-term approach of some central issues. Always well written, it provides not only the specialist but also the general reader with a fresh and clear overview of new insights into the history of French universities. As such it raises new questions, for example about the incongruity of the early modern French universities: their time-worn structure and conservative recruitment patterns contrast sharply with their ability to assimilate the new science, better and faster than historians have assumed until quite recently.

The volume doesn't pretend to be a general synthesis but even so it shows a somewhat peculiar deviation towards the end. After the creation of the Napoleonic university the importance of the sociological, external approach and the weight of the political factor seem to increase more and more. Is this a logical consequence of the editor's choice, since he has entrusted the modern and contemporary chapters to sociologists, not historians? Or does it testify to a real change either within the university or in its relation to society? It is, of course, always difficult to decide whether and until what point a historical narrative is the result of a research option or a reflection of reality. Yet there is some reason to believe that the final chapters are biased by the author's options. The history of the French universities after 1950, in particular, as written in this book by Passeron, reflects a preconception of university history in which the university is a pure product of the socio-economic forces and its whole evolution is exclusively seen from the country's centre, Paris. Is it really too early for a more balanced, historian's view of this period?

There are no footnotes in this volume, but a short bibliography at the end of each chapter. A chronology and a useful index conclude the book.

Willem Frijhoff
Erasmus University, Rotterdam

Die Universität zu Prag. Munich: Verlaghaus Sudetenland (Schriften der Sudetendeutschen Akademie der Wissenschaften, Vol.7), 1986. 207 pp.

This volume is the second book published in Germany in the last decade giving a broad survey of the results of research into problems concerning the history of Prague university. The first discussed the division into Czech and German universities in 1882, and was published on the occasion of the anniversary of this event in 1982 (*Die Teilung der Prager Universität 1882 und die intellektuelle Desintegration in den böhmischen Ländern*, Munich, Oldenbourg, 1984, 220pp.) Individual monographic studies have also been published but *Die Universität zu Prag* has broader aspirations; it attempts to cover all periods of the university's history. Its aims are expressed in the chronological survey of six centuries of university life (with two surprising errors in the dates of the division of the University in 1882 and the abolition of the German university in 1945) and in the broad, good bibliography of the literature of Prague university history published in German (pp. 190–203). Nevertheless the volume does not succeed in giving equally sophisticated articles for all historical periods; its most important part, much more than a half of the whole volume, is the article by Peter Moraw, 'Die Universität Prag im Mittelalter. Grundzüge ihrer Geschichte im europäischen Zusammenhang' (pp. 9–134). Moraw's article is the first real broad and deep synthesis of the earlier history of Prague university produced in German since Tomek's *Geschichte der Prager Universitât*, written before 1848.

The first question in Moraw's study is for whom was the first Central European university founded and why was it situated in Prague when in other parts of the Empire it could be based on older school traditions and a more developed cultural and economic infrastructure? The answer is, according to Moraw, quite simple; the decision was taken according to the wishes of the ruling dynasty and in the interests of the local church organization. The Luxemburg dynasty and Bohemian church hierarchy became the most important sponsors and protectors of the new *studium generale* in the first decades of its existence.

The University was during the period before the Hussite wars – according to the strict interpretation of the foundation *Bulla* of Charles IV – divided into two corporations: the Juridical University and the University of the other three faculties among which the Faculty of Arts was dominant. The members of both Prague universities followed their studies for the same reason; they prepared them for further church, or rarely lay, careers.

Teaching activities in the university were not attractive for them, even when the monarch and the archbishop were solicitous to attract them to the benefices within the colleges.

Moraw analyses another of the specific features of Prague University, its system of university 'nations', which was at that time to some degree anachronistic. These complicated and somewhat clumsy institutions became in Prague the centre of many conflicts within the university. The most important among them, those ended by the secession in 1409, had, according to Moraw's opinion, first of all social origins. They were connected with the immediate dependence of the university on both local powers, the dynasty and the archbishop. The deteriorating position of both of them was exploited by the members of the domestic, but least numerous, university nation to change the internal order of the university. Moraw, in agreement with other authors (F. Kavka, F. Seibt), takes the events connected with the edict of Kutná Hora as caused mostly by the unsatisfied social aspirations of the teachers of the arts faculty.

Moraw's study contains many new interesting ideas concerning the history of Prague university, based on a new interpretation of some more or less well known data about the administrative and institutional structure of the university and on a full knowledge of the literature published during the last years both in Czech and German. The problem that was for many decades a centre of the dispute between Czech and German historians has found in Peter Moraw an objective author who is able to integrate the history of Prague university into the social context of the Bohemian lands and the whole of Central Europe. The reader would prefer to find in this study in individual cases evidence in the footnotes. The list of sources and literature at the end can help in general orientation, but it does not give enough detail for individual conclusions.

The article by Karl Schnith, 'Zum Wesen und Bedeutung des Lollardentums im Zeitraum von 1382 bis 1414', is an attempt to find comparative material for the social and religious contents of Hussitism in the simultaneous English movement that was also under the strong influence of the ideas of the Oxford reformer, John Wyclif. The author looks for parallels between the Hussite revolution and the Oldcastle uprising, and finds them in the causes and in the course of events of both. His interest is especially in the description of the contacts between the Czech and English Wyclifists, which were so important for events in the Bohemian lands.

The biography of a highly learned member of the Augustinian order is the subject of the article written by Ernst Nittner, 'Von Mainz nach Prag. Jordan Simon (1719–1776)'. The monastery of the Augustinians in the Lesser Town of Prague at St. Thomas Church was very important for the Catholic German students in Prague between 1918 and 1938, but this monastery had for the German-speaking Bohemians an importance even earlier. Jordan Simon, born into a teacher's family, entered the Augustinian order and studied in Mainz. After being ordained he spent two years travelling throughout Europe but afterwards he came back obediently to his monastery. He taught at the university of Erfurt, but because of his reformist Catholic opinions he came into conflict with his superior, the archbishop of Mainz. Nevertheless he found a supporter in Kosmas Schmalfus, the first professor of the theology of St. Augustine at Prague university. The chairs of Augustinian theology were, together with the chairs of Thomist theology, established in the Austrian universities by the decision of the *Hofstudienkomission* to diminish the monopoly of the Jesuit order in theological instruction. When Schmalfus went to Rome to become the general assistant of the Augustinian order, he removed all obstacles and prepared for Simon, who condemned in a very overt form both Free Thought and superstition disguised as devoutness, the way to the Prague chair of Augustinian theology and to his last quiet years in St. Thomas monastery.

The article discussing the history of the Prague university insignia brings little valuable information about the new insignia of the German university that were given by the Czechoslovak government to this university when it conveyed the historical ones to the Czech university in 1934 (Gisela Hüttisch-Maximilian Hüttisch, 'Zur Geschichte der Insignien der Prager Universität'). These insignia were used between 1937 and 1939. After 15 March the German university took at once the old insignia from its Czech partner a few months before the Czech universities were closed by Hitler's authorities. The new insignia were not used any more and could not be found later. Maximilian Hüttisch gives information about their origins and provides illustrations. Unfortunately other information in this article only reproduces the official version presented by the German university at that time.

Aleš Zelenka entitles his article, 'Bemerkungen zum Siegel der mittelalterlichen Universität Prag.' It contains no real analysis, only a few remarks about the oldest Prague university seal without any knowledge of the fundamental analytical article of Josef Krása, published in the memorial volume *Karolus Quartus* in 1978; this contains an analysis of fourteenth century seals from the point of view of art history. Krása with his broad knowledge did not dare to give the name of any possible designer, whereas Zelenka tries to identify the goldsmith Gerhard from Dortmund as a probable designer of the seal. It is difficult to deny his hypothesis, but these reviewers do not find any real reason for its acceptance. So only the list of the early university seals used by the university of Paris brings information not contained in Krása's article. At the end of the book, the chronology of probably the most important events in the history of Prague university and

a selective bibliography of the German literature on the history of the
university can be found.

Jan Havránek and Michal Svatoš
University of Prague

Mariano Peset and Salvador Albiñana (eds), *Claustros y Estudiantes*. Valencia: Universidad de Valencia, 1989. 2 vols xxxii + 432 pp; vii + 426 pp.

These two volumes bring together forty-six essays on the history of Spanish, Portuguese, and Spanish-American universities. They are the fruit of a conference held at Valencia in 1987. They continue the good work initiated by Professor Peset in a seminar at Valencia which has already brought forth the important book, *Universidades Españolas y Americanas* (1987; see *ante* vol. x (1991), 288–9). In his prologue Professor Peset sets out his objectives under five heads. He wants the historians of universities to break free from their isolation. He wishes students of the history of particular universities to be aware of where their study fits into the analysis of the roots of power in university corporations; he insists that the people who worked in universities are more worthy of study than a static consideration of the institution to which they belonged; he hopes that new emphasis on what was studied at universities and how the syllabus changed will prove revealing, and finally he believes that a study of the financial aspects of universities, from the salaries of the staff to the income and expenditure of the universities themselves, is an essential preliminary to the understanding of their development.

It is clear that the authors of the essays in this collection have borne these aspirations well in mind and that these aims have produced particularly fruitful results. Naturally the history of the University of Valencia is well represented (eleven essays), and especial emphasis is placed on the development of its school of medicine. On the other side of the Atlantic the University of Mexico in which Professor Peset is especially interested is also well to the fore (nine essays). But the range is wide and reaches to Alcalá de Henares, Cervera, Gandía, Salamanca, Santiago de Compostela, and Valladolid in the peninsula and to Argentina, Chile, Colombia, Cuba, Ecuador, Peru, and Venezuela in Spanish America.

The chronological range stretches from the sixteenth to the early nineteenth century but the bulk of the essays belong to the eighteenth. They are

particularly concerned with the Enlightenment of the reign of Charles III
and its effects in Spain and overseas. The stimulus provided by the seizure of
the property of the Jesuits in 1767 is a recurring theme. An essay which
bears out splendidly Professor Peset's aims is that by J. Rodríguez-San
Pedro Bezares and others – a very detailed analysis of the rise and fall of the
income and expenditure of the University of Salamanca in relation to the
fiscal and economic policies of the governments of seventeenth-century
Spain.

J. R. L. Highfield
Merton College
Oxford

R. C. Schwinges, *Deutsche Universitätsbesucher im. 14 und 15.
Jahrhundert. Studien zur Sozialgeschichte des alten Reiches.* Stuttgart: Franz Steiner Verlag 1986. xviii + 732 pp.

Recent years appear to have seen the revival of 'blockbuster' studies
concerned with university history published in Germany. In the case of the
present volume we must doubt whether it was necessary to reproduce
around 150 pages of tables of computer print-outs that add to the bulk –
and expense – of this book. What may have been a necessity for a
Habilitationsschrift produces a cumbersome and somewhat daunting study
for the busy university historian. Readers must also be warned that they
must face – or merely ignore – large chunks of sociological analysis before
reaching the central core of historical information and interpretation. Nor
must they be deceived by the title given to this volume; some two hundred
pages are devoted solely to the examination of the university of Cologne.
There are perhaps here three studies in one book!

Nevertheless, we are given in the historical section of this volume the
details of an investigation that no historian of European universities can
ignore. Schwinges has taken the printed editions of the various matriculation records of the German universities and subjected them to computer
analysis. He investigates the 'demography' of attendance, ranking the
German universities in the order of their popularity, showing how the
number of entrants rose and fell and suggesting why, investigating the
geographical and social background of the students, analysing the distribution of the intake into the various faculties, making suggestions about the
role of 'poverty' and 'nobility' and associating this analysis with the
different periods of university foundation, expansion and contraction. The

result is a mass of detail that no reviewer can hope to summarise but can only urge his readers themselves to consult. Especially for the university of Cologne, we are given the statistics of student life that enable us to construct with greater confidence a picture of the structure of that interesting city-university.

Naturally, there are some caveats that must be considered. How sound is the evidence on which this study is based? Many of the editions of the German university matriculation records – where they exist in full – date from an earlier and perhaps less critical scholarly age: misreadings and omissions are not uncommon. More important is the question of how many students escaped entry in the matriculation register and how many enrolled *causa honoris* without intending to study. Such factors may not alter comparative conclusions since they affected all universities in a generally similar manner. But when considering such subjects as 'poverty' and 'nobility', they become more important. Both the 'poor' and the 'nobility' formed minority groups within the German universities and any serious omissions in the matriculation records could have grave consequences for the analyst. The 'poor', for example, could be expected to try and avoid entry in the records both to escape the fee required and because they might be doubtful as to their ability to remain at the university. The 'nobles' would, of course, be those that the university would most like to honour by including their names in its registers and, in turn, nobles would themselves appreciate the opportunity to associate themselves with what was often a local university, especially at the time of its foundation or on occasions when commemorations were celebrated. Such nobles may never have attended a single lecture! It must also be said that the results of Schwinges' analysis also often fall into the category of telling us what we already knew or strongly suspected. For instance, it is not especially unexpected to find that there were more foreign students in German universities that were nearer to foreign countries! Nor can we be surprised at the large intake at Cologne from the city and surrounding areas themselves. Nevertheless, even here it must be accepted that what was earlier merely surmise is now supported by a mass of evidence.

While this is certainly not a work to be read for pleasure, it will remain as an essential reference book for many years. Will someone from those dead figures now bring to life the German universities? Behind the cold computer analysis must lie many human stories of pain and pleasure, of failure and success, of expectations achieved and ambitions thwarted.

John M. Fletcher
Aston University

Armin Gerl, *Trigonometrisch-astronomisches Rechnen kurz vor Copernicus. Der Briefwechsel Regiomontanus-Bianchini.* Stuttgart: Steiner, 1989.358 pp. DM 70.

Johannes Regiomontanus has long been something of a figurehead for the scientific side of the Renaissance – and yet it clearly does no harm to associate the name of Copernicus with his, so as to catch the ignorant reader. Giovanni Bianchini is less well known. Astronomer to the Duke of Ferrara, he composed among other things a *Flores Almagesti*, that is, one of the many abbreviated versions of Ptolemy's *Almagest*, and various astronomical tables and collections of tables based largely on the Alfonsine. Regiomontanus' great reputation also owed much in a way to Ptolemy: as a young prodigy at the University of Vienna he had been appointed a colleague of Georg Peurbach, and their careers became more closely linked after the arrival of Cardinal Bessarion in Vienna in 1460. Bessarion persuaded Peurbach to undertake an *Epitome* of the *Almagest*. Peurbach died before completing it. Regiomontanus pledged himself to continue, and seems to have had the manuscript ready early in 1463. It was not to be printed until 1496, twenty years after his relatively early death, but quickly became a valued textbook with an unusually vivid style that served astronomy well.

Although his scientific originality has been much exaggerated there is no doubt that he had a pervasive influence on the course and style of European learning. It is not simply that a man like Copernicus could be stimulated by his reading of the *Epitome* to modify the Ptolemaic system, but that armed with fluency in Greek, and encouraged by Bessarion to get back to the purity of his originals, Regiomontanus helped to persuade his readers to think for themselves on the basis of those originals.

I should like to say that the correspondence with Bianchini reveals some of the springs of Regiomontanus' magic, but for all but the dedicated astronomical calculator it will make obscure reading. (It should be emphasized that Armin Gerl's is only a summary and analysis based on earlier editions.) It opened with a lost letter from Bianchini announcing an observation he had made (5 April 1463) on an unknown star. Regiomontanus replied on 27 July 1463 – the post with Italy was better in those days – with a detailed calculation of coordinates. Mr Gerl, whose Inaugural Dissertation this book represents, follows the original calculation with his own digest of it, annotates it heavily along the way, and allows us to savour fully the style of trigonometric-astronomical calculation on the eve of Copernicus. He does this all told for five letters, the last of February 1464. One has the feeling that the two correspondents were perhaps really engaged in a trial of strength: at times the correspondence seems to hint at the problem-challenge genre of later centuries. They both emerge as highly competent mathematicians. In all this we learn something of new decimal styles in tabulation. We learn that there were some new trigonometrical formulae in use, how precession calculations were done, that then as now people occasionally erred, and many such things. At all events, the promise of the title of this new volume is fulfilled.

As a piece of book-production it is unimaginative: there is much white space in the notes, and there is alas no index. As a work of scholarship it takes the reader through every difficulty with a resolution that would have made Regiomontanus shudder. 'Regiomontanus now multiplies 28905 by 60 000 and obtains 1 734 300 000, and divides by 55 585, to obtain 31 201.' There are neater (and therefore cheaper) ways of expressing such truths, but perhaps they are not true to history, and there is, to be sure, a class of reader that prefers the truth to be spelled out in full. To them, and to those in a hurry, I commend the note that runs from p. 157 to 167, with its potted history of trigonometry. Many a doctoral thesis has less substance.

John D. North
University of Groningen

Antinino Poppi, *Introduzione All 'Aristotelismo Padovano*. Padova: Editrice Antenore, 1991. Second edition. 143 pp.

In this welcome second edition of Antinino Poppi's *Introduzione All 'Aristotelismo Padovano*, the two papers published in the 1970 edition are each supplemented by an appendix with new material. The first paper, 'Lineamenti di Storia della Scuola Padovana di Filosofia', provides a sketch of the development of philosophy at the University of Padua and places in context two fundamental Paduan issues, those of immortality and scientific method. This paper is supplemented by a newly added study of the transition from Aristotelian natural philosophy to modern science, considering, in particular, developments of Zaberella and Galileo. Poppi briefly reviews and puts into perspective the discussion of this issue since it was introduced by Randall more than thirty years ago.

The second paper, 'Studi Recenti Sull 'Aristotelismo Italiano del Rinascimento (1958–1969)', provides a review of the discussion of Italian Aristotelianism from Renan's *Averroes et l'Averroisme* published in 1852 to C. B. Schmitt's paper 'Comparison of Zabarella's View with Galileo's in *De Motu*' of 1969. This is supplemented by a consideration of activities of the *Centro aristotelico* of Padua. Poppi, in this newly added appendix, briefly reviews the contemporary discussion of the origin and context of Paduan Aristotelianism, Paduan epistemology, metaphysics, logic, and the problem raised by Pomponazzi. He examines a number of publications of the *Centro per la storia della tradizione aristotelica nel veneto*, including, among other texts, P. Marangon's 1977 monograph on the origin of Paduan Aristotelianism, M. L. Pine's 1986 monograph on Pietro Pomponazzi, and Galileo's *Tractatio de praecognitionibus et praecognitis* and *Tractatio de demonstratione*, transcribed from the Latin autograph by W.F. Edwards, with an introduction, notes and commentary by W. A. Wallace.

During the Renaissance, the University of Padua, renowned for its distinguished medical school, was one of the most important universities in Europe, and it was the centre of a distinctive philosophic tradition. Poppi's monograph is a valuable source of information for those interested in an introduction to Renaissance Aristotelianism as it developed at the University of Padua, and it is a useful guide to works about Paduan Aristotelianism.

Emily Michael
Brooklyn College
City University of New York
USA

Quaderni per la Storia dell'Università di Padova, 20 (1987) and 21 (1988). Padua: Editrice Antenore.

These two volumes continue the Quaderni's admirable coverage of Paduan history. A number of pieces relate to the fifteenth century. In vol. 20, Donato Gallo contributes fresh material to the published series of degree records (1419–28), while Annalisa Belloni, investigating Johannes Heller's period of study at Padua later in the century, adds substantially to her important study of the organization and conduct of law teaching. Vol. 21 includes a study by Roland Hissette of the relationship of two Paduan teachers, Giovanni Marcanova and Nicoletto Vernia, to the Averroist tradition, as well as editions of the grant of citizenship to Antonio Niccolò Loschi (by Dieter Girgensohn) and a university oration of Pietro Marcello given in 1417 (by Donato Gallo). The other main focus of the two volumes is the late seventeenth and eighteenth century. Dante Nardo provides a concise presentation of the philosopher, Latinist and editor Giovanni Antonio Volpi (vol. 20); Brendan Dooley's study of Italian university medical teaching from Sbaraglia to Vallisnieri (vol. 21) informs sensitively of classroom practices and pedagogical attitudes; Cinzio Gibin publishes correspondence of the 1790s between the medical professor Stefano Gallini and Giuseppe Olivi (vol. 21). As usual the bibliographical section is rich and meticulous, and together with the notice section and the reviews – which include an extensive article by Tiziana Pesenti on recent work on Paduan scholastic medicine (vol. 20) – maintains the high standards of information and scholarly assistance for which this journal is known.

Peter Denley
Department of History
Queen Mary and Westfield College
University of London
Hampstead Campus
London NW3 7ST

Rudolph Stichweh, *Der frühmoderne Staat und die europäische Universität*. Frankfurt am Main: Suhrkamp, 1991. 427pp.

Professor Stichweh's *Habilitation* thesis is an extensive analysis of state, society, and university in the early modern period. Stichweh is a sociologist with a background in eighteenth and nineteenth century intellectual and scientific history. The principal sources are contemporary writings about universities and states, the treatment being literary and qualitative rather than quantitative. After establishing the historical context of universities from the thirteenth century, Stichweh focuses on the sixteenth, seventeenth and eighteenth centuries, ranging over many important issues: for example, the educational 'system' as a whole; the effect of the political and ideological climate on learning; education of the nobility; religious influences on universities. The sections on education, socialization, and social class are particularly interesting. The argument is that medieval universities were formed mainly by interaction with the church. Sixteenth- and seventeenth-century universities were not sleepy backwaters but influenced, and were affected by, wider developments within state and society. Relations with the church weakened and secular interactions became much more significant. Only during the eighteenth and nineteenth centuries did universities become increasingly insular, academic institutions. The book touches on all parts of Europe but the emphasis is on the German lands, England, and France: this is reflected in the extensive bibliography of printed primary sources and secondary literature. The writing style is complex and demanding, aimed at an academic rather than a student audience, though the short, headed sections make the book easy to use. The author makes explicit use of theory and forms wide-ranging generalisations which, despite the lack of detailed examples from the very different societies of early modern Europe, are usually accurate and never less than thought provoking. This book is likely to be well received by non-specialists. Historians of universities will find it most stimulating even if there are times when they may be cautious about the way the intellectual coherence of the whole has been achieved at the expense of a comprehensive recognition of the intractability of some of the parts.

R. A. Houston
Department of Modern History
University of St Andrews

David Stevenson, *King's College, Aberdeen, 1560–1641: From Protestant Reformation to Covenanting Revolution*. Aberdeen: Aberdeen University Press, 1990. x + 180 pp. £8.90.

This is the third in a series of quincentennial studies in the history of the University of Aberdeen, which was founded in 1495. A range of monographs is promised on different aspects of the university's evolution. The university's authorities are to be congratulated on commissioning the series – a bold decision in these times of shrinking financial resources.

As its title suggests, this volume is primarily a study of the religious history of King's College Aberdeen from the Scottish Reformation to the successful revolt of the covenanters against Charles I. The principal developments during these years were the establishment of Protestantism in the college in the 1560s, the implementation in subsequent decades of intellectual and institutional changes linked to Andrew Melville's drive to reform the Scottish universities, the many years of feuding over the legitimacy of the old constitution against the new (essentially Melvillian) foundation, and the rearguard action fought by the 'Aberdeen doctors' against the covenanters in the late 1630s. King's was the only college in the university at the start of this period but was joined by a second foundation, Marischal College, in 1593. The relationship of the two institutions is another of the themes covered by the book.

Dr Stevenson describes and analyses these events in detail, drawing his evidence from a wide range of primary and secondary sources. Where records have not survived – particularly those of the later sixteenth century –

his reconstructions are cautious and thoughtful. Most of the surviving evidence concerns institutional, political/religious and intellectual developments and their interrelationship. Due to the lack of extant material there is very little about students and their everyday life. The description of the college's constitutional changes and the conflicts surrounding them is particularly thorough and there is a translation of the 'New Foundation' by G. Patrick Edwards among the appendices. Everything is set in its context within the history of the Scottish universities, the country's religious evolution, and shifts in political power and patronage – all of which had their impact on King's College.

Although this is a short book it is an admirably thorough piece of scholarship and will be very useful to any historian interested in the universities of the early modern period, whatever their particular focus of study. It can be recommended especially to those researching the history of the two English universities who – like this reviewer – all too often forget the British context of their subject.

John Twigg
London

Mordechai Feingold (ed.), *Before Newton. The life and times of Isaac Barrow*. Cambridge: Cambridge University Press, 1990. 380 pp.

The role of the universities in the Scientific Revolution of the seventeenth century has for long been the subject of a continuing debate. The earlier view that the universities adhered to a conservative and anti-scientific attitude has more recently been replaced by a more positive appraisal of their contributions. The universities, it is said, at least provided a number of talented individuals with a stimulating intellectual atmosphere, proper means of living and working facilities. Galileo and Newton both laid the foundations of their enormous *oeuvre* while being employed in their respective universities. This more positive turn of mind, however, is hardly a more apt appreciation of whatever it was the universities stood for. In fact, assigning a role to the universities in the Scientific Revolution already presupposes that the universities were directly and consciously involved. A more balanced understanding of the academic milieu should in the first place be concerned with the particular intellectual and educational project the universities were trying to carry out. If universities are to be labelled conservative after all, it is certainly worth while finding out what exactly they were conserving. The work of Isaac Barrow (1630–1677) lends itself perfectly to analyse the academic aspirations in the face of the advent of the new science.

Where does Barrow stand in the historiography of the Scientific Revolution? Foremost, Barrow plays a role in the intellectual debt of Newton to his university background. As the first Lucasian professor of mathematics at the university of Cambridge, he is said to have 'discovered' Newton's mathematical gifts and to have helped him pursuing an academic career. However, in a strict sense Newton was no pupil of Barrow and his work shows no traces of any 'Barrovian' heritage. In the development of mathematical analysis, Barrow holds a place as a forerunner with some original contributions of his own but without any direct influence on those who superseded him. Furthermore, he was rather conservative in matters of natural philosophy and warned his students against a too great adherence to the new doctrines. In 1669 he gave up his Lucasian professorship (to the benefit of Newton) to devote himself to what he considered his real vocation, 'to serve God and the Gospel of his Son.' It is easy to see how Barrow, overshadowed by the creative genius of Newton, could slip from the attention of historians of science to become the perfect example of a traditional, conservative university professor, for whom the study of natural science was only of secondary interest. A first reappraisal of Barrow should then obviously set him free from the Newtonian context which does not give him a fair deal. The book under review, appropriately called *Before Newton* does a fine job to bring finally back to life the scholar and divine Isaac Barrow and the intellectual world he stood for.

Before Newton contains seven papers by six authors. The first long paper by Feingold paints an intellectual biography of Barrow. Without in any way underrating the original contributions of the other authors, Feingold's paper can be regarded as a synthesis of the book's message, which is elaborated more fully but also in a more demanding way in the other papers. The scientific and mathematical work of Barrow is studied in great detail by Alan E. Shapiro (optics) and Michael S. Mahoney (mathematics). Both these papers are quite difficult and tedious for anyone not versed in the history of science. It is to be feared that this could deter university historians from going into this matter, which, however, would be to miss much of the value of this book. John Gascoigne gives an illuminating view of the intellectual atmosphere at Cambridge during the Interregnum and the Restoration. The book closes with three shorter papers on Barrow as a scholar (A. Grafton), Barrow as a preacher (I. Simon), and Barrow's library (Feingold).

The combination of papers on history of universities, history of science, and history of ideas makes *Before Newton* a very stimulating book. Its main argument concerns an evaluation of Barrow's defence of classical learning (including Aristotelian philosophy), founded on a genuine concern for a solid, rational education and the preservation of Christian faith. The new science certainly put a strain on this educational programme, but it did not disturb Barrow's strong views on the higher calling of scholars. For Barrow, science was evidently a second choice, an outlet for his higher ambitions which could not be realised, and only to be valued in as much as it led to 'the contemplation of the truth'. Still, science, both in its mathematical and philosophical aspects, was not underestimated by Barrow and received his full attention.

How well could science thrive in this university environment? Interestingly, the respective images of Barrow as a scientist presented here differ a lot. Shapiro brings out the innovative contributions of Barrow to the theory of optical imagery, fully adopted by Newton, while Mahoney on the other hand shows how far Barrow was still removed from the fundamentally new concepts of late seventeenth century mathematics. The mathematical work of Barrow may indeed provide an inventory of the materials available to Newton and Leibniz, but is not a prototype of the calculus. Even then, Barrow's mathematical writings are clearly more than simple academic expositions of classical theories. Barrow was indeed convinced that university lectures should bring students in close enough contact with the current problems of contemporary scientific endeavours. He evidently was aware of the inherent limitations set to such a programme; one cannot teach advanced mathematics to students who still need to make the first steps into the field. This may in fact account for the amount of vagueness and superficiality in some of his mathematical lectures. Shapiro, however, points out without any reserve that the *Optical Lectures* of 1669 represented 'the most advanced treatise on geometrical optics yet published.' He concludes that their contents 'are so sophisticated that they were surely above the head of any student'. It is puzzling to hear Barrow assert that with these *Optical Lectures* he deliberately planned to avoid the too difficult subject of Pure Geometry 'and to stray forthwith into pleasanter fields'! It is evident that the university lectures given by Barrow were of a surprisingly high scientific standard, to say the least. In this sense, Newton would not belie the standards set by his predecessor.

Before Newton gives the reader a good inside view of university life and the intellectual climate in seventeenth century Cambridge. It is certainly too early to formulate a coherent view on the relationship between university scholars and their attitudes towards the new science. This book at least does not offer a conclusive or definitive argument but it touches upon all the relevant material and pays attention to the different areas of research

involved. Barrow will not be the only one who has greatly benefited from the
work of these authors.

Geert H. W. Vanpaemel
Economische Hogeschool Sint-Aloysius
Stormstraat 2
1000 Brussels
Belgium

John Twigg, *The University of Cambridge and the English Revolution, 1625–1688.* The History of the University of Cambridge Texts and Studies I. Boydell Press/Cambridge University Library, 1990. xiii + 325pp.

John Twigg's meticulously researched and carefully considered work fills an obvious lacuna in the well-tilled field of seventeenth-century English historiography. For few institutions were more closely involved in the ideological and political upheavals of that turbulent century than the two universities: institutions which largely served to shape and define the theological debates which coloured the age and which also helped to mould the mentality of the governing elite in Church and State. Thanks to Twigg's labours we now have a detailed account of Cambridge's role in the events between 1625 and 1688 – a period which Twigg understandably links together under the general heading of 'the English Revolution' – and the forthcoming history of the University of Oxford in the seventeenth century should complement his work with a detailed study of the 'Other Place' during the same period.

Cambridge has long been associated with Puritanism but Twigg's account brings out the extent to which the university, in the ideologically charged period of the pre-Civil War years, also acted as a centre for the promotion of Puritanism's theological *bête noir*: Arminianism. Thanks to royal patronage and the sledgehammer tactics of Laud the Arminians made rapid strides within the university, so much so that Twigg suggests that for the Laudians 'Complete dominance was only a matter of time' (p.41), though adding the important caveat that 'Time, however, was not on the Laudians' side'. The extent of the Laudians' penetration within the university also accounts for the massive scale of ejections which followed the parliamentary visitation of the university in 1644–5, Twigg's patient investigations showing that about half the fellowship of the university were expelled. Another culling of dons followed in 1650–1, with about 29 being ejected but thereafter the Interregnum governments were in some ways less inclined to meddle in the universities' affairs than their Stuart counterparts were both before and after the Restoration. Twigg's detailed analysis of the use of royal mandates indicates the extent of royal intrusion throughout the seventeenth century, making James II's attempts to advance his academic protégés appear much less unprecedented than commonly thought. The extent of royal involvement in university life also underlines the significance that the universities were seen as having in the establishment of ideological support for the constituted order in Church and State, something of which Charles II and his ministers were particularly aware with their largely successful endeavours to ensure that college heads were appointed who could be relied upon to support the cause of the restored Church and King. So successful was Charles that, as Twigg brings out, the university's loyalties were to be sorely tested under James II as Cambridge dons vainly attempted to reconcile Passive Obedience to the Lord's Anointed with hostility to a popish monarch.

Twigg's work offers, then, much commendable detail on some of the major currents of the age. Its origins as a Ph.D are, however, still rather evident and the reader is often left to discern for him/herself how the material presented relates to the larger themes which are immanent in the work. Thus Chapter One provides much useful background but does not set out to establish firmly in the reader's mind the underlying themes which inform the work; similarly the overall coherence of the book would have been improved by a conclusion drawing together its major threads. The author's interests lie primarily in the political-cum-ecclesiastical history of the age and the book is therefore rather summary in its account of the changes in the university's intellectual life (particularly in areas other than theology) but to ask for more on such subjects is to ask the author to widen the scope of the book beyond its already wide limits. For in providing a clear account of how the reverberations of the great political and religious upheavals of the seventeenth century were reflected in miniature in the microcosm of Cambridge Twigg has greatly enhanced both our understanding of Cambridge's past and the character and dynamics of 'the century of revolution'.

John Gascoigne
School of History
University of New South Wales
Kensington. NSW 2033
Australia

Matti Klinge, Rainer Knapas, Anto Leikola, and John Strömberg, *Kungliga Akademien i Åbo 1640–1808; Kejserliga Alexanders Universitet 1808–1917* (Helsingfors Universitet 1640–1990 I–II). Otava: Helsingfors, 1988–9. 740pp., 944pp.

In 1990 Finland's oldest university, now situated in the country's capital city, celebrated its 350th anniversary. In association with the event a lavish three-volume history of the institution from its foundation was planned. The first two volumes, here reviewed, carry the story up to the attainment of Finnish independence during the First World War. The country's only university throughout this period, it has been a focus of national cultural, and at some periods also of political, life to a much greater extent than have the universities of larger countries and indeed than those in the rest of Scandinavia. All the great figures in the country's public life have been associated with it in one way or another.

It began in what was until the nineteenth century Finland's chief town of Turku (in Swedish Åbo), like its eight-year older sister university in Dorpat, as one of the *gymnasia* founded by king Gustavus Adolphus to train the growing number of bureaucrats needed to run the expanding Swedish empire and raised to university status largely by the efforts of the then governor-general count Per Brahe in an effort to encourage the culture and scholarship thought fitting for Sweden's new position in Europe. In its early years, however, it appears to have differed little from a gymnasium with regard to syllabus or quality of teaching, and was long as important for the training of priests as of civil servants; a large proportion of its students were sons of the manse, and the young nobles who attended rarely graduated. It was not until after it resumed its life following the end of the Russian occupation of Finland the Great Northern War (during which professors and students took refuge in Sweden) that it began to acquire academic distinction not only in Finland (still part of the Swedish monarchy) but also in Northern Europe. In the later part of the century, although it still lay in the shadow of the University of Uppsala, with which its ties were close, it boasted a number of distinguished scholars and national figures like Henrik Gabriel Porthan, first its librarian and then one of its professors, who helped to make it the centre for the new consciousness of Finnish national identity.

But it really blossomed after Finland in 1809 was lost to the Swedish monarchy to become a grand duchy under the Russian tsar. Tsar Alexander I made most generous provision for the institution, which in 1828, after a disastrous fire had destroyed a large part of Turku, moved to Helsinki, now the grand duchy's capital, and was rewarded by having his name attached to it. The new building designed for it by Carl Engel faced the centre of administration across Senate Square as a symbol of its close ties with the State; the heir to the throne was usually to be its chancellor, and most of the country's civil servants were recruited from its students. Yet throughout the Russian period the university, although the student radicals occasionally caused the authorities some headaches, enjoyed a privileged status, and appears to have suffered little during the process of Russification of Finland instituted by Nicholas II in the 1890s. Indeed it grew markedly around the turn of the century, to become the largest university in Scandinavia with some 3,000 students. Both in its faculty and student life were reflected the language battles of the nineteenth century, whose main protagonists were among the professoriate.

The approach in each volume, particularly in the first, is topical rather than chronological with each scholar involved in the enterprise contributing chapters on, for example, administration, the teaching body, curriculum, student life and buildings. Some of these are, it must be admitted, more readable than others. The creation of new chairs and the succession of professors in the nineteenth and early twentieth century does become a rather dull chronicle, and could have been as well treated in tabular form. But a patient reading of the whole does provide an excellent impression of all aspects of university life over the quarter of a millenium covered. It represents a great deal of time and effort as well as of patient scholarship, and is richly illustrated (although it is regrettable that only one pictorial record of the old buildings in Turku appears to have survived). Each anniversary in the university's life has been made the subject of elaborate celebrations, but such a history is the best of all possible monuments.

Stewart Oakley
University of East Anglia

L. W. B. Brockliss, *French Higher Education in the Seventeenth and Eighteenth Centuries. A Cultural History*. Oxford Clarendon Press: 1987. xvi + 544 pp.

Until the publication of this seminal book, French higher education in the early modern period was regarded either as an outdated educational system that had missed its connection with modernity or as a pure instrument for the reproduction of the monarchy's élites. On both fronts Laurence Brockliss strongly suggests a refreshing new vision, based on an extensive research in original, mostly neglected, documents and some new questions. His research material includes hundreds of textbooks, scholarly exercises, theses, note-books, disputes and examinations, most of which had never been used before, at least not in a national survey. Indeed, Brockliss's third major contribution to French university history is his decidedly national approach, with due attention paid to such university mammoths like Paris and Montpellier, but without overstating their importance. This national approach is rooted in the two leading questions that Brockliss asks himself throughout his study. Firstly, what was, in the different arts and sciences as elements of the university curriculum, the teachers' capacity to assimilate and hence to disseminate new science (science being used in this book in the broad sense of the word, including the liberal arts)? Secondly, how did institutionalized science teaching contribute to the formation of what he calls the French 'liberal professional élite'? Both questions involve not so much the few top-ranking scholars and administrators surrounding the monarch as the average educated intellectuals of which there were tens of thousands all over the kingdom.

Brockliss organizes his treatment along two lines of unequal importance: institutional elements and curricular developments. To begin with, he rightly points out that there was no real division between the *collèges de plein exercice* (public grammar schools with a superstructure of at least some courses in philosophy) and the universities. His detailed sketch of the whole higher education system (including rival institutions as the theological seminaries and 18th-century alternatives as the private boarding-schools or the technical colleges) and of the main aspects of student life at the beginning of the book is illuminating, in spite of the questionable postulate of student boredom, allegedly a cause of student violence. Besides, the reader should keep in mind that Brockliss's integration of the *collèges* and the universities into one single higher education system, quite plausible in itself, increases the importance of age disparities. Student life and science teaching are not quite the same at the age of 11 as of 25. It is, for example, difficult to put on the same footing the teaching of elementary arithmetics and of sophisticated mathematics. With regard to the author's final concern, however, more explicit attention could have been paid to the tensions inherent to the early modern higher education system: élitist recruitment and the ascription of results according to social standing (as desired by the parents and most of the pupils themselves) *versus* essentially non-élitist pedagogical aims (as expressed by the teachers); science-oriented teaching *versus* practical professional experience; the requirements of status, ritual, and ceremony in a society of orders (such as expressed in expensive graduation, often meaningless from a scientific point of view) *versus* the need for well-trained executives of the absolutist state.

In the second part of his book, by far the more important and indeed the most innovative one, Brockliss examines successively the elements of the institutional curriculum of the French higher education system. The author emphasizes that extra-curricular lessons may have corrected important curricular gaps, as we know for certain in the case of the late-18th-century boarding schools. But unfortunately very little is known of those informal teaching procedures. With regard to the basic questions of the book it is, on the other hand, somewhat surprising to find the curriculum torn up into single disciplines, only marginal attention being paid to the *ratio studiorum* as such or to the repeated endeavours to create new blueprints for important parts of the higher education system, especially at the end of the *Ancien régime*. In fact, the reader should realize that the book is not so much concerned with educational values as with the transfer of knowledge. Brockliss's disciplinary approach, though masking somehow the cohesion of the human perception and of the movement of thinking in an age when common philosophical references explicitly underpinned the theories of theology, law, medicine and natural sciences, is particularly suited to show the dynamics of assimilation and repulsion within a limited, institutionalized body of science. Brockliss excels in the analysis of such evolutions and in his best chapters he achieves a fundamentally new picture: he shows convincingly how basic loyalty to, for example, Aristotelism or Galenism did not prevent the teachers from introducing into their teaching or even their publications the debates with alternative or new theories. Once acquainted with the new science, professors more or less consciously picked up bits of explanation suitable for still unsolved questions and thus piecemeal corroded their basic theory from within, until the new science imposed itself in its full strength as a new paradigm. That is how it went with Cartesianism and Newtonism in physics, with mechanicism and vitalism in medicine, and, until a certain point, also with Jansenism and Gallicanism, materialism and utilitarianism in ethics and theology. Without ever being quoted, Thomas Kuhn is continuously present in these chapters. This dynamic way of looking at the evolution of science teaching in France is not only refreshing, it also does justice to the teachers themselves in that it breaks with the old caricatures and stereotypes of ideological thinking. The results of the assimilation process of the new sciences being known, it is the process itself that Brockliss unfolds in a marvellously perceptive way.

Yet some questions remain. In fact, the question that really matters to Brockliss himself is not asked until the very end of the book. For in spite of its apparent stability France was finally shaken by a Revolution in which intellectuals played a major role and science could impose itself through a variety of brand-new institutions. How can we explain that such an excessive law-and-order society as was the early modern French monarchy proved suddenly its ability and readiness to embrace on a very large scale not only the ideas and ideals, but also the categories of observation, representation and thinking, and the basically experimental approach, in short the 'mental structures' as Lucien Febvre has put it, of Enlightenment and Revolution? It is on this point that Brockliss's approach may rightly be called a 'cultural history'. He seeks the answer to this question in the divergent evolution of the teaching of the ethical and metaphysical sciences on the one hand, and of that of the natural sciences and medicine on the other. Whereas the latter developed within 'an academic environment that was relatively dynamic and even original' and became the paragons of revolutionary science, the former had to cope with 'a university and college world that was generally intellectually sterile and establishment-orientated' (p. 444). Of course, the political interests of the monarchy and the theological censorship of the church loom heavily here. As long as atheism (Spinoza!) and other deadly sins could be avoided, the natural sciences were barely confronted with such harsh forms of censorship. One problem remains however unsolved. If college teaching prepared the bulk of the students for a changing world-view, why exactly did a particular member of the educated élite make up his choice in favour or against the new ideals? Huge numbers of lawyers, not physicians or scientists represented the Third Estate. A convincing answer to this question, correctly asked by the author but not yet solved, might well involve a return to social history and to some of those forms of quantitative research about which Brockliss shows himself so sceptical in this book. His scepticism echoes the present-day shift from a socio-economic to a cultural paradigm in historical writing, and reflects the uneasiness experienced at present by many social historians about their former explanations of what is now perceived as a primarily cultural evolution.

Without denying the importance of institutionalized education for the construction of the child's world-view, at least two supplementary points should be born in mind. Firstly, the early modern university was not quite the happy symbiosis between the matters taught by the teachers and those assimilated by obedient and actively present students that the author tends to assume. Most likely, higher education might better be perceived as the interconnection of two profoundly different educational networks: the professorial realm of science teaching and the students' realm of education, the latter being only partly reducible to instruction by teachers. Many incongruities of the functioning of the early modern university itself (such as student absenteeism, or the disjunction of courses and degrees) can be explained by this dichotomy. Therefore many other factors may play a decisive role in the assimilation process of new science by large élites, such as alternative teaching, sociability or reading culture. Secondly, the falling student numbers at all levels of the higher education system in the second half of the 18th century may contradict Brockliss's thesis of a mentality change through curricular innovation. As long as good prosopographical knowledge of the education of those involved in the revolutionary process does not exist, we can barely go beyond some basic assumptions of a very questionable nature.

Willem Frijhoff
Erasmus University
Rotterdam

Anthony J. La Vopa, *Grace, Talent, and Merit. Poor Students Clerical Careers, and Professional Ideology in Eighteenth-Century Germany.* Cambridge: Cambridge University Press, 1988. viii + 412 pp.

Despite the title this is principally a study of the poor student in eighteenth-century Protestant Germany. The author defines a poor student as one unable to pursue his studies without financial assistance from sources outside his immediate family. The first part of the book charts the presence of such students in the Latin schools and universities. Their number is impossible to quantify for university matriculation records give no indication of social status before the last decades of the century. La Vopa, however, is convinced that they were always a significant minority, if one that fluctuated according to economic cycles. It was a longstanding tenet of Lutheranism that the bright children of the poor should be educated through the aid of the community, and it was a commonplace for well-to-do patrons to sponsor the indigent scholar. In addition, schools and universities in Lutheran states, especially the University of Halle, provided institutional support for the poor student, often in the form of free meals. Most of these poor students, La Vopa shows, were in fact 'insiders', the sons of educated but down-at-heel clergymen and local officials. Some, on the other hand, were genuine 'outsiders' whose fathers were artisans, and it was from this group that many of the most original minds of the century emerged, such as Kant and Fichte.

The second part of the book examines the way in which the poor student was viewed by contemporaries. At no time in the century was it felt that the poor should be present in higher education or the poor scholar allowed to compete with his social superiors for the best positions in Church and state. This was particularly the case in the first half of the century when attitudes towards the poor scholar were determined by Pietist theologians. While emphasizing the Lutheran doctrine of the calling, the Pietists argued that the poor scholar should forgo ambition and accept inferior livings in the

Church as part of Christian suffering. Admittedly, the rationalist apologists of the German Enlightenment made much greater play of the individual's right to self-fulfilment. They, too, though, insisted on the individual's subordination to the community and its needs, and accepted that entrance to higher education should be carefully controlled for the general good. Moreover, by reducing the emphasis on a Latin education and giving greater play to elegant German, civility, etc., the rationalist made it more difficult for the poor student to enter the ranks of the *Gelehrten*.

As the third part of the book reveals, on the other hand, there were some cultural developments in the course of the century which suggested that the status of the poor scholar was not eternally fixed. At the end of the century, the neohumanist movement seemed to provide the ideal ideological support for an opening-up of higher education. The neohumanists rejected the rationalists' insistence that educational provision should be determined by the community's needs and promoted a conception of individual self-realisation (or *Bildung*). Earlier in the century, moreover, the rationalists had willy-nilly helped to enhance the dignity of poor students by stressing the importance to the community of their traditional careers as teachers and rural clergymen. These developments, however, should not be exaggerated. Indeed, the neohumanists as much as the rationalists ensured that higher education would be monopolized by the elite by associating *Humanität* with a comprehensive acquaintance with the culture of Ancient Greece. The one really radical educationalist, insists La Vopa, was Fichte, the subject of his final chapter. Fichte rejected Ancient Greece's claim to be the paradigmatic civilisation and looked forward to an age when all men were equal and released from manual labour. Germany was to lead the way in this great enterprise and its key would lie in the education of the young in isolation from their parents. Even Fichte, however, was an elitist. If the ranks of the men of science were to be filled indiscriminately, their number would be few.

La Vopa has written a rich and informative work, one that is far more ambitious in scope than the complementary study of eighteenth-century France by Harvey Chisick (*The Limits of Reform in the Enlightenment* (Princeton N.J., 1981)). In fact, the work is as much about the German Enlightenment *tout court* as the poor student in the eighteenth century. As a result, if a criticism could be levelled against the book it would be that the author's interest in the German Enlightenment often seems to dominate the text. This is a book that will interest the eighteenth-century historian of ideas more than the historian of universities. As the author himself admits this is not a work based on detailed archival research. A reader would search in vain for a substantial account of the provision for poor scholars at particular institutions. La Vopa is primarily informative about the way that the exceptionally-gifted but poor made sense of their educational experience and limited job opportunities. La Vopa's expertise lies in the sensitive reading of autobiographical fragments. The author, of course, is not to be blamed for the absence of hard institutional data. He set out to write a book which was a social history of educational ideas. On the other hand, the book tends to suggest that he does not feel that detailed archival research would be very valuable. La Vopa believes that 'reality' is the product of cultural assumptions. Since the eighteenth-century cultural climate was predominantly hostile to poor students, *ergo* their numbers must be small and achievements limited. This may well be true, but it would still be useful if one day (providing the sources exist) the potential for educational mobility could be studied statistically for Germany in the way it has been for France by Dominique Julia and Willem Frijhoff (*Ecole et société dans la France d'ancien-régime* (Paris, 1975)).

L. W. B. Brockliss,
Magdalen College,
Oxford, OX1 4AU

F. M. L. Thompson (ed.), *The University of London and the World of Learning, 1836–1986* London and Ronceverte: Hambledon Press, 1990 xxviii + 260 pp.

Symposia always seem like a good idea at the time. If detail is needed on a complex problem or institution, why not adopt the subsidiarity principle and devolve it down the line to the expert in that particular area? It's then, of course, that the problems begin to crowd in on the editor – of which sheer lethargy in submission of drafts is by no means the worst. There is the world authority who, when called to write on his department or discipline, contents himself with a brief dive into some handy work of reference; the missionary who converts the same putative general overview into an impassioned plea for some good idea like world government; the doctoral student whose text collapses under the weight of its footnotes. Worst of all, there is the thirteenth fairy, the one who wasn't invited to contribute but (since all the others have *ipso facto* disqualified themselves) always gets the book to review.

The present reviewer is not in this position, but he doesn't envy Professor Michael Thompson's task. Editing *The University of London and the World of Learning* – which stems from a series of lectures delivered in 1986 as a consequence of the sesquicentenary of the University – must have been made even more complex by the fact that the identity of the University of London has been as vague as its boundaries have been vast. Negley Harte's concise *The University of London, 1836–1986* (1986) supplied the skeleton of the history of the University and its constituent colleges. Thompson and his contributors have tried, almost completely on a faculty basis, to assess its contribution to scholarship and teaching in – and beyond – Britain.

They have not been helped, either, by the changing structure of the University. From its foundation in 1836 to its reform in 1890 it was 'a mere examining board' – which is all that Robert Lowe, one of the most pugnacious Benthamite educational reformers of the nineteenth century (and the University's MP, 1867–1874) believed a university should be. Between 1890 and 1960 its remit broadened into a 'federative' examining structure, the creation of central institutions for fostering research in the arts, sciences, and area studies. With affiliated colleges and associated students its writ truly ran world-wide, and was appropriately capped – New Delhi fashion – by Sir Charles Holden's grandly-planned university precinct north of the British Museum in the 1930s. Since 1960 it has been subject to the same process as the former empire. The commonwealth colleges have, for better or worse, received independence; at the same time the 'nationalism' of the constituent colleges has reasserted itself and pushed the University in a confederal direction. Recently we have had the prospect of the London School of Economics sallying out of Houghton Street to capture the former County Hall for the training of well-heeled Indonesian accountants who seem to have replaced the colonial liberationists who once flocked to Harold Laski's lectures. This would not only symbolically commemorate the victory of Hayek over Sidney Webb, but the marginalizing of the University by the college which, Lord MacGregor of Durris reminds us, dominated its Social Science Faculty.

MacGregor's contribution manages to square the intellectual and institutional requirements of the project. Though it's difficult to see how he could fail, the LSE being, from 1918 to the 1960s, from Tawney, T. H. Marshall and Beveridge to Laski and Titmuss, at the centre of British 'welfarist' ideological development. Throughout this time its accommodation, however, was literally Dickensian (in the sense that not one in ten of the visitors to 'The Old Curiosity Shop' were aware of the LSE): something reflective, as J. Mordaunt Crook's engaging architectural study suggests, of fluctuations between the University's own lack of self-confidence and the bold, not to say megalomaniac, projects of various individuals – a high proportion of them Scots, like Haldane and Swinton – who took it upon themselves to plan for it. As a result, there can be few single institutions with so many semi-completed building projects, so many architectural waifs and strays (that the 'Museum of Mankind' which backs up the Royal Academy at Burlington House was once the University's central office, was news to me) and so many 'casualties', like Colcutt's lamented Imperial Institute. Elsewhere, the principle of devolving the lectures to 'faculty spokespersons' can produce rather awkward results. The editor himself faces fearful odds when he deals with the Humanities (which Thatcherite newspeak has now christened 'Cost Centres 34 and 35'). Professor Thompson performs a near-miracle of condensation with a vast and fecund archipelago of teaching and research. Succinct, funny, and legitimately indignant in his comments on history, classics, literature, and philosophy, and their appraisal by successive policy-makers, the sheer size of his task means that his essay can be no more than a sketch. Still, like a sketch by Turner or Constable, it means a lot. Which can't be said of Sir Herman Bondi's piece on 'The Sciences' – a quick wheech through the *DNB*, thank you and good night. This performance must have been as embarrassing to listen to as it is to read. Not embarrassing enough, alas: Bondi ought to have been well and truly beached.

By contrast, L. P. Le Quesne on Medicine, Harold Billett on Engineering, Sir William Taylor on Education and the late Rev Sydney Hall Evans on Theology are adequately-presented, if conventional, institutional accounts. W. L. Twining on the Law Faculty is elegant and has a coherent intellectual case to argue, about the dialectic between legal philosophy and rationalizations derived from actual practice, which is only slightly diminished by the University's inability, before 1914, to produce more than a handful of Law graduates. Brian Trowell on Music (an area of fierce controversy in the recent past) provides a bonus, in the 'University Song' composed in 1925 by John Ireland to words by John Drinkwater. Starting 'Pilgrims from many paths we came / To where the roods of Empire meet . . .', it has, unsurprisingly, vanished from view. Gillian Sutherland's contribution 'The Plainest Principles of Justice', on women and the University, is the most original, and represents an impressive piece of research. Indeed, the best essays – by Crook, Twining, Sutherland and Thompson – suggest that the whole project could have benefited from being disarticulated after the lecture-series, and reassembled by non-institutional writers on thematic lines.

This might have raised important issues which are only sketchily covered, if at all. How did the influence of London graduates compare with the products of Oxford and Cambridge? Why, given Hayek, Oakeshott, and Tawney (and reckoning one Laski equal to one Cole as energetic if unoriginal *politicos*), was Oxford still so far ahead of the LSE in producing actual political leaders? How did London compare, as a force in the nation, with other metropolitan universities such as Berlin, Columbia, and the Sorbonne? Finally, why does there not seem to be a 'literary imagination' to the University, or at the very least a 'London University novel'? Surely this benevolent academic mastodon deserves better than the only candidate which springs to mind, if one accepts Senate House rather than the BBC as the model for MINILUV – Orwell's *1984*?

Christopher Harvie
University of Tübingen

Lindy Moore, *Bajanellas and Semilinas: Aberdeen University and the Education of Women*. Aberdeen: Aberdeen University Press, 1991. 192 pp. £8.95

'Bajanellas' and 'Semilinas' were the names given to the early women students at Aberdeen University – the feminine equivalents to 'bajans' and 'semis' – male first and second year students. Lindy Moore traces the development of women's education at Aberdeen University from its origins in the 1870s and 1880s to 1920, when women made up almost half of the student body. Moore chronicles the debates over women's higher education which persisted throughout this period, and explores how the admission of women affected the university and the women students themselves.

Moore's task is a difficult one because of the scarcity of primary source materials about women's experience at Aberdeen, or for that matter about women's higher education in Scotland as a whole. Unlike the historians of the English women's colleges, she could not mine the rich archival sources almost always produced by independent institutions. Moore is forced to concentrate on attitudes towards women students, which were expressed volubly by the student newspaper *Alma Mater*. She was, however, able to interview several former women students, and more significantly, to assemble valuable data about the social origins, education, and careers of Aberdeen women students, based primarily on T. Watt's *Roll of Graduates* (1935).

Aberdeen University was unique in that it made no special provision for its women students. The creation of a separate college for women was opposed by those who believed men and women should be treated identically, and those who feared that the cost of such an institution would exclude the many local and poorer women whom the university wished to serve. Indeed, when Castleton House, a residence for women students was founded in the mid-1890s, not one person applied. Instead over 50 percent of Aberdeen women students lived in lodgings, where they were free to come and go as they wished. In contrast, students at the English residential women's colleges were carefully chaperoned, and living in lodgings was usually considered unacceptable. Moore suggests that this different approach can be explained by the lower-middle class and working-class origins of many Aberdeen women students; in these groups the physical and social separation of men and women was less strictly enforced.

Moore demonstrates that while women students were personally almost always treated with politeness, they were criticised at an abstract level. The *Alma Mater* made women students the objects of ridicule, representing them as 'concerned only with men, marriage, clothes, hats, fashion, and gossip.' Later as the women's suffrage movement gained strength, women student activists were portrayed as unfeminine and aggressive. Moore shows that despite the rising numbers of women students at Aberdeen, the male student ethos, occasionally manifested in drunkenness and rowdiness, remained dominant. Although women were officially welcome in many university societies, a reluctance to challenge the male-dominated atmosphere kept most of them from active participation. The representation of women in the Student Representative Council was a recurring source of controversy. Although women gained more confidence during the First World War, when they found themselves virtually running student activities, during the 1920s and 1930s, the proportion of women students declined and the election of a woman, Mary Esslemont, as president of the Student Representative Council in 1922, would not be repeated for another sixty-eight years. Furthermore, few women held academic posts at Aberdeen, where the first woman professor was appointed only in 1964.

Moore's book helps fill the need for research on Scottish women's higher education, as well as being one of only a few works on women at coeducational universities. (Mabel Tylecote's *The Education of Women at Manchester University*, published in 1941, was an early precursor.) Aberdeen was distinctive in its policy of not making any special provision for women students. Women's 'equality' at Aberdeen was, however, somewhat illusory. Moore's analysis of the difficulties women had in reaching positions of influence in the university suggests that coeducation was perhaps not the best way to prepare women for leadership roles.

Fernanda Perrone
Special Collections Library
Rutgers University
New Brunswick
NJ 08901
USA

Ivo Tertera, *J. F. Herbart a jeho stoupenci na pražské univerzitě* (*J. F. Herbart and his followers at Prague University*), Charles University: Prague 1989. 474pp. Kcs 53.50.

This massive hardback volume devotes 115 pages to the anti-Hegelian philosopher and pedagogical theoretician J.F. Herbart himself, then traces the development of his influence in German-speaking circles, especially in Prague (pp. 129–208), before concluding with a fairly extended (pp. 209–388) treatment of the analogous phenomenon among the Czech-speaking Prague professors whose photographs are reproduced. A summary (p. 439–454) is provided in German but not in any other language. At the same time the book provides a lot of information about university life in Prague in the second half of the nineteenth century, and so is likely to be a useful source book to researchers in this field, too. Although Herbart himself is correctly described as a philosopher, the book will be of little interest to anyone who regards philosophy as an analytical and dialogical activity. Any potential general reader in the UK may well be put off by the home-spun typography and book production. Such a reader should also note that muscular vigour is required for handling the weighty tome (1.342 kg), and that its mental counterpart is needed for dealing with the somewhat stodgy prose. It is rather a pity that in England there are so few general readers whose Czech is in good enough trim for reading the book. For it is liable to be an *avis rara* here since only 600 copies in all have been printed. Otherwise the review copy, if sold by the reviewer's heirs for its rarity value (the advertised publication price amounts to £1.05 at the current rate) could have made the family fortune.

Lubor Velecky

Diane Rubenstein, *What's Left? The Ecole Normale Supérieure and the Right*. Madison: University of Wisconsin Press, 1990. xvi + 215 pp.

Diane Rubenstein's book appears in a series called 'rhetoric of the human sciences', and she defines it as a study of 'the politics of writing', and a 'reading of the Ecole Normale as a text'. We thus have fair warning that this is a work whose dense theoretical framework is that of post-modernist literary theory. Historians have generally managed to avoid paying much attention to post-modernism: they have profited from reading Foucault or

Bourdieu, but the thought of Derrida, who is Rubenstein's main inspiration, seems remarkably ahistorical. What then can the historian of French higher education gain from a battle with the tiresome word-play (e.g. between 'write', 'rite', and 'right'), with the thicket of jargon (phronesis, etymon, habitus, hexis, the amnesia of genesis, Greimas' Semiotic Rectangle . . .), with the forced binary contrasts and oracular banalities which characterize the deconstructionist style – admittedly peculiarly appropriate in this case since so many of its pioneers were themselves *normaliens*?

Perhaps three themes can be isolated. First, Rubenstein seeks a 'rightist reinscription' of the Ecole Normale as a corrective to the 'leftist caricature' of its history; although the school's output of right-wing writers in the twentieth century has hardly been ignored in previous accounts, there is value in her systematic treatment of them. Some went all the way to fascism, and Rubenstein has a chapter (though it is the least penetrable in the book) on the post-war trials of intellectual collaborators. Secondly, she relates the intellectual style of these right-wing *normaliens* to their experiences at the school itself and to permanent features of its internal life. It is in the 'élite discourse' which they learnt there, and the 'institutional authority' with which the Ecole Normale clothed them, that we can find the underlying kinship with their left-wing contemporaries. Thirdly, Rubenstein analyses the literary and publishing networks of the inter-war period, paying special attention to Robert Brasillach and the journal *Je Suis Partout*.

There is plenty of interesting material here, and the book is based on a wide range of archives, private papers and interviews. Yet the result is far from a conventional work of history, and even those who might welcome a dialogue between disciplines are likely to feel uneasy with this somewhat combative and uncompromising book, in which language and writing seem to replace human beings as the actors in history.

R.D. Anderson
University of Edinburgh

Notker Hammerstein, *Die Johann Wolfgang Goethe-Universität Frankfurt am Main. Von der Stiftungsuniversität zur staatlichen Hochschule*, Band I. *Die Universitätsgeschichte von der Gründung 1914 bis zu den fünfziger Jahren.* Frankfurt am Main: Alfred Metzner Verlag, 1989. 909 pp. DM 78.

This weighty and informative work was commissioned to celebrate the seventy-fifth anniversary of the founding of the University of Frankfurt.

Considering that the author, a noted authority on early-modern university history, had only two years to complete the book, it is in many ways a remarkable achievement.

Hammerstein does not treat the origins of the university in any depth, arguing that Paul Kluke's 1972 account *Die Stiftungsuniversität Frankfurt am Main, 1914–1932* does a thorough enough job. Thus nearly half the book dwells on the National Socialist era, with almost as much more on the period from 1945 to the early 1950s.

Hammerstein makes clear that he is not a fan of the 'new history of education.' The main weight in his story falls on the professors, administrators, and benefactors of the university, not on the student body or matters that might be called the social history of education. Numbers and statistics 'can take a back seat, especially since they contribute nothing to the illumination of recent German university history that cannot be reached on the path I have chosen.' (p. 12.)

The Nazi years were arguably harder on Frankfurt's university than most others: it had been founded in no small part through the efforts of civic-minded Jews and with a consciously experimental, forward-looking attitude, all of which was anathema to National Socialists. Nearly a third of the Frankfurt faculty was purged by the Nazis, starting with the distinguished Kurator, Kurt Riezler, and among them such illustrious names as Ernst Kantorowicz, Max Horkheimer, Martin Buber, Paul Tillich, Theodor Adorno, and Karl Mannheim. Hammerstein's approach to this tragedy is carefully to document the way in which persons were purged, but he is much less sure-footed in describing the scholarly and scientific work of the survivors, who are generally assumed to have been keeping a low profile. The even further decline, almost to the vanishing point, of the university during the war years is given in full and depressing detail. The difficulties of rebuilding the ruined university for the first four years after the war are well-documented in the last section of the book.

It would perhaps be too much to expect that a 'commissioned' history, even of a university with such progressive traditions as Frankfurt, would match the sharp tone of questioning raised by outside university historians in Germany and abroad (whose work is seldom cited by Hammerstein). In a work which devotes as much time to the university in the Nazi period as many other whole monographs, the author manages to avoid deep probing into the activities of the avowed National Socialists and collaborators on the faculty, noting frequently that their ideas were confused and written in miserable German – a patrician view not uncommon among the academic establishment in West Germany since 1945. In an attempt to dwell on the career of one Nazi professor, presumably meant to use *pars pro toto*, the author describes the decline and fall of the dean of medicine, Hans Holfelder (pp. 463–9). This career seemed vexed by the combination of infighting

among Holfelder's fellow Nazis and the quiet resistance of the city administration and non-Nazi medical colleagues. It ended on the Russian front
with an SS unit. One can still wonder: was this a typical case?

Brief career biographies of professors, in any case, do typify the working
method of this book, and there is much interesting material. For researchers
interested in the 'new history of education,' Hammerstein and his student
assistants have assembled, one might conclude metaphorically, an excellent
set of maps and topographies that can be immensely useful for future
digging below the surface of German university history. Although this may
not be the final word, it is a far richer and more satisfying approach than the
usual university-jubilee offering.

Charles E. McClelland
University of New Mexico

Ben Siegel (ed.), *The American Writer and the University*. Newark:
University of Delaware Press, 1989. 195 pp. £22.50.

The campus novel is attracting growing scholarly interest in Europe and
North America, with at least three books on the subject appearing in the last
twelve months alone. Because this collection of essays antedated the boom,
having originated in MLA programmes on 'The American Writer and the
University' in the late 1980s, it suffers from a certain lack of focus and
coherence. Although its contributors were aware of Proctor's (1957) and
Lyons's (1962) pioneering work, they were unable to set their ideas against
the diachronic and comparative backgrounds established by Weiss (1986)
and Carter (1990) respectively. The result is a collection of ten essays – seven
by literary critics and three by writers-in-residence – which, though individually interesting, either evince little sense of the overall subgeneric
context with which they are dealing or fail to develop the broader implications of their principal insights.

Thus, although the seven critical essays discuss campus novelists who are
also recognized as major authors of non-campus fiction (Oates (pp. 39–53);
Malamud (pp. 54–67); Roth (pp. 68–87); Barth (pp. 88–100); Heller (pp.
101–13); Bellow (pp. 114–35) and Federman (pp. 136–45)), none of their
authors seems to know very much about those hundreds of novels by
unknowns which have set the classic patterns of North American campus
fiction or why patterns should have been established in North America
which are radically different from their superficially similar British counterparts. Consequently, whether their chosen author deals with Academe

positively or negatively, the seven critics seem not to be aware of the potential of the material with which they are working. When Stanley Trachtenberg highlights the negative nature of the academics in Oates's *Hungry Ghosts* (1978), he does not seem to realize how extreme her vision is within the context of post-McCarthy campus fiction. When James Mellard discusses Malamud's *A New Life* (1961), he only half realizes that Cascadia College is a hick aberration and by no means metonymic of the system as a whole. When Eric Solomon indicates (p. 70) that Roth's treatment of academics becomes increasingly positive between *Goodbye, Columbus* (1959) and *Professor of Desire* (1977), he does not grasp that this up-grading was part of a more general trend which is particularly visible in the more popular media, and so omits to explain why Roth did not produce more devastating novels about campus life even though he could have done so. When James Nagel documents Heller's deletions from *Catch-22* (1961) (pp. 103–6), he never explains why a writer who believes that 'the better educated a character is, the less he is likely to understand' (p. 102) should have removed some hyper-vitriolic passages which are directed precisely at one of his (recurrent) main targets. When Melvin Friedman shows that Federman has refused 'to concentrate on the ungenerous, unseemly aspects of university life' (p. 141), he relates this refusal not to the high status or cultural significance of North American universities, but simply to Federman's own professional commitment (p. 142). Elaine Safer and Ben Siegel, discussing Barth's and Bellow's excoriating visions of the modern North American university, have a more developed sense that larger issues are at stake – that both novelists are attacking a *trahison des clercs* (pp. 94–7 and 121–6). But neither explains how those visions can co-exist with a host of contemporary campus novels which presents Academe, for all its flaws, as a thoroughly good thing.

Clues which enable us to develop the above insights; answer the un- or partially answered questions; and explain the gaping chasm between Federman's silence and Barth's and Bellow's ire are provided by Theodore Weiss and James Ragan – teachers of creative writing at the Universities of Princeton and Southern California respectively. The modern North American multi-versity (or as Weiss calls it, 'per-ver-sity') may, as Bellow claims, have become so absorbed into the fabric of society that it commodifies and acceptably packages subjects which ought to involve criticism, if not subversion of prevailing values, but Weiss and Ragan can see its other, more positive side. The university is said to provide the last remaining refuge for the independently creative mind (p. 153); to serve as a context in which alternative values may, occasionally, blossom (p. 154); and to form an ordered enclave which is relatively exempt from 'post-Kennedy anti-intellectualism' (p. 162), media imperialism (pp. 164–5) and 'the rape and aberrations of language' (p. 165). Fictional academics, as in the novels of

Oates, Barth, and Bellow, may be deeply flawed instruments of a system which has lost its way; and fictional universities, as in the novels of Malamud and Heller, may be breeding grounds of provincialism and moral insensitivity, but both Roth and Federman, like a host of lesser-known writers of the post-McCarthy era, understand and promote the positive virtues of the North American higher education system. Since *Lucky Jim* (1954), the handful of British novelists who have apologized for universities have done so largely in the name of an antique, Oxbridge-centred model. In contrast, a much larger number of North American novelists has attempted that task over the same period, and their apologias have focussed less on a particular institution which is accessible only to an elite and more on abstract values which can be fostered anywhere: freedom of speech, generosity of spirit, personal development, and open access to all who desire it. It is true that some modern American novels by major writers present the contemporary university as a monstrous travesty. But against those novels and in contrast with their British counterparts we need to set novels which depict the university and its employees as a countervailing power to the media-dominated consumerism which typifies so much of North American society.

Richard Sheppard
Magdalen College
Oxford OX1 4AU

A.E. Firth, *Goldsmiths' College: A Centenary Account*. London: Athlone Press, 1991. 160 pp.

In his excellent study *The University of London* (London 1986) Negley Harte makes the observation that 'All universities are different, but some are more different than others. The University of London is the most different of them all'. The same could be said with even greater pathos of London's constituent schools. Few of them have been more different than Goldsmiths'.

Mr Firth traces Goldsmiths' distinctiveness to two complex and inter-twined relationships. The first is a mission to serve the local community through core provision of teacher training, fine art, and adult education. The second is Goldsmiths' complicated relationship with the University of London.

Goldsmiths' was established in 1891. It was a community college. In 1896 over 7000 students were enrolled on some 78 courses ranging from Applied

Mathematics to Wood Carving. But in 1904 the worshipful company of Goldsmiths', concerned by the implications of the 1902 Education Act, announced that it no longer wished to run an institution subject to, 'the inspection and control of another body'. It offered the college as a gift to the University of London. The University accepted. It agreed that Goldsmiths' should house a Teacher Training College serving local authorities in the London area, and in this capacity should become an, 'Institution with Recognised Teachers'. So began Goldsmiths' emergence as a constitutional curiosity. The IRT scheme allowed students studying at an independent institution, who were taught by staff recognized by the University as competent teachers, to read for University degrees. But Goldsmiths' was not independent. It was owned by the University.

Furthermore it maintained strong community links by teaching subjects for which it received funding from a range of external sources. This haphazard relationship, the subject of much heated debate, became gradually unsustainable in the post Robbins era. The college responded to sectoral trends by shifting an increasing proportion of its efforts to degree-level work, but from 1972 the IRT scheme began to be phased out, putting the College's degree programmes under threat. A range of potential mergers with Bedford and Royal Holloway, QMC, Thames Polytechnic, and Avery Hill College were discussed, until in 1988 Goldsmiths' was incorporated as a School of the University.

The book is arranged chronologically in two parts, the division being drawn in 1960. Both parts contain chapters on six sub-themes; the site, government and constitution, social life, and one of each of the three core educational activities. Mr Firth maintains that his work is 'not a full scholarly history' and, indeed, it does not in any detailed way analyse the growth of the College within the wider political, social, economic, and educational context. But this beautifully illustrated book is based on a meticulous search of the College archives, and does provide a clear path through a potentially confusing chronology. Illuminated by Mr Firth's light wit, it will be treasured by members as a valued contribution to the College's centenary celebrations.

P. R. H. Slee
University of Aston

Publications on University History since 1977: A Continuing Bibliography

Edited by John M. Fletcher
With the assistance of Christopher A. Upton

Produced with the co-operation of the International
Commission for the History of Universities

Preface

Our reports show a growing interest in the history of universities, especially with conferences, resulting in published papers, in many countries. We can usually locate this material, but we ask any scholars who publish relevant articles in journals or in such volumes as commemorative or anniversary essays that we may miss to send us note of their work. We are grateful to all who have supplied to us information during the past year. May we remind new readers that lists for 1977–81 were published in *History of European Universities: Work in Progress and Publications* in five volumes available from the address below. These lists have been expanded and lists for 1982 onwards printed in this journal from volume 7 (1988); back numbers of the journal can be obtained from the publishers.

The following have contributed reports for this issue; membership of the International Commission is indicated by an asterix. A. Kernbauer (Austria), H. de Ridder-Symoens* and J. Paquet* (Belgium, The Netherlands and Luxembourg), C. A. Upton and E. S. Leedham-Green (British Isles), M. Svatoš (Czechoslovakia), J. Verger* (France), L. Szögi (Hungary), D. Maffei*, P. Maffei and G. Minnucci (Italy), J. Basista (Poland), A. García y García*, A. M. Carabias Torres, D. L. M. Gutierrez Torrecilla and M. Augusto Rodrigues (Spain and Portugal), Marcia G. Synnott (U.S.A.). Copy has been prepared by Pauline A. Fletcher. We are most grateful to all for their assistance.

Databases relating to university history

The following information has been received:
Aberdeen (Scotland), Univ. of:
  Students of Aberdeen Univ. Their student and subsequent careers.
  In progress: Period 1860–80 well advanced; plans to move backwards and
  forwards in time.

Prof. P. L. Payne, Department of History, University of Aberdeen, King's College, Aberdeen AB9 2UB, Scotland.
Alcalá (Spain), Univ. of:
Teachers at the Univ. of Alcalá 16th–18th centuries.
In progress.
Prof. L. M. Gutiérrez Torrecilla, University de Alcalá, Archivo General, Pza San Diego S/N, 28801 Alcalá de Henares, Spain.
———:
Bibliography and records of the Univ. of Alcalá.
In progress.
Prof. L. M. Gutiérrez Torrecilla (Address as above).
———:
Members of the colleges of San Ildefonso (1508–1770), San Ciriaco y Santa Paula (1611–1834) and Santa Catalina (1663–1764) of Univ. of Alcalá.
Complete: approx. 2,200 names.
Prof. L. M. Gutiérrez Torrecilla, C/Samaca No. 2 lo A, 28033, Madrid, Spain.
Birmingham (England), Univ. of:
Students of Birmingham Univ. 1900–56, with sample extension to 1980.
In progress.
Dr D. Drummond, Leverhulme Project Higher Education and Society 1880–1980, University of Birmingham, School of History, Birmingham B15 2TT, England.
Coimbra (Portugal), Univ. of:
Professors of the Univ. of Coimbra.
In progress.
Prof. M. Augusto-Rodrigues, Arquivo da Universidade de Coimbra, 3000 Coimbra, Portugal.
Dublin (Ireland), Trinity Coll.:
Students of Trinity Coll., Dublin, 1638–1700, from matriculation and degree lists.
In progress.
Dr Alan Ford, Department of Theology, Abbey House, Palace Green, University of Durham, Durham DH1 3RS, England.
Ireland, students of:
See entry following.
Leuven (Belgium), Univ. of:
Irish students at the Univ. of Leuven 1616–1797.
In progress.
Mr J. Nilis, Neremweg 164, 3700 Tongeren, Belgium.
Liège (Belgium), parish priests of the northern part of the diocese of:
Univ. educ. of parish priests of the northern part of the diocese of Liège 1400–1570.
In progress.
Mr A.-J. Bijsterveld, Van Heutszstraat 69, 6521 CS Nijmegen, The Netherlands.
Salamanca (Spain), Univ. of:

The careers in church and state of members of the *colegiales mayores* of Salamanca, 15th–19th centuries.
In progress.
Prof. A. M. Carabias Torres, Universidad de Salamanca, Dpto de Historia Medieval, Moderna y Contemporánea, C/. Cervantes s/n, 37007 Salamanca, Spain.
The Netherlands, students of:
The *peregrinatio academica* of students from the Netherlands 1300–1800.
In progress: approx. 10,000 names.
Prof. H. de Ridder-Symoens, Grote Baan 98, B-9920 Lovendegem, Belgium.

For further details, please contact the addresses given.

We would appreciate any additions to this list for inclusion in the next issue of the journal. Please send any information to the address below. Scholars recorded above will be contacted concerning revisions of their entries before the appearance of our next volume. We thank all who have assisted in this work of collection.

Dr John M. Fletcher
Dept of Modern Languages
Aston University
Aston Triangle
Birmingham B4 7ET
England

Austria

Additions to Earlier Lists

For 1988
Litsch, K.: Zur Rechtsstellung d. Prager Universitätsprof. in d. ersten Hälfte d. 19. Jh., in *Bildungsgeschichte, Bevölkerungsgeschichte, Gesellschaftsgeschichte in den böhmischen Ländern und in Europa*, Vienna/Munich (henceforth noted as *Bildungsgeschichte*): 3–16.
Natter, G.: Icones rectorum. Werden und Eigenart der Rektorengalerie an der Universität Wien. Thesis. Innsbruck.
Schuler, D.: Die Universitätsbiblioth. Innsbruck u. ihr Personal im Jahrzehnt vor 1914, *Tiroler Heimat*, 51/52: 81–108.
Uiblein, P.: Johannes von Gmunden, seine Tätigkeit an d. Wiener Univ., *Sitzungsber. d. Österr. Akad. d. Wiss. Wien. Phil.-hist. Klasse*, 497: 11–64.
Zwahr, H.: Die Univ. Leipzig im Revolutionsjahr 1830. Durchbrüche zu einem neuen Wissenschaftsverständnis u. zu bürgerlicher pol. Praxis, in *Bildungsgeschichte*: 17–31.

For 1989

Busek, E., Mantl, W. and Peterlik, M. eds: *Wissenschaft und Freiheit. Ideen zu Universität und Universalität. Symposion vom 23. bis 25. Oktober 1987*, Vienna/Munich.

Hrubi, F. R. ed.: *Universität-Bildung-Humanität. Festschrift für Alois Eder zum 70. Geburtstag*, Vienna.

Kellermann, P.: Uber d. Entwicklung d. Univ. in Österr. 1945–89, *Österr. Z. f. Soziol.*, 14(4): 46–49.

Kuschey, B.: Univ. am Ende?—Eine Konfrontation, *Aufrisse. Z. f. pol. Bildung*, 10: 8–16.

Lichtenberger-Fenz, B.: Die Vertreibung d. Vernunft, *Wiener Tagebuch*, 7/8: 32–33.

Mairold, M.: Steirische Studenten an d. Salzburger Benediktineruniv., *Z. d. hist. Vereins f. Steiermark*, 80: 167–211.

Mroczkowski, P.: John Henry Newman's 'The Idea of a Univ.' and the present sociocult. context, *Innovation*, 3(1): 13–23.

Putzer, P.: Sceptra Univ. Salisburgensis (Ein Nachtrag), *Mitt. d. Gesellschaft f. Salzburger Landeskunde*, 129: 217–26.

For 1990

Seewann, H.: *Zirkel und Zionsstern. Bilder und Dokumente aus der versunkenen Welt des jüdisch-nationalen Korporationswesens. Ein Beitrag zur Geschichte des Zionismus auf akademischem Boden*, Graz.

Belgium, The Netherlands and Luxembourg

Additions to Earlier Lists

For 1980

Os, M. van and Wieringa, W. J. eds: *Wetenschap en rekenschap 1880–1980. Een eeuw wetenschapsbeoefening en wetenschaps-beschouwing aan de Vrije Universiteit. Gedenkboek bij het honderdjarig bestaan van de Vrije Universiteit te Amsterdam* (Scholarship and responsibility 1880–1980. A cent. of scholarly study and scholarly contemplation at the V.U. Memorial for the 100 yr existence of the V.U. of A.), Kampen.

For 1982

Langham, I.: *The building of British social anthropology. W. H. R. Rivers and his Cambridge disciples in the development of kinship studies*, Dordrecht.

For 1986

Pastoret, P.-P., Mees, G. and Mammerickx, M.: *De l'art à la science ou 150 ans de méd. vétérin. à Cureghem*, Brussels.

For 1988

Balthazar, H.: *Een kwarteeuw democratisering en expansiebeleid van het Belgisch hoger onderwijs* (A quarter of a cent. of democratisation and expansion pol. in B. higher education), Ghent.

Bouquegneau, C.: Le 150e anniv. de la fac. polytech. de Mons, *Hainaut tourisme*, 246: 3–6.

Desmeuraux, J.: Wervikse univ. studenten te Leuven tijdens het ancien régime (Univ. students of W. at L. during the a. r.), *Jb. stedelijke oudheidkundige comm. Wervik*, 13–22.

Noël, F.: *1894. L'univ. de Bruxelles en crise*, Brussels.

Persyn, J.-M.: Oudart de Bersacques et Louvain, *Bull. de la soc. des antiquaires de Morinie*, 23: 345–48.

Rotsaert, K.: Brugge universiteitsstad. Twee gemiste kansen (B. univ. city. 2 missed chances), *Het Brugs ommeland*, 28: 159–66.

Schaik, A. H. M. van: *Dr Hendrik Moller 1869–1940. Een ongemakkelijk initiator van onderwijs en cultuur in Noord Brabant* (Dr H.M. 1869–1940. An uneasy initiator of educ. and cult. in N.B.), Tilburg.

Simon-Van der Meersch, A. M., Langendries, E. and Vandenabeele, J.: *20 Jaar Rijksuniversiteit-studenten in actie 1968–88* (20 yrs of action by students of the RUG 1968–88), Ghent. (Cat. of an exhib.).

Stevens, F.: *Geschiedenis van de Leuvense rechtsfaculteit 1425–1914* (Hist. of the fac. of law of L. univ.), Leuven.

Verhulst, A.: Univ. jongeren over 'De Nieuwe Orde' van Maurice de Wilde (Univ. students' reactions to The New Order of M. de W.), in G. Peeters and M. de Moor eds: *Arbeid in veelvoud. Een huldeboek voor J. Craeybeckx en E. Scholliers*, Brussels: 324–30. (Concerns T.V. programme about Flemish co-op. with Germans during World War 2).

Vermeiren, K.: *Mei '68, twintig jaar later* (May 1968, 20 yrs later), Wevelgem.

For 1989

Bragard-Desoroux, E.: Le financement du système univ. belge, *Courrier hebdomadaire du CRISP*, number 1261–62.

Dievoet, G. van, Auweele, D. van den and Oosterbosch, M.: Henricus de Piro en de Leuvense Univ. 1428–31 (H. de P. and the univ. of L.), *Ex officina*, 6: 139–68.

Lavis, E.: Un Cinacien fondateur de la fac. de méd. de l'Univ. de Liège: Nicolas-Gabriel-Antoine Ansiaux 1780–1834, *Cercle cult. cinacie*, 81: 24–25.

Maanen, R. C. J. van and Otterspeer, O.: Onderwijs en wetenschap (Teaching and science), in I. W. L. Moerman and R. C. J. van Maanen eds: *Leiden in gaslicht. Een staat in verandering 1800–1900*, Utrecht: 53–65.

Raaij, B. J. M. van: Het Brabants Studentengilde van Onze Lieve Vrouw. Een regionale kath. studentenbeweging tussen anti-modernisme en modernisme 1926–70 (The B. student soc. of Our Lady. A local cath. student movt between anti-modernism and modernism 1926–70), *Noordbrabants hist. jb.*, 6: 155–96.

Schippers, H.: Van tusschenlieden tot ingenieurs. De geschiedenis van het hoger technisch onderwijs in Nederland (From artisans to engineers. The hist. of higher tech. education in the Neths), Hilversum.

322   History of Universities

Struyker-Boudier, C. E. M.: *De filosofie van Leuven* (Phil. from L.), Nijmegen/Baarn.
Vis, G. J.: Leiden ontzet, Leuven in last. Ned. letterkunde aan de univ. 1850–80 (L. appalled, L. in trouble. Neth. literature in the univ. 1850–80), *Handelingen van de konink. Zuidned. maatschappij voor taal- en letterkunde en gesch.*, 43: 65–78.
Wesselius, J. W.: Johannes Drusius the younger's last journey to England and his Hebrew letter-book, *Lias*, 16: 159–76. (J.D. had close connections with Oxford).

For 1990
Ashmann, M.: Collegia en colleges. Juridisch onderwijs aan de Leidse Universiteit 1575–1630 in het bijzonder het disputeren (Colleagues and colls. The teaching of law at L. univ. 1575–1630, especially by disputations). Thesis. Leiden.
Auweele, D. van den and Oosterbosch, M.: Consilia juridica Lovaniensia. A propos de trois recueils d'avis juridiques du 15e s., in F. Stevens and D. van den Auweele eds.: *'Houd voet bij stuk'. Xenia iuris historiae G. van Dievoet oblata*, Leuven (henceforth noted as *Houd voet bij stuk*): 105–48.
Boag, J. W., Rubinin, P. E. and Shoenberg, D.: *Kapitza in Cambridge and Moscow. Life and letters of a Russian physicist*, Amsterdam.
Bruneel, C.: La fête à la charnière de deux régimes: le 'primus' de l'année 1794, *Lias*, 17: 135–43.
Canoy-Olthoff, A. M. M. and Nève, P. L.: *Holländische Eleganz gegenüber deutschen Usus Modernus Pandectarum? Ein Vergleich des privatrechtlichen Unterrichts in Leiden und an einigen deutschen Universitäten anhand einiger holländischer und deutscher juristischer Dissertationen über locatio-conductio 1650–1750*, Nijmegen.
Centenaire de la fondation de l'Instit. Sup. de Phil. (de l'Univ. de Louvain), *Rev. phil. de Louvain*, 88: 145–310.
Colen, C. and Clerck, M. de: Het archeol. onderzoek van het coll. de Bay te Leuven (Archeol. research at Bay coll. in L.), *Jb. van de gesch.- en oudheidkundige kring voor Leuven en omgeving*, 30: 40–111.
Delsaerdt, P.: Les règlements sur la production et la vente des livres, promulgués par l'ancienne univ. de Louvain. Ed. critique, *Lias*, 17: 64–89.
Derez, M.: Enkele geschiedkundige en architect. aantekeningen over de Leuvense cisterciënzercolls van Aulne en Villers (Some hist. and architect. notes on the Cistercian colls of A. and V. at L.), in M. Sabbe, M. Lamberigts and F. Gistelinck eds: *Bernardus en de Cisterciënzerfamilie in België*, Leuven (henceforth noted as *Cisterciënzerfamilie*): 335–46.
Dhondt, U.: Het hoger instit. voor wijsbegeerte. Honderd jaar. Een korte gesch. (The advanced instit. for phil. 100 yrs. A short hist.), *Onze alma mater*, 14: 156–62. (Refers to Leuven).
Donnelly, J. P.: Padua, Louvain and Paris. Three cases of univ.-Jesuit confrontation 1591–96, *Louvain studies*, 15: 47–63.
Frijhoff, W.: L'Ec. de Chirurgie de Paris et les Pays-Bas: analyse d'un recrutement 1752–91, *Lias*, 17(2): 185–239.

—— and Drie, R. van: Het wapenboek van de Ned. studentenvereniging te Angers 1614–1617 (The book of the coats-of-arms of the Neth. student soc. at A. 1614–1617), *Jb. van het Centraal Bureau voor Geneal. en het Iconografisch Bureau*, 44: 115–48.

Gent, J. J. M. van: 'Minder nut dan bij ons'. Collectie-vorming in de universiteitsbiblioth. te Franeker en Groningen omstreeks 1815 ('Not so much useful as with us'. The formation of univ. library collections at F. and G. around 1815), in L. J. Engels etc. eds: *Bibliotheek, wetenschap en cultuur. Opstellen aan W. R. H. Koops bij zijn afscheid als bibliothecaris der Rijksuniversiteit te Groningen*, Groningen: 408–416.

Heesakkers, C. L.: Het Ned. Album Amicorum in de periode 1556–1700 (Neths A.A. 1556–1700), *Batavia acad.*, 8(2): 37–47. (Many from students and profs).

Jansen, C. J. H.: Het 18-eeuwse onderwijs in de statistiek aan de juridische fac. van de Repub. der Verenigde Ned. (18th cent.-teaching of statistics in the Repub. of the United Neths), *Tijdsch. voor Rechtsgesch.*, 58(1–2): 111–28.

Jong, O. J. de: De univ. en hun hist. recht (Univs and their hist. rules), in D. Tiemersma ed.: *Wijsbegeerte, universiteit en maatschappij. Liber Amicorum voor Jan Sperna Weiland*, Baarn: 152–59. (Concerns acad. ritual).

Lamberigts, M.: De cisterciënzers en Leuven (The Cistercians in L.), in *Cisterciënzerfamilie*: 295–331.

Leuven university 1425–1985, Leuven. (Eng. trans of 1988 ed.).

Magits, M.: De invoering van de praktische oefeningen in het rechtsonder- wijs: meer dan een acad. discussie? (The introd. of practical exercises in the teaching of law. More than an acad. discussion?), in *Houd voet bij stuk*: 67–74.

Mellaerts, W.: Taalgebruik in overheidsdienst en onderwijs te Leuven 1829– 42 (The use of public officials in teaching at L. 1829–42), *Wetenschappe- lijke tijdingen*, 49(2): 84–102.

Roelevink, J.: Het Babel van de geleerden. Latijn in het Ned. univ. onderwijs van de 18 en de 19 eeuw (Learned Babel. Latin in Neth. univ. teaching from the 18th to the 19th cent.), *Jb. van de maatschappij der Ned. letterkunde te Leiden*, 1989–90: 33–43.

Rummel, E.: Erasmus and the Louvain theologians. A strategy of defense, *Ned. arch. voor kerkgesch.*, 70(1): 2–12.

Ruuls, A. N.: Disputaties binnen het juridisch onderwijs aan de Kwartier- lijke Acad. te Nijmegen verdedigd onder leiding van Petrus de Greve (periode 1663–76) (Disputations in the legal teaching at the K.A. of N. defended under the direction of P. de G. around 1663–76), in D. Lambrecht ed.: *Lopend rechtshistorisch onderzoek. Handelingen van het tiende Belgisch-Nederlands rechtshistorisch colloquium*, Brussels: 91–114.

Tiggelen, B. van: Le regard d'un prof. viennois sur la fac. des arts de Louvain: le rapport de Joseph Ernst Mayer (ou Meyer, 1751?–après 1818?), *Lias*, 17(2): 241–93.

Verstegen, R.: L'enseignement du droit en Belgique. Evol. de la législation aux 19e et 20e s., in *Houd voet bij stuk*: 149–92.

Vries, H. de: De universiteitsarch. in de Ned. vanaf de 19de eeuw, in het bijzonder te Groningen (Univ. archives in the Neths from the 19th cent., with special ref. to G.), Ned. archievenblad, 94(1): 30–43.

Walckiers, M.: La méd. arabe aux Pays-Bas méridionaux du 15e au 17e s., Acta Belgica hist. medicinae, 3(4): 147–52. (Notes situation in Leuven).

Winges, M.: Jeugdige lichtzinnigheid en losbandigheid. Seksueel gedrag en seksuele beleving van studenten ten tijde van de Ned. Repub. (Youthful frivolity and profligacy. Sexual behaviour and sexual experience of students at the time of the Neths Repub.), in G. Hekma, D. Kraakman and W. Melching eds: Grensgeschillen in de seks. Bijdragen tot een culturele geschiedenis van de seksualiteit, Amsterdam/Atlanta: 7–28.

Publications 1991

Auweele, D. van den: De univ. en de Europ. cult.: een hist. beschouwing (Univs and Europ. cult.: a hist. view), Onze alma mater, 45(1): 70–85.

Bakker, M. and Hooff, G. van eds: Gedenkboek Technische Universiteit Eindhoven 1956–91 (Memorial volume for the Tech. Univ. of E. 1956–91), Eindhoven.

Berkel, K. van: Dirk Huizinga als redacteur van Isis (1872–75). Een Groninger bijdrage aan de popularisering van de natuurwetenschap in 19de-eeuws Ned. (D.H. as ed. of Isis 1872–75. A G. contrib. to the popularisation of science in 19th-cent. Neths), in K. van Berkel, H. Boels and W. R. H. Koops eds: Nederland en het Noorden. Opstellen aangeboden aan prof. dr M. G. Buist, Assen/Maastricht (henceforth noted as Ned. en het Noorden): 184–208.

Berg, A. J. van den: De Nederlanse Christen-Studenten Vereniging 1896–1985 (The Neths Christian Student Soc. 1896–1985), 's-Gravenhage.

Buist, M. G.: Terugblik. MO-opleidingen en de vernieuwing van de Groninger letterenfac. na de Tweede Wereld-oorlog (In retrospect. Secondary educ. training and the renewal of the G. fac. of literature after the 2nd World War), in Ned. en het Noorden: 224–43.

Cameron, J. K.: Some students from the Neths at the univ. of St Andrews in the late 16th and early 17th cents, in C. G. F. de Jong and J. van Sluis eds: Gericht verleden. Kerkhistorische opstellen aangeboden aan prof. dr W. Nijenhuis, Leiden: 49–72.

Derez, M.: Leuven, Tielt/Leuven. (Text and photos, with full descriptions of univ. buildings).

Despy-Meyer, A., Dierkens, A. and Scheelings, F. eds: 25-11-1941. De Université Libre de Bruxelles sluit haar deuren (25-11-1941. The free univ. of B. closes its doors), Brussels. (Also pub. in Fr.).

Engels, L. J.: Petrarca's dichterkrans en de jonge universiteit (P.'s poetic garland and the young univ.), Groningen. (Concerns medieval univ.).

Hees, P. van: Een 'Groot-Nederlands' schilderij afkomstig uit de Utrechtse studentenwereld van de jaren dertig (A 'Great Neths' picture from the U. student world of the 30s), Wetenschappelijke tijdingen, 50(4): 239–44.

Hunin, J.: Leuven Vlaams 1912–22 (Flemish L. 1912–22), Wetenschappelijke tijdingen, 50(3): 129–57.

Jansen, C. J. H.: De verhouding tussen wetenschap en praktijk in de jurid. opleiding van de 18de en 19de eeuw (The relationship between scholarship and practice in the teaching of law in the 18th and 19th cents), *Ned. juristenblad*, 66(13): 564–70.

——— and Klomp, R. J. Q.: Over de knie van de student. Jurid. onderwijs aan de univ. van Amsterdam tussen 1876 en 1915 (Over the head of the students. Legal teaching at the univ. of A. between 1876 and 1915), *Ned. juristenblad*, 66(13): 934–42.

Krul, E.: Archiefwetenschap of cultuurgesch. ? P. J. Blok en de Groninger leerstoel voor gesch. in 1905 (Archival scholarship or cultural hist. ? P.J.B. and the G. chair of hist. in 1905), in *Ned. en het Noorden*: 209–23.

Lenders, P.: *Ontstaan en groei van de universiteit van Antwerpen* (The origin and growth of the univ. of A.), Leuven.

Mulder, M. J.: Hebraïci van eertijds. De illustere schl van Deventer (Hebraists of former times. The renowned schl of D.), *Alef beet*, 1(1): 23–26.

Musschoot, A. M. ed.: *Jong, en Vlaams, en vrij. De Gentse Rijksuniversiteit in de spiegel van de literatuur* (Young, Flemish and free. The RUG as shown in literature), Ghent.

Poulain, N. and Zabeau-Van der Verren, L. eds: *De universiteit bouwt 1918–40* (The univ. builds 1918–40), Ghent. (Cat. of an exhib. at Ghent).

Roegiers, J.: P. S. van Eupen 1744–1804: van ultramontaan tot revolutionair (P.S. van E. 1744–1804. From ultramontanist to revolutionary), in P. Lenders ed.: *Het einde van het ancien régime in België*, Kortrijk-Heule: 263–328. (Considers univ. of Leuven).

Sybrandy, S.: Learlingen fan Johannes Schrader, heechlearaar yn it Latyn te Frjentsjer (Pupils of J.S. Latin teacher at Franeker), *De Vrije Fries*, 71: 84–97. (J.S. 1721–83).

Veen, T.: Studiosus sine studio sus est: visitatie van een jurid. fac. (S.s.s.s.e. Examination of a fac. of law), *Ned. juristenblad*, 66(13): 572–80.

Vermij, R.: Promoveren te Utrecht aan het eind van de 17de eeuw (Graduations at U. at the end of the 17th cent.), *Maandblad oud-Utrecht*, 64(4): 33–38.

Verstappen, L.: *Geschiedenis studeren in Gent en Groningen 1958–82* (Hist. studies in G. and G. 1958–82), Ghent.

Vogelzang, F.: Een reiziger in Utrecht. Thomas Pennant op de Grand Tour 1765 (A traveller in U. T.P. on the Grand Tour), *Maandblad oud-Utrecht*, 64: 73–75.

Zijlstra, S.: Studie en carrière van de Friezen 1200–1650: Problemen en perspectieven (Study and careers of Frisians 1200–1650: problems and perspectives), *Batavia acad.*, 9(1): 3–12.

The British Isles

Additions to Earlier Lists

For 1977
Everett, M.: Merton chapel in the 19th cent., *Oxoniensia*, 42: 247–55.
Haslam, J. A. G.: *Cambridge University Aeronautics Department. An account of the conduct and development of research in flight 1921 to 1939*, Cambridge.

For 1978
Griffith, W. P.: Richard Fletcher of Bangor: an early 17th-cent. Welsh student at Cambridge, *Caernarvonshire hist. soc. trans*, 39: 44–73.
Underwood, E. A.: The first and final phases of the Irish med. students at the univ. of Leyden, in E. O'Brien ed.: *Essays in honour of J. D. H. Widdess*, Dublin: 5–42.

For 1979
Beecham, J.: The universities and the development of public, further and higher education in England and Wales. Thesis. Univ. of Wales.
Clark, B. N.: The influence of the continent upon the development of higher education and research in Chemistry in Great Britain in the later half of the 19th century. Thesis. Manchester.

For 1980
Maxwell, I.: *Universities in Partnership: the Inter-University Council and the growth of higher education in developing countries 1946–70*, Edinburgh.
Walker, A.: The evolution of the university settlement movement and some aspects of its development. Thesis. Edinburgh.
Walker, H. C.: The informal curriculum available at the University of Cambridge 1550–1650. Thesis. London.

For 1981
Toms, V. T.: Scholarship endowments to universities with special reference to Tudor merchants. Thesis. London.

For 1982
Searby, P.: *The training of teachers in Cambridge university: The first 60 years 1879–1939*, Cambridge.
Steers, J. A.: St Catharine's Coll. in, and immediately after, the First World War, *St Catharine's Coll. soc. magazine*.

For 1983
Chippendale, P. R.: The debate on the idea of the university in England and

Ireland 1825–c.1850, and its implications for the creation and early development of the idea of the university in New South Wales, 1845–c.1860. Thesis. Lancaster.

Fraser, J. M.: The decline of the autonomy of British universities in the Robbins era 1963–83. Thesis. Stirling.

Mawditt, R. M.: Universities in Great Britain: A study of comparative costs to 1975. Thesis. Bath.

Morrison, A.: Samuel Taylor Coleridge's Greek Prize Ode on the Slave Trade, in J. R. Watson ed.: *An infinite complexity: Essays in romanticism*, Edinburgh: 145–60.

Stubbings, F.: *Forty-nine lives: an anthology of portraits of Emmanuel men*, Cambridge.

For 1984

Evans, R. A.: The universities and the city: a socio-historical study of the East End Settlements 1884–1914 with special reference to Toynbee Hall. Thesis. London.

Keeble, S. P.: University education and business management from the 1890s to the 1950s: a reluctant relationship. Thesis. London.

Lowe, K. J. P.: Card. Francesco Soderini's proposal for an Ital. coll. at Paris in 1524, *Hist. of univs*, 4: 167–78.

Mangan, J. A.: 'Oars and the man'. Pleasure and purpose in Victorian and Edwardian Cambridge, *Brit. jnl of sports hist.*, 1(3): 245–71.

O'Day, R.: Room at the top: Oxford and Cambridge in the Tudor and Stuart age, *Hist. today*, 34(2): 31–38.

Robertson, P.: Scott. univs and Scott. indust. 1860–1914, *Scott. econ. and soc. hist.*, 4: 39–54.

Searby, P.: A failure at Cambridge: Cavendish Coll. 1877–92, *Procs of the Cambridge Antiquarian Soc.*, 72: 106–20.

Underwood, M. G.: A tutor's lot, *The eagle*, 69: 3–8. (Activities of James Wood at St John's, Cambridge, 1789–1814).

Wilkes, J. R.: The development of history as an academic subject at English universities c.1840–70. Thesis. Ulster.

For 1985

Bottrall, M.: *Hughes Hall 1885–1985*, Cambridge. (Graduate hall at Cambridge).

Humphery-Smith, C. etc. eds: *The Cambridge Armorial*, London. (The arms of the univ. and colleges).

Payne, I.: The musical estab. at Trinity Coll., Cambridge, 1546–1644, *Procs of the Cambridge Antiquarian Soc.*, 74: 53–69.

Raven, R. J.: Viscount Townshend and the Cambridge prize for trade theory, *Hist. jnl*, 28(3): 535–55. (Attempt to encourage univ. interest in commercial studies in 1750s).

Topolski, D.: *Boat race: The Oxford revival*, London.

For 1986

Baker, J. H.: 'Doctors wear scarlet': the festal gowns of the univ. of Cambridge, *Costume*, 20: 33–43.

Becher, H. W.: Voluntary science in 19th-cent. Cambridge Univ. to the 1850s, *Brit jnl for the hist. of science*, 19: 57–87.

Chitnis, A. C.: *The Scottish Enlightenment and early Victorian English society*, London. (Section on Scott. univs).

Doyle, B. A.: English and Englishness: a cultural history of English studies in British higher education 1880–1980. Thesis. Thames Polytechnic.

Knox, R. G.: Prof. John Gibb and Westminster Coll., Cambridge, *Jnl of the United Reformed Church Hist. Soc.*, 3(8): 328–37.

McCrone, K.: The 'lady blue'. Sport at the Oxbridge women's colls from their fndation to 1914, *Brit. jnl of sports hist.*, 3(2): 191–215.

Platt, C.: *The most obliging man in Europe: Life and times of the Oxford scout*, London. (Oxford coll. room servants).

Rogers, N. J.: The Old Proctor's Book: a Cambridge MS of *c*.1390, in W. M. Ormrod, ed.: *England in the fourteenth century*, Woodbridge: 213–23.

Wedermann, G.: Alesius in Cambridge 1535, *Jnl of eccles. hist.*, 37(1): 15–41.

Wieland, J.: John Henry Newman, 'The Tamworth Reading Room': Towards *The Idea of a University, Downside rev.*, 103: 127–36.

For 1987

Brockliss, L. W. B. and Ferté, P.: Irish clerics in Fr. in the 17th and 18th cents: a statistical survey, *Procs of the Ryl Irish Acad. Section C*, 87*(C.9)*: 527–72. (Names taken from records of Fr. univs and colls).

Caenegem, R. C. van: *Judges, legislators and professors. Chapters in European legal history*, Cambridge.

Chablo, D.: University architecture in Britain 1950–75. Thesis. Oxford.

Griffith, W. P.: William Hughes and the 'Decensus' controversy of 1567, *Bull. of the Board of Celtic Studies*, 74: 185–99. (W.H. charged with heresy before Vice-Chancellor's court, Cambridge).

Harrow, J. R.: The development of university settlements in England 1884–1939. Thesis. London.

Lowe, R.: Structural change in Eng. higher educ. 1870–1920, in D. K. Müller etc. eds: *The rise of the modern educational system: Structural change and social reproduction 1870–1920*, Cambridge: 163–78.

Payne, I.: Music at Jesus Coll. *c*.1557–1679, *Procs of the Cambridge Antiquarian Soc.*, 76: 97–103.

Phillipson, L.: Quakerism in Cambridge before the Act of Toln 1653–89, *Procs of the Cambridge Antiquarian Soc.*, 76: 1–25.

Ringrose, J. S.: Coll. servants in the 18th cent., *Pembroke coll., Cambridge, soc. Annual gazette*: 25–29.

Sicca, C. M.: *Committed to classicism. The building of Downing College, Cambridge*, Cambridge.

For 1988

Alsop, J.: A letter relating to Thomas Baker's Cambridge Univ. Collections,

Procs of the Cambridge Antiquarian Soc., 77: 151. (A 1709 request from T.B.).

Eward, S. M.: 'Alma Mater Cantabrigia': A device in print and plaster, *Procs of the Cambridge Antiquarian Soc.*, 77: 137–43. (Concerns device of John Legate, univ. printer *c*.1600).

Mayr-Harting, H.: The fndation of Peterhouse, Cambridge 1284 and the Rule of St Benedict, *Eng. hist. rev.*, 103: 318–38.

Payne, I.: George Loosemore at Trinity Coll., Cambridge 1660–82, *Procs of the Cambridge Antiquarian Soc.*, 77: 145–50.

Phillipson, L.: Quakerism in Cambridge from the Act of Toln to the end of the 19th cent. 1689–1900, *Procs of the Cambridge Antiquarian Soc.*, 77: 1–33.

Pickles, J. D.: The Haddon Library, Cambridge, *Library hist.*, 8(1): 1–9.

Sanderson, M.: The Eng. civic univs and the 'indust. spirit' 1870–1914, *Hist. research*, 61: 90–104.

Soffer, R. N.: The devel. of disciplines in the modern Eng. univ., *Hist. jnl*, 31(4): 933–47.

Wayment, H.: *King's College chapel Cambridge: The side-chapel glass. An introduction and a catalogue*, Cambridge.

For 1989

Clark, G.: *Prehistory at Cambridge and beyond*, Cambridge.

Coones, P. and Stoddart, D.: Early geog. at Oxford and Cambridge, *Geog. jnl*, 155: 13–32.

Forgan, S.: The architect. of science and the idea of a univ., *Studies in the hist. and philos. of science*, 20(4): 405–34. (Considers univs and colls in late 19th cent.).

Frankel, W. and Miller, H. eds: *Town and Tallith. In commemoration of the 50th anniversary of the founding of the Cambridge University Jewish Society*, London. (Studies of the Jews in Cambridge).

French, S.: *Aspects of Downing history*, 2, Cambridge.

Gascoigne, J.: Church and state allied: the failure of parliamentary reform of the Eng. univs, in L. Beier, D. Cannadine and J. Rosenheim eds: *The first modern society: Essays in English history in honour of Lawrence Stone*, Cambridge: 401–29.

Hall, C. and Lovatt, R.: The site and fndation of Peterhouse, *Procs of the Cambridge Antiquarian Soc.*, 78: 5–46.

Stewart, W. A. C.: *Higher education in postwar Britain*, Basingstoke.

For 1990

Bennett, D.: *Emily Davies and the liberation of women 1830–1921*, London. (E.D. fnder of Girton Coll. Cambridge).

Brockliss, L. W. B.: Copernicanism in the univ.: The Fr. experience, in S. Hutton and J. Henry eds: *New perspectives on renaissance thought. Festschrift for Charles Schmitt*, London: 190–213.

Cameron, J. K.: A trilingual coll. for Scotland: the fnding of St Mary's Coll., in D. W. D. Shaw ed.: *In divers manners. A St Mary's miscellany*, St Andrews (henceforth noted as *In divers manners*): 29–42. (Coll. of univ. of St Andrews).
——— St Mary's Coll. 1547–74—The second fndation. The principalship of John Douglas, in *In divers manners*: 43–57. (Coll. of univ. of St Andrews).
——— Andrew Melville in St Andrews, in *In divers manners*: 58–72. (A.M. head of St Mary's Coll. at end of 16th cent.).
Denley, P.: Govts and schls in late medieval Italy, in T. Dean and C. Wickham eds: *City and countryside in late medieval and renaissance Italy*, London: 93–107. (Many schls administered by universities).
Feingold, M. ed.: *Before Newton: The life and times of Isaac Barrow*, Cambridge. (I.B. 1630–77 master of Trinity Coll., Cambridge).
Freeman, G.: *Alma Mater: Memoirs of Girton College 1926–29*, Cambridge.
Gareth Evans, W.: *Education and female emancipation: The Welsh experience 1847–1914*, Cardiff.
Posthumus Meyjes, G. H. M.: *Quasi stellae fulgebunt*. On the position and function of the Dr of Divinity in mediaeval church and soc., in *In divers manners*: 11–28.
Roberts, J. M.: *'The idea of a university'* revisited, in I. Ker and A. G. Hill eds: *Newman after a hundred years*, London: 193–222.
Stewart, M. A.: The origins of the Scott. Greek chairs, in E. M. Craik ed.: *'Owls to Athens'. Essays on classical subjects presented to Sir Kenneth Dover*, Oxford: 391–400.
Taunton, N.: Did John Fletcher the playwright go to univ.?, *Notes and queries*, 235(2): 171–72.
Thompson, M. W.: *The Cambridge Antiquarian Society 1840–1990*, Cambridge.
Twigg, J.: *The university of Cambridge and the English revolution*, Woodbridge.
Underwood, M. G.: Restructuring a household, *The eagle*, 72: 9–18. (The household econ. of St John's, Cambridge, in 19th cent.).

Publications 1991
Anderson, R. D.: Univs and elites in modern Britain, *Hist. of univs*, 10: 225–50.
Cobban, A. B.: Pembroke Coll.: its educ. significance in late medieval Cambridge, *Trans of the Cambridge bibliog. soc.*, 10(1): 1–16.
Denley, P.: The coll. movt in Ital. univs in the late middle ages, *Hist. of univs*, 10: 29–91.
Dunbabin, J.: Meeting the costs of univ. educ. in north. France c.1240–1340, *Hist. of univs*, 10: 1–27.
Firth, A. E.: *Goldsmith's College: a centenary account*, London.
García y García, A.: The medieval students of the Univ. of Salamanca, *Hist. of univs*, 10: 93–115.

Greatrex, J.: Monk students from Norwich cathedral priory at Oxford and Cambridge *c*.1300–1530, *Eng. hist. rev.*, 105: 555–83.

Kendall, C. M.: Higher educ. and the emergence of the professional woman in Glasgow *c*.1890–1914, *Hist. of univs*, 10: 199–223.

Leedham-Green, E., Rhodes, D. E. and Stubbings, F. H. eds: *Garrett Godfrey's Accounts c.1527–33*, Cambridge. (A 16th-cent. bookseller of Cambridge).

Moore, L.: *Bajanellas and Semilanas: Aberdeen University and the education of women 1860–1920*, Aberdeen.

Nève, P.: Disputs of Scots students attending univs in the north. Neths, in W. M. Gordon and T. D. Fergus: *Legal history in the making. Proceedings of the Ninth British Legal History Conference Glasgow 1989*, London: 95–108.

Nockles, P. B.: The acad. counter-revoln: Newman and Tractarian Oxford's idea of a univ., *Hist. of univs*, 10: 137–97.

Owen, D. M.: *The medieval canon law: Teaching, literature and transmission*, Cambridge. (Especially concerned with Cambridge).

Page, R. I.: Audits and replacements in the Parker Library: 1590–1650, *Trans of the Cambridge bibliog. soc.*, 10(1): 17–39. (Refers to books left to Corpus Christi Coll., Cambridge).

Passmore, R. etc. eds: *William Cullen and the 18th-century medical world*, Edinburgh. (W.C. prof. at Glasgow and Edinburgh).

Pešek, J.: The Univ. of Prague, Czech Latin Schls and soc. mobility 1570–1620, *Hist. of univs*, 10: 117–36.

Purvis, J.: *A history of women's education in England*, Milton Keynes.

Rosner, L.: *Medical education in the age of improvement. Edinburgh students and apprentices 1760–1826*, Edinburgh.

Virgoe, R.: Hugh atte Fenne and books at Cambridge, *Trans of the Cambridge bibliog. soc.*, 10(1): 92–98. (H. a. F. died *c*.1476).

Waterman, A. M. C.: A Cambridge 'via media' in late Georgian Anglicanism, *Jnl of eccles. hist.*, 42: 419–36.

Publications 1992

Jones, M. K. and Underwood, M. G.: *The king's mother. Lady Margaret Beauford, Countess of Richmond and Derby*, Cambridge. (M.B. active in educ. work at Oxford and Cambridge at end of 15th cent.).

Ridder Symoens, H. de. ed.: *A history of the university in Europe. 1. Universities in the middle ages*, Cambridge.

Czechoslovakia

Additions to Earlier Lists

For 1986

Bagin, A. etc.: *Facultas theologica SS. Cyrilli et Methodii Bratislavae 1936–86. Sborník studií* (Contribs to the hist. of the fac. of theol. of the univ. of B.), Bratislava.

Pešek, J.: Manuál rektora Curia-Dvorského: kniha záhadná (Reg. of the
rect. C.-D.: an enigmatical book), *Acta Univ. Carolinae—Hist. Univ.
Carolinae Pragensis* (henceforth noted as *AUC–HUCP*), 26(1): 97–108.

For 1987

Čičaj, V. ed.: *Trnavská univerzita v slovenských dejinách* (The univ. of T. in
the hist. of Slovakia), Bratislava.
Pohorský, M. ed.: *Karel Čapek. Univerzitní studie* (Univ. studies of K.Č.),
Prague.
Tříška, J.: *Pražská rétorika. Rhetorica Pragensis* (Rhet. at P.), Prague.

For 1988

Adamec, J. etc.: *Biografický slovník pražské lékařské fakulty 1348–1939. Díl
l. A-K* (Biograph. reg. of the Prague fac. of med., 1: A-K), Prague.
(Summary in German).
Folta, J., Rotter, M. and Těšínská, E.: *Fyzika na Karlově univerzitě* (The
level of physics at the Charles univ.), Prague. (Text also in Eng. and
Russian).
*Jan Evangelista Purkyně in science and culture. Scientific conference. Prague
26–30 August 1987.* Vols 1–2, Prague.

For 1989

Hlaváček, I. ed.: *Josef Emler (1836–99) Příspěvky k jeho učitelské, vědecké a
organizátorské* činnosti (Contribs to pedagog., scientif. and organis.
activity by prof. J.E. 1836–99), Prague.
Porubčinová, Z.: *Lékařská fakulta v Brně, její přínos a pokrokové tradice*
(The fac. of med. of the univ. of Brno, its hist.), Brno.
Tretera, I.: *J. F. Herbart a jeho stoupenci na pražské univerzitě* (J.F.H. and
his adherents at Prague univ.), Prague. (Summary in German).

Publications 1990

Blümlová, D.: Formováni osobnosti Václava Tilleho—podněty a inspirace
(The making of the personality of prof. V.T.), *AUC–HUCP*, 30(2): 59–
80. (Summary in German).
Hlaváčková, L. and Svobodný, P.: *Dějiny všeobecné nemocnice v Praze
1790–1952 (k 200. výročí založení nemocnice)* (The hist. of the teaching
hospital at Prague 1790–1952), Prague. (Summaries in Eng. and
German).
Hojda, Z.: Coll. Nordica v Olomouci a Branievě 1578–1619 (The Coll.
Nordica at O. and B. 1578–1619), *AUC–HUCP*, 30(1): 49–95. (Sum-
maries in Germ. and Swedish).
Hůrský, J.: Organizace českých zahraničních studentů v Praze v letech
1930–40 (K 60. výročí založení spolku) (The assoc. of foreign students
of Czech origin at Prague 1930–40), *AUC–HUCP*, 30(2): 81–87.
(Summary in German).

Bibliography 333

Kejř, J.: Příspěvky k dějinám pražské právnické univ. (Two contribs to the hist. of Prague law univ. 1377–81), *AUC–HUCP*, 30(2): 9–24. (Summary in English).

Moškoř, M.: Studentské nadace a jejich zakladatelé v Čechách 1583–1754 (The exhibitions for students and their fnders in Bohemia 1583–1754), *Folia hist. Bohemica*, 14: 229–55. (Summary in German).

Neřoldová, L.: Hospodářská správa Karlovy a Rečkovy koleje (80. léta 16. st.–1622) (Admin. of the econ. of the Charles' and Reček's colls between the 1580s and 1622), *AUC–HUCP*, 30(1): 31–48. (Summary in German).

Pešek, J.: Univ. správa městských latinských škol v Čechách a na Moravě na přelomu 16. a 17. st. (The univ. admin. of the town schls in Bohemia and Moravia at the turn of the 16th and 17th cents), *AUC–HUCP*, 30(2): 41–58. (Summary in German).

——— Nad rekonstruovanou matrikou graduovaných pražské univ. let 1588–1620 (On the reconstructed reg. of the grads of the Univ. of Prague), *Studia Comeniana et hist.*, 42(20): 84–88.

Pešková, J.: Ordines lectionum jako pramen poznání výuky na artistické fak. pražské univ. 1570–1619 ('Ordines lectionum' as a source of knowledge of instruction in the fac. of arts at Prague univ. 1570–1619), *AUC–HUCP*, 30(1): 9–30. (Summary in German).

Sborník referátů druhého sympozia o českém architektu, staviteli, zakladateli nadání a podporovateli věd a umění Josefu Hlávkovi konaného ve dnech 14. a 15. září 1989 v Praze. Část 1–2 (J.H. as a sponsor of sciences and arts. Vols 1–2), *Acta polytech. Práce ČVUT v Praze*, 6(3–4). (Summaries in German).

Svatoš, M.: Regionální hist. a dějiny Univ. Karlovy (Regional hist. and the hist. of the Charles univ. at Prague), *Muzeum a současnost*, 11: 7–14. (Summaries in Germ. and Russian).

Uhlíř, Z.: Prokopa Písaře, 'Liber de arte moriendi' (The 'Liber de arte moriendi' in univ. lectures of P.P.), *AUC–HUCP*, 30(2): 25–40. (Summary in German).

France

Additions to Earlier Lists

For 1982
Nivet, J.: La Salle des Thèses de l'Univ. d'Orléans, *Bull. de la soc. archéol. et hist. de l'Orléanais*, 8: 1–52.

For 1983
Reitel, F.: L'enseignement sup. en France: évolution 1945–81, *Mosella*, 13: 1–48.

For 1986
Reulos, M.: L'univ. de Paris et les Tourangeaux, *Bull. de la soc. archéol. de Touraine*, 41: 397–403.

For 1987
Devaux, O.: Entre la mort de l'univ. et la naissance de l'Ec. centrale: l'"Instit. Paganel' et la difficile survie de l'enseignement du droit à Toulouse en 1794, *Rev. d'hist. des facs de droit et de la sc. juridique*, 5: 23–32.

Flament, P.: Le clergé de Séez et l'univ. de Paris dans la seconde moitié du 18e s., 1751–90, *Cahiers Léopold Delisle*, 35/36: 77–92.

Pillorget, R.: Richelieu, rénovateur de la Sorbonne, in *Richelieu et la culture*, Paris: 43–45.

Reulos, M.: La 'Nation' de Normandie à l'univ. de Paris, *Cahiers Léopold Delisle*, 35/36: 37–44.

Revel, J.: Les univs fr. du 16e au 18e s.: l'innovation par surcroît? in *La ville et l'innovation. Relais et réseaux de diffusion en Europe, 14e–19e siècles*, Paris: 75–88.

Ventre-Denis, M.: La fac. de droit de Paris et la vie pol. sous la Restauration: l'affaire Bavoux, *Rev. d'hist. des facs de droit et de la sc. juridique*, 5: 33–64.

For 1988
Bouard, M. de: Heurs et malheurs de l'univ. de Caen 1939–1944–1957. Réflexions et souvenirs, *Etudes normandes*, 37: 4–14.

Carbasse, J.-M.: L'enseignement du droit fr. à l'univ. de Perpignan 1683–1791, *Soc. agricole, scientif. et litt. des Pyrénées-Orientales*, 96: 131–41.

Caron, J.-C.: Révoltes étudiantes, révoltes agissantes? Le poids des révoltes étudiantes dans la vie pol. fr. 1815–48, in *Révolte et sociétés* (= *Sources-Travaux hist.*, 17/18), Paris: 194–204.

Catalogue de l'exposition 'L'Université de Strasbourg, 13e–20e siècle, la ville, la région, l'Europe', organisée par la Bibliothèque nationale et universitaire de Strasbourg, 14 oct.–30 nov. 1988, Strasbourg.

Dreyfus-Armand, G. and Gervereau, L. eds: *Mai 68. Les mouvements étudiants en France et dans le monde*, Paris.

Dulieu, L.: *La Médecine à Montpellier. 4. De la Première à la Troisième République. 1ère partie*, Avignon.

Gontard, M.: La naissance de l'enseignement sup. à Lyon: les trois facs du Premier Empire, *Mémoires de l'Acad. des sciences, belles-lettres et arts de Lyon*, s.3, 42: 92–93.

Maffre, P.: Jacques Siegfried, patron de l'enseignement commercial sup., *Rev. d'hist. moderne*, 35: 594–613.

Mandin, A. and Lavabre-Bertrand, T.: L'Ec. de santé de Montpellier à partir du 14 frimaire an 3, in M. Peronnet ed.: *Chaptal*, Toulouse: 113–118.

Monchablon, A.: Syndicalisme étudiant et génération algérienne, *Cahiers de l'Instit. d'hist. du temps présent*, 10: 119–29.

Rev. d'hist. des facs de droit et de la sc. juridique, 7 = *Les facultés de droit dans les révolutions françaises 18e–19e s.*

Simonetti, P.: 'Vive la Charte, vive le roi', cris séditieux? L'exemple des manifestations d'étudiants de la fac. de droit de Toulouse en 1822, in *Révolte et sociétés* (= *Sources-Travaux hist.*, 17/18), Paris: 81–87.

Sirinelli, J.-F.: *Géneration intellectuelle. Khâgneux et normaliens dans l'entre-deux-guerres*, Paris.

Thuillier, G.: Aux origines de l'ENA, le projet des *Nouveaux Cahiers* en mai 1938, *La rev. admin.*, 246: 517–20.

For 1989
Cahiers pour l'hist. du CNRS, 3, 4, 5.

Danguy des Deserts, P.: Origines et destinées des étudiants en droit inscrits à la fac. de Rennes à la fin de l'Ancien Régime, in *La révolution et les juristes à Rennes*, Paris: 159–217.

Deyon, S.: Les acads protestantes en France, *Bull. de la soc. d'hist. du protestantisme fr.*, 135: 77–85.

Grelon, A.: Les univs et la formation des ingénieurs en France 1870–1914, *Formation—Emploi*, 27/28: 65–88.

Joyaux, F.: Quelques étudiants siamois à Paris dans les années 20 et leur influence pol. à Bangkok, in *Le Paris des étrangers depuis un siécle*, Paris: 183–92.

Kintz, J.-P.: Le cahier de doléances de l'univ. protestante de Strasbourg, *Saisons d'Alsace*, 104: 91–101.

Laquièze, A.: L'inspection générale des facs de droit dans la seconde moitié du 19e s., 1852–88, *Rev. d'hist. des facs de droit et de la sc. juridique*, 9: 7–43.

Laspougeas, J.: L'univ. de Caen face à la Révoln, in *L'Eglise et la Révolution*, Caen: 37–51.

Le Coll. de France. Quelques données de son hist. et de son caractère propre, in *Annuaire du Collège de France*, Paris: 5–72. (Hist. and list of profs since 1800).

Luciani, G.: Grenoble et ses étudiants étrangers: le comité de patronage des étudiants étrangers de 1896 à nos jours, *Bull. de l'Acad. delphinale*, s. 10, 4: 80–89.

Quatre cent cinquantième anniversaire de la fondation du gymnase Jean Sturm et de l'université de Strasbourg 1538–1988, Strasbourg.

For 1990
Arnold, M. ed.: *La Faculté de théologie protestante de l'Université de Strasbourg de 1919 à 1945*, Strasbourg.

Bergougnioux, A.: L'enseignement de la linguistique et de la philol. en France au 19e s. d'aprés les affiches de cours des facs de lettres 1845–97, *Archives et docs de la soc. d'hist. et d'épistémologie des sc. du langage*, s.2,2: 1–105.

Blanchard, A. ed.: *Ecoles et universités dans la France méridionale á l'époque moderne*, Montpellier.

Bressolette, C. and Doré, J.: La lente fondation d'une fac. de théol. à Paris. Les cent ans de la fac. de théol. de l'Instit. cath. de Paris, *Rev. de l'Instit. cath. de Paris*, 36: 5–84.

Bull. de la soc. d'hist. du protestantisme fr., 136 = *Actes du colloque organisé à l'occasion du 450e anniversaire de la fondation de la faculté de théologie protestante et de l'université de Strasbourg.*

Burlats-Brun, P.: Profs de droit à Montpellier du 15e au 18e s., *Bull. hist. de la ville de Montpellier*, 13: 32–38.

Cahiers pour l'hist. du CNRS, 6, 7.

Mouchel, C.: Théodore Marcile et le cicéronianisme à l'univ. de Paris sous le règne d'Henri III, *Nouvelle rev. du 16e s.*, 8: 51–62.

Tanaka, M.: *La nation anglo-allemande de l'Université de Paris à la fin du Moyen Age*, Paris.

Publications 1991

Caron, J.-C.: *Générations romantiques. Les étudiants de Paris et le Quartier latin 1814–51*, Paris.

Gorochov, N.: Le coll. du cardinal Lemoine au 16e s., *Paris et Ile-de-France. Mémoires*, 42: 219–59. (A coll. of Paris).

Grés-Gayer, J. M.: *Théologie et pouvoir en Sorbonne. La Faculté de théologie de Paris et la bulle 'Unigenitus' 1714–21*, Paris.

Hist. de l'éduc., 51–52 = *Bibliographie d'histoire de l'éducation française. Titres parus au cours de l'année 1988 et suppléments des années antérieures.*

Huguet, F.: *Les professeurs de la faculté de médecine de Paris. Dictionnaire biographique 1794–1939*, Paris.

Les fonds anciens des bibliothèques du Quartier latin = *Mèl. de la Bibl. Sorbonne*, 11. (8 articles on the libraries of the facs and colleges).

Sorbier, F. du ed.: *Oxford 1919–39*, Paris.

Verger, J.: Jean XXII et Benoît XII et les univs du Midi, *Cahiers de Fanjeaux* (Toulouse), 26: 199–219.

——— La mobilité étudiante au Moyen Age, *Hist. de l'éduc.*, 50: 65–90.

——— Moines, chanoines et colls réguliers dans les univs du Midi au Moyen Age, in *Naissance et fonctionnement des réseaux monastiques et canoniaux*, Saint-Etienne: 511–49.

Hungary

Additions to Earlier Lists

For 1989

Rajczi, P.: A 'Maurinum'. A pécsi egyetemi Szt Mór koll. történetéből (The 'M.' From the hist. of the St Maurice Coll. of the univ. of P.), *Baranya történelmi és honismereti évfeles folyóirat*, 1–2: 122–32.

For 1990

Balázs, M. and Monok, I.: *Pápai szemináriumok magyarországi alumnusai* (Hungarian seminarists at the papal seminaries), Szeged.

Barcza, J.: Református kollégiumok (Reformed colls), *História*, 5–6: 54–55.

Katona, T. and Latzkovits, M. eds: *Lőcsei stipendiánsok és literátusok. 1. Külföldi tanulmányutak dokumentumai 1550–1699* (Stipendiarists and litterati from L. Docs of study tours abroad 1550–1699), Szeged.
Klaniczay, T.: Egyetem Magyarországon Mátyás korában (The univ. in Hungary during the reign of M.), *Irodalomtörténeti Közlemények*, 5–6: 575–613.
Mészáros, I.: Pázmány Péter oktatáspolitikája (P.P.'s educ. pol.), *Magyar Tudomány*, 4: 420–32.
Pintér, G.: *Horváti Békés János diáknaplója* (J.B.H.'s diary), Szeged.
Sluis, J. van and Postma, F.: *Hermann Alexander Röell und seine ungarischen Studenten*, Szeged.
Szögi, L.: A pozsonyi Erzsébet Tudományegyetem kezdetei (The beginnings of the Elizabeth Univ. of P.), in I. Pénzes ed.: *Évfordulóink a műszaki és természettudományokban 1991*, Budapest: 151–52.
——— ed.: *Dokumentumok a magyar állatorvosi oktatás történetéhez. 2. 1817–49* (Docs for the hist. of veterinary educ. in Hungary), Budapest.
Vincze, L.: Klebelsberg—Tiz év közoktatásügyünk történetéből (K.—10 yrs of the hist. of our public educ.), *Magyar Tudomány*, 9: 1080–88.

Publications 1991

Bíró, J.: Egy sajátos egyetemi szerep: a magántanárság (Unique univ. role: Private professorship), *Magyar Felsőoktatás*, 6–7: 49–50.
Boda, M.: A középkori pécsi egyetem alapításának előzményei (The antecedents of the fndation of the medieval univ. in P.), *Baranya történelmi és honismereti évfeles folyóirat*, 1–2: 71–87.
Bolberitz, P.: A Pázmány Péter Római Katolikus Hittudományi Akad. (The P.P.R.C. theol. coll.), in G. Ujváry ed.: *Hittudományi fakultások és tanintézetek a 20. századi magyar egyetemeken*, Budapest (henceforth noted as *Hittudományi*): 48–53.
Borsodi, C.: A hittudományi fak. leválasztása a tudományegyetemekről 1950 nyarán (The detachment of the theol. facs from the univs in Summer 1950), in *Hittudományi*: 105–25.
Csohány, J.: Református teológiai fak. Debrecenben 1914–50 (The reformed theol. fac. in Debrecen 1914–50), in *Hittudományi*: 65–75.
Fabinyi, T.: Evangelikus teológiai fak. Sopronban 1923–50 (The evangelical theol. fac. in S. 1923–50), in *Hittudományi*: 84–95.
Jankovics, J. ed.: Teleki Sámuel albuma (S.T.'s album), Szeged.
Kiss, J. M.: Párhuzamos utak. A kolozsvári és a pozsonyi egyetem válságos időszakának történetéhez (Collateral ways. On the hist. of a critical period for the univ. in K. and P.), in J. M. Kiss ed.: *Tanulmányok a magyar felsőoktatás 19.–20. sz. történetéből*, Budapest (henceforth noted as *Tanulmányok*): 123–63.
——— A Pázmány Péter Tudományegyetem felvidéki birtokai visszaszerzéséért inditott perek (Legal actions for the recovery of P.P.'s univ. estates in Upper Hungary), *Levéltári Szemle*, 3: 31–43.
Kiss, M.: Műegyetem alapítási kísérlet Győrött az 1960-as években (Attempts to fnd a polytech at G. in the 60s), in *Tanulmányok*: 163–209.

Ladányi, A.: *A felsőoktatás irányításának történeti alakulása* (The hist. formation of the direction of higher educ.), Budapest.

Ladányi, S.: A református teológiai akad. helye felsőoktatásunkban (The place of the reformed theol. colls in our higher educ.), in *Hittudományi*: 53–65.

Micheller, M.: Diákszálló vagy koll.? Értékrend a kollégiumban a rendszerváltások tükrében (Students' hostel or coll.?), *Magyar Felsőoktatás*, 6–7: 47–48.

Pröhle, K.: Az evangelikus teológia és lelkészképzés helye és szerepe a magyar felsőoktatásban (The place and role of evangelical theol. and the pastor's training in Hungarian higher educ.), in *Hittudományi*: 75–84.

Rozs, A.: A 'Foederatio Emericana' Pécsett (The 'F.E.' in P.), *Baranya történelmi és honismereti évfeles folyóirat*, 1–2: 200–217.

Schweitzer, J.: Az Országos Rabbiképző Intézet helye a magyar felsőoktatásban (The place of the Hungarian Rabbi seminary in Hungarian higher educ.), in *Hittudományi*: 95–105.

Szabó, M. and Tonk, S.: *Erdélyiek egyetemjárása a korai újkorban 1521–1700* (Transylvanian students abroad 1521–1700), Szeged.

Szögi, L.: Katolikus egyetemalapítási törekvések Magyarországon (Attempts to found cath. univs in Hungary), in *Hittudományi*: 10–40.

——— Korai magyar egyetemek (Early Hungarian univs), in I. Pénzes ed.: *Évfordulóink a műszaki és természettudományokban 1992*, Budapest: 55–57.

——— Az olmützi egyetemen tanult magyarországi, erdélyi és horvátországi születésű hallgatók 1576–1850 (Hungarian, Transylvanian and Croatian students at the univ. of O. 1576–1850), in E. Kovács etc. eds: *Unger Mátyás Emlékkönyv*, Budapest: 191–225.

——— A temesvári és kassai műegyetem létesítésének tervei 1918 előtt (Plans for the fndation of polytechs in K. and T. before 1918), in *Tanulmányok*: 105–23.

Tonk, S. ed.: *Albizálás erdélyi városokban és falvakban. Kiss Sámuel enyedi diák gyűjtőútja 1797* (S.K., a student from Nagyenyed. His journey for the purposes of collecting), Szeged.

Török, J.: A római katolikus Hittudományi Kar a budapesti egyetemen 1913–50 között (The R.C. theol. fac. at the univ. of B. 1913–50), in *Hittudományi*: 40–48.

Ujváry, G.: Egyetemek képviselete az országgyűlésen (The representation of univs in parliament), in *Tanulmányok*: 7–71.

——— Egyetemi és főiskolai egyesületek a két világháború közötti Magyarországon (Univ. and coll. assocs in Hungary between the 2 world wars), *Magyar Felsőoktatás*, 6–7: 45–46.

Zsidi, V.: Magyar ösztöndíjasok és volt kereskedelmi főiskolai hallgatók keleten. Forrásközlés (Hungarian scholars and students of commercial colls in the east. Sources), in *Tanulmányok*: 71–105.

Italy

Additions to Earlier Lists

For 1983

Kiene, M.: L'architett. del Coll. di Spagna di Bologna: organ. dello spazio e influssi sull' edilizia univ. europ., *Il carrobbio*, 9: 234–42.

For 1984

Baldini, U. and Coyne, G. V.: The Louvain lectures (Lectiones Lovanienses) of Bellarmine and the autograph copy of his 1616 declaration to Galileo, in G. V. Coyne ed.: *Studi Galileiani*, 1(2), Rome: 1–48.

Zanetti, D. E.: Univ. e classi soc. nella Lombardia spagnola, in A. Tagliaferri ed.: *I ceti dirigenti in Italia in età moderna e contemporanea. Atti del convegno Cividale del Friuli 1983*, Udine: 229–45.

For 1986

Kiene, M.: Die Bautätigkeit in d. ital. Univ. von d. Mitte d. Trecento bis zur Mitte d. Quattrocento, *Mitt. d. Kunsthist. Instit. in Florenz*, 30(3): 433–92.

For 1988

Agrimi, J. and Crisciani, C.: *Edocere medicos. Medicina scolastica nei secoli 13–15*, Naples.

Alma mater librorum. Nove secoli di editoria bolognese per l'Università, Bologna. (Cat. of exhib. at B.).

Brizzi, G. P. and Accorsi, M. L.: *Annali del Collegio Ungaro-Illirico di Bologna 1553–1764*, Bologna.

D'Amato, A.: *I Domenicani e l'Università di Bologna*, Bologna.

Manno Tolu, R.: La 'Domus pauperum scolarium Italorum' a Parigi nell 1334, *Arch. storico ital.*, 146: 49–56.

For 1989

Maschietto, F. M.: *Benedettini professori all' Università di Padova (secc. 15–18). Profili biografici*, Cesena/Padua.

Paticchia, V.: *80 centenario dell' Università di Bologna 1886–88. Progetto culturale e opinione pubblica a confronto negli anni di Crispi*, Bologna.

For 1990

Ascheri, M.: La nobiltà dell' Univ. medievale nella Glossa e in Bartolo da Sassoferrato, in A. de Benedictis ed.: *Sapere e/è potere. Discipline dispute e professioni nell' Università medievale e moderna. Il caso bolognese a confronto. 3. Dalle discipline ai ruoli sociali*, Bologna (henceforth noted as *Sapere 3*): 239–68.

Battelli, G.: I documenti dell' istit. dello Studium Generale in Macerata, *Annali della fac. di lettere e fil. dell' univ. di Macerata*, 22–23 (1989–90): 57–73.

Black, R.: Umanesimo e scl. nell' Arezzo Rinascimentale, *Atti e memorie della accad. Petrarca*, 50 (1988): 87–112.

Boris, F.: Lo Studio e la Mercanzia: i 'Signori dottore cittadini' giudici del Foro dei Mercanti nel Cinquecento, in *Sapere 3*: 179–201. (With lists and bibliog. notes).

Botgia, G. C. etc. eds: *I libri dell' ingegnere*, Bologna. (Concerns engineering studies at Bologna).

Caputo, V. and Caputo, R.: *L'università degli scolari di medicina e d'arti dello Studio ferrarese (sec. 15–18)*, Ferrara.

Catoni, G., Leoncini, A. and Vannozzi, F. eds: *L'Archivio dell' Università di Siena. Inventario della sezione storica*, Siena.

Colli, V.: Cattedre minori, letture univ. e coll. dei dottori di diritto civile a Bologna nel sec. 15, in *Sapere 3*: 135–78.

Fabbrini, F. ed.: *Statuti dell' Università medievale di Arezzo, 1255*, Arezzo.

Ghezzo, M. P. ed.: *Acta graduum academicorum Gymnasii patavini ab anno 1451 ad annum 1460*, Padua.

Gherardi, R.: Scienza e pol. nella proposta di organ. disciplinare di Luigi Ferdinando Marsili, in *Sapere 3*: 403–410. (L.F.M. fnder of Istit. delle Scienze in early 18th cent.).

Hammerstein, N.: Univ. e Stato nel Sacro Romano Impero della Nazione Tedesca, in *Sapere 3*: 269–84.

Lewanski, R. C.: *Laudatio Bononiae. Atti del Convegno storico italo-polacco svoltosi a Bologna del 26 al 31 maggio 1988 in occasione del Nono Centenario dell' Alma Mater Studiorum*, Bologna. (Essays discussing relationship between Bologna and Poland).

Massetto, G. P.: La cult. giuridica civilistica, in *Storia de Pavia*, 3(2), Milan: 475–531.

Monfasani, J.: L'insegnamento univ. e la cult. bizantina in Italia nel Quattrocento, in L. Avellini: *Sapere e/è potere. Discipline dispute e professioni nell' Università medievale e moderna. Il caso bolognese a confronto. 1. Forme e oggetti della disputa delle arti*, Bologna: 43–65.

Musiedlak, D.: *Université privée et formation de la classe dirigeante. L'université L. Bocconi de Milan 1902–25*, Rome.

Pesenti, T.: Le origini dell' insegnamento med. a Pavia, in *Storia di Pavia*, 3(2), Milan: 453–74.

Prodi, P.: Il giuramento univ. tra corporazione, ideologia e confessione religiosa, in *Sapere 3*: 23–35.

Quaglioni, D.: Autosufficienza e primato del diritto nell' educ. giuridica preumanistica, in A. Cristiani ed.: *Sapere e/è potere. Discipline dispute e professioni nell' Università medievale e moderna. Il caso bolognese a confronto. 2. Verso un nuovo sistema del sapere*, Bologna: 125–34.

Sottili, A.: Univ. e cult. a Pavia in età visconteo-sforzesca, in *Storia di Pavia*, 3(2), Milan: 359–451.

Trombetti Budriesi, A. L.: *Gli statuti del collegio dei dottori, giudici e avvocati di Bologna 1393–1467 e la loro matricola (fino al 1776)*, Bologna.

Verger, J.: Les étudiants slaves et hongrois dans les univs occident. 13e–15e s., in *L'église et le peuple chrétien dans les pays de l'Europe du Centre-Est et du Nord 14e–15e siècles*, Rome: 83–106.

Zito, G. ed.: *Insegnamenti e professioni. L'Università di Catania e le città di Sicilia*, Catania.

Publications 1991

Brizzi, G. P. and Varni, A. eds: *L'università in Italia fra età moderna e contemporanea. Aspetti e momenti*, Bologna.

Bucci, O.: Lo Studium Romanae Curiae Lateranense e gli Studi giuridici dal 1853 al 1931. Il ruolo avuto dal Pontificato di Leone XIII nella formazione del Pontificium Institutum Utriusque Juris, *Apollinaris*, 64: 151–226.

Castelli, P. ed.: *La rinascita del sapere. Libri e maestri dello Studio ferrarese*, Venice.

Claudia Toniolo Fascione, M.: Il Coll. della Sapienza di Pisa nella Toscana del Seicento: provenienza cult., soc. e geog. delle richieste di ammissione, in D. Maffei and H. de Ridder-Symoens eds: *I collegi universitari in Europa tra il 14 e il 18 secolo*, Milan (henceforth noted as *I collegi universitari*): 33–45.

Colao, F.: Leggi romane e leggi patrie nella fac. legale senese alla fine del Settecento, in M. Ascheri ed.: *Scritti di storia del diritto offerti dagli allievi a Domenico Maffei*, Padua: 455–80.

—— L'univ. ital. nell' età liberale in alcuni recenti studi, *Studi senesi*, 103: 350–58.

Compère, M.-M.: Les colls de l'univ. de Paris au 16e s.: Structure institut. et fonctions éduc., in *I collegi universitari*: 101–118.

Cuart Moner, B.: Extracción soc. de los cols de San Clemente de los españoles de Bolonia 1500–1800, in *I collegi universitari*: 53–79.

Decennale dell' Università degli Studi della Basilicata—Potenza 1981–91. Una università per lo sviluppo, Potenza.

Fletcher, J. M.: The hist. of acad. colls: Problems and prospects, in *I collegi universitari*: 13–22.

Frijhoff, W.: Conclusions: Vers une autre hist. des colls univ., in *I collegi universitari*: 185–96.

Hammerstein, N.: Protestant colls in the Holy Roman Empire, in *I collegi universitari*: 163–72.

Leeuwen, C. van ed.: *Studi Belgi e Olandesi per il 9 centenario dell' Alma Mater Bolognese*, Bologna. (Essays discussing relationship between the Low Countries and Bologna).

Maesschalck, E. de: Fndation and evoln of colls at Louvain in the late middle ages, in *I collegi universitari*: 155–62.

Martin Hernández, F.: Los cols univ. españoles como signo de reforma (s. 14–16), in *I collegi universitari*: 81–100.

Minnucci, G.: La vita nel Coll. della Sapienza di Siena durante la seconda metà del 15 sec., in *I collegi universitari*: 23–32.

Müller, R. A.: The colls of the 'Societas Jesu' in the German Empire, in *I collegi universitari*: 173–84.

Nicolini, U.: La 'Domus Sancti Gregorii' o 'Sapienza Vecchia' di Perugia. Nota sul periodo delle origini, in *I collegi universitari*: 47–52.

Pizzi, A. ed.: *L'Università di Siena. 750 anni di storia*, Siena.

Storia dell' Ateneo. Bilancio del primo venticinquennio. 1965–91: 25o di fondazione, Chieti. (Hist. of G. d'Annunzio univ.).
Svatoš, M. and Havránek, J.: Univ. colls at Prague from the 14th to the 18th cents, in *I collegi universitari*: 143–54.
Upton, C. A.: The closed soc. and its enemies: Andrew Melville and his circle 1580–1603, in *I collegi universitari*: 119–29. (Concerns St Mary's Coll., St Andrews).
Verger, J.: Coll. e univ. tra Medio Evo ed Età Moderna, in *I collegi universitari*: 1–12.
——— L'hist. des institutions scolaires et les études de phil. médiévale, in *Gli studi di filosofia medievale fra otto e novecento*, Rome: 361–77.
Wyrozumski, J.: Les colls et les internats de l'univ. Jagellonne aux 15e et 16e s., in *I collegi universitari*: 131–42.

Publication 1992
Caputo, V.: Gli statuti di Leonello d'Este per gli scolari giuristi (a. 1447), *Atti (dell') accad. delle scienze di Ferrara*, 68–69 (1990–92): 3–23.

Poland

Additions to Earlier Lists

For 1985
Wryk, R.: *AZS 1908–83. Wspomnienia i pamiętniki* (The Acad. Sports Club 1908–83. Memories), Poznań.

For 1988
Quirini-Popławska, D. ed.: *Commentationes historicae: Almae Matri Studiorum Bononiensis novem saecula feliciter celebranti ab Universitate Iagiellonica cracoviensi oblatae*, Warsaw/Cracow. (Studies on relations between Poland and the univ. of Bologna. Mostly in Italian).

For 1989
Karolewicz, G.: *Katolicki Uniwersytet Lubelski w latach 1925–39 we wspomnieniach swoich pracowników i studentów* (The Cath. Univ. of Lublin 1925–39 as remembered by its profs and students), Lublin.

Publications 1990
Basaj, M. and Urbańczyka, S. eds: *Slawistyka na przełomie 19 i 20 wieku* (Slavonic studies at the turn of the 19th–20th cent.), Wrocław. (Many refs to univ. scholars and depts).
Dudkowa, R.: *Uniwersytet Jagielloński: czasy współczesne* (The J.U.: contemporary hist.), Cracow.

Gorlach, E. ed.: *Profesorowie i Docenci Studium Rolniczego i Wydziału Rolnego UJ oraz Wyższej Szkoły Rolniczej oraz Akademii Rolniczej im Hugona Kołłątaja 1890–1990* (Profs and associate profs of the agricult. fac. of the J.U. and the Hugon Kollataj Cracow Acad. of Agricult. in the yrs 1890–1990), Cracow.

Pollo, I.: *Nauka i szkolnictwo wyższe w Polsce a odzyskanie niepodległości w 1918 roku* (Science and univ. educ. in Poland and the gaining of independence in 1918), Lublin.

Walasek, S. ed.: *Z historii szkolnictwa i myśli pedagogicznej w Polsce 1773–1939* (From the hist. of educ. and pedagog. thought in Poland in the yrs 1773–1939), Warsaw/Wrocław. (Summary in English).

Walczak, J.: *Ruch studencki w Polsce 1944–84* (Student movts in Poland in the yrs 1944–84), Wrocław.

Publications 1991

Anusz, A.: *Niezależne Zrzeszenie Studentów w latach 1980–89* (The independent student union in the yrs 1980–89), Warsaw.

Beauvois, D.: *Szkolnictwo polskie na ziemiach litewsko-ruskich 1803–32, 1. Uniwersytet Wileński* (Polish educ. in the Lithuanian-Ruthenian territories in the yrs 1803–32, I. Vilnius Univ.), Lublin. (Trans from French ed. of 1977).

Bednarska-Ruszajowa, K.: *Od Homera do J. J. Rousseau; w kręgu lektur profesorów krakowskich okresu Oświecenia* (From H. to J.J.R., in the milieu of authors read by Cracow profs in the period of the Enlightenment), Cracow. (Summary in German).

Bobińska, C.: Les generations d'étudiants en tant que groupes soc., in M. Kulczykowski ed.: *Les étudiants-liens sociaux, culture, moeurs du moyenage jusqu'au 19e siècle*, Cracow (henceforth noted as *Les étudiants*): 135–45.

Brzozowski, S.: Soz. Aktivität Polnischer Auslandstudenten 1860–1918, in *Les étudiants*: 165–78.

Czepulis-Rastenis, R.: Le rôle de l'univ. de Vilna dans la période suivant sa suppression, in *Les étudiants*: 189–96.

Fletcher, J. M.: The age of entry of students to the Eng. univs before the Refn, in *Les étudiants*: 65–66.

Frijhoff, W.: Le rôle des études univ. dans une société locale: la ville de Zutphen en Gueldre du moyen-age au debut du 19e s. Premier bilan d'une recherche, in *Les étudiants*: 87–114.

Hajdukiewicz, L.: Autour de problematique de la jeunesse de l'univ. cracovienne du 15e jusqu'au 18e s., in *Les étudiants*: 29–42.

Heppner, H.: Die Galizischen Studenten in Graz 1848–1918, in *Les étudiants*: 147–56.

Kaniewska, I.: Die Struktur d. Studenten d. Krakauer Akad. vom 15.–18. Jh., in *Les étudiants*: 43–63.

Kubik, K.: Peregrinanten-Wanderstudenten d. Stadt Gdańsk im 17. Jh.-Kult. u. Sitten, in *Les étudiants*: 81–85.

Mayeur, F.: Naissance de l'étudiant en sciences et en lettres à la fin du 19e s. en France, in *Les étudiants*: 157–63.

Mokrzecki, L., Burzyńska, L. and Puchowski, K.: Die Eduk. d. Pommer-schen Jugend u. Studenten u. d. Integrationsprobleme d. 17.–19. Jh., in *Les étudiants*: 115–28.
Natio Polona: Le Università in Italia e in Polonia. *Secc*. 13–20: *Mostra documentaria*, Cracow/Rome.
Pešek, J. and Svatoš, M.: Die soz. Zusammensetzung d. Prager Studenten-schaft im 14.–16. Jh., in *Les étudiants*: 19–28.
Podraza, A.: Jugend plebejischer Herkunft an d. Jagiellonen Univ. im 19. u. 20. Jh., in *Les étudiants*:179–88.
Siciński, Z.: *Wkład Politechniki Lwowskiej w polska elektronikę* (The contrib. of Lwow Polytech. to Polish electronics), Wrocław/Warsaw/Cracow. (Summary in English).
Wyrozumski, J.: Les étudiants au moyen-age, in *Les étudiants*: 13–18.
Zemanek, A.: *Dzieje nauczania botaniki w U.J.* (The hist. of the teaching of botany at the J.U. 1783–1917), Cracow.

Spain and Portugal

Additions to Earlier Lists

For 1985
Barredo de Valenzuela, A.: Extremadura en la Univ. de Alcalá, *Hidalguía*, 32 (1984–85): 497–522.

For 1986
Belenguer Calpe, E. and González Luis, M. L. C.: La falacia del tratamiento ilustrado de un antiilustrado, *Hist. de la educ.*, 5: 149–58.
Böhm, W.: El declive de la Univ., *Hist. de la educ.*, 5: 23–39.
Capitán Díaz, A.: *Historia del pensamiento pedagógico en Europa. 2: Pedagogia contemporanea*, Madrid.
Rodríguez-San Pedro Bezares, L. E.: La matrícula de la Univ. de Salamanca 1598–1625, *Hist. de la educ.*, 5: 71–105.
Ruiz Berrio, J.: Algunas reflexiones sobre la hist. de las Univ., *Hist. de la educ.*, 5: 7–22.
Santoni Rugiu, A.: Líneas de desarrollo y contradicción en la univ. ital. de los dos último s.: *Hist. de la educ.*, 5: 119–29.
Svatoš, M.: Estructura soc. de la Univ. de Praga, *Hist. de la educ.*, 5: 61–70.
Zorzuli, M. C.: La carrera del prof. de derecho en Pavía durante la etapa españ. (s. 16–17), *Hist. de la educ.*, 5: 107–118.

For 1987
Fariña Casaldarnos, M. del C.: La cátedra de latinidad a través de los planes de estudios 1845–52, *Hist. de la educ.*, 6: 183–91.
Guillamón Alvarez, F. G. and Velázquez Martinez, M.: La significación de la econ. pol. en la España ilustrada: Los orígenes de las cátedras de

Econ. y Comercio, in *Homenaje al Prof. Torres Fontes*, Murcia (2 vols) (henceforth noted as *Homenaje*): 751–65.
Santamaría, A.: Consideraciones sobre la Univ. Luliana de Mallorca, in *Homenaje*: 1547–62.
Scanlon, G. M.: La mujer y la instrucción púb.: De la Ley Moyano a la 2 Repúb., *Hist. de la educ.*, 6: 193–207.

For 1988
Martin Lamouroux, F.: *La revelación contable en la Salamanca histórica: la Universidad de Salamanca en la encrucijada contable de los siglos 15 y 16 a través de sus cuentas*, Salamanca.

For 1989
Campos y Fernández de Sevilla, F. I.: Memorial de Felipe V. La Univ. de Alcalá solicita, a principios del s. 18, se mantenga la enseñanza del Derecho Común, in *Recuerdo de la profesora Sylvia Romeu Alfaro*, Valencia, 1: 211–23.

For 1990
Alejo Montes, F. J.: *La reforma de la Universidad de Salamanca a finales del siglo 16. Los Estatutos de 1594*, Salamanca.
——— La Univ. de Salamanca en el s. 16: La ref. educ. de D. Juan de Zúñiga 1594, *Studia hist. Hist. moderna*, 8: 151–62.
Amasuno Sarraga, M. V.: *La escuela de medicina en el estudio salmantino (siglos 13–15)*, Salamanca.
Arias González, L. and Chocarro Martin, F. J.: El Col. Trilingüe en el s. 18. Estudio y análisis de las becas y becas-pensiones, *Studia hist. Hist. moderna*, 8: 279–303.
Benítez i Riera, J. M.: La contribució intelectual dels Jesuites a la Universitat de Cervera. Thesis. Cervera.
Carabias Torres, A. M. ed.: *Historia de la Universidad de Salamanca hecha por el maestro Pedro Chacon 1569*, Salamanca.
——— etc.: Cat. de colegiales del Col. Mayor de San Bartolomé en el s. 17, *Studia hist. Hist. moderna*, 8: 183–265.
Esteve Perandreu, F.: Las bulas de Calixto III sobre el Estudio general de Lérida, *Analecta sacra tarraconensia*, 63–64: 257–84.
Palmero Cámara, M. del C.: *Educación y sociedad en la Rioja Republicana 1931–36*, Salamanca.
Pérez, A. M.: *Historia de la educación en España: textos y documentos. T.V. Nacional-Catolicismo y educación en la España de posguerra*, Madrid.
Polo Rodríguez, J. L.: El absentismo del prof. en la Univ. salmantina de la pre-Ilustración 1700–50, *Studia hist. Hist. moderna*, 8: 305–311.
Rodríguez Cruz, A. M.: Juan de Lorenzana, univ. salmantino y catedrático de la Univ. de San Marcos de Lima, in *Los Dominicos y el Nuevo Mundo. Actas del 2 Congreso Internacional*, Salamanca: 381–401.
Rodríguez Díez, J.: La tutela jurídica de la identidad de los centros docentes confesionales ante la legislación españ. de enseñanza. Libertad de

enseñanza y libertad de cátedra, *Anu. jurídico y econ. Escurialense*, 22: 159–96.

Rodríguez San Pedro, L. E. ed.: *Estatutos hechos por la Universidad de Salamanca 1625*, Salamanca. (Facsimile ed.).

Valero García, P. and Pérez Martín, M.: Pedro de Luna y el Estudio Salmantino. Aspecto instit.: su Constitución, *Studia hist. Hist. moderna*, 8: 131–49.

Valle López, A. del: *La Universidad Central y su distrito en el primer decenio de la Restauración Borbónica 1875–85*, Madrid.

Weruaga Prieto, A.: El Col. de San Pelayo de Salamanca. Procedencia soc. de sus miembros 1660–80, *Studia hist. Hist. moderna*, 8: 267–78.

Publications 1991

Alaustre, I.: *Alcalá de Henares y sus fiestas públicas 1503–1675*, Alcalá.

Baldo Lacomba, M.: La Ilustración en la Univ. de Córdoba y el Col. de San Carlos de Buenos Aires 1767–1810, *Estudios de hist. soc. y econ. de América*, 7: 31–54.

Ballesteros Torres, P. L.: Univ. alcalaínos en el Consejo de las Indias 1701–1800, *Estudios de hist. soc. y econ. de América*, 7: 240–64.

Bosco Amores Carredano, J.: La Univ. de la Habana en el s. 18: Trad. y renovación, *Estudios de hist. soc. y econ. de América*, 7: 207–217.

Carabias Torres, A. M.: Excol. mayores en la admin. españ. y americana durante el reinado de Felipe V, *Estudios de hist. soc. y econ. de América*, 7: 55–93.

Carretero Egido, B.: Los oficios en indias de los col. del Col. de San Pelayo de Salamanca, *Estudios de hist. soc. y econ. de América*, 7: 225–39.

Casado Arbonies, M.: Dos arzobispados americanos para el estudiante de Alcalá Don Antonio Claudio Alvarez de Quiñones, *Estudios de hist. soc. y econ. de América*, 7: 268–83.

Cuart Moner, B.: *Colegios Mayores y limpieza de sangre durante la Edad Moderna*, Salamanca.

——— De Bolonia a las Indias: los col. de San Clemente en la admin. americana durante el s. 18, *Estudios de hist. soc. y econ. de América*, 7: 170–89.

Escandell Bonet, B.: La ref. de Cisneros y su influencia en el pensiamento de San Ignacio, in *San Ignacio de Loyola en Alcalá de Henares*, Alcalá (henceforth noted as *San Ignacio*): 13–50. (C. fnder of Univ. of Alcalá).

Felipo Orts, A.: *La Universidad de Valencia durante el siglo 17 1611–1707*, Valencia.

Fernández Alvarez, M., Rodríguez San Pedro, L. E. and Alvarez Villar, J.: *La Universidad de Salamanca. Ocho siglos de magisterio*, Salamanca.

Ferrero Mico, R.: Intentos de reorgan. en la Univ. de Caracas al final del s. 18, *Estudios de hist. soc. y econ. de América*, 7: 150–69.

Garcia Castro, M. D. and Mediano Benito, J. M.: La legislación univ. de España y América durante los tres primeros Borbones, *Estudios de hist. soc. y econ. de América*, 7: 190–206.

González González, E.: El rechazo de la Univ. de México a las ref. Ilustradas 1763–77, *Estudios de hist. soc. y econ. de América*, 7: 94–124.

Bibliography 347

González Navarro, R.: Ignacio de Loyola y el Col. Mayor de San Ildefonso: dos realidades coincidentes en los albores del S. de Oro Complutense, in *San Ignacio*: 73–126.

Herráez Hernández, J. M.: Las informaciones de col. como fuente para el estudio de la proyección univ., *Estudios de hist. soc. y econ. de América*, 7: 218–24.

Molas Ribalta, P.: Dos catedráticos de Cervera en la América borbónica. La familia Moixó, *Estudios de hist. soc. y econ. de América*, 7: 22–30.

Peset Reig, M.: Análisis de las constituciones de 1817 de Caracas, *Estudios de hist. soc. y econ. de América*, 7: 125–49.

Pumar Martínez, C.: Las becas para americanos en el plan de ref. de los Cols Mayores de 1816, *Estudios de hist. soc. y econ. de América*, 7: 265–67.

Rodrigues, M. A.: *A Universidade de Coimbra. Marcos da sua historia*, Coimbra.

Rodríguez San Pedro Bezares, L. E.: Vinculación univ. de los carmelitas salmantinos 1564–68. Nuevas precisiones sobre los estudios de San Juan de la Cruz, *Salmanticensis*, 38: 155–66.

Royón Lara, E. S. J.: Ignacio de Loyola en Alcalá: algo más que un estudiante, in *San Ignacio*: 127–44.

The United States

Additions to Earlier Lists

For 1979
Hayden, D. L.: A history of the external degree in Britain and the U.S.A. Thesis. Univ. of Alabama.

Rolph, R. S.: Emmanuel College, Cambridge, and the puritan movements of old and New England. Thesis. Univ. of South California.

For 1981
Baker, W. J.: *Beyond port and prejudice: Charles Lloyd of Oxford*, Orono, Maine. (C.L. prof. of theol. in mid-1820s).

Gavroglu, K.: Certain features of higher educ. in Greece and the failure of the attempts to reform it, *Jnl of the Hellenic Diaspora*, 8: 95–108.

For 1982
Arnaldi, G.: Students and profs in 13th-cent. Italy, *Italian quarterly*, 23(89): 73–82. (Ital. version in *La cultura*, 20 (1982)).

Burson, M. C.: Emden's *Registers* and the prosopog. of medieval Eng. univs, *Medieval prosopog.*, 3: 35–51.

For 1983
Osmund Lewry, P.: Rhet. at Paris and Oxford in the mid-13th cent., *Rhetorica*, 1: 45–63.

348 *History of Universities*

For 1985
McMurtry, J.: *English Language, English Literature: the creation of an academic discipline*, Hamden, Conn.

For 1986
Green, L. D.: *John Rainold's Oxford lectures on Aristotle's Rhetoric 1572–78*, Cranbury, NJ.

For 1987
Boyer, E. L.: *Carnegie foundation for the advancement of teaching staff*, New York.
Clark, B. R. ed.: *The academic profession—National, disciplinary and institutional settings*, Berkeley/Los Angeles, Calif./London. (Survey of post-World War 2 events).
Gabriel, A. L.: Paris, Univ. of, in J. R. Strayer ed.: *Dictionary of the Middle Ages*, 9, New York: 408–10.
Jacobson, T. C.: *Making medical doctors. Science and medicine at Vanderbilt since Flexner*, Tuscaloosa, Ala.

For 1988
Budlong, A. H. and Martinec, E. L.: *Midwest College of Engineering, 20 years of engineering education innovation*, Glen Ellyn, Ill.
Feldman, P. H.: *Recruiting an elite: Admissions to Harvard College*, New York.
Home, D. W.: The Cambridge Platonists of old England and the Cambridge Platonists of New England, *Church hist.*, 57: 470–85.
Lee, D. C.: *The people's universities of the USSR*, New York.
Smith, R. A.: *Sports and freedom: The rise of big-time college athletics*, New York.
Stricker, F.: American profs in the progressive era: Incomes, aspirations, and professionalism, *Jnl of interdisciplinary hist.*, 19: 231–57.

For 1989
Ashmore, H. S.: *Unseasonable truths: The life of Robert Maynard Hutchins*, Boston, Mass.
Ball, C. and Eggins, H. eds: *Higher Education in the 1990s: New Dimensions*, New York.
Bator, P. G.: The formation of the Regius Chair of Rhet. and Belles Lettres, the univ. of Edinburgh, *Quart. jnl of speech*, 75(1): 40–64. (Mid 18th-cent. Edinburgh).
Bensimon, E. etc.: *Making sense of administrative leadership: The 'L' word in higher education*, Washington, DC.
Bostert, R. H. ed.: *Newhall and Williams College: Selected papers of a history teacher at a New England college 1917–73*, New York.
Bowen, W. G. and Sosa, J. A.: *Prospects for faculty in the Arts and Sciences: A study of factors affecting demand and supply 1987–2012*, Princeton, NJ.
Bradley, D. and Grantham, S. eds: *Dartmouth*, Hanover, NH.

Butcher, P. S.: *Education for equality: Women's rights periodicals and higher education 1849–1920*, New York.

Chu, D.: *The character of American higher education and intercollegiate sport*, Albany, NY.

Clinchy, B. M.: The level of thoughtfulness in coll. women: Integrating reason and care, *American behavioral scientist*, 32: 647–57.

Conway, J.: Higher educ. for women: Models for the 21st cent., *American behavioral scientist*, 32: 633–39.

De Bary, W. T. and Chaffee, J. W. eds: *Neo Confucian education: The formative stage*, Berkeley, Calif.

DeVitis, J. L. and Sola, P. A. eds: *Building bridges for educational reform. New approaches to teacher education*, Ames, Iowa.

Dooley, B.: Soc. control and the Ital univs: From Renaiss. to Illuminismo, *Jnl of modern hist.*, 61: 205–39.

Emans, R. L.: *Understanding undergraduate education*, Vermillion, SD.

Fairweather, J. S.: *Entrepreneurship in higher education: Lessons for colleges, universities, and industry*, College Station, Tex.

Finkelstein, B.: Conveying messages to women: Higher educ. and the teaching profession in hist. perspective, *American behavioral scientist*, 32: 680–99.

Harding, S.: Women as creators of knowledge: New environments, *American behavioral scientist*, 32: 700–707.

Harvey, A. M. etc.: *A model of its kind. 1. A centennial history of medicine at Johns Hopkins; A model of its kind. 2. A pictorial history of medicine at Johns Hopkins*, Baltimore, Md.

Herbst, J.: *And sadly teach: Teacher education and professionalization in American culture*, Madison, Wisc.

Jarausch, K. H. and Arminger, G.: The Germ. teaching profession and Nazi party membership: A demographic logit model, *Jnl of interdisciplinary hist.*, 20: 197–225.

Kassow, S. D.: *Students, professors and the state in Tsarist Russia*, Berkeley, Calif.

Lee, R. A.: McCarthyism at the univ. of South Dakota, *South Dakota hist.*, 19: 424–38.

Lindsay, A.: *The challenge for research in higher education: Harmonizing excellence and utility*, College Station, Tex.

Lux, D. S.: *Patronage and royal science in 17th-century France: The Académie de Physique in Caen*, Ithaca, NY.

Marsh, P. T. ed.: *Contesting the boundaries of liberal and professional education: The Syracuse experiment*, New York.

Melosh, B.: 'Not merely a profession': Nurses and resistance to professionalization, *American behavioral scientist*, 32: 668–79.

Moffatt, M.: *Coming of age in New Jersey: College and American culture*, New Brunswick, NJ. (Student life at Rutgers Coll. in 1970s and 1980s).

Olivas, M.: *The law of higher education*, Durham, NC.

Rasmussen, W. D.: *Taking the university to the people: 75 years of Cooperative Extension*, Ames, Iowa.

Rothschild, J.: Technol. and educ.: A feminist perspective, *American behavioral scientist*, 32: 708–718.

Schiebinger, L.: *The mind has no sex? Women in the origins of modern science*, Cambridge, Mass.

Solomon, B.: Demog. changes and women on campus, *American behavioral scientist*, 32: 640–46.

Sprague, R.: *Longwood College: A history*, Richmond, Va.

Synnott, M. G.: Federalism vindicated: Univ. desegregation in South Carolina and Alabama 1962–63, *Jnl of policy hist.*, 1(2): 292–318.

Thelin, J. R. and Wiseman, L. L.: *The old college try: Balancing academics and athletics in higher education*, Washington, DC.

Tierney, W. G.: *Curricular landscapes, democratic vistas: Transformative leadership in higher education*, New York.

Vander Waerdt, L.: *Affirmative action in higher education: A sourcebook*, Denver, Colo.

Yllo, K.: Revisions: How the new scholarship on women and gender transforms the coll. curriculum, *American behavioral scientist*, 32: 658–67.

For 1990

Altenbaugh, R. J.: *Education for struggle: The American labor colleges of the 1920s and 1930s*, Philadelphia, Pa.

Alexander, M. van C.: *The growth of English education 1348–1648: A social and cultural history*, University Park, Pa.

Barone, D.: An introd. to William Smith and rhet. at the coll. of Philadelphia, *Procs of the American Philos. Soc.*, 134: 111–60.

Barnes, S. H. ed.: *Points of view on American higher education: A selection of important contributions appearing in 'The chronicle of higher education'*, 3 vols, Lewiston, NY.

Barnett, R.: *Idea of higher education*, Philadelphia, Pa.

Bok, D.: *Universities and the future of America*, Durham, NC.

Boney, F. N.: 'The rising hope of our land': Univ. of Georgia students over 2 cents, *Georgia hist. quart.*, 74: 117–33.

Bruce Leslie, W.: When profs had servants: Prestige, pay and professionalization 1860–1917, *Hist. of higher educ. annual*, 10: 19–30.

Clark, M. E. and Wawrytko, S. A. eds: *Rethinking the curriculum: Toward an integrated, interdisciplinary college education*, New York.

Counelis, J. S.: *Higher learning and orthodox Christianity*, Scranton, Pa.

Desjarlais-Lueth, C.: Brown Univ. and acad. library hist., *Libraries and cult.*, 25: 218–42.

Durkin, J. S. J. ed.: *Swift Potomac's lovely daughter: Two centuries at Georgetown through students' eyes*, Washington, DC.

Faulk, O. B. and Faulk, L. E.: 'Of light, liberty, and learning': Lloyd Noble and the OU Board of Regents, *Chronicles of Oklahoma*, 68: 116–37.

Fitzpatrick, E.: *Endless crusade: Women social scientists and progressive reform*, New York.

Flawn, P. T.: *A primer for university presidents: Managing the modern university*, Austin, Tex.

Gambino, R.: *Racing with catastrophe: Rescuing higher education in America*, New York.

Giamatti, A. B.: *Free and ordered space: The real world of the university*, New York.

Goldman, S.: Hebrew at the early colls: Orations at Harvard, Dartmouth and Columbia, *American Jewish archives*, 42: 23–26.

Gordon, L. D.: *Gender and higher education in the progressive era*, New Haven, Conn./London.

Gordon, W. A.: *The fourth of May: Killings and coverups at Kent State*, Buffalo, NY.

Greenberg, M. and Zenchelsky, S.: The confrontation with Nazism at Rutgers: Acad. bureaucracy and moral failure, *Hist of educ. quart.*, 30: 325–49.

Grendler, P. F.: The univ. of Padua 1405–1600: A success story, *Hist. of higher educ. annual*, 10: 7–17.

Gunter, H. C.: A young Latin scholar: Univ. Life in the 1920s, *Palimpsest*, 71: 38–48.

Hood, A. B. and Arconeaux, C.: *Key resources in student services: A guide to the field and its literature*, San Francisco, Calif.

Kennedy, R.: The alliance between Puritanism and Cartesian logic at Harvard 1687–1735, *Jnl of hist. of ideas*, 51: 549–72.

Kimball, R.: *Tenured radicals: How politics has corrupted higher education*, New York.

Kingston, P. and Lewis, L. S. eds: *The high-status track: Studies of elite schools and stratification*, Albany, NY.

Laabs, T. R.: The history and development of Karl Marx university at Leipzig. Thesis. Univ. of North Texas.

Lane, M. ed.: *Black Mountain College: Sprouted seeds: An anthology of personal accounts*, Knoxville, Tenn.

Light, R. J. etc.: *By design: Planning research on higher education*, Cambridge, Mass.

McArthur, B.: A gamble on youth: Robert M. Hutchins, the univ. of Chicago and the pol. of presidential selection, *Hist. of educ. quart.*, 30: 161–86.

McFadden, W. C. ed.: *Georgetown at two hundred: Faculty reflections on the university's future*, Washington, DC.

Marcus, L. R. and Stickney, B. D. eds: *Politics and policy in the age of education*, Springfield, Ill.

Markowitz, R. J.: Subway scholars at concrete campuses: Daughters of Jewish immigrants prepare for the teaching profession. New York city 1920–40, *Hist. of higher educ. annual*, 10: 31–50.

Nauert, C. G. Jr: Humanistic infiltration into the acad. world: Some studies of north. univs, *Renaissance quarterly*, 43(4): 799–824.

Parnell, D.: *Dateline 2000: The new higher education agenda*, Washington, DC.

Perlstein, D.: Teaching freedom: SNCC and the creation of the Mississippi freedom schls, *Hist. of educ. quart.*, 30: 297–324.

Persons, S.: *The university of Iowa in the 20th century: An institutional history*, Iowa City.

Robertson, P. L.: The devel. of an urban univ.: Glasgow 1860–1914, *Hist. of educ. quart.*, 30: 47–78.

Rudolph, F.: *The American college and university: A history*, Athens, Ga. (Reissue, with supplementary inform., of R.'s 1962 book).

Schaefer, D.: *Education without compromise: From chaos to coherence in higher education*, San Francisco, Calif.

Schwider, D.: The Iowa State Coll. Cooperative Extension Service through two World Wars, *Agricult. hist.*, 64: 219–30.

Scott, B. A.: *The Liberal Arts in a time of crisis*, Westport, Conn.

Sherman, R. G.: Constitutionalism and the Illinois Community Coll. system: A case of dissenting taxpayers 1966–68, *Illinois hist. jnl*, 83: 85–96.

Simpson, E. L.: *Faculty renewal in higher education*, Malabar, Fla.

Solinger, J. W. ed.: *Museums and universities: New paths for continuing education*, New York.

Steeples, D. W. ed.: *Managing change in higher education*, San Francisco, Calif.

Sulek, R. P.: *Hoosier Honor: Bob Knight and academic success at Indiana university*, New York.

Sykes, J.: *The hollow men: Politics and corruption in higher education*, Washington, DC.

Townsend, L.: The gender effect: The early curricula of Beloit Coll. and Rochford Female Seminary, *Hist. of higher educ. annual*, 10: 69–90.

Varga, N.: *Baltimore's Loyola, Loyola's Baltimore 1851–1986*, Baltimore, Md.

Walton, C. C.: Acad. freedom at the Cath. univ. of America during the 1970s, *Cath. hist. rev.*, 76: 555–63.

Waugh, L. J. and Stitzel, J. G.: 'Anything but cordial': Coeduc. and West Virginia Univ's early women, *West Virginia hist.*, 49: 69–80.

Williams, F. B. Jr: East Tennessee State Univ. The beginning, *Tennessee hist. quart.*, 49: 218–29.

Wilson, S. H.: Window on the mountains: Berea's Appalachia 1870–1930, *Filson club hist. quart.*, 64: 384–400.

Publications 1991

Crowther, E. R.: Antebellum community support for Judson and Howard colls, *Alabama rev.*, 44: 17–35.

Denley, P.: Career, springboard or sinecure? Univ. teaching in 15th-cent. Italy, *Medieval prosop.*, 12(2): 95–114.

D'Souza, D.: *Illiberal education: The politics of race and sex on campus*, New York.

Weneck, B.: Soc. and cult. stratification in women's higher educ.: Barnard Coll. and Teachers Coll. 1898–1912, *Hist. of educ. quart.*, 31: 1–25.

Index to Continents, Towns and Institutions